CONGRESS WITH
A CROCODILE

EDITED BY
TAHIR SHAH

CONGRESS WITH A CROCODILE

AND OTHER
FOOTNOTES FROM
SIR RICHARD BURTON'S
BOOK OF THE THOUSAND
NIGHTS AND A NIGHT

EDITED BY
TAHIR SHAH

MMXXI

Secretum Mundi Publishing Ltd
Kemp House
City Road
London
EC1V 2NX
United Kingdom

www.secretum-mundi.com
info@secretum-mundi.com

First published by Secretum Mundi Publishing Ltd, 2021
Version 09112020

CONGRESS WITH A CROCODILE

EDITED BY TAHIR SHAH

Tahir Shah asserts the right to be identified as the Author of the Work
in accordance with the Copyright, Designs and Patents Act 1988.

A CIP catalogue record for this title is available from the British Library.

Visit the author's website at:

Tahirshah.com

ISBN 978-1-912383-69-6

In memory of Oliver –
Who shared my delight in the bizarre,
magical underbelly of it all.

'The more I study religions the more I am convinced that man never worshipped anything but himself.'

'Conquer thyself, till thou hast done this, thou art but a slave; for it is almost as well to be subjected to another's appetite as to thine own.'

'Of the gladdest moments in human life, methinks, is the departure upon a distant journey into unknown lands. Shaking off with one mighty effort the fetters of Habit, the leaden weight of Routine, the cloak of many Cares and the slavery of Civilization, man feels once more happy.'

Sir Richard Francis Burton

A WORD OF CAUTION

This book will be offensive to absolutely everyone
in whose hands it is held.

Whoever you are – irrespective of your gender,
age, race, nationality, or faith – please be warned
that you will be offended by the musings of
Sir Richard Francis Burton.

Please note: The opinions of Sir Richard Burton
are most definitely not those of the editor,
and that the material contained in this book
is presented for scholarly interest,
and for that alone.

INTRODUCTION

I AM SITTING at a circular mahogany desk with an emerald-green leather top.

Positioned in a pool of light beside the window, it is in the South Library of The Athenaeum Club, on London's Pall Mall. It's hard to imagine a more glorious or, indeed, a more secretive library – one that's changed as little as it has in the last century and a half.

The annals of the Club record that it was at this desk that Sir Richard Burton laboured for years, translating his celebrated and scandalous *Book of The Thousand Nights and a Night*. My own enthusiasm to become a member of the Athenaeum was fuelled by an urge to write at the same desk as Burton.

In the twenty years I've worked there, I've often pondered upon what was going through Sir Richard's mind. It's a question I'm sure many of the greats of the Victorian age, some of whom toiled in the very same room, wondered about too.

Most writers are quickly forgotten when they die.

The few who are remembered are fortunate, singled out for the genius of their work, or for being towering characters – or both.

1

A handful of the great Victorian gentlemen authors, such as Dickens, Thackeray, and Trollope, are still read. All members of the Athenaeum Club, who overlapped with Burton, their work is studied as literature from another age.

In this pantheon of writers, there's a plinth on which stands a writer whose work is known and celebrated, but almost never actually read. This plinth belongs to Sir Richard Francis Burton – a polymath shockingly current for his oddball eccentricities.

All over the world there are experts who pore over the life and work of Sir Richard. There are connoisseurs who collect his first editions, his correspondences, and rare ephemera associated with him. Each year, scholarly papers are published about the titanic hero – a man who stood against the system, lampooned and chided for his entire adult life.

At this point I must nail my colours to the mast.

You see, I am one of the connoisseurs, or rather a would-be connoisseur. I like nothing more than to pore over the thick biographies, and shuffle my way through his published works.

A long time ago, when a rare windfall graced my bank account, I blew the lot on a short, secret handwritten report by Burton on the wealth of the Sultan of Zanzibar. Alas, hard times forced me to sell. But, for a dozen or so years, I owned it. I'd place it beneath my pillow at night, and press my face to it by day, in a desperate bid to draw some kind of magical inspiration from the connection to Burton.

CONGRESS WITH A CROCODILE

I've published a great deal on stories and storytelling, and about *The Thousand and One Nights*, and so I'll refrain from adding to the communal wordage on that subject here. Rather, I'd like to indulge myself with a swift amble through the twists and turns of Sir Richard's association with *The Nights*, as he liked to call them.

Arabian Nights mania ran the entire duration of the Victorian age, with increasingly extravagant editions being released as the nineteenth century progressed. Advances in literacy, communication, illustration and printing techniques led to a voracious surge in tales from the mysterious Orient. For the Victorians, there was nothing quite so mysterious or exotic as tales of jinns, flying carpets, and caves packed with treasure.

Until the last decade of his life, Richard Burton was a man whose industrial work ethic was very much in line with the time, but whose indescribable oddity was most definitely not.

When it came to defining the peoples he'd encountered on his travels, or voicing his private thoughts on his superiors, he just couldn't help but be shamelessly outspoken.

The fact that he'd been passed over for promotion in the military and in the diplomatic corps, blackballed from learned institutions and lampooned by his peers was a subject on which he waxed lyrical to anyone who would listen.

His substantial body of work was of little importance to Victorian society. Regarded as esoteric, arcane and irrelevant, it encompassed all manner of subjects – from swordsmanship to exploration and topography, to linguistics and poetry.

A mishmash of preoccupation and obsession, Burton's books didn't sell well and, on the whole, the print runs were terribly small – which explains why his first editions cost a fortune.

While sitting at that circular table in the Athenaeum's library, I've often imagined the *Eureka*! moment in which all the points joined up in Burton's mind. For years, he'd watched his arch-rival, the Orientalist Edward Lane, bask in the limelight of what he considered to be a meagre three-volume edition of *The Arabian Nights*. It was a work in which he'd developed a great interest, having helped his friend, John Payne, on a nine-volume translation.

Others were securing fame and fortune for themselves, while Burton clearly regarded himself as the most expert Arabist alive. He'd soaked up a lifetime of material on the region – studying the literature, folklore, and etiquette, as well as the obscurest cultural practices imaginable.

Throw into the mix the fact that Burton had a work ethic to end all work ethics, and you have the reason why he couldn't resist rising to the challenge of producing his own monumental translation of *The Thousand and One Nights*.

Masses has been written by scholars about the so-called 'orphan' stories Burton added to his version of *The Nights*, as well as the plagiarisms. As someone who applauds oral storytelling far more than that of written tales, I have no problem at all with adding to, or changing, a narrative. Plagiarism, though, is another matter – and one that's very serious.

If I'm honest, I admit that – while I salute Sir Richard's colossal sixteen-volume achievement – I don't rate it as the best.

It's almost impossible to read – and I'm saying that as a diehard fan.

But what fascinates me is why Burton undertook the mother of all translation projects. In my opinion, there were two clear reasons.

One: to bask in his own share of limelight, and to capitalize on the Victorian mania for *The Nights*.

Two: as a way of shoehorning a lifetime's worth of extraneous material on the Arab world and beyond into a single project in his twilight years.

For well over a century, scholars have raked over the reasons why Burton wrote his version of *The Nights* in such an impossibly abstruse style. A concoction of his own making, it was a hybrid of Old Testament English, Gothic prose, and Burtonian jibberish.

My own opinion is that, again, there were two reasons:

First: he'd got into character. Not the character of the protagonists, but the character of the whacky oddball polymath who was cornering the market in Oriental literary translations.

Second: because making the text near-impossible to understand meant that those who'd bought the volumes would find themselves diverted... to the footnotes.

As far as I'm concerned, the footnotes are the thing of real wonder in Burton's *Book of The Thousand Nights and a Night*. Stretching to some 350,000 words (a full-length novel is about 80,000), they cover every conceivable subject, theory, idea, and obscenity.

If you've got this far, you hopefully read my warning in the preliminary pages – that Burton's translation is truly offensive.

This is a point I can't layer on thickly enough.

The thing that's impressive is that he offends absolutely everyone you could imagine. His *Arabian Nights* is a last hoorah in offending – rounding on gender, race, nationality, age, and every other section and subsection of humanity.

Some of the footnotes are monstrously long. Others are so sordid in their subject matter that they cause readers to blush in the twenty-first century. God knows what effect they must have had to the prudish sensibilities of Burton's time.

While many of the footnotes consider Burton's favourite subjects – among them castration, eunuchs, farting, sodomy, pederasty, bastinadoing, circumcision, 'savages', and gelding – many are less outrageous.

A central point that fascinates me is this:

Specific terminology and the subjects that were so absolutely abhorrent for Victorian readers are largely acceptable in our own time. We don't think twice about discussing sex or themes that Victorians classed as perversions of the most repugnant nature. For instance, we've come a million miles from a time that railed against gay love and culture.

I like to think that Sir Richard would be thrilled to bits by the world we inhabit – a world freed from many of the inhibitions that so fascinated him.

Of course, we don't all go on about castration the whole time, but if we did, I suppose we'd still be on relatively safe ground – that is if the observations were respectful, and not made to denigrate others.

At the same time, certain words and subjects that were so acceptable as to be standard fare for the Victorians are well beyond the furthest boundaries of acceptability to you and me – and quite rightly so.

As someone who embodies a hybrid of cultures, and who has found himself at the sharp end of racism far more often than I care to remember, I'm elated that the racist-speak of Sir Richard's age is no longer the *lingua franca*. But of course it was, until a handful of years ago – well into my lifetime at least.

For Burton, there was only one major danger zone – the Obscene Publications Act of 1857. Ruthless in its clout and reach, it gave the authorities the right to seize the entire stock, close down the publisher, the printer, and hold the author, as well as readers, to account.

Burton shunned established publishers, as I myself have done in recent years, and he released his multi-volume edition of *The Arabian Nights* himself. As someone who delights in sticking two fingers up to the literary establishment when I get the opportunity, I can only applaud that Sir Richard set himself up as a publisher – The Kama Shastra Society – and that he claimed the books were printed in Benares, India, when in actual fact they were printed in Stoke Newington, North London.

There's no doubt that a great many editions of *The Book of The Thousand Nights and a Night* were purchased, as they were on private subscription, by gentlemen eager to pick their way through the peculiarities of the translator's footnotes rather than the main text.

And what a feast they got for their money – that is if they understood what they were reading. After all, the language Sir Richard used was encoded. At best it was convoluted to decipher – even to those who'd studied the classics and were familiar with Burton-speak.

There are not only plenty of archaic terms of a perverse nature, such as 'onanism', but other words of a far less racy nature that had gone out of fashion centuries before… that is, if they were ever in common use at all. These included a catalogue of terms most dictionaries would be challenged to define – such as chevisance (a chivalrous adventure), cark (to worry), vivisepulture (act of burying someone alive), and kemperley (a struggle).

I can only imagine the titilation of the well-heeled subscribers who received their volumes over the months and years they appeared, between 1885 and 1888. The sublime limited-edition bindings, festooned with Arabic calligraphy and gold, were a kind of literary Trojan horse. Although magnificent to hold, admire, and peruse, they were indescribably challenging to understand.

Or, at least, the main text was.

My suggestion is that relatively few subscribers ever bothered with the stories – it was the footnotes they were after. By their archaic nature these nuggets of scholarship and scandal are equally opaque. But they serve up wonder to anyone investing the time and energy in decoding them.

On the publication of his sixteen-volume edition of *The Nights*, Burton was quoted as saying to his beloved wife, Isabel, 'Now that I know the tastes of England, we need never be without money again.'

Alas, though, not long after the final Supplementary volume had been dispatched to subscribers, the legendary Orientalist was dead. He was interred above ground in his Bedouin tent mausoleum, made from fine Carrara marble, in the churchyard of St. Mary Magdalen, Mortlake. Five years after his funeral, on 15th June 1891, his wife Isabel was interred there, by his side.

In death, Burton is a character remembered for his ability to follow the path that enlivened him, and for not being a prude when all about him were - or at least pretended they were.

The fact that Sir Richard had explored vast tracts of five continents, and had done so on his own terms, would have been enough to make him the legend he deserved to be. But more worthy still was that, even in death, he never sold out to the establishment. That is for me the greatest epitaph of all.

Tahir Shah

BIBLIOGRAPHIES

Burton's Main Publications:

Goa and the Blue Mountains, or Six Months of Sick Leave,
    1851
Scinde or, The Unhappy Valley (two volumes), 1851
Sindh, and the Races that Inhabit the Valley of the Indus,
    1851
Falconry in the Valley of the Indus, 1852
A Complete System of Bayonet Exercise, 1853
*Personal Narrative of a Pilgrimage to El-Medinah and
    Meccah* (three volumes), 1855-6
First Footsteps in East Africa, or, an Exploration of Harar,
    1856
The Lake Regions of Central Equatorial Africa (two
    volumes), 1859
The Lake Regions of Central Africa, 1859
*The City of the Saints, and Across the Rocky Mountains to
    California*, 1861
Wanderings in West Africa, From Liverpool to Fernando Po
    (two volumes), 1863
Abeokuta and the Cameroons Mountains (two volumes),
    1863

A Mission to Gelele, King of Dohomé (two volumes), 1864
The Nile Basin (with James McQueen), 1864
Wit and Wisdom From West Africa, 1865
Stone Talk (as Frank Baker), 1865
The Guide-Book: A Pictorial Pilgrimage to Mecca and Medina, 1865
Explorations of the Highlands of the Brazil (two volumes), 1869
Letters From the Battle-fields of Paraguay, 1870
Vikram and the Vampire or Tales of Hindu Devilry, 1870
Unexplored Syria (two volumes), 1872
Zanzibar; City, Island, and Coast (two volumes), 1872
The Lands of the Cazembe: Lacerda's Journey to the Cazembe in 1798 (translated and edited by Burton), 1873
Ananga River of The Hindu Art of Love (with F.F. Arbuthnot), 1873
The Captivity of Hans Stade of Hesse, in A.D. 1547-1555, Among the Wild Tribes of the Eastern Brazil (translated by Albert Tootal and annotated by Burton), 1874
Ultima Thule; or A Summer in Iceland (two volumes), 1875
A New System of Sword Exercise for Infantry, 1876
Two Trips to Gorilla Land and the Cataracts of the Congo, 1876
Etruscan Bologna: A Study, 1876
Sind Revisited (two volumes), 1877
The Gold Mines of Midian, 1878
The Land of Midian (revisited) (two volumes) 1879

Os Lusiadas (The Lusiads) (two volumes), 1880
The Kasîdah of Haji Abdu El-Yezdi, 1880
A Glance at the 'Passion Play', 1881
Lord Beaconsfield: A Sketch, 1882
To the Gold Coast for Gold, A Personal Narrative (with
   Verney Lovett Cameron) (two volumes), 1883
The Kama Sutra of Vatsyayana (with F.F. Arbuthnot), 1883
Camoens: His Life and His Lusiads, 1883
Camoens: Lyricks (two volumes), 1884
The Book of the Sword, 1884
The Book of the Thousand Nights and a Night (ten
   volumes), 1885
The Perfumed Garden of Cheikh Nefzaoui, 1886
*The Supplemental Nights to the Thousand Nights and a
   Night* (six volumes), 1886-8
The Gulistan or Rose Garden of Sa'di (with Edward
   Rehatsek), 1887
Priapeia, 1890

Posthumously Published:

The Carmina of Catullus, 1894
The Jew, the Gypsy and El Islam, 1898
Wanderings in Three Continents, 1901
The Sentiment of the Sword, 1911

Bibliographies:

Annotated Bibliography, Norman Moseley Penzer, 1923
Sir Richard F. Burton: A Bibliographical Study, James A.
  Casada, 1990
Catalogue of Richard Burton's Library, B.J. Kirkpatrick,
  1978

Main Biographies:

The Life of Captain Sir Richard F. Burton, Isabel Burton,
  1893
The True Life of Captain Sir Richard F. Burton, Georgiana
  M. Stisted, 1896
The Real Sir Richard Burton, Walter Dodge, 1907
Arabian Nights Adventurer, Fairfax Downey, 1931
Captain Sir Richard Burton, Edward Rice, 1936
Richard Burton, Explorer, Hugh Schonfield, 1936
The Arabian Knights, Seton Dearden, 1953
The Devil Drives, Fawn Brodie, 1967
Richard Burton: A Biography, John Cotteral, 1971
Sir Richard Burton, Michael Hastings, 1978
Burton: A Biography of Sir Richard Francis Burton, Byron
  Farwell, 1990
A Rage to Live, Mary S. Lovell, 1998

A NOTE ON
THE FOOTNOTES

The footnotes presented here have been selected for their
scholarly, folkloric, or wider cultural interest.

They keep to the general order of the original volumes,
with each entry offered in full facsimile. Where useful, the
line of text to which the footnote refers has been provided
in italics.

Please note that the capitalized title of each entry is
the work of the editor.

THE FOOTNOTES

IMPOSING PARTS

DEBAUCHED WOMEN PREFER negroes on account of the size of their parts. I measured one man in Somali-land who, when quiescent, numbered nearly six inches. This is a characteristic of the negro race and of African animals: *e.g.* the horse; whereas the pure Arab, man and beast, is below the average of Europe; one of the best proofs by the by, that the Egyptian is not an Asiatic, but a negro partially whitewashed. Moreover, these imposing parts do not increase proportionally during erection; consequently, the "deed of kind" takes a much longer time and adds greatly to the woman's enjoyment. In my time no honest Hindi Moslem would take his womenfolk to Zanzibar on account of the huge attractions and enormous temptations there and thereby offered to them. Upon the subject of Imsák = retention of semen and "prolongation of pleasure," I shall find it necessary to say more.

*

GENIES

THE ARAB SINGULAR (whence the French "génie"); fem. Jinniyah; the Div and Rakshah of old Guebre-land and the "Rakshasa," or "Yaksha," of Hinduism. It would be interesting to trace the evident connection, by no means "accidental," of "Jinn" with the "Genius" who came to the Romans through the Asiatic Etruscans, and whose name

I cannot derive from "gignomai" or "genitus." He was unknown to the Greeks, who had the Daimon (δαίμον), a family which separated, like the Jinn and the Genius, into two categories, the good (Agatho-dæmons) and the bad (Kako-dæmons). We know nothing concerning the status of the Jinn amongst the pre-Moslemitic or pagan Arabs: the Moslems made him a supernatural anthropoid being, created of subtile fire (Koran, chapts. xv. 27; lv. 14), not of earth like man, propagating his kind, ruled by mighty kings, the last being Ján bin Ján, missionarised by Prophets and subject to death and Judgement. From the same root are "Junún" = madness (*i.e.*, possession or obsession by the Jinn) and "Majnún" = a madman. According to R. Jeremiah bin Eliazar in Psalm xli. 5, Adam was excommunicated for one hundred and thirty years, during which he begat children in his own image (Gen. v. 3) and these were Mazikeen or Shedeem — Jinns. Further details anent the Jinn will presently occur.

*

A-FRIT

Not "A-frit," pronounced Aye-frit, as our poets have it. This variety of the Jinn, who, as will be shown, are divided into two races like mankind, is generally, but not always, a malignant being, hostile and injurious to mankind (Koran xxvii. 39).

*

THE DIABOLOS

"IBLIS," VULGARLY WRITTEN "Eblis," from a root meaning The Despairer, with a suspicious likeness to Diabolos; possibly from "Balas," a profligate. Some translate it The Calumniator, as Satan is the Hater. Iblis (who appears in the Arab. version of the N. Testament) succeeded another revolting angel Al-Haris; and his story of pride, refusing to worship Adam, is told four times in the Koran from the Talmud (Sanhedrim 29). He caused Adam and Eve to lose Paradise (ii. 34); he still betrays mankind (xxv. 31), and at the end of time he, with the other devils, will be "gathered together on their knees round Hell" (xix. 69). He has evidently had the worst of the game and we wonder, with Origen, Tillotson, Burns and many others, that he does not throw up the cards.

*

ROYAL HERB

OCYMUM BASILICUM, THE "royal herb," so much prized all over the East, especially in India, where, under the name of "Tulsi," it is a shrub sacred to the merry god Krishna. I found the verses in a MS. copy of the Nights.

*

RICHARD BURTON

JERKING THE DATE-STONE

TRAVELLERS TELL OF a peculiar knack of jerking the date-stone, which makes it strike with great force: I never saw this "Inwá" practised, but it reminds me of the water-splashing with one hand in the German baths.

*

CONCUBINES

ORIGINALLY IN AL-ISLAM the concubine (Surriyat, etc.) was a captive taken in war and the Koran says nothing about buying slave-girls. But if the captives were true believers the Moslem was ordered to marry not to keep them. In modern days concubinage has become an extensive subject. Practically the disadvantage is that the slave-girls, knowing themselves to be the master's property, consider him bound to sleep with them; which is by no means the mistress's view. Some wives, however, when old and childless, insist, after the fashion of Sarah, upon the husband taking a young concubine and treat her like a daughter — which is rare. The Nights abound in tales of concubines, but these are chiefly owned by the Caliphs and high officials who did much as they pleased. The only redeeming point in the system is that it obviated the necessity of prostitution which is, perhaps, the greatest evil known to modern society.

*

CONGRESS WITH A CROCODILE

MAN VERSUS JINN

THE INTELLECT OF man is stronger than that of the Jinni; the Ifrit, however, enters the jar because he has been adjured by the Most Great Name and not from mere stupidity. The seal-ring of Solomon according to the Rabbis contained a chased stone which told him everything he wanted to know.

*

POWDERED ANTIMONY

ARAB "KOHL," IN India, Surmah, not a "collyrium," but powdered antimony for the eyelids. That sold in the bazars is not the real grey ore of antimony but a galena or sulphuret of lead. Its use arose as follows. When Allah showed Himself to Moses on Sinai through an opening the size of a needle, the Prophet fainted and the Mount took fire: thereupon Allah said, "Henceforth shalt thou and thy seed grind the earth of this mountain and apply it to your eyes!" The powder is kept in an étui called Makhalah and applied with a thick blunt needle to the inside of the eyelid, drawing it along the rim; hence etui and probe denote the sexual *rem in re* and in cases of adultery the question will be asked, "Didst thou see the needle in the Kohl-pot?" Women mostly use a preparation of soot or lamp-black (Hind. Kajala, Kajjal) whose colour is easily distinguished from that of Kohl. The latter word, with the article (Al-Kohl) is the origin of our "alcohol;" though even M. Littré fails to show how "fine powder" became "spirits of wine." I found this powder (wherewith Jezebel "painted" her eyes) a great preservative from ophthalmia in desert-travelling: the use in India was universal, but now European example is gradually abolishing it.

*

UNDER THY PROTECTION

ARAB. "ATADAKHKHAL". WHEN danger threatens it is customary to seize a man's skirt and cry "Dakhíl-ak!" (= under thy protection). Among noble tribes the Badawi thus invoked will defend the stranger with his life. Foreigners have brought themselves into contempt by thus applying to women or to mere youths.

*

BLACK LASHES

ARAB. "KAHÍLAT AL-TARAF" = lit. eyelids lined with Kohl; and figuratively "with black lashes and languorous look." This is a phrase which frequently occurs in The Nights and which, as will appear, applies to the "lower animals" as well as to men. Moslems In Central Africa apply Kohl not to the thickness of the eyelid but upon both outer lids, fixing it with some greasy substance. The peculiar Egyptian (and Syrian) eye with its thick fringes of jet-black lashes, looking like lines of black drawn with soot, easily suggests the simile.

In England I have seen the same appearance amongst miners fresh from the colliery.

*

STRANGE WOMEN

ARAB. "DASTÚR" (FROM Persian) = leave, permission. The word has two meanings (see Burckhardt, Arab. Prov. No. 609) and is much used, *e.g.* before walking up stairs or entering a room where strange women might be met. So "Tarík" = Clear the way (Pilgrimage, iii., 319). The old Persian occupation of Egypt, not to speak of the Persian-speaking Circassians and other rulers has left many such traces in popular language. One of them is that horror of travellers — "Bakhshísh" pron. bakhsheesh and shortened to shísh from the Pers. "baksheesh." Our "Christmas *box*" has been most unnecessarily derived from the same, despite our reading: —

Gladly the boy, with Christmas box in hand.

And, as will be seen, Persians have bequeathed to the outer world worse things than bad language, *e.g.* heresy and sodomy.

*

SHEDDING TEARS

Quoth the King, "Thou art excused, O youth; so look upon me as thy guest come hither on an especial object. I would thou acquaint me with the secrets of this tarn and its fishes and of this palace and thy loneliness therein and the cause of thy groaning and wailing." When the young man heard these words he wept with sore weeping: till his bosom was drenched with tears and began reciting...

This readiness of shedding tears contrasts strongly with the external stoicism of modern civilization; but it is true to Arab character; and Easterns, like the heroes of Homer and Italians of Boccaccio, are not ashamed of what we look upon as the result of feminine hysteria — "a good cry."

*

THICKER THAN WATER

An Arab holds that he has a right to marry his first cousin, the daughter of his father's brother, and if any win her from him a death and a blood-feud may result. It was the same in a modified form amongst the Jews and in both races the consanguineous marriage was not attended by the evil results (idiotcy, congenital deafness, etc.) observed in mixed races like the English and the Anglo-American. When a Badawi speaks of "the daughter of my uncle" he means wife; and the former is the dearer title, as a wife can be divorced, but blood is thicker than water.

*

GARDEN HEMP

THE ARAB "BANJ" and Hindú "Bhang" (which I use as most familiar) both derive from the old Coptic "Nibanj" meaning a preparation of hemp (*Cannabis sativa* seu *Indica*); and here it is easy to recognise the Homeric "Nepenthe." Al-Kazwini explains the term by "garden hemp" (Kinnab bostáni or Sháhdánaj). On the other hand not a few apply the word to the henbane (*hyoscyamus niger*) so much used in mediæval Europe. The Kámús evidently means henbane distinguishing it from "Hashish al haráfísh" = rascals' grass, *i.e.* the herb Pantagruelion. The "Alfáz Adwiya" (French translation) explains "Tabannuj" by "Endormir quelqu'un en lui faisant avaler de la jusquiame." In modern parlance Tabannuj is = our anæsthetic administered before an operation, a deadener of pain like myrrh and a number of other drugs. For this purpose hemp is always used (at least I never heard of henbane); and various preparations of the drug are sold at an especial bazar in Cairo. See the "powder of marvellous virtue" in Boccaccio, iii., 8; and iv., 10. Of these intoxicants, properly so termed, I shall have something to say in a future page.

The use of Bhang doubtless dates from the dawn of civilisation, whose earliest social pleasures would be inebriants. Herodotus (iv. c. 75) shows the Scythians burning the seeds (leaves and capsules) in worship and becoming drunken with the fumes, as do the S. African Bushmen of the present day. This would be the earliest form of smoking: it is still doubtful whether the pipe was used or not. Galen also mentions intoxication by hemp. Amongst Moslems, the Persians adopted the drink as an ecstatic, and about our thirteenth century Egypt, which began the practice, introduced a number of preparations to be noticed in the course of The Nights.

*

TOWERING HEAPS

I rose and followed her as she left the palace and she threaded the streets until she came to the city gate, where she spoke words I understood not, and the padlocks dropped of themselves as if broken and the gate-leaves opened. She went forth (and I after her without her noticing aught) till she came at last to the outlying mounds and a reed fence built about a roundroofed hut of mud-bricks.

The rubbish heaps which outlie Eastern cities, some (near Cairo) are over a hundred feet high.

*

COOLNESS OF THE EYE

ARAB. "KURRAT AL-AYN;" coolness of eyes as opposed to a hot eye ("sakhin") *i.e.* one red with tears. The term is true and picturesque so I translate it literally. All coolness is pleasant to dwellers in burning lands: thus in Al-Hariri Abu Zayd says of Bassorah, "I found there whatever could fill the eye with coolness." And a "cool booty" (or prize) is one which has been secured without plunging into the flames of war, or simply a pleasant prize.

*

THE UNION OF CONTRASTS

So she ate and drank and washed her hands, and went and lay down by the side of the slave, upon the cane-trash and, stripping herself stark naked, she crept in with him under his foul coverlet and his rags and tatters. When I saw my wife, my cousin, the daughter of my uncle, do this deed "I clean lost my wits, and climbing down from the roof, I entered and took the sword which she had with her and drew it, determined to cut down the twain…"

There is a terrible truth in this satire, which reminds us of the noble dame who preferred to her handsome husband the palefrenier laid, ord et infâme of Queen Margaret of Navarre (Heptameron No. xx.) We have all known women who sacrificed everything despite themselves, as it were, for the most worthless of men. The world stares and scoffs and blames and understands nothing. There is for every woman one man and one only in whose slavery she is "ready to sweep the floor." Fate is mostly opposed to her meeting him but, when she does, adieu husband and children, honour and religion, life and "soul." Moreover Nature (human) commands the union of contrasts, such as fair and foul, dark and light, tall and short; otherwise mankind would be like the canines, a race of extremes, dwarf as toy-terriers, giants like mastiffs, bald as Chinese "remedy dogs," or hairy as Newfoundlands. The famous Wilkes said only a half-truth when he backed himself, with an hour's start, against the handsomest man in England; his uncommon and remarkable ugliness (he was, as the Italians say, *un bel brutto*), was the highest recommendation in the eyes of very beautiful women.

*

FREQUENTING THE CEMETERY

EVERY MOSLEM BURIAL-GROUND has a place of the kind where honourable women may sit and weep unseen by the multitude. These visits are enjoined by the Apostle: — Frequent the cemetery, 'twill make you think of futurity! Also: — Whoever visiteth the graves of his parents (or one of them) every Friday, he shall be written a pious son, even though he might have been in the world, before that, a disobedient. (Pilgrimage ii., 71.) The buildings resemble our European "mortuary chapels." Saíd, Pasha of Egypt, was kind enough to erect one on the island off Suez, for the "use of English ladies who would like shelter whilst weeping and wailing for their dead." But I never heard that any of the ladies went there.

30

CONGRESS WITH A CROCODILE

*

BURIED ON HILL-SLOPES

"THE DYING BADAWI to his tribe" (and lover) appears to me highly pathetic. The wild people love to be buried upon hill-slopes whence they can look down upon the camp; and they still call out the names of kinsmen and friends as they pass by the grave-yards.

*

NAVEL BEAUTY

Her throat recalled the antelope's, and her breasts, like two pomegranates of even size, stood at bay as it were; her body rose and fell in waves below her dress like the rolls of a piece of brocade, and her navel Would hold an ounce of benzoin ointment. In fine she was like her of whom the poet said...

A large hollow navel is looked upon not only as a beauty, but in children it is held a promise of good growth.

*

ALIF

ARAB. "KÁMAT ALFIYYAH" = like the letter Alif, a straight perpendicular stroke. In the Egyptian hieroglyphs, the origin of every alphabet (not syllabarium) known to man, one form was a flag or leaf of water-plant standing upright. Hence probably the Arabic Alif-shape; while other nations preferred other modifications of the letter (ox's head, etc.), which in Egyptian number some thirty-six varieties, simple and compound.

*

UNPOISONED WINE

Then sat she down, she and her sisters, placing amidst them the Porter who kept deeming himself in a dream; and she took up the wine flagon, and poured out the first cup and drank it off, and likewise a second and a third.

She drinks first, the custom of the universal East, to show that the wine she had bought was unpoisoned. Easterns, who utterly ignore the "social glass" of Western civilisation, drink honestly to get drunk; and, when far gone are addicted to horseplay (in Pers. "Badmasti" = *le vin mauvais*) which leads to quarrels and bloodshed. Hence it is held highly irreverent to assert of patriarchs, prophets and saints that they "drank wine;" and Moslems agree with our "Teatotallers" in denying that, except in the case of Noah, inebriatives are anywhere mentioned in Holy Writ.

*

DEBAUCHERY OF THE MIND

LANE (I. 124) IS scandalized and naturally enough by this scene, which is the only blot in an admirable tale admirably told. Yet even here the grossness is but little more pronounced than what we find in our old drama (*e.g.*, Shakspeare's King Henry V.) written for the stage, whereas tales like The Nights are not read or recited before both sexes. Lastly "nothing follows all this palming work:" in Europe the orgie would end very differently. These "nuns of Theleme" are physically pure: their debauchery is of the mind, not the body. Galland makes them five, including the two doggesses.

*

REFORMATION

WINE-DRINKING, AT all times forbidden to Moslems, vitiates the Pilgrimage-rite: the Pilgrim is vowed to a strict observance of the ceremonial law and many men date their "reformation" from the "Hajj." Pilgrimage, iii., 126.

*

GARDEN OF DELIGHTS

ARAB. "AL-NA'IM;" in full "Jannat al-Na'im" = the Garden of Delights, *i.e.* the fifth Heaven made of white silver. The generic name of Heaven (the place of reward) is "Jannat," lit. a garden; "Firdaus" being evidently derived from the Persian through the Greek παράδεισος, and meaning a chase, a hunting-park. Writers on this subject should bear in mind Mandeville's modesty, "Of Paradise I cannot speak properly, for I was not there."

*

THE BLINDING OF PRINCES

IN THE EAST blinding was a common practice, especially in the case of junior princes not required as heirs. A deep perpendicular incision was made down each corner of the eyes; the lids were lifted and the balls removed by cutting the optic nerve and the muscles. The later Caliphs blinded their victims by passing a red-hot sword blade close to the orbit or a needle over the eyeball. About the same time in Europe the operation was performed with a heated metal basin — the well-known *bacinare* (used by Ariosto), as happened to Pier delle Vigne (Petrus de Vineâ), the "godfather of modern Italian."

*

DISGRACING A MAN

STRIKING WITH THE shoe, the pipe-stick and similar articles is highly insulting, because they are not made, like whips and scourges, for such purpose. Here the East and the West differ diametrically. "Wounds which are given by instruments which are in one's hands by chance do not disgrace a man," says Cervantes (D. Q. i., chapt. 15), and goes on to prove that if a Zapatero (cobbler) cudgel another with his form or last, the latter must not consider himself cudgelled. The reverse in the East where a blow of a pipe-stick cost Mahommed Ali Pasna's son his life: Ishmail Pasha was burned to death by Malik Nimr, chief of Shendy (Pilgrimage, i., 203). Moreover, the actual wound is less considered in Moslem law than the instrument which caused it: so sticks and stones are venial weapons, whilst sword and dagger, gun and pistol are felonious. See *ibid.* (i., 336) for a note upon the weapons with which nations are policed.

*

ABOMINATION

INCEST IS NOW abominable everywhere except amongst the overcrowded poor of great and civilised cities. Yet such unions were common and lawful amongst ancient and highly cultivated peoples, as the Egyptians (Isis and Osiris), Assyrians and ancient Persians. Physiologically they are injurious only when the parents have constitutional defects: if both are sound, the issue, as amongst the so-called "lower animals," is viable and healthy.

*

RICHARD BURTON

SUN TO ROAST AN EGG

Dwellers in the Northern Temperates can hardly imagine what a dust-storm is in sun-parched tropical lands. In Sind we were often obliged to use candles at midday, while above the dust was a sun that would roast an egg.

*

ARAB RACES

Arab. "Urban," now always used of the wild people, whom the French have taught us to call *les Bedouins*; "Badw"being a waste or desert; and Badawi (fem. Badawíyah, plur. Badáwi and Bidwán), a man of the waste. Europeans have also learnt to miscall the Egyptians "Arabs": the difference is as great as between an Englishman and a Spaniard. Arabs proper divide their race into sundry successive families. "The Arab al-Arabá" (or al-Aribah, or al-Urubíyat) are the autochthones, prehistoric, proto-historic and extinct tribes; for instance, a few of the Adites who being at Meccah escaped the destruction of their wicked nation, but mingled with other classes. The "Arab al-Muta'arribah," (Arabised Arabs) are the first advenæ represented by such noble strains as the Koraysh (Koreish), some still surviving. The "Arab al-Musta'aribah," (insititious, naturalised or instituted Arabs, men who claim to be Arabs) are Arabs like the Sinaites, the Egyptians and the Maroccans descended by intermarriage with other races. Hence our "Mosarabians" and the "Marrabais" of Rabelais (not, "a word compounded of Maurus and Arabs"). Some genealogists, however, make the Muta'arribah descendants of Kahtan (possible the Joktan of Genesis x., a comparatively modern document, B.C. 700?); and the Musta'aribah those descended from Adnán the origin of Arab genealogy. And, lastly, are the "Arab al-Musta'ajimah," barbarised Arabs, like the present population of Meccah and Al-Medinah. Besides these there are other tribes whose origin is still unknown; such as the Mahrah tribes of Hazramaut, the "Akhdám" (= serviles) of Oman (Maskat); and the "Ebná" of Al-Yaman: Ibn Ishak supposes the latter to be descended from the Persian soldiers of Anushirwan who expelled the Abyssinian invader from Southern Arabia. (Pilgrimage, iii., 31, etc.).

*

PILLARS OF SAND

ARAB. "SADD" = WALL, dyke, etc. the "bund" or "band" of Anglo-India. Hence the "Sadd" on the Nile, the banks of grass and floating islands which "wall" the stream. There are few sights more appalling than a sandstorm in the desert, the "Zauba'ah" as the Arabs call it. Devils, or pillars of sand, vertical and inclined, measuring a thousand feet high, rush over the plain lashing the sand at their base like a sea surging under a furious whirlwind; shearing the grass clean away from the roots, tearing up trees, which are whirled like leaves and sticks in air, and sweeping away tents and houses as if they were bits of paper. At last the columns join at the top and form, perhaps three thousand feet above the earth, a gigantic cloud of yellow sand which obliterates not only the horizon but even the midday sun. These sand-spouts are the terror of travellers. In Sind and the Punjab we have the dust-storm which for darkness, I have said, beats the blackest London fog.

*

PALM CRUCIFICATION

Quoth the Ifrit, "These words are absurd; thou harlot! thou strumpet!" Then he stripped her stark naked and, stretching her upon the floor, bound her hands and feet to four stakes, like one crucified; and set about torturing and trying to make her confess.

This penalty is mentioned in the Koran (chapt. v.) as fit for those who fight against Allah and his Apostle; but commentators are not agreed if the sinners are first to be put to death or to hang on the cross till they die. Pharaoh (chapt xx.) threatens to crucify his magicians on palm-trees, and is held to be the first crucifier.

*

VILLAINS FOREIGNERS

Arab. "Ajami" = foreigner, esp. a Persian: the latter in The Nights is mostly a villain. I must here remark that the contemptible condition of Persians in Al-Hijáz (which I noted in 1852, Pilgrimage i. 327) has completely changed. They are no longer, "The slippers of Ali and hounds of Omar": they have learned the force of union and now, instead of being bullied, they bully.

*

EVIL EYE

The smiter with the evil eye is called "A'in" and the person smitten "Ma'ín" or "Ma'ún."

*

POMEGRANATE FROM EDEN

Thereupon the eagle changed into a piebald wolf and these two battled in the palace for a long time, when the cat, seeing himself overcome, changed into a worm and crept into a huge red pomegranate, which lay beside the jetting fountain in the midst of the palace hall.

The pomegranate is probably chosen here because each fruit is supposed to contain one seed from Eden-garden.

Hence a host of superstitions (Pilgrimage iii., 104) possibly connected with the Chaldaic-Babylonian god Rimmon or Ramanu. Hence Persephone or Ishtar tasted the "rich pomegranate's seed." Lenormant, loc. cit. pp. 166,182.

*

CRYING FOR THE DEAD

Then came in the Chamberlains and Grandees and were amazed to find two heaps of ashes and the Sultan in a fainting fit; so they stood round him till he revived and told them what had befallen his daughter from the Ifrit; whereat their grief was right grievous and the women and the slave-girls shrieked and keened, and they continued their lamentations for the space of seven days.

I use this Irish term = crying for the dead; as English wants the word for the præfica or myrialogist. The practice is not encouraged in Al-Islam; and Caliph Abu Bakr said, "Verily a corpse is sprinkled with boiling water by reason of the lamentations of the living," *i.e.* punished for not having taken measures to prevent their profitless lamentations. But the practice is from Negroland whence it reached Egypt; and the people have there developed a curious system in the "weeping-song": I have noted this in "The Lake-Regions of Central Africa." In Zoroastrianism (Dabistan, chapt. xcvii.) tears shed for the dead form a river in hell, black and frigid.

CONGRESS WITH A CROCODILE

*

LIKE THE DRIED CROCODILE

Patient I'll bide without complaint, a wronged and vanquisht man;
Patient as sunparcht wight that spans the desert's sandy sea:
Patient I'll be till Aloe's self unwittingly allow,
I'm patient under bitterer things than bitterest aloë:

These lines are hardly translateable. Arab. "Sabr" means "patience" as well as "aloes," hereby lending itself to a host of puns and double entendres more or less vile. The aloe, according to Burckhardt, is planted in grave-yards as a lesson of patience: it is also slung, like the dried crocodile, over house-doors to prevent evil spirits entering; "thus hung without earth and water," says Lane (M. E., chapt. xi.), "it will live for several years and even blossom. Hence (?) it is called *Sabr*, which signifies patience." But Sibr as well as Sabr (a root) means "long-sufferance." I hold the practise to be one of the many Inner African superstitions. The wild Gallas to the present day plant aloes on graves, and suppose that when the plant sprouts the deceased has been admitted to the gardens of Wák, the Creator. (Pilgrimage iii. 350).

*

RICHARD BURTON

RIVER OF PEACE

Every city in the East has its specific title: this was given to Baghdad either on account of its superior police or simply because it was the Capital of the Caliphate. The Tigris was also called the "River of Peace (or Security)."

*

BLINDED BY BILE

Arab. "Samn," (Pers. "Raughan" Hind. "Ghi") the "single sauce" of the East; fresh butter set upon the fire, skimmed and kept (for a century if required) in leather bottles and demijohns. Then it becomes a hard black mass, considered a panacea for wounds and diseases. It is very "filling": you say jocosely to an Eastern threatened with a sudden inroad of guests, "Go, swamp thy rice with Raughan." I once tried training, like a Hindu Pahlawan or athlete, on Gur (raw sugar), milk and Ghi; and the result was being blinded by bile before the week ended.

*

DATING PREGNANCY

Arabs date pregnancy from the stopping of the menses, upon which the fœtus is supposed to feed. Kalilah wa

Dimnah says, "The child's navel adheres to that of his mother and thereby he sucks" (i. 263).

*

DESERT SANDS

At this I rejoiced making certain of my safety; so I arose and fording what little was left of the water got me to the main land, where I fell in with great heaps of loose sand in which even a camel's hoof would sink up to the knee.

I have heard of such sands in the Desert east of Damascus which can be crossed only on boards or camel furniture; and the same is reported of the infamous Region "Al-Ahkáf" ("Unexplored Syria").

*

BARK OF A DOG

However I emboldened my soul and wading through the sand behold, a fire shone from afar burning with a blazing light.

Hence the Arab. saying "The bark of a dog and not the gleam of a fire;" the tired traveller knows from the former that the camp is near, whereas the latter shows from great distances.

*

RICHARD BURTON

COLOUR OF MOURNING

Dark blue is the colour of mourning in Egypt as it was of the Roman Republic. The Persians hold that this tint was introduced by Kay Kawús (B.C. 600) when mourning for his son Siyáwush. It was continued till the death of Husayn on the 10th of Muharram (the first month, then representing the vernal equinox) when it was changed for black. As a rule Moslems do not adopt this symbol of sorrow (called "Hidád"), looking upon the practice as somewhat idolatrous and foreign to Arab manners. In Egypt and especially on the Upper Nile women dye their hands with indigo and stain their faces black or blacker.

*

ROC

Lastly they gave me a knife saying, "Take this skin and stretch thyself upon it and we will sew it around thee; presently there shall come to thee a certain bird, hight Rukh, that will catch thee up in his pounces and tower high in air and then set thee down on a mountain…"

The older Roc, of which more in the Tale of Sindbad. Meanwhile the reader curious about the Persian Símurgh (thirty bird) will consult the Dabistan, i., 55, 191 and iii., 237, and Richardson's Diss. p. xlviii. For the Anka (Enka or Unka = long-necked bird) see Dab. iii., 249 and for the

44

Humá (bird of Paradise) Richardson lxix. We still lack details concerning the Ben or Bennu (nycticorax) of Egypt which with the Article pi gave rise to the Greek "phœnix."

*

KNOCKER RING

THE KNOCKER RING is an invention well known to the Romans.

*

LIQUID BLACK EYES

"O our lord, choose from amongst us her who shall be thy bed-fellow this night and not lie with thee again till forty days be past." So I chose a girl fair of face and perfect in shape, with eyes Kohl-edged by nature's hand…

This may mean "liquid black eyes"; but also, as I have noticed, that the lashes were long and thick enough to make the eyelids appear as if Kohl-powder had been applied to the inner rims.

*

RICHARD BURTON

TEETH BEAUTY

A SLIGHT PARTING between the two front incisors, the upper only, is considered a beauty by Arabs; why it is hard to say except for the racial love of variety. "Sughr" (Thugr) in the text means, primarily, the opening of the mouth, the gape: hence the front teeth.

*

FLYING HORSE

When he felt the blow, he neighed a neigh with a sound like deafening thunder and, opening a pair of wings flew up with me in the firmament of heaven far beyond the eyesight of man.

The flying horse is Pegasus which is a Greek travesty of an Egyptian myth developed in India.

*

SHREDDING

ARAB. "SHARMUTAH" (PLUR. Sharámít) from the root Sharmat, to shred, a favourite Egyptian word also applied in vulgar speech to a strumpet, a punk, a piece. It is also the popular term for strips of jerked or boucaned meat hung up in the sun to dry, and classically called "Kadíd."

*

MAN TO MONKEY

ARAB. "MASKHÚT," MOSTLY applied to change of shape as man enchanted to monkey, and in vulgar parlance applied to a statue (of stone, etc.). The list of metamorphoses in Al-Islam is longer than that known to Ovid. Those who have seen Petra, the Greek town of the Haurán and the Roman ruins in Northern Africa will readily detect the basis upon which these stories are built. I shall return to this subject in The City of Iram (Night cclxxvi.) and The City of Brass (dlxvii.).

*

PEARL WEALTH

THE PEARL IS supposed in the East to lose 1% per ann. of its splendour and value.

*

SOFT-SIDED BEAUTY

IN ARAB TALES beauty is always "soft-sided," and a smooth skin is valued in proportion to its rarity.

*

RICHARD BURTON

DISPLAYING THE BRIDE

ARAB. "JILÁ" (THE Hindostani Julwa) = the displaying of the bride before the bridegroom for the first time, in different dresses, to the number of seven which are often borrowed for the occasion. The happy man must pay a fee called "the tax of face-unveiling" before he can see her features. Amongst Syrian Christians he sometimes tries to lift the veil by a sharp movement of the sword which is parried by the women present, and the blade remains entangled in the cloth. At last he succeeds, the bride sinks to the ground covering her face with her hands and the robes of her friends: presently she is raised up, her veil is readjusted and her face is left bare.

*

CLAPPING

I NEED HARDLY say that in the East, where bells are unused, clapping the hands summons the servants. In India men cry "Quy hye" (Koi hái?) and in the Brazil whistle "Pst!" after the fashion of Spain and Portugal.

*

PRECAUTION

IN THE MOSLEM East a young woman, single or married, is not allowed to appear alone in the streets; and the police has a right to arrest delinquents. As a preventive of intrigues the precaution is excellent. During the Crimean war hundreds of officers, English, French and Italian, became familiar with Constantinople; and not a few flattered themselves on their success with Turkish women. I do not believe that a single *bonâ fide* case occurred; the "conquests" were all Greeks, Wallachians, Armenians or Jewesses.

*

PECCADILLO OF BEHEADING

But he looked on me with eyes of wrath, and began repeating:
Tell her who turneth from our love to work it injury sore,
And taketh her a fine new love the old love tossing o'er:
We cry enough o' thee ere thou enough of us shalt cry!
What past between us doth suffice and haply something more.

Such an execution would be contrary to Moslem law: but people would look leniently upon the peccadillo of beheading or sacking a faithless wife. Moreover the youth was of the blood royal and *A quoi bon être prince?* as was said by a boy of viceroyal family in Egypt to his tutor who reproached him for unnecessarily shooting down a poor old man.

*

49

RICHARD BURTON

BASTINADOED

WHEN A WOMAN is bastinadoed in the East they leave her some portion of dress and pour over her sundry buckets of water for a delicate consideration. When the hands are beaten they are passed through holes in the curtain separating the sufferer from mankind, and made fast to a "falakah" or pole.

*

SERVILE VILLAINIES

IT IS SUPPOSED that slaves cannot help telling these fatal lies. Arab story-books are full of ancient and modern instances and some have become "Joe Millers." Moreover it is held unworthy of a freeborn man to take over-notice of these servile villanies; hence the scoundrel in the story escapes unpunished. I have already noticed the predilection of debauched women for these "skunks of the human race;" and the young man in the text evidently suspected that his wife had passed herself this "little caprice." The excuse which the Caliph would find for him is the *pundonor* shown in killing one he loved so fondly.

*

CHIVALROUS ROMANCES

ARAB. "KHILA'AH" PROP. what a man strips from his person: gen. an honorary gift. It is something more than the "robe of

50

honour" of our chivalrous romances, as it includes a horse, a sword (often gold-hilted), a black turban (amongst the Abbasides) embroidered with gold, a violet-coloured mantle, a waist-shawl and a gold neck-chain and shoe-buckles.

*

BRIDE PRICE

ARAB. "MAHR," THE money settled by the man before marriage on the woman and without which the contract is not valid. Usually half of it is paid down on the marriage-day and the other half when the husband dies or divorces his wife. But if she take a divorce she forfeits her right to it, and obscene fellows, especially Persians, often compel her to demand divorce by unnatural and preposterous use of her person.

*

HOLINESS

ARAB. "AL-KUDS" = holiness. There are few cities which in our day have less claim to this title than Jerusalem; and, curious to say, the "Holy Land" shows Jews, Christians and Moslems all in their worst form. The only religion (if it can be called one) which produces men in Syria is the Druse. "Heiligen-landes Jüden" are proverbial and nothing can be meaner than the Christians while the Moslems are famed for treachery.

RICHARD BURTON

*

SMELLING THE AIR

ARAB. "SHAMM AL-HAWÁ." In vulgar parlance to "smell the air" is to take a walk especially out of town. There is a peculiar Egyptian festival called "Shamm al-Nasím" (smelling the Zephyr) which begins on Easter-Monday (O.S.), thus corresponding with the Persian Nau-roz, vernal equinox and introducing the fifty days of "Khammasín" or "Mirisi" (hot desert winds). On awaking, the people smell and bathe their temples with vinegar in which an onion has been soaked and break their fast with a "fisikh" or dried "búri" = mullet from Lake Menzalah: the late Hekekiyan Bey had the fish-heads counted in one public garden and found 70,000. The rest of the day is spent out of doors "Gypsying," and families greatly enjoy themselves on these occasions. For a longer description see a paper by my excellent friend Yacoub Artin Pasha, in the Bulletin de l'Institut Égyptien, 2nd series, No. 4, Cairo, 1884. I have noticed the Mirisi (Southwester) and other winds in the Land of Midian, i., 23.

*

CARRIED ACROSS

When the Wazir heard the door-keeper's words he arose forthright; and, mounting his horse, rode to the Khan and went in to Nur al-Din who, seeing the Minister making towards him, rose to his feet and advanced to meet him and saluted him.

So in the days of the "Mameluke Beys" in Egypt a man of rank would not cross the street on foot.

*

WHALES AND LIZARDS

ARAB. BASRAH. THE city now in decay and not to flourish again till the advent of the Euphrates Valley R.R., is a modern place, founded in A.H. 15, by the Caliph Omar upon the Aylah, a feeder of the Tigris. Here, according to Al-Hariri, the "whales and the lizards meet;" and, as the tide affects the river,
Its stream shows prodigy, ebbing and flowing.
In its far-famed market-place, Al-Marbad, poems used to be recited; and the city was famous for its mosques and Saint-shrines, fair women and school of Grammar which rivalled that of Kúfah. But already in Al-Hariri's day (nat. A.H. 446 = A.D. 1030) Baghdad had drawn off much of its population.

*

FUMIGATION

So the Wazir sent for the Kazi and legal witnesses and they wrote out the marriage contract, after which the slaves

53

perfumed the guests with incense, and served them with sherbet of sugar and sprinkled rose-water on them and all went their ways.

This fumigation (Bukhúr) is still used. A little incense or perfumed wood is burnt upon an open censer (Mibkharah) of earthenware or metal, and passed round, each guest holding it for a few moments under his beard. In the Somali Country, the very home of incense, both sexes fumigate the whole person after carnal intercourse. Lane (Mod. Egypt, chapt. viii.) gives an illustration of the Mibkharah.

*

NOT TO BE VITUPERATED

THE READER OF The Nights will remark that the merchant is often a merchant-prince, consorting and mating with the highest dignitaries. Even amongst the Romans, a race of soldiers, statesmen and lawyers, "mercatura" on a large scale was "not to be vituperated." In Boccaccio (x. 19) they are netti e delicati uomini. England is perhaps the only country which has made her fortune by trade, and much of it illicit trade, like that in slaves which built Liverpool and Bristol, and which yet disdains or affects to disdain the trader. But the unworthy prejudice is disappearing with the last generation, and men who formerly would have half starved as curates and ensigns, barristers and *carabins* are now only too glad to become merchants.

CONGRESS WITH A CROCODILE

*

A PASSPORT TO FAVOURS

The world's best joys long be thy lot, my lord!
And last while darkness and the dawn o'erlap:
O thou who makest, when we greet thy gifts,
The world to dance and Time his palms to clap.

Such an address to a royalty (Eastern) even in the present day, would be a passport to future favours.

*

CARRYING OR CARRIED

I had sworn I would not marry my daughter to any but to him; so when he came I married him to her.

In England the man marries and the woman is married: there is no such distinction in Arabia.

*

SULTAN

"Sultan" (and its corruption "Soldan") etymologically means lord, victorious, ruler, ruling over. In Arabia it is a not uncommon proper name; and as a title it is taken by a host of petty kinglets. The Abbaside Caliphs (as Al-Wásik who has been noticed) formally created these Sultans as their regents. Al-Tá'i bi'llah (regn. A.H. 363 = 974), invested the famous Sabuktagin with the office; and, as Alexander-Sikandar was wont to do, fastened for him two flags, one of silver, after the fashion of nobles, and the other of gold, as Viceroy-designate. Sabuktagin's son, the famous Mahmúd of the Ghaznavite dynasty in A.H. 393 = 1002, was the first to adopt "Sultan" as an independent title some two hundred years after the death of Harun al-Rashid. In old writers we have the Soldan of Egypt, the Soudan of Persia, and the Sowdan of Babylon; three modifications of one word.

*

BY HEART

I.E. HE WAS a "Háfiz," one who commits to memory the whole of the Koran. It is a serious task and must be begun early. I learnt by rote the last "Juzw" (or thirtieth part) and found that quite enough. This is the vulgar use of "Hafiz": technically and theologically it means the third order of Traditionists (the total being five) who know by heart 300,000 traditions of the Prophet with their ascriptions. A curious "spiritualist" book calls itself "Hafed, Prince of Persia," proving by the very title that the Spirits are equally ignorant of Arabic and Persian.

*

CONGRESS WITH A CROCODILE

PROFESSIONAL BEAUTIES

And they blessed him aloud as he passed and called upon Almighty Allah to bless him.

This naïve admiration of beauty in either sex characterised our chivalrous times. Now it is mostly confined to "professional beauties" of what is conventionally called the "fair sex"; as if there could be any comparison between the beauty of man and the beauty of woman, the Apollo Belvidere with the Venus de Medici.

*

WINE OF DATES

ARAB. "NABÍZ" = WINE of raisins or dates; any fermented liquor; from a root to "press out" in Syriac, like the word "Talmiz" (or Tilmiz, says the Kashf al-Ghurrah) a pupil, student. Date-wine (fermented from the fruit, not the Tádi, or juice of the stem, our "toddy") is called Fazikh. Hence the Masjid al-Fazikh at Al-Medinah where the Ansar or Auxiliaries of that city were sitting cup in hand when they heard of the revelation forbidding inebriants and poured the liquor upon the ground (Pilgrimage ii. 322).

*

RICHARD BURTON

SERVING TRUE BELIEVERS

ALSO CALLED "GHILMÁN" = the beautiful youths appointed to serve the True Believers in Paradise. The Koran says (chapt. lvi. 9 etc.) "Youths, which shall continue in their bloom for ever, shall go round about to attend them, with goblets, and beakers, and a cup of flowing wine," etc. Mohammed was an Arab (not a Persian, a born pederast) and he was too fond of women to be charged with love of boys: even Tristram Shandy (vol. vii. chapt. 7; "No, quoth a third; the gentleman has been committing — —") knew that the two tastes are incompatibles. But this and other passages in the Koran have given the Chevaliers de la Paille a hint that the use of boys, like that of wine, here forbidden, will be permitted in Paradise.

*

FEMININE DEVILRY

When she had reached the age of nineteen, the Sultan of Egypt heard of her and, sending for the Wazir her father, said to him: — Hear me, O Wazir: it hath reached mine ear that thou hast a daughter and I wish to demand her of thee in marriage.

Which, by the by, is the age of an oldish old maid in Egypt. I much doubt puberty being there earlier than in England where our grandmothers married at fourteen. But Orientals are aware that the period of especial feminine devilry is between the first menstruation and twenty when, according to some, every girl is a "possible murderess." So they wisely marry her and get rid of what is called the "lump of grief," the "domestic calamity" — a daughter. Amongst them we never hear of the abominable egotism and cruelty of the English mother, who disappoints her daughter's womanly cravings in order to keep her at home for her own comfort; and an "old maid" in the house, especially a stout, plump old maid, is considered not "respectable." The ancient virgin is known by being lean and scraggy; and perhaps this diagnosis is correct.

*

BARMECIDES

"Know that I have brought thee hither, meaning to do thee a good turn for the love of Allah: so take this torch and mingle with the people at the Hammam-door and walk on with them without stopping till thou reach the house of the wedding-festival; then go boldly forward and enter the great saloon; and fear none, but take thy stand at the right hand of the Hunchback bridegroom; and, as often as any of the nurses and tirewomen and singing-girls come up to thee, put thy hand into thy pocket which thou wilt find filled with gold..."

This is the custom with such gentry, who, when they see a likely man sitting, are allowed by custom to ride astraddle upon his knees with most suggestive movements, till he buys them off. These Ghawází are mostly Gypsies who pretend to be Moslems; and they have been confused with the Almahs or Moslem dancing-girls proper (Awálim, plur. of Alimah, a learned feminine) by a host of travellers. They call themselves Barámikah or Barmecides only to affect Persian origin. Under native rule they were perpetually being banished from and returning to Cairo (Pilgrimage i., 202). Lane (M. E., chapts. xviii. and xix.) discusses the subject, and would derive Al'mah, often so pronounced, from Heb. Almah, girl, virgin, singing girl, hence he would translate Al-Alamoth shir (Psalm xlvi.) and Nebalim al-alamoth (1 Chron., xv. 20) by a "song for singing-girls" and "harps for singing-girls." He quotes also St. Jerome as authority that Alma in Punic (Phœnician) signified a virgin, not a common article, I may observe, amongst singing-girls. I shall notice in a future page Burckhardt's description of the Ghawazi, p. 173, "Arabic Proverbs;" etc., etc. Second Edition. London: Quaritch, 1875.

*

THE CAT'S MIAO

"What ails thee?"; and the mouse grew and grew till it became a coal-black cat and caterwauled "Meeao! Meeao!"

"Miao" or "Mau" is the generic name of the cat in the Egyptian of the hieroglyphs.

*

REVERSED BEAUTY

A GREAT BEAUTY in Arabia and the reverse in Denmark, Germany and Slav-land, where it is a sign of being a werewolf or a vampire. In Greece also it denotes a "Brukolak" or vampire.

*

CONCEPTIONS

"O thou whore! What is this thou tellest me? Where be thy wits?" "O my father," she rejoined, "thou breakest my heart; enough for thee that thou hast been so hard upon me! Indeed my husband who took my virginity is but just now gone to the draught house and I feel that I have conceived by him."

This is not physiologically true: a bride rarely conceives the first night, and certainly would not know that she had conceived. Moreover the number of courses furnished by the bridegroom would be against conception. It is popularly said that a young couple often undoes in the morning what it has done during the night.

*

RICHARD BURTON

CHARM OF THE DESERT

I see their traces and with pain I melt,
And on their whilome homes I weep and yearn:
And Him I pray who dealt this parting-blow
Some day he deign vouchsafe a safe return.

To the English reader these lines would appear the reverse of apposite; but Orientals have their own ways of application, and all allusions to Badawi partings are effective and affecting. The civilised poets of Arab cities throw the charm of the Desert over their verse by images borrowed from its scenery, the dromedary, the mirage and the well, as naturally as certain of our bards who hated the country, babbled of purling rills, etc. Thoroughly to feel Arabic poetry one must know the Desert (Pilgrimage iii., 63).

*

MODERN WRITING

So he took the document and, repairing with it to the Sultan, acquainted him with what had passed, from first to last; whereat the King marvelled and commanded the case to be at once recorded.

In those days the Arabs and the Portuguese recorded everything which struck them, as the Chinese and Japanese do in our times. And yet we complain of the amount of our modern writing!

*

MINOR MIRACLES

Thou hast some art the hearts of men to clip;
Close-veiled, far-hidden mystery dark and deep:
O thou whose beauties shame the lustrous moon,
Wherewith the saffron Morn fears rivalship!
Thy beauty is a shrine shall ne'er decay;
Whose signs shall grow until they all outstrip;
Must I be thirst-burnt by that Eden-brow
And die of pine to taste that Kausar lip?

Alluding to the τήρατα ("minor miracles which cause surprise") performed by Saints' tombs, the mildest form of thaumaturgy. One of them gravely recorded in the Dabistan (ii. 226) is that of the holy Jamen, who opened the Sámran or bead-bracelet from the arm of the beautiful Chistápá with member erect, "thus evincing his manly strength and his command over himself"(!)

*

RICHARD BURTON

FOUNT OF MERCY

THE RIVER OF Paradise, a *lieu commun* of poets (Koran, chapt. cviii.): the water is whiter than milk or silver, sweeter than honey, smoother than cream, more odorous than musk; its banks are of chrysolite and it is drunk out of silver cups set around it thick as stars. Two pipes conduct it to the Prophet's Pond which is an exact square, one month's journey in compass. Kausar is spirituous like wine; Salsabil sweet like clarified honey; the Fount of Mildness is like milk and the Fount of Mercy like liquid crystal.

*

IMPURITY

THE MOSLEM DOES not use the European basin because water which has touched an impure skin becomes impure. Hence it is poured out from a ewer ("ibrík" Pers. Abríz) upon the hands and falls into a basin ("tisht") with an open-worked cover.

*

SMALL STONES

ARAB. "JUDRI," LIT. "small stones" from the hard gravelly feeling of the pustules (Rodwell, p. 20). The disease is generally supposed to be the growth of Central Africa where it is still a plague and passed over to Arabia about the birth-time of Mohammed. Thus is usually explained the "war of the elephant" (Koran, chapt. cv.) when the Abyssinian army of Abrahah, the Christian, was destroyed by swallows (Abábíl which Major Price makes the plural of Abilah = a vesicle) which dropped upon them "stones of baked clay," like vetches (Pilgrimage ii. 175). See for details Sale (*in loco*) who seems to accept the miraculous defence of the Ka'abah. For the horrors of small-pox in Central Intertropical Africa the inoculation, known also to the Badawin of Al-Hijáz and other details, readers will consult "The Lake Regions of Central Africa" (ii. 318). The Hindus "take the bull by the horns" and boldly make "Sítlá" (small-pox) a goddess, an incarnation of Bhawáni, deëss of destruction-reproduction. In China small pox is believed to date from B.C. 1200; but the chronology of the Middle Kingdom still awaits the sceptic.

*

SON OF GOD

ARAB. "UZAYR." ESDRAS was a manner of Ripp van Winkle. He was riding over the ruins of Jerusalem when it had been destroyed by the Chaldeans and he doubted by what means Allah would restore it; whereupon he died and at the end of a hundred years he revived. He found his basket of figs and cruse of wine as they were; but of his ass only the bones remained. These were raised to life as Ezra looked on and the ass began at once to bray. Which was a lesson to Esdras. (Koran, chapt. ii). The oath by the ass's hoofs is to ridicule the Jew. Mohammed seems to have had an *idée fixe* that "the Jews say, Ezra is the son of God" (Koran ix.); it may have arisen from the heterodox Jewish belief that Ezra, when the Law was utterly lost, dictated the whole anew to the scribes of his own memory. His tomb with the huge green dome is still visited by the Jews of Baghdad.

*

HUNCHBACK

THE HUNCHBACK, IN Arabia as in Southern Europe, is looked upon by the vulgar with fear and aversion: The reason is that he is usually sharper-witted than his neighbours.

*

MAKING WATER

IN THE EAST women stand on minor occasions while men squat on their hunkers in a way hardly possible to an untrained European. The custom is old. Herodotus (ii., 35) says, "The women stand up when they make water, but the men sit down." Will it be believed that Canon Rawlinson was too modest to leave this passage in his translation? The custom was perpetuated by Al-Islam because the position prevents the ejection touching the clothes and making them ceremonially impure; possibly they borrowed it from the Guebres. Dabistan, Gate xvi. says, "It is improper, whilst in an erect posture, to make water; it is therefore necessary to sit at squat and force it to some distance, repeating the Avesta mentally."

*

GUARDING THE BAZAARS

ARAB. "WALI" = GOVERNOR; the term still in use for the Governor-General of a Province as opposed to the "Muháfiz," or district-governor. In Eastern Arabia the Wali is the Civil Governor opposed to the Amir or Military Commandant. Under the Caliphate the Wali acted also as Prefect of Police (the Indian Faujdár), who is now called "Zábit." The older name for the latter was "Sáhib al-Shartah" (= chief of the watch) or "Mutawalli"; and it was his duty to go the rounds in person. The old "Charley," with his lantern and cudgel, still guards the bazars in Damascus.

*

LONG DROP

Forthwith they set up a gallows under which they made the Nazarene stand and the torch-bearer, who was hangman, threw the rope round his neck and passed one end through the pulley, and was about to hoist him up when lo! the Reeve, who was passing by, saw the Broker about to be hanged; and, making his way through the people, cried out to the executioner, "Hold! Hold! I am he who killed the Hunchback!"

RICHARD BURTON

I need hardly say that the civilised "drop" is unknown to the East where men are strung up as to a yardarm. This greatly prolongs the suffering.

*

LEFTIE

THE LEFT HAND is used throughout the East for purposes of ablution and is considered unclean. To offer the left hand would be most insulting and no man ever strokes his beard with it or eats with it: hence, probably, one never sees a left-handed man throughout the Moslem east. In the Brazil for the same reason old-fashioned people will not take snuff with the right hand. And it is related of the Khataians that they prefer the left hand, "Because the heart, which is the Sultan of the city of the Body, hath his mansion on that side" (Rauzat al-Safá).

*

TWO HORNS

ARAB. "BAYÁZ AL-SULTÁNÍ," the best kind of gypsum which shines like polished marble. The stucco on the walls of Alexandria, built by Alexander of the two Horns, was so exquisitely tempered and beautifully polished that men had to wear masks for fear of blindness.

*

INNER LIP

"Kɪssɪɴɢ ᴡɪᴛʜ ᴛʜ' inner lip," as Shakespeare calls it; the French *langue fourrée*; and Sankrit "Samputa." The subject of kissing is extensive in the East. Ten different varieties are duly enumerated in the "Ananga-Ranga;" or, The Hindu Art of Love (Ars Amoris Indica) translated from the Sanscrit, and annotated by A. F. F. and B. F. R. It is also connected with unguiculation, or impressing the nails, of which there are seven kinds; morsication (seven kinds); handling the hair and tappings or pattings with the fingers and palm (eight kinds).

*

THEFT

Cᴜᴛᴛɪɴɢ ᴏꜰꜰ ᴛʜᴇ right hand is the Koranic punishment (chapt. v.) for one who robs an article worth four dinars, about forty francs to shillings. The left foot is to be cut off at the ankle for a second offence and so on; but death is reserved for a hardened criminal. The practice is now obsolete and theft is punished by the bastinado, fine or imprisonment. The old Guebres were as severe. For stealing one dirham's worth they took a fine of two, cut off the ear-lobes, gave ten stick-blows and dismissed the criminal who had been subjected to an hour's imprisonment. A second theft caused the penalties to be doubled; and after that the right hand was cut off or death was inflicted according to the proportion stolen.

RICHARD BURTON

*

PUSTULES

When I ended my verses I wept, and she cried out with an exceeding loud cry, "What is the cause of thy tears? Thou burnest my heart! What makes thee take the cup with thy left hand?" Quoth I, "Truly I have on my right hand a boil;" and quoth she, "Put it out and I will open it for thee."

Boils and pimples are supposed to be caused by broken hair-roots and in Hindostani are called Bál-tor.

*

POSSESSION OF SPOILS

HE INTENDED TO bury it decently, a respect which Moslems always show even to the exuviæ of the body, as hair and nail parings. Amongst Guebres the latter were collected and carried to some mountain. The practice was intensified by fear of demons or wizards getting possession of the spoils.

*

COMPELLED TO PAY

Then she sent for the Kazi and witnesses and said to them, "Write my contract of marriage with this young man, and bear ye witness that I have received the marriage-settlement."

70

Without which the marriage was not valid. The minimum is ten dirhams (drachmas) now valued at about five francs to shillings; and if a man marry without naming the sum, the woman, after consummation, can compel him to pay this minimum.

*

GO-BETWEENS

Quoth I "It is nothing!" Then giving the eunuch some of the gold pieces, I begged him to be go-between in the matter; but he laughed and said, "She is more in love with thee than thou with her: she hath no occasion for the stuffs she hath bought of thee and did all this only for the love of thee; so ask of her what thou wilt and she will deny thee nothing."

The eunuch is the best possible go-between on account of his almost unlimited power over the Harem.

*

STOCK TOPIC

SMUGGLING MEN INTO the Harem is a stock "topic" of eastern tales. "By means of their female attendants, the ladies of the royal harem generally get men into their apartments in the disguise of women." Says Vatsyayana in The Kama Sutra,

RICHARD BURTON

Part V., London: Printed for the Hindoo Kamashastra Society, 1883. For private circulation only.

*

EPICENES

A MOST IMPORTANT Jack in office whom one can see with his smooth chin and blubber lips, starting up from his lazy snooze in the shade and delivering his orders more peremptorily than any Dogberry. These epicenes are as curious and exceptional in character as in external conformation. Disconnected, after a fashion, with humanity, they are brave, fierce and capable of any villany or barbarity (as Agha Mohammed Khan in Persia 1795-98). The frame is unnaturally long and lean, especially the arms and legs; with high, flat, thin shoulders; big protruding joints and a face by contrast extraordinarily large, a veritable mask; the Castrato is expert in the use of weapons and sits his horse admirably, riding well "home" in the saddle for the best of reasons; and his hoarse thick voice, which apparently does not break, as in the European "Cáppone," invests him with all the circumstance of command.

*

72

AVERTING THE EYE

ARAB. "BI'L-SALÁMAH" = IN safety (to avert the evil eye). When visiting the sick it is usual to say something civil; "The Lord heal thee! No evil befal thee!" etc.

*

DANGER OF WASHING

However I felt his pulse and wrote him a prescription and continued to visit him for ten days, at the end of which time he recovered and went to the Hammam, whereupon the Viceroy gave me a handsome dress of honour and appointed me superintendent of the hospital which is in Damascus.

Washing during sickness is held dangerous by Arabs; and "going to the Hammam" is, I have said, equivalent to convalescence.

*

ABODE OF THE CHAINED

ARAB. "MÁRISTÁN" (PRONOUNCED Múristan) a corruption of the Pers. "Bímáristán" = place of sickness, a hospital much affected by the old Guebres (Dabistan, i., 165, 166). That of Damascus was the first Moslem hospital, founded by Al-Walid Son of Abd al-Malik the Ommiade in A.H. 88 = 706-7.

Benjamin of Tudela (A.D. 1164) calls it "Dar-al-Maraphtan" which his latest Editor explains by "Dar-al-Mora-bittan" (abode of those who require being chained). Al-Makrizi (Khitat) ascribes the invention of "Spitals" to Hippocrates; another historian to an early Pharaoh "Manákiyush;" thus ignoring the Persian Kings, Saint Ephrem (or Ephraim) Syru etc. In modern parlance "Maristan" is a madhouse where the maniacs are treated with all the horrors which were universal in Europe till within a few years and of which occasional traces occur to this day. In A.D. 1399 Katherine de la Court held a "hospital in the Court called Robert de Paris;" but the first madhouse in Christendom was built by the legate Ortiz in Toledo A.D. 1483, and was therefore called Casa del Nuncio. The Damascus "Maristan" was described by every traveller of the last century: and it showed a curious contrast between the treatment of the maniac and the idiot or omadhaun, who is humanely allowed to wander about unharmed, if not held a Saint. When I saw it last (1870) it was all but empty and mostly in ruins. As far as my experience goes, the United States is the only country where the insane are rationally treated by the sane.

*

GLANCE OF A SPY

ARAB. "NARJÍS." THE Arabs borrowed nothing, but the Persians much, from Greek Mythology. Hence the eye of Narcissus, an idea hardly suggested by the look of the daffodil (or asphodel) flower, is at times the glance of a spy and at times the die-away look of a mistress. Some scholars explain it by the form of the flower, the internal calyx resembling the iris, and the stalk being bent just below the petals suggesting drooping eyelids and languid eyes. Hence a poet addresses the Narcissus: —

O Narjis, look away! Before those eyes;
I may not kiss her as a-breast she lies.
What! Shall the lover close his eyes in sleep;
While thine watch all things between earth and skies?

The fashionable lover in the East must affect a frantic jealousy if he does not feel it.

*

IN WANT OF FURNITURE

In Egypt there are neither bedsteads nor bed-rooms: the carpets and mattresses, pillows and cushions (sheets being unknown) are spread out when wanted, and during the day are put into chests or cupboards, or only rolled up in a corner of the room (Pilgrimage i., 53).

*

SANGUINARY JEALOUSY

The women of Damascus have always been famed for the sanguinary jealousy with which European story-books and novels credit the "Spanish lady." The men were as celebrated for intolerance and fanaticism, which we first read of in the days of Bertrandon de la Brocquière and which culminated in the massacre of 1860. Yet they are a notoriously timid race and make, physically and morally, the worst of soldiers: we proved that under my late friend Fred. Walpole in the Bashi-Buzuks during the old Crimean war. The men looked very fine fellows and after a month in camp fell off to the condition of old women.

*

BITING FINGERS

IN SIGN OF disappointment, regret, vexation; a gesture still common amongst Moslems and corresponding in significance to a certain extent with our stamping, wringing the hands and so forth. It is not mentioned in the Koran where, however, we find "biting fingers' ends out of wrath" against a man (chapt. iii).

*

NO UNMERITED SCANDAL

When she grew up, I sent her to Cairo and married her to her cousin, my brother's son. After a while he died and she came back: but she had learnt wantonness and ungraciousness from the people of Cairo; so she visited thee four times and at last brought her younger sister.

This is no unmerited scandal. The Cairenes, especially the feminine half (for reasons elsewhere given), have always been held exceedingly debauched. Even the modest Lane gives a "shocking" story of a woman enjoying her lover under the nose of her husband and confining the latter in a madhouse (chapt. xiii.) With civilisation, which objects to the good old remedy, the sword, they become worse: and the Kazi's court is crowded with would-be divorcees. Under English rule the evil has reached its acme because it goes unpunished: in the avenues of the new Isma'iliyah Quarter, inhabited by Europeans, women, even young women, will threaten to expose their persons unless they receive "bakhshísh." It was the same in Sind when husbands were assured that they would be hanged for cutting down adulterous wives: at once after its conquest the women broke loose; and in 1843-50, if a young officer sent to the bazar for a girl, half-a-dozen would troop to his quarters. Indeed more than once the professional prostitutes threatened to memorialise Sir Charles Napier because the "modest women," the "ladies" were taking the bread out of their mouths. The same was the case at Kabul (Caboul) of Afghanistan in the old war of 1840; and here the women had more excuse, the husbands being notable sodomites as the song has it: —

The worth of slit the Afghan knows;
The worth of hole the Kábul-man.

*

RICHARD BURTON

THREE SISTERS GERMAN

"...See then, O my son, what hath come to pass; and now I desire thee not to thwart me in what I am about to offer thee, and it is that I purpose to marry thee to my youngest daughter; for she is a virgin and born of another mother; and I will take no dower of thee but, on the contrary, will appoint thee an allowance, and thou shalt abide with me in my house in the stead of my son."

So that he might not have to do with three sisters german. Moreover amongst Moslems a girl's conduct is presaged by that of her mother; and if one sister go wrong, the other is expected to follow suit. Practically the rule applies everywhere: "like mother like daughter."

*

PASSING THE BLADE

THE "MUZAYYIN" OR barber in the East brings his basin and budget under his arm: he is not content only to shave, he must scrape the forehead, trim the eyebrows, pass the blade lightly over the nose and correct the upper and lower lines of the mustachios, opening the central parting and so forth. He is not a whit less a tattler and a scandalmonger than the old Roman tonsor or Figaro his *confrère* in Southern Europe. The whole scene of the Barber is admirable, an excellent specimen of Arab humour and not over-caricatured. We all have met him.

CONGRESS WITH A CROCODILE

*

SCALPS

KORAN XLVIII., 8. It may be observed that according to the Ahádis (sayings of the Prophet) and the Sunnat (sayings and doings of Mahommed), all the hair should be allowed to grow or the whole head be clean shaven. Hence the "Shúshah," or topknot supposed to be left as a handle for drawing the wearer into Paradise; and the Zulf, or side-locks, somewhat like the ringlets of the Polish Jews, are both vain "Bida'at," or innovations, and therefore technically termed "Makrúh," a practice not laudable, neither "Halál" (perfectly lawful) nor "Harám" (forbidden by the law). When boys are first shaved, generally in the second or third year, a tuft is left on the crown and another over the forehead: but this is not the fashion amongst adults. Abu Hanifah, if I am rightly informed, wrote a treatise on the Shushah or long lock growing from the Násiyah (head-poll) which is also a precaution lest the decapitated Moslem's mouth be defiled by an impure hand; and thus it would resemble the chivalry-lock by which the Redskin brave (and even the "cowboy" of better times) facilitated the removal of his own scalp. Possibly the Turks had learned the practice from the Chinese and introduced it into Baghdad (Pilgrimage i., 240). The Badawi plait their locks in Kurún (horns) or Jadáil (ringlets) which are undone only to be washed with the water of the she-camel. The wild Sherifs wear Haffah, long elf-locks hanging down both sides of the throat, and shaved away about a finger's breadth round the forehead and behind the neck (Pilgrimage iii., 35-36). I have elsewhere noted the *accroche-cœurs*, the "idiot-fringe," etc.

*

BLOOD OF REDEMPTION

MEATS ARE RARELY coloured in modern days; but Persian cooks are great adepts in staining rice for the "Puláo" (which we call after its Turkish corruption "pilaff"): it sometimes appears in rainbow-colours, red, yellow and blue; and in India is covered with gold and silver leaf. Europe retains the practice in tinting Pasch (Easter) eggs, the survival of the mundane ovum which was hatched at Easter-tide; and they are dyed red in allusion to the Blood of Redemption.

*

CABBAGING

THE TAILOR IN the East, as in Southern Europe, is made to cut out the cloth in presence of its owner to prevent "cabbaging."

*

MINERAL DYES

HAIR-DYES, IN the East, are all of vegetable matter, henna, indigo-leaves, galls, etc.: our mineral dyes are, happily for them, unknown. Herklots will supply a host of recipes. The Egyptian mixture which I quoted in Pilgrimage (ii., 274) is sulphate of iron and ammoniure of iron one part and gall nuts two parts, infused in eight parts of distilled water. It is innocuous but very poor as a dye.

*

LOST EYE

"... Then she will bid thee doff thy clothes and run; and she will run before thee as if she were flying from thee; and do thou follow her from place to place till thy prickle stands at fullest point, when she will yield to thee;" adding, "Strip off thy clothes at once." So he rose, well nigh lost in ecstacy and, doffing his raiment, showed himself mother-naked. — And Shahrazad perceived the dawn of day and ceased to say her permitted say.

This scene used to be enacted a few years ago in Paris for the benefit of concealed spectators, a young American being the victim. It was put down when one of the lookers-on lost his eye by a pen-knife thrust into the "crevice."

*

WEAK-EYED

THE BLIND IN Egypt are notorious for insolence and violence, fanaticism and rapacity. Not a few foreigners have suffered from them (Pilgrimage i. 148). In former times many were blinded in infancy by their mothers, and others blinded themselves to escape conscription or honest hard work. They could always obtain food, especially as Mu'ezzins; and were preferred because they could not take advantage of the minaret by spying into their neighbours' households. The Egyptian race is chronically weak-eyed, the effect of the damp hot climate of the valley, where ophthalmia prevailed even during the pre-Pharaohnic days. The great Sesostris died stone-blind and his successor lost his sight for ten years (Pilgrimage ii., 176). That the Fellahs are now congenitally weak-eyed, may by seen by comparing them with negroes imported from Central Africa. Ophthalmia rages, especially during the damp season, in the lower Nile-valley; and the best cure for it is a fortnight's trip to the Desert where, despite glare, sand and wind, the eye readily recovers tone.

*

ONE-EYED MEN

A FORMULA FOR averting "Al-Ayn," the evil eye. It is always unlucky to meet a one-eyed man, especially the first thing in the morning and when setting out on any errand. The idea is that the fascinated one will suffer from some action of the physical eye. Monoculars also are held to be rogues: so the Sanskrit saying "Few one-eyed men be honest men."

*

HALF WAY TO GOD

ARAB. "SADAKAH" (SINCERITY), voluntary or superogatory alms, opposed to "Zakát" (purification), legal alms which are indispensable. "Prayer carries us half way to Allah; fasting brings us to the door of His palace and alms-deeds (Sadakah) causes us to enter." For "Zakát" no especial rate is fixed; but it should not be less than one-fortieth of property or two and a half per cent. Thus Al-Islam is, as far as I know, the only faith which makes a poor-rate (Zakát) obligatory and which has invented a property-tax, as opposed to the unjust and unfair income-tax upon which England prides herself.

*

THE VAULT

ARAB. "SARDÁBEH" (PERSIAN) = an underground room used for coolness in the hot season. It is unknown in Cairo but every house in Baghdad, in fact throughout the Mesopotamian cities, has one. It is on the principle of the underground cellar without which wine will not keep: Lane (i., 406) calls it a "vault."

*

RICHARD BURTON

ACTING SWISS

As he was on the road he suddenly caught sight of a large and handsome mansion, with a detached building wide and lofty at the entrance, where sat sundry eunuchs bidding and forbidding.

The Castrato at the door is still (I have said,) the fashion of Cairo and he acts "Suisse" with a witness.

*

TAKING SALT

"Nahnu málihín" = we are on terms of salt, said and say the Arabs. But the traveller must not trust in these days to the once sacred tie; there are tribes which will give bread with one hand and stab with the other. The Eastern use of salt is a curious contrast with that of Westerns, who made it an invidious and inhospitable distinction, *e.g.* to sit above the salt-cellar and below the salt. Amongst the ancients, however, "he took bread and salt" means he swore, the food being eaten when an oath was taken. Hence the "Bride cake" of salt, water and flour.

*

COOLING BARLEY

BARLEY IN ARABIA is, like our oats, food for horses: it fattens at the same time that it cools them. Had this been known to our cavalry when we first occupied Egypt in 1883-4 our losses in horse-flesh would have been far less; but official ignorance persisted in feeding the cattle upon heated oats and the riders upon beef, which is indigestible, instead of mutton, which is wholesome.

*

LIFE IN THE BALANCE

THE KING'S BARBER is usually a man of rank for the best of reasons that he holds his Sovereign's life between his fingers. One of these noble Figaros in India married an English lady who was, they say, unpleasantly surprised to find out what were her husband's official duties.

*

POWER OF THE PEN

THE BUL. EDIT. gives the lines as follows: —
    The lance was his pen, and the hearts of his foes
    His paper, and dipped he in blood for ink;
    Hence our sires entitled the spear Khattíyah,
    Meaning that withal man shall write, I think.

The pun is in "Khattíyah" which may mean a writer (feminine) and also a spear, from Khatt-Hajar, a tract in the province Al-Bahrayn (Persian Gulf), and Oman, where the best Indian bamboos were landed and fashioned into lances. Imr al-Kays (Mu'allakah v. 4.) sings of "our dark spears firmly wrought of Khattiyan cane;" Al-Busírí of "the brown lances of Khatt;" also see Lebid v. 50 and Hamásah pp. 26, 231: Antar notes the "Spears of Khatt" and "Rudaynian lances." Rudaynah is said to have been the wife of one Samhár, the Ferrara of lances; others make her the wife of Al-Ka'azab and hold Samhár to be a town in Abyssinia where the best weapons were manufactured. The pen is the Calamus or Kalam (reed cut for pen) of which the finest and hardest are brought from Java: they require the least nibbing. The rhetorical figure in the text is called Husn al-Ta'alíl, our ætiology; and is as admirable to the Arabs as it appears silly to us.

*

MOONLIGHT

"THE SUN SHALL not smite thee by day, nor the moon by night" (Psalm cxxi. 6). Easterns still believe in the blighting effect of the moon's rays, which the Northerners of Europe, who view it under different conditions, are pleased to deny. I have seen a hale and hearty Arab, after sitting an hour in the moonlight, look like a man fresh from a sick bed; and I knew an Englishman in India whose face was temporarily paralysed by sleeping with it exposed to the moon.

*

LOST MAN

A moon which blights you if you dare behold;
A branch which folds you in its waving fold:
Locks of the Zanj and golden glint of hair;
Sweet gait and form a spear to have and hold:
Ah! hard of heart with softest slenderest waist,
That evil to this weal why not remould?

i.e. Why not make thy heart as soft as thy sides! The converse of this was reported at Paris during the Empire, when a man had by mistake pinched a very high personage: "Ah, Madame! if your heart be as hard as (what he had pinched) I am a lost man."

*

UNPLEASANT PLEASANTRIES

"NA'ÍMAN" IS said to one after bathing or head-shaving: the proper reply, for in the East every sign of ceremony has its countersign, is "Allah benefit thee!" (Pilgrimage i. II, iii. 285; Lane M. E. chapt. viii.; Caussin de Perceval's Arabic Grammar, etc., etc.). I have given a specimen (Pilgrimage i., 122) not only of sign and countersign, but also of the rhyming repartee which rakes love. Hanien! (pleasant to thee! said when a man drinks). Allah pleasure thee (Allah yuhanník which Arnauts and other ruffians perverted to Allah yaník,

Allah copulate with thee); thou drinkest for *ten*! — I am the cock and thou art the *hen*! (*i.e.* a passive catamite) — Nay, I am the thick one (the penis which gives pleasure) and thou art the *thin*! And so forth with most unpleasant pleasantries.

*

DISGRACE

AMONGST MOSLEMS, I have said, it is held highly disgraceful when the sound of women's cries can be heard by outsiders.

*

FUNERAL PRAYER

PRAYERS OVER THE dead are not universal in Al-Islam; but when they are recited they lack the "sijdah" or prostration.

*

FEAST OF THE CIRCUMCISION

IN ONE MATTER Moslems contrast strongly with Christians, by most scrupulously following the example of their law-giver: hence they are the model Conservatives. But (European) Christendom is here, as in other things, curiously contradictory: for instance, it still keeps a "Feast of the Circumcision," and practically holds circumcision in horror. Eastern Christians, however, have not wholly abolished it, and the Abyssinians, who find it a useful hygienic precaution, still practise it. For ulcers, syphilis and other venereals which are readily cured in Egypt become dangerous in the Highlands of Ethiopia.

*

THE CITADEL

HENCE THE KHEDIVIAL Palace near Cairo "Kasr al-Nuzhah;" literally "of Delights;" one of those flimsy new-Cairo buildings which contrast so marvellously with the architecture of ancient and even of mediæval Egypt, and which are covering the land with modern ruins. Compare Mohammed Ali's mosque in the citadel with the older Sultan Hasan. A popular tale is told that, when the conquering Turk, Yáwúz Sultan Selim, first visited Cairo, they led him to Mosque Al-Ghúri. "This is a splendid Ká'ah (saloon)!" quoth he. When he entered Sultan Hasan, he exclaimed, "This is a citadel!"; but after inspecting the Mosque Al-Mu'ayyad he cried, "'Tis a veritable place of prayer, a fit stead for the Faithful to adore the Eternal!"

*

SENSITIVE

ARAB. GARDENERS ARE very touchy on this point. A friend of mine was on a similar occasion addressed, in true Egyptian lingo, by an old Adam-son, "Ya ibn al-Kalb! beta'mil ay?" (O dog-son, what art thou up to?).

*

TURTLE-DOVES

IN MOSLEM WRITINGS the dove and turtle-dove are mostly feminine, whereas the female bird is always mute and only the male sings to summon or to amuse his mate.

*

FOOD TO HIS CAMELS

A TREE WHOSE coals burn with fierce heat: Al-Hariri (Vth Séance). This Artemisia is like the tamarisk but a smaller growth and is held to be a characteristic of the Arabian Desert. A Badawi always hails with pleasure the first sight of the Ghazá, after he has sojourned for time away from his wilds. Mr. Palgrave (i. 38) describes the "Ghadá" as an Euphorbia with a woody stem often 5-6 feet high and slender flexible green twigs (?), "forming a feathery tuft, not ungraceful to the eye, while it affords some shelter to the traveller, and food to his camels."

*

ILL-OMENED

THE ASS IS held to be ill-omened. I have noticed the braying elsewhere. According to Mandeville the Devil did not enter the Ark with the Ass, but he left it when Noah said "Benedicite." In his day (A.D. 1322) and in that of Benjamin of Tudela, people had seen and touched the ship on Ararat, the Judi (Gordiæi) mountains; and this dates from Berosus (S.C. 250) who, of course, refers to the Ark of Xisisthrus. See Josephus Ant. i. 3, 6; and Rodwell (Koran, pp. 65, 530).

*

MOON-FACED

Round with big and little, the bowl and cup,
Take either that moon in his sheen hath crowned:
Nor drink without music, for oft I've seen,
The horse drink best to the whistle's sound!

i.e. the Sáki, cup-boy or cup-bearer. "Moon-faced," as I have shown elsewhere, is no compliment in English, but it is in Persian and Arabic.

*

BENEATH THE VEIL

ARAB. "LISÁM," THE end of the "Kúfiyah," or head-kerchief passed over the face under the eyes and made fast on the other side. This mouth-veil serves as a mask (eyes not being recognisable) and defends from heat, cold and thirst. I also believe that hooding the eyes with this article, Badawi-fashion, produces a sensation of coolness, at any rate a marked difference of apparent temperature; somewhat like a pair of dark spectacles or looking at the sea from a sandy shore. Pilgrimage i., 210 and 346. The woman's "Lisám" (chin-veil) or Yashmak is noticed in i., 337.

*

TAKING A CRAFT

"It passed through my thought, O Commander of the Faithful," said the fisherman, *"that, since thou wishest to learn fishing so thou mayest have in hand an honest trade whereby to gain thy livelihood, this my gaberdine besitteth thee right well."*

Most characteristic is this familiarity between the greatest man then in the world and his pauper subject. The fisherman alludes to a practise of Al-Islam, instituted by Caliph Omar, that all rulers should work at some handicraft in order to spare the public treasure. Hence Sultan Mu'ayyad of Cairo was a calligrapher who sold his handwriting, and his example was followed by the Turkish Sultans Mahmúd, Abd al-Majíd and Abd al-Aziz. German royalties prefer carpentering and Louis XVI. watch-making.

*

GENEROSITY

And warned me to flee from the city afar,
Disappear, disappoint what my enemies planned:
Then we fled from our home 'neath the wing of the night,
And sought us a refuge by Baghdad strand:
Of my riches I've nothing on thee to bestow,
O Fisher, except the fair gift thou hast scanned:
The loved of my soul, and when I from her part,
Know for sure that I give thee the blood of my heart.

Such an act of generosity would appear to Europeans well-nigh insanity, but it is quite in Arab manners. Witness the oft-quoted tale of Hátim and his horse. As a rule the Arab is the reverse of generous, contrasting badly, in this point, with his cousin the Jew: hence his ideal of generosity is of the very highest. "The generous (*i.e.* liberal) is Allah's friend, aye, though he be a sinner; and the miser is Allah's foe, aye, though he be a saint!" Indian Moslems call a skin-flint Makhi-chús = fly-sucker (Pilgrimage i. 242).

*

BEARING THE DEAD

ARAB. "JANÁZAH," so called only when carrying a corpse; else Na'ash, Sarír or Tábút: Irán being the large hearse on which chiefs are borne. It is made of plank or stick-work; but there are several varieties (Lane, M. E. chapt. xxviii).

RICHARD BURTON

*

CANNIBAL TRIBES

"See," said Kafur, "now it is shut and barred." "How weak are your wits!" cried the third who bore the adze and his name was Bukhayt, "know ye not that the owners of the gardens use to come out from Baghdad and tend them and, when evening closes upon them, they enter this place and shut the door, for fear lest the wicked blackmen, like ourselves, should catch them and roast 'em and eat 'em.'

There are, as I have shown, not a few cannibal tribes in Central Africa and these at times find their way into the slave market.

*

EGYPTIAN BLOOD

My purchaser had a daughter three years old, with whom I was brought up, and they used to make mock of me, letting me play with her and dance for her and sing to her, till I reached the age of twelve and she that of ten; and even then they did not forbid me seeing her.

This familiarity with blackamoor slave-boys is common in Egypt and often ends as in the story: Egyptian blood is sufficiently mixed with negro to breed inclination for miscegenation. But here the girl was wickedly neglected by her mother at such an age as ten.

*

CLOSE INSPECTION

On the night of consummation they cut the throat of a pigeon-poult and sprinkled the blood on her shift.

This ancient and venerable practice of inspecting the marriage-sheet is still religiously preserved in most parts of the East; and in old-fashioned Moslem families it is publicly exposed in the Harem to prove that the "domestic calamity" (the daughter) went to her husband a clean maid. Also the general idea is that no blood will impose upon the experts, or jury of matrons, except that of a pigeon-poult which exactly resembles hymeneal blood — when not subjected to the microscope. This belief is universal in Southern Europe and I have heard of it in England. Further details will be given in Night ccxi.

*

ADDRESSED TO A EUNUCH

"Agha" Turk. = sir, gentleman, is, I have said, politely addressed to a eunuch.

RICHARD BURTON

*

LONG PERFORMANCE

After a while they seized me unawares and gelded me; and, when they brought her to her bridegroom, they made me her Agha, her eunuch, to walk before her wheresoever she went, whether to the bath or to her father's house. I abode with her a long time enjoying her beauty and loveliness by way of kissing and clipping and coupling with her, till she died, and her husband and mother and father died also; when they seized me for the Royal Treasury as being the property of an intestate, and I found my way hither, where I became your comrade.

As Bukhayt tells us he lost only his testes, consequently his *erectio et distensio penis* was as that of a boy before puberty and it would last as long as his heart and circulation kept sound. Hence the eunuch who preserves his penis is much prized in the Zenanah where some women prefer him to the entire man, on account of his long performance of the deed of kind. Of this more in a future page.

*

CORNICING

IT IS OR rather was the custom in Egypt and Syria to range long rows of fine China bowls along the shelves running round the rooms at the height of six or seven feet, and they formed a magnificent cornice. I bought many of them at Damascus till the people, learning their value, asked prohibitive prices.

*

NOSE-BAGS

Now when it was the Fortieth Night…

The tale is interesting as well as amusing, excellently describing the extravagances still practised in middle-class Moslem families on the death of the pater familias. I must again note that Arab women are much more unwilling to expose the back of the head covered by the "Tarhah" (head-veil) than the face, which is hidden by the "Burka" or nose-bag.

*

HYSTERICS

The first to address my owner were his wife and children; and when he saw them he was confounded and laughed and said to them, "How is it with all of you and what befel you in the house and what hath come to pass to you?" When they saw him they exclaimed, "Praise be to Allah for thy preservation!"

The usual hysterical laughter of this nervous race.

RICHARD BURTON

*

UNWANTED FREEDOM

"…When this is done, go down with me to the slave-market and sell me as thou boughtest me to whoso will buy me with my blemish; but thou shalt not manumit me, for I have no handicraft whereby to gain my living; and this my demand is a matter of law which the doctors have laid down in the Chapter of Emancipation."

Here the slave refuses to be set free and starve. For a master so to do without ample reason is held disgraceful. I well remember the weeping and wailing throughout Sind when an order from Sir Charles Napier set free the negroes whom British philanthropy thus doomed to endure if not to die of hunger.

*

MANUMISSION

MANUMISSION WHICH IS founded upon Roman law, is an extensive subject discussed in the Hidáyah and other canonical works. The slave here lays down the law incorrectly, but his claim shows his true impudence.

*

SECRET SATISFACTION

Then my master returned home and found his house in ruins, and it was I who had laid waste the greater part of it, having broken things which were worth much money, as also had done his wife, who said to him, "'Twas Kafur who broke the vessels and chinaware."

This is quite true to nature. The most remarkable thing in the wild central African is his enormous development of "destructiveness." At Zanzibar I never saw a slave break a glass or plate without a grin or a chuckle of satisfaction.

*

THE TWO EGGS

ARAB. "KHASSÁ-NI"; KHUSYATÁNI (vulg.) being the testicles, also called "bayzatán" (the two eggs) a *double entendre* which has given rise to many tales. For instance in the witty Persian book "Dozd o Kazi" (The Thief and the Judge) a footpad strips the man of learning and offers to return his clothes if he can ask him a puzzle in law or religion. The Kazi (in folk-lore mostly a fool) fails, and his wife bids him ask the man to supper for a trial of wits on the same condition. She begins with compliments and ends by producing five eggs which she would have him distribute equally amongst the three; and, when he is perplexed, she gives one to each of the men taking three for herself. Whereupon the "Dozd" wends his way, having lost his booty as his extreme stupidity deserved. In the text the eunuch, Kafur, is made a "Sandali" or smooth-shaven, so that he was of no use to women.

*

SWEET NAMES

But no one answered her, so she turned her and cried out, "Ho Sabíhah! Shajarat al-Durr! Núr al-Hudá! Najmat al-Subh! be ye awake? Shahwah, Nuzhah, Halwá, Zarífah, out on you, speak!..."

Names of her slave-girls which mean (in order), Garden-bloom, Dawn (or Beautiful), Tree o' Pearl (P. N. of Saladin's wife), Light of (right) Direction, Star o' the Morn, Lewdness (= Shahwah, I suppose this is a chaff), Delight, Sweetmeat and Miss Pretty.

*

DISPOSAL OF A RIVAL

"O my lady," he replied, "three slave-eunuchs came here bearing this chest;" and related to her the whole of what had befallen him, and how evening having closed upon him had proved the cause of her preservation, otherwise she had died smothered.

CONGRESS WITH A CROCODILE

This mode of disposing of a rival was very common in Harems. But it had its difficulties and on the whole the river was (and is) preferred.

*

DINGY DRINKING

An Eastern dislikes nothing more than drinking in a dim dingy place: the brightest lights seem to add to his "drinkitite."

*

PRUDENCE

They ceased not to carouse after this fashion till near upon dawn when drowsiness overcame them and they slept where they were, apart each from other, till the morning.

He did not sleep with her because he suspected some palace-mystery which suggested prudence, she also had her reasons.

*

FAWNING DOGS

Arab. "Maragha" lit. rubbed his face on them like a fawning dog. Ghanim is another "softy" lover, a favourite character in Arab tales; and by way of contrast, the girl is masterful enough.

*

LEAVE OF ABSENCE

THE MOST TERRIBLE part of a *belle passion* in the East is that the beloved will not allow her lover leave of absence for an hour.

*

WRETCHED PUNS

From eyelids driven sleep by deputy:
Passion thou hast infused in every heart,
From eyelids driven sleep by deputy:
Erst was (I wot) the spray made thin of leaf
O Cassia-spray! Unlief thy sin I see...

It is hard to preserve these wretched puns. In the original we have "O spray" (or branch) of capparis-shrub (*aráki*) which has been thinned of leaf and fruit (*tujna, i.e.*, whose fruit, the hymen, has been plucked before and not by me) I see thee (*aráka*) against me sinning (*tajní*).

*

BADGE OF MOURNING

We will dig a grave for it midmost the palace and there bury it: then do thou build an oratory over it and set therein lighted candles and lamps, and order each and every in the palace to be clad in black.

Apparently the writer forgets that the Abbaside banners and dress were black, originally a badge of mourning for the Imám Ibrahim bin Mohammed put to death by the Ommiade Caliph Al-Marwán. The modern Egyptian mourning, like the old Persian, is indigo-blue of the darkest; but, as before noted, the custom is by no means universal.

*

ARRIVAL FROM THE ROAD

A SERVANT RETURNING from a journey shows his master due honour by appearing before him in travelling suit and uncleaned.

*

LOOT

When the missive came to the viceroy, he kissed it and laid it on his head; then he let proclaim in the bazars, "Whoso is desirous to plunder, away with him to the house of Ghanim son of Ayyub."

These plunderings were sanctioned by custom. But a few years ago, when the Turkish soldiers mutinied about arrears of pay (often delayed for years) the governing Páshá would set fire to the town and allow the men to loot what they pleased during a stated time. Rochet (*soi-disant* D'Héricourt) amusingly describes this manœuvre of the Turkish Governor of Al-Hodaydah in the last generation (Pilgrimage iii. 381).

*

WEEPING AND WAILING

So they flocked thither, when they found that Ghanim's mother and sister had built him a tomb in the midst of the house and sat by it weeping for him; whereupon they seized the two without telling them the cause and, after spoiling the house, carried them before the viceroy.

Another cenotaph whose use was to enable women to indulge in their pet pastime of weeping and wailing in company.

*

PAUPER LODGINGS

THE LODGING OF pauper travellers, as the chapel in Iceland is of the wealthy. I have often taken benefit of the mosque, but as a rule it is unpleasant, the matting being not only torn but over-populous. Juvenal seems to allude to the Jewish

Synagogue similarly used: — "in quâ te quæro proseuchâ"? (iii. 296) and in Acts iii. we find the lame, blind and impotent in the Temple-porch.

*

THE FIRST LOUSE

There he lay till dawn, his heart fluttering for want of food; and, owing to his sweating, the lice coursed over his skin; his breath waxed fetid and his whole condition was changed.

This foul sort of vermin is supposed to be bred by perspiration. It is an epoch in the civilised traveller's life when he catches his first louse.

*

KIND-HEARTED

THE MOSLEM PEASANT is a kind-hearted man and will make many sacrifices for a sick stranger even of another creed. It is a manner of "pundonor" with the village.

*

IN THE PRESENT

Next day the villagers brought a camel and said to the cameleer, "Set this sick man on thy beast and carry him to

Baghdad and put him down at the Spital-door; so haply he may be medicined and be healed and thou shalt have thy hire."

This may also mean, "And Heaven will reward thee;" but camel-men do not usually accept any drafts upon futurity.

*

LIKE THE DEAD

Presently, he woke and finding himself bound with ropes on a camel's back, he began to weep and complain, and the village-people saw his mother and sister weeping over him, albeit they knew him not.

He felt that he was being treated like a corpse.

*

TAKING TO THE PILLOW

THE IMPORTANCE OF the pillow (wisádah or makhaddah) to the sick man is often recognised in The Nights. "He took to his pillow" is = took to his bed.

*

PROGNOSTICATIONS

When she heard his words her heart fluttered and her vitals yearned, and she said to him, "Send with me one who shall guide me to thy house."

The reader will notice in The Nights the frequent mention of these physical prognostications, with which mesmerists are familiar.

*

SATISFACTION

For he had built twelve pavilions, after the number of the months, each containing thirty private chambers, which thus numbered three hundred and three score, wherein he lodged his handmaids: and he appointed according to law for each one her night, when he lay with her and came not again to her for a full year; and on this wise he abode for a length of time.
This is a Moslem law (Koran chapt. iv. bodily borrowed from the Talmud) which does not allow a man to marry one wife unless he can carnally satisfy her. Moreover he must distribute his honours equally and each wife has a right to her night unless she herself give it up. This was the case even with the spouses of the Prophet; and his biography notices several occasions when his wives waived their rights in favour of one another. M. Riche kindly provides the King with *la piquante française* (p. 15).

107

RICHARD BURTON

*

A SCANDALOUS GIFT

So THE CELEBRATED mosque in Stambul, famed for being the largest church in the world, is known to the Greeks as "Agia (pron. Aya) Sophia" and to Moslems as "Aya Sofiyeh" (Holy Wisdom) *i.e.* the Logos or Second Person of the Trinity (not a Saintess). The sending a Christian girl as a present to a Moslem would, in these days be considered highly scandalous. But it was done by the Mukaukis or Coptic Governor of Egypt (under Heraclius) who of course hated the Greeks. This worthy gave two damsels to Mohammed, one called Sírín and the other Máriyah (Maria) whom the Prophet reserved for his especial use and whose abode is still shown at Al-Medinah. The Rev. Doctor Badger (loc. cit. p. 972) gives the translation of an epistle by Mohammed to this Mukaukis, written in the Cufic character (??) and sealed "Mohammed, The Apostle of Allah." My friend seems to believe that it is an original, but upon this subject opinions will differ. It is, however, exceedingly interesting, beginning with "Bismillah," etc., and ending (before the signature) with a quotation from the Koran (iii. 57); and may be assumed as a formula addressed to foreign potentates by a Prophet who had become virtually "King of Arabia."

*

THE GROANING-CHAIR

EXODUS I. 16, quoted by Lane (M. E., chapt. xxvii.). Torrens in his Notes cites Drayton's "Moon-calf": —
Bring forth the birth-stool — no, let it alone;
She is so far beyond all compass grown,
Some other new device us needs must stead,
Or else she never can be brought to bed.
It is the "groaning-chair" of Poor Robin's Almanac (1676) and we find it alluded to in Boccaccio, the classical sedile which according to scoffers has formed the papal chair (a curule seat) ever since the days of Pope Joan, when it has been held advisable for one of the Cardinals to ascertain that His Holiness possesses all the instruments of virility. This "Kursí al-wiládah" is of peculiar form on which the patient is seated. A most interesting essay might be written upon the various positions preferred during delivery, *e.g.* the wild Irish still stand on all fours, like the so-called "lower animals." Amongst the Moslems of Waday, etc., a cord is hung from the top of the hut, and the woman in labour holds on to it standing with her legs apart, till the midwife receives the child.

*

LULLILOOING

SOME ORIENTALISTS CALL "lullilooing" the trilling cry, which is made by raising the voice to its highest pitch and breaking it by a rapid succession of touches on the palate with the tongue-tip, others "Ziraleet" and Zagaleet, and one traveller tells us that it began at the marriage-festival of Isaac and Rebecca(!). Arabs term it classically Tahlíl and vulgarly Zaghrutah (Plur. Zaghárit) and Persians "Kil." Finally in Don Quixote we have "Lelilies," the battle-cry of the Moors (Duffield iii. 289). Dr. Buchanan likens it to a serpent uttering human sounds, but the good missionary heard it at the festival of Jagannath (Pilgrimage iii. 197).

*

PRELIMINARY MOVE

When the appointed three days were ended, the army drew out to the suburbs of Baghdad city; and King Omar came forth to take leave of his son who kissed the ground before him and received from the King seven parcels of money.

This preliminary move, called in Persian Nakl-i-Safar, is generally mentioned. So the Franciscan monks in California, when setting out for a long journey through the desert, marched three times round the convent and pitched tents for the night under its walls.

*

110

CONGRESS WITH A CROCODILE

WILD BEASTS DURING NOON-HEATS

ARAB. "GHÁBAH" NOT a forest in our sense of the word, but a place where water sinks and the trees (mostly Mimosas), which elsewhere are widely scattered, form a comparatively dense growth and collect in thickets. These are favourite places for wild beasts during noon-heats.

*

FATHER OF FARTS

ARAB. "ZIRT," A low word. The superlative "Zarrát" (fartermost) or, "Abu Zirt" (Father of farts) is a facetious term among the bean-eating Fellahs and a deadly insult amongst the Badawin (Night ccccx.). The latter prefer the word Taggáa (Pilgrimage iii. 84). We did not disdain the word in farthingale = pet en air.

*

UNLEAPING

When the damsel saw him she sprang to her feet and, taking firm stand on the bank of the stream, whose breadth was six ells, the normal cubits, made one bound and landed clear on the farther side, where she turned and cried out with a loud voice, "Who art thou, O thou fellow..."

Arab horses are never taught to leap, so she was quite safe on the other side of a brook nine feet broad.

RICHARD BURTON

*

MAN'S SEED

Then he sware to her by all she named and tied his steed to a tree; but he was drowned in the sea of thought, saying in himself, "Praise be to Him who fashioned her from dirty water!"

The allusion is Koranic: "O men, if ye be in doubt concerning the resurrection, consider that he first created you of the dust of the ground (Adam); afterwards of seed" (chapt. xxii.). But the physiological ideas of the Koran are curious. It supposes that the Mani or male semen is in the loins and that of women in the breast bone (chapt. lxxxvi.); that the mingled seed of the two (chapt. lxxvi.) fructifies the ovary and that the child is fed through the navel with menstruous blood, hence the cessation of the catamenia. Barzoi (Kalilah and Dímnah) says: — "Man's seed, falling into the woman's womb, is mixed with her seed and her blood: when it thickens and curdles the Spirit moves it and it turns about like liquid cheese; then it solidifies, its arteries are formed, its limbs constructed and its joints distinguished. If the babe is a male, his face is placed towards his mother's back; if a female, towards her belly. (P. 262, Mr. I. G. N. Keith-Falconer's translation.) But there is a curious prolepsis of the spermatozoa-theory. We read (Koran chapt. vii.), "Thy Lord drew forth their posterity from the loins of the sons of Adam;" and the commentators say that Allah stroked Adam's back and extracted from his loins

112

all his posterity, which shall ever be, in the shape of small ants; these confessed their dependence on God and were dismissed to return whence they came." From this fiction it appears (says Sale) that the doctrine of pre-existence is not unknown to the Mohammedans; and there is some little conformity between it and the modern theory of generatio ex animalculis in semine marium. The poets call this Yaum-i-Alast = the Day of Am-I-not (-your Lord)? which Sir William Jones most unhappily translated "Art thou not with thy Lord?" (Alasta bi Rabbi-kum); and they produce a grand vision of unembodied spirits appearing in countless millions before their Creator.

*

FAIR FALL

Then each approached the adversary and he set his breast against hers, but when he felt waist touch waist, his strength failed him; and she, waxing ware of this, lifted him with her hands swiftlier than the blinding leven-flash, and threw him to the ground. He fell on his back, and then she said to him, "Rise: I give thee thy life a second time…"

In Eastern wrestling this counts as a fair fall. So Ajax fell on his back with Ulysses on his breast (Iliad XXXii., 700, etc.).

*

RICHARD BURTON

BARING TEETH

"...but I charge thee, if there be in the Moslem army sent by Omar bin al-Nu'uman to succour the King of Constantinople, a stronger than thou, send him hither and tell him of me: for in wrestling there are shifts and trips, catches and holds, such as the feint or falsing and the snap or first grip, the hug, the feet-catch, the thigh-bite the jostle and the leg-lock."

So biting was allowed amongst the Greeks in the ἀνακλινοπάλη, the final struggle on the ground.

*

SPOILS OF WAR

KORAN IV., XXII. etc., meaning it is lawful to marry women taken in war after the necessary purification although their husbands be still living. This is not permitted with a free woman who is a True Believer. I have noted that the only concubine slave-girls mentioned in the Koran are these "captives possessed by the right hand."

*

AMAZONS

"Now by the virtue of thy faith," she replied, "did I not fear lest the news of me be bruited abroad that I am of the daughters of Roum, I would adventure myself and sally forth single-handed

114

against the ten thousand horsemen and slay their leader, the Wazir Dandan and vanquish their champion Sharrkan."

The Amazonian dame is a favourite in folk-lore and is an ornament to poetry from the Iliad to our modern day. Such heroines, apparently unknown to the Pagan Arabs, were common in the early ages of Al-Islam as Ockley and Gibbon prove, and that the race is not extinct may be seen in my Pilgrimage (iii. 55) where the sister of Ibn Rumi resolved to take blood revenge for her brother.

*

QUEEN OF SHEBA

AND SOLOMON SAID, "O nobles, which of you will bring me her throne?" A terrible genius (*i.e.* an Ifrit of the Jinn named Dhakwan or the notorious Sakhr) said, "I will bring it unto thee before thou arise from thy seat (of justice); for I am able to perform it, and may be trusted" (Koran, xxvii. 38-39). Balkís or *Bilkís* (says the Durrat al-Ghawwás) daughter of Hozád bin Sharhabíl, twenty-second in the list of the rulers of Al-Yaman, according to some murdered her husband, and became, by Moslem ignorance, the Biblical "Queen of Sheba." The Abyssinians transfer her from Arabian Saba to Ethiopia and make her the mother by Solomon of Menelek, their proto-monarch; thus claiming for their royalties an antiquity compared with which all reigning houses in the world are of yesterday. The dates of the Tabábi'ah or Tobbas

115

prove that the Bilkís of history ruled Al-Yaman in the early Christian era.

*

BEDFELLOWS

She was clad in brocades befitting Kings; her breasts were like twin pomegranates, a woven zone set with all kinds of jewels tightly clasped her waist which expanded below into jutting hips; and her hinder cheeks stood out as a mound of crystal supporting a silvern shaft.

This prominence of the glutæi muscles is always insisted upon, because it is supposed to promise well in a bedfellow. In Somali-land, where the people are sub-steatopygous, a rich young man, who can afford such luxury, will have the girls drawn up in line and choose her to wife who projects furthest behind.

*

FOUNTAIN OF PARADISE

THE FOUNTAIN IN Paradise whose water shall be drunk with "pure" wine mixed and sealed with musk (for clay). It is so called because it comes from the "Sanam" (Sanima, to be high) boss or highest ridge of the Moslem Heaven (Koran lv.

78 and lxxxiii. 27). Mr. Rodwell says "it is conveyed to the highest apartments in the Pavilions of Paradise."

*

BEAST OF AFRICA

ARAB. "AL-FIL," the elephant = the French fol or fou and our bishop. I have derived "elephant" from Píl (old Persian, Sansk. Pilu) and Arab. Fil, with the article Al-Fil, whence the Greek ἐλέφας the suffix — as being devoted to barbarous words as Obod-as (Al-Ubayd), Aretas (Al-Háris), etc. Mr. Isaac Taylor (The Alphabet i. 169), preserves the old absurdity of "eleph-ant or ox-like (!) beast of Africa." Prof. Sayce finds the word al-ab (two distinct characters) in line 3, above the figure of an (Indian) elephant, on the black obelisk of Nimrod Mound, and suggests an Assyrian derivation.

*

EASTERN ATTACK

When he heard this, he sprang to his feet and made for them with his sword and battle-gear; and Masurah, the Knight, also sprang up and bore down upon him. Sharrkan met him like a lion and delivered a shoulder cut which clove him to the middle, and the blade came out gleaming and glittering from his back and bowels.

117

Lit. "smote him on the tendons of his neck." This is the famous shoulder-cut (Tawashshuh) which, with the leg-cut (Kalam), formed, and still forms, the staple of Eastern attack with the sword.

*

THRESHING

ARAB. "DIRÁS." EASTERNS do not thresh with flails. The material is strewed over a round and smoothed floor of dried mud in the open air and threshed by different contrivances. In Egypt the favourite is a chair-like machine called "Norag," running on iron plates and drawn by bulls or cows over the corn. Generally, however, Moslems prefer the old classical Τρίβολον, the Tribulum of Virgil and Varro, a slipper-shaped sled of wood garnished on the sole with large-headed iron nails, or sharp fragments of flint or basalt. Thus is made the "Tibn" or straw, the universal hay of the East, which our machines cannot imitate.

*

KEEPING SCORE

Then she took reckoning of the dead and found that he had slain fourscore of the Knights, and other twenty had taken to flight.

These numbers appear to be grossly exaggerated, but they were possible in the days of sword and armour: at the battle of Saffayn the Caliph Ali is said to have cut down five hundred and twenty-three men in a single night.

*

THE RAVISHER

RICHARDSON IN HIS excellent dictionary (note 103) which modern priggism finds "unscientific," wonderfully derives this word from Arab. "Khattáf," a snatcher (*i.e.* of women), a ravisher. It is an evident corruption of "captivus" through Italian and French.

*

THE WRECKER

Thereupon we sallied forth and, looking on them as spoil driven to us by Fate, boarded and took them; and, slaying the men, made prize of the wreck, wherein we found the treasures and rarities in question and forty maidens, amongst whom was the King's daughter, Sophia.

The "wrecker" is known all over the world; and not only barbarians hold that ships driven ashore become the property of the shore.

119

RICHARD BURTON

*

SHADES OF HORSEFLESH

ARAB. "ASHHAB." NAMES of colours are few amongst semi-civilised peoples, but in Arabia there is a distinct word for every shade of horseflesh.

*

HOCUSSING

"... When the hour of ending the carousal shall draw near, fill her a last cup and dropping therein the Bhang, give it to her to drink, and she will not reach her sleeping-chamber ere the drug take effect on her. Then do thou go in to her and take thy will of her; and such is my advice."

This is not Badawi sentiment: the honoratioren amongst wild people would scorn such foul play; but amongst the settled Arabs honour between men and women is unknown; and such "hocussing" would be held quite fair.

*

WINE-SERVICE

THE TABLE OF wine, in our day, is mostly a japanned tray with glasses and bottles, saucers of pickles and fruits and, perhaps, a bunch of flowers and aromatic herbs. During the Caliphate the "wine-service" was on a larger scale.

*

KNOWN TO SOME

HERE THE "BHANG" (almost a generic term applied to hellebore, etc.) may be hyoscyamus or henbane. Yet there are varieties of Cannabis, such as the Dakha of South Africa, capable of most violent effect. I found the use of the drug well known to the negroes of the Southern United States and of the Brazil, although few of their owners had ever heard of it.

*

COLD AND CONCUPISCENCE

THE NEGRO SKIN assumes this dust-colour in cold, fear, concupiscence and other mental emotions.

Ho thou, Abrizah, mercy! leave me not for I
Of thy love and Yamáni glance the victim lie
My heart is cut to pieces by thy cruelty,
My body wasted and my patience done to die...

He compares her glance with the blade of a Yamani sword, a *lieu commun* of Eastern poetry. The weapons are famous in The Nights; but the best sword-cutlery came from Persia as the porcelain from China to Sana'á. Here, however, is especial allusion as to the sword "Samsam" or "Samsamah." It belonged to the Himyarite Tobba, Amru bin Ma'ad Kurb, and came into the hands of Harun al-Rashid. When the Emperor of the Greeks sent a present of superior sword-blades to him by way of a brave, the Caliph, in the presence of the Envoys, took "Samsam" in hand and cut the others in twain as if they were cabbages without the least prejudice to the edge of "Samsam."

*

SUCKLING IN DEATH

Such was the case with AlGhazban; but as regards Abrizah, she gave birth to a son, like the moon, and Marjanah took the babe and did him the necessary offices and laid him by his mother's side; and lo and behold! the child fastened to its mother's breast and she dying.

This touch of pathos is truly Arab. So in the "Romance of Dalhamah" (Lane, M. E. xxiii.) the infant Gundubah sucks the breast of its dead mother and the King exclaims, "If she had committed this crime she would not be affording the child her milk after she was dead."

*

SICKLY PERFUME

Arab. "Má al-Khaláf"(or "Khiláf") a sickly perfume but much prized, made from the flowers of the Salix Ægyptiaca.

*

ARABS OF THE DESERT

Then she walked on, weeping and turning right and left as she went, when behold, there espied her an old Badawi who had come into the town from the desert with wild Arabs other five.

The word has been explained (vol. i. 112). It is trivial, not occurring in the Koran which uses "Arabs of the Desert;" "Arabs who dwell in tents," etc. (chapt. ix. and xxxiii.). "A'arábi" is the classical word and the origin of "Arab" is disputed. According to Pocock (Notæ Spec. Hist. Arab.): "Diverse are the opinions concerning the denomination of the Arabs; but the most certain of all is that which draws it from Arabah, which is part of the region of Tehamah, (belonging to Al-Medinah, Pilgrimage ii. 118), which their father Ismail afterwards inhabited." Tehamah (tierra caliente) is the maritime region of Al-Hijaz, the Moslem's Holy Land; and its "Arabah," a very small tract which named a very large tract, must not be confounded, as some have done, with the Wady Arabah, the ancient outlet of the Dead Sea. The derivation of "Arab" from "Ya'arab" a fancied son of Joktan is mythological.

RICHARD BURTON

In Heb. Arabia may be called "Eretz Ereb" (or "Arab") = land of the West; but in Arabic "Gharb" (not Ereb) is the Occident and the Arab dates long before the Hebrew.

*

TO CUT OR TO KISS

Then she bowed down over his feet and kissed them; and he left beating her and began reviling her and said, "By the rights of my bonnet, if I see or hear thee weeping, I will cut out thy tongue and stuff it up thy coynte, O thou city-filth!"

"When thine enemy extends his hand to thee, cut it off if thou can, or kiss it," wisely said Caliph al-Mansúr.

*

BUFFOON HEADWEAR

THE TARTUR WAS a peculiar turban worn by the Northern Arabs and shown in old prints. In modern Egypt the term is applied to the tall sugar-loaf caps of felt affected mostly by regular Dervishes. Burckhardt (Proverbs 194 and 398) makes it the high cap of felt or fur proper to the irregular cavalry called Dely or Delaty. In Dar For (Darfour) "Tartur" is a conical cap adorned with beads and cowries worn by the Manghwah or buffoon who corresponds with the Egyptian "Khalbús" or "Maskharah" and the Turkish "Sutari." For an illustration see Plate iv. fig. 10 of Voyage au Darfour par Mohammed El-Tounsy (The Tunisian), Paris, Duprat, 1845.

*

SWEATING GOLD

"…So if he take the girl, I will weigh thee out her price at once."
"I agree with thee to this condition," answered the Badawi.

This mention of weighing suggests the dust of Dean Swift and the money of the Gold Coast. It was done, I have said, because the gold coin, besides being "sweated" was soft and was soon worn down.

*

ROGUE AND FOOL

Thereupon the Badawi waxed angry and answered, "Thou wilt turn me the girl's head with this talk! Why dost thou say that she is noble, while she is of the scum of slave-girls and of the refuse of folk? I will not sell her to thee!"

The Badawi, who was fool as well as rogue, begins to fear that he has kidnapped a girl of family.

*

RICHARD BURTON

CERTAINTY

Cried the Badawi, "And what hath the baggage to do with clothes? By Allah, this camlet in which she is wrapped is ample for her." "With thy leave," said the merchant, "I will unveil her face and examine her even as folk examine slave-girls whom they think of buying."

These examinations being very indecent are usually done in strictest privacy. The great point is to make sure of virginity.

*

AVERTING THE GAZE

Replied the other, "Up and do what thou wilt and Allah keep thy youth! Examine her outside and inside and, if thou wilt, strip off her clothes and look at her when she is naked." Quoth the trader, "Allah forfend! I will look at naught save her face."

This is according to strict Moslem law: the purchaser may not look at the girl's nakedness till she is his, and he ought to manage matters through an old woman.

*

THE IGNORANCE

THE CELEBRATED COMPANION of Mohammed who succeeded Abu Bakr in the Caliphate (A. H. 13-23 = 634-644). The

Sunnis know him as Al-Adil, the Just; and the Shiahs detest him for his usurpation, his austerity and harshness. It is said that he laughed once, and wept once. The laugh was caused by recollecting how he ate his dough-gods (the idols of the Hanifah tribe) in The Ignorance. The tears were drawn by remembering how he buried alive his baby daughter who, while the grave was being dug, patted away the dust from his hair and beard. Omar was doubtless a great man, but he is one of the most ungenial figures in Moslem history which does not abound in genialities. To me he suggests a Puritan, a Covenanter of the sourest and narrowest type; and I cannot wonder that the Persians abhor him, and abuse him on all occasions.

*

CLEANSING

"...Then quoth Mu'awiyah: — Enter, O Abu Bahr, and drew a curtain between himself and Maysun, that she might hear what they said without being seen herself; then he said to Al-Ahnaf: — O Son of the Sea, draw near and tell me what counsel thou hast for me. Quoth Al-Ahnaf, Part thy hair and trim thy moustachio and pare thy nails and pluck thine armpits and shave thy pubes and ever use the toothstick because therein be two-and-seventy virtues, and make the Ghusl or complete ablution on Friday, as an expiation for all between the Fridays."

This is essential for cleanliness in hot lands: however much the bath may be used, the body-pile and lower hair, if submitted to a microscope, will show more or less sordes adherent. The axilla-hair is plucked because if shaved the growing pile causes itching and the depilatories are held deleterious. At first vellication is painful but the skin becomes used to it. The pecten is shaved either without or after using depilatories, of which more presently. The body-pile is removed by "Takhfíf"; the Libán Shámi (Syrian incense), a fir-gum imported from Scio, is melted and allowed to cool in the form of a pledget. This is passed over the face and all the down adhering to it is pulled up by the roots (Burckhardt No. 420). Not a few Anglo-Indians have adopted these precautions.

*

FATTED ASS

She said, It hath reached me, O auspicious King, that Ahnaf bin Kays replied to Al-Mu'awiyah's question, "And ever use the toothstick, because therein be two-and-seventy virtues and make the complete Friday ablution as an expiation for all between the two Fridays."

This Caliph was a tall, fair, handsome man of awe-inspiring aspect. Omar used to look at him and say, "This is the Cæsar of the Arabs," while his wife called him a "fatted ass."

128

CONGRESS WITH A CROCODILE

*

WHEN READY

"I bid her perfume herself and kiss her till she is moved to desire; then, should it be as thou knowest, I throw her on her back..."

i.e., "When ready and in erection."

*

LYNCH LAW

Then Othman cried, And where wilt thou find the like of Omar? Again Zayd bin Aslam relates of his father that he said: — I went out one night with Omar till we approached a blazing fire.

The seditions in Kufah were mainly caused by the wilful nepotism of Caliph Othman bin Asákir which at last brought about his death. His main quality seems to have been personal beauty: "never was seen man or woman of fairer face than he and he was the most comely of men:" he was especially famed for beautiful teeth which in old age he bound about with gold wire. He is described as of middling stature, large-limbed, broad shouldered, fleshy of thigh and long in the fore-arm which was hairy. His face inclined to yellow and was pock-marked; his beard was full and his curly hair, which he dyed yellow, fell below his ears. He is called "writer of the Koran" from his edition of the MS., and "Lord of the two Lights" because he married two of the Prophet's daughters, Rukayyah and Umm Kulthum; and, according to the Shi'ahs who call him Othman-i-Lang or "limping Othman," he vilely maltreated them. They justify his death as the act of an Ijmá' al-Muslimin, the general consensus of Moslems which ratifies "Lynch law." Altogether Othman is a mean figure in history.

*

THE OLD SHE-HYÆNA

ABU BAKR ORIGINALLY called Abd al-Ka'ahah (slave of the Ka'abah) took the name of Abdullah and was surnamed Abu Bakr (father of the virgin) when Mohammed, who before had married only widows, took to wife his daughter, the famous or infamous Ayishah. "Bikr" is the usual form, but "Bakr," primarily meaning a young camel, is metaphorically applied to human youth (Lane's Lex. *s. v.*). The first Caliph was a cloth-merchant, like many of the Meccan chiefs. He is described as very fair with bulging brow, deep-set eyes and thin-cheeked, of slender build and lean-loined, stooping and with the backs of his hands fleshless. He used tinctures of Henna and Katam for his beard. The Persians who hate him, call him "Pir-i-Kaftár," the old she-hyæna, and believe that he wanders about the deserts of Arabia in perpetual rut which the males must satisfy.

*

THE DAY OF ARAFAT

WHEN THE "DAY of Arafat" (9th of Zú'l-Hijjah) falls upon a Friday. For this Hajj al-Akbar see my Pilgrimage iii. 226. It is often confounded by writers (even by the learned M. Caussin de Perceval) with the common Pilgrimage as opposed to the Umrah, or "Lesser Pilgrimage" (ibid. iii. 342, etc.). The latter means etymologically cohabiting with a woman in her father's house as opposed to 'Ars or leading her to the husband's home: it is applied to visiting Meccah and going through all the pilgrim-rites but not at the Pilgrimage-season. Hence its title "Hajj al-Asghar" the "Lesser Hajj." But "Umrah" is also applied to a certain ceremony between the hills Safá (a large hard rock) and Marwah (stone full of flints), which accompanies the Hajj and which I have described (ibid. iii. 344). At Meccah I also heard of two places called Al-Umrah, the Greater in the Wady Fátimah and the Lesser half way nearer the city (ibid. iii. 344).

*

WRETCHED EGOTISM

Then he summoned his sons who numbered twelve, and when he beheld them his eyes dropped tears and presently he said to them, Your Father is between two things; either ye will be well to do, and your parent will enter the fire, or ye will be poor

131

and your parent will enter Paradise; and your father's entry into Paradise is liefer to him than that ye should be well to do.

A fair specimen of the unworthy egoism which all religious systems virtually inculcate. Here a pious father leaves his children miserable to save his own dirty soul.

*

REPUGNANCE

Then Sharrkan went in unto her and took her maidenhead; and she at once conceived by him and, when she announced it, he rejoiced with exceeding joy and commanded the savants to record the date of her conception.

This gratuitous incest in ignorance injures the tale and is as repugnant to Moslem as to Christian taste.

*

THE NAMING

Allah made the child-birth easy to her and she bare a daughter, whereupon she sent for Sharrkan and seeing him she said to him, "This is thy daughter: name her as thou wilt." Quoth he, "It is usual to name children on the seventh day after birth."

CONGRESS WITH A CROCODILE

The child is named either on the day of its birth or on that day week. The father whispers it in the right ear, often adding the Azán or prayer-call, and repeating in the left ear the "Ikámah" or Friday sentence. There are many rules for choosing names according to the week-day, the ascendant planet, the "Sortes Coranicæ," etc.

*

DEADLY SINS

Amongst Moslems as amongst Christians there are seven deadly sins: idolatry, murder, falsely charging modest women with unchastity, robbing orphans, usury, desertion in Holy War and disobedience to parents. The difference between the two creeds is noteworthy. And the sage knows only three, intemperance, ignorance and egoism.

*

DECREED BY DESTINY

Then he fell to comforting her and kissing her head and she asked him, "What wilt thou call the girl?" "Call her Kuzia-Fakan," answered he.

Meaning, "It was decreed by Destiny; so it came to pass," appropriate if not neat.

RICHARD BURTON

*

TWO-HUMPED

THE SHORT, STOUT, dark, long-haired and two bunched camel from "Bukhtar" (Bactria), the "Eastern" (Bakhtar) region on the Amu or Jayhún (Oxus) River; afterwards called Khorasan. The two-humped camel is never seen in Arabia except with northern caravans, and to speak of it would be a sore test of Badawi credulity.

*

BEAUTY SLEEP

"KAYLÚLAH" IS THE "forty-winks" about noon: it is a Sunnat or Practice of the Prophet who said, "Make the mid-day siesta, for verily at this hour the devils sleep not." "Aylúlah" is slumbering after morning prayers (our "beauty-sleep"), causing heaviness and idleness: "Ghaylúlah" is dozing about 9 a.m. engendering poverty and wretchedness: "Kaylúlah" (with the guttural Kaf) is sleeping before evening prayers and "Faylúlah" is slumbering after sunset — both held to be highly detrimental. (Pilgrimage ii. 49.)

*

CONGRESS WITH A CROCODILE

RISING SUN

WHEN THEY SAY, The leven flashes bright on the hills of Al-Yaman, the allusion is to the south quarter, where summer-lightning is seen. Al-Yaman (always with the article) means, I have said, the right-hand region to one facing the rising sun and Al-Sham (Syria) the left-hand region.

*

THE VEILED SEX

He brimmed a bowl of merest pine,
And made me drain the dregs, did he:
I see me, sweetheart, dead and gone
Ere I again shall gaze on thee.

Time! prithee bring our childhood back, ✿ Restore our happy infancy,
Again "he" for "she," in delicacy and jealousy of making public the beauty or conditions of the "veiled sex." Even public singers would hesitate to use a feminine pronoun. As will be seen, however, the rule is not invariably kept and hardly ever in Badawi poetry.

*

RICHARD BURTON

KEEPING PLACE

"Alas the pity of his youth! To-morrow they will hang him."
And he ceased not following them till he approached their
station, without any observing him. Then he stood still and
said, "How base it will be of him, if he say it was I who bade
him recite the verses!"

In such caravans each party must keep its own place under
pain of getting into trouble with the watchmen and guards.

*

SORE-FOOTED

ARAB. "AL-HÁFI," WHICH in Egyptian means sore-footed as
well. He was an ascetic of the eighth and ninth centuries
(A.D.). He relates a tradition of the famous soldier-saint Khálid
bin Walíd who lies buried like the poet Ka'ab al-Ahbár near
Hums (Emessa) once the Bœotia, Phrygia, Abdera, Suabia of
Syria now Halbun (pronounced Halbáun) near Damascus.
I cannot explain how this Kuraysh noble (a glorious figure
in Moslem history) is claimed by the Afghans as one of their
countrymen and made to speak Pukhtu or Pushtu, their
rough old dialect of Persian. The curious reader will consult
my Pilgrimage iii. 322 for the dialogue between Mohammed
and Khalid. Again there is general belief in Arabia that the
English sent a mission to the Prophet, praying that Khalid
might be despatched to proselytise them: unfortunately

CONGRESS WITH A CROCODILE

Mohammed was dead and the "Ingriz" ratted. It is popularly held that no armed man can approach Khalid's grave; but I suppose my revolver did not count.

*

WEAL-BRINGING LIE

Then rose a man of tattered appearance and said, O folk, beware of a truth which bringeth unweal, for there is no harm in a lie bringing weal, and in time of need no choice we heed: speech booteth not in the absence of good qualities even as silence hurteth not in the presence of good.

A favourite sentiment in the East: we find it at the very beginning of Sa'di's Gulistan: better a weal-bringing lie than a harm-dealing truth.

*

MOUNTED ON CLOUDS

ARAB. "RIJÁL AL-GHAYB," somewhat like the "Himalayan Brothers" of modern superstition. See Herklots (Qanoon-e-Islam) for a long and careful description of these "Mardán-i-Ghayb" (Pers.), a "class of people mounted on clouds," invisible, but moving in a circular orbit round the world; and suggesting the Hindu "Lokapálas." They should not be in front of the traveller nor on his right, but either behind or on his left hand. Hence tables, memorial couplets and hemistichs are required to ascertain the station, without which precaution journeys are apt to end badly.

*

HINGES OF STONE

Door-hinges in the east are two projections for the top and bottom of the leaf playing in hollows of the lintel and threshold. It appears to be the primitive form, for we find it in the very heart of Africa. In the basaltic cities of the Hauran, where the doors are of thick stone, they move easily on these pins. I found them also in the official (not the temple) City of Palmyra, but all broken.

*

RED MEN

Arab. "Banu 'l-Asfar;" which may mean "Pale faces," in the sense of "yaller girls" (New Orleans) and that intended by North American Indians, or, possibly, the peoples with yellow (or rather tow-coloured) hair we now call Russians. The races of Hindostan term the English not "white men," but "red men;" and the reason will at once be seen by comparing a Britisher with a high-caste Nágar Brahman whose face is of parchment-colour as if he had drunk *exsangue cuminum*.

The Yellow-faces of the text correspond with the Sansk. "Svetadvipa" — Whiteman's Land.

*

IN THE SHAPE OF MEN

ARAB. "AL-MUSAKHKHAM." No Moslem believes that Isa was crucified and a favourite fancy is that Judas, changed to the likeness of Jesus, thus paid for his treason. (Evangel. Barnabæ). Hence the resurrection is called not "Kiyámah" but "Kumámah" = rubbish. This heresy about the Cross they share with the Docetes, "certain beasts in the shape of men" (says Ignatius), who held that a phantom was crucified. So far the Moslems are logical, for "Isa," being angelically, miraculously and immaculately conceived, could not die; but they contradict themselves when they hold a vacant place near Mohammed's tomb for the body of Isa after his second coming as a forerunner to Mohammed and Doomday (Pilgrimage ii. 89).

*

EAT SAND!

Hearing of it Kings would pay a thousand gold pieces for every dram and they sent for and sought it to fumigate brides withal; and the Chief Priests and the great Kings were wont to use a little of it as collyrium for the eyes and as a remedy in

139

sickness and colic; and the Patriarchs used to mix their own skite...

Again the coarsest word "Khara." The allusion is to the vulgar saying, "Thou eatest skite!" (*i.e.* thou talkest nonsense). Decent English writers modify this to, "Thou eatest dirt:" and Lord Beaconsfield made it ridiculous by turning it into "eating *sand.*"

*

HOLY MERDE

...with it, for that the skite of the Chief Patriarch could not suffice for ten countries. So, as soon as dawn was seen and the morning shone with its shine and sheen, the horsemen ran to their spears full keen...

These silly scandals, which cause us only to smile, excite Easterns to fury. I have seen a Moslem wild with rage on hearing a Christian parody the opening words of the Koran, "Bismillahi 'l-Rahmáni 'l-Rahím, Mismish wa Kamar al-din," roughly translated, "In the name of Allah, the Compassionating, the Compassionate! Apricots and marmalade." The idea of the Holy Merde might have been suggested by the Hindus: see Mandeville, of the archiprotopapaton (prelate) carrying ox-dung and urine to the King, who therewith anoints his brow and breast, &c. And, incredible to relate, this is still practised after a fashion by the Parsis, one of the most progressive and the sharpest witted of Asiatic races.

*

LEFT-HANDED LAND

SYRIA, THE "LEFT-HAND land" as has before been explained. The popular saying about its people is "Shámi shúmi!" — the Syrian is small potatoes (to render the sense Americanicè). Nor did Syrus, the slave in Roman days, bear the best of names. In Al-Hijaz the Syrian is addressed "Abú Shám" (Father of Syria) and insulted as "Abuser of the Salt" a (traitor). Yet many sayings of Mohammed are recorded in honour of Syria, and he sometimes used Syriac words. Such were "Bakh, bakh" (= euge, before noticed), and "Kakh," a congener of the Latin Cacus and Caca which our day has docked to "cack." (Pilgrimage iii. 115).

*

SEVERING THE LEGS

Then army met army and breasts fell under hoof, whilst spear and sword ruled the day and fore-arms and wrists grew weak and the coursers seemed created without legs; nor did the herald of war cease calling to fight, till arms were aweary and day took flight and night came on with darkness dight.

RICHARD BURTON

The leg-cut is a prime favourite with the Eastern Sworder,
and a heavy two-handed blade easily severs a horse's leg.

*

HAIR LENGTH

Laud not long hair, except it be dispread
In two-fold locks, on day of fight and fray,
O'er youth who bears his lance 'twixt flank and thigh,
From many a whiskered knight to win the day.

Mohammed allowed his locks to grow down to his ear-lobes
but never lower.

*

TURNING FACE

ARAB. "LISÁM" I have explained as a covering for the lower
face, made by drawing over it the corner of the head-
kerchief (Pilgrimage i. 346). The Lisám of the African
Tawárik hoods the eyes so that a man must turn up his face
to see, and swathes all the lower half, leaving only the nose
exposed. And this is worn by many men by night as well as
by day, doubtless to avoid the evil eye. The native Sultans
of Darfur, like those of Bornu and others further west, used
white muslin as a face-wrap: hence, too, the ceremonies
when spitting, etc., etc. The Kúfiyah or head-kerchief of

the Arabs soon reached Europe and became in Low Latin Cuphia; in Spanish Escofia; in Ital. Cuffia or Scuffia; in French Escoffion, Scofion (Reine Marguerite) Coëffe (une pellicule, marque de bonheur), Coiffe and Coife, &c.; the Scotch Curch or Coif, opposed to the maiden snood; and, lastly our Sergeant-at-Law's Coif. Littré, the Learned, who in erudition was *né coiffé*, has missed this obvious derivation.

*

SLASHING BLADES

Moreover, they took their ships, with all the money and treasure and cargo, save a score of keel, and the Moslems got that loot whose like was never gotten in bygone years; nor was such cut and thrust ever heard of by men's ears.

"Cutting," throughout the book, alludes to the scymitar with which Arabs never give point; and "thrusting" to the footman's spear and the horseman's lance.

*

MAGIC

But she had studied the scriptures of Al-Islam and had made the Pilgrimage to the Holy House of Meccah and all this that she might come to the knowledge of the Mohammedan ordinances and the miraculous versets of the Koran; and she

143

RICHARD BURTON

had professed Judaism in the Holy City of Jerusalem for two years' space, that she might master the magic of men and demons; so that she was a plague of plagues and a pest of pests, wrong-headed as to belief and to no religion lief.

Clearly alluding to the magic so deeply studied by mediæval Jews.

*

ONANISM

ARAB. "SAHÁKAH," LIT. rubbing. The Moslem Harem is a great school for this "Lesbian (which I would call Atossan) love"; but the motive of the practice lies deeper. As amongst men the mixture of the feminine with the masculine temperament leads to sodomy, so the reverse makes women prefer their own sex. These tribades are mostly known by peculiarities of form and features, hairy cheeks and upper lips, gruff voices, hircine odour and the large projecting clitoris with erectile powers known to the Arabs as "bazar" (رظ), hence Tabzír = circumcision or amputation of such clitoris. Burckhardt (Prov. 436) translates "Bazarah" by slut or wench. He adds "it originally signifies the labia which the Cairenes also entitle Zambúr and which are cut off in girlhood." See also Lane, Lex. s. v.; Tabzír. Both writers confuse excision of the nymphæ with circumcision of the clitoris (Zambúr). Al-Siyúti (Kitab al-Izá' fi 'Ilm al-Nikah) has a very interesting chapter on Sapphic venery, which is well

144

known to Europe as proved by such works as "Gamiani," and "Anandria ou Confessions de Mademoiselle Sappho, avec la Clef," Lesbos, 1778. Onanism is fatally prevalent: in many Harems and girls' schools tallow-candles and similar succedania are vainly forbidden and bananas when detected are cut into four so as to be useless; of late years, however, China has sent some marvellous artificial phalli of stuffed bladder, horn and even caoutchouc, the latter material of course borrowed from Europe.

*

TWO REDS

Now the chief reason of her sojourn with her son, King Hardub of Greece, was on account of the slave virgins at his court: for she was given to tribadism and could not exist without sapphism or she went mad: so if any damsel pleased her, she was wont to teach her the art of rubbing clitoris against clitoris and would anoint her with saffron till she fainted away for excess of volupty.

This is considered a powerful aphrodisiac in the East. Hence male devotees are advised to avoid the "two reds," *i.e.* meat and wine; while the "two reds," which corrupt women, are gold and saffron, that is perfumery. Hence also the saying of Mohammed: — "Perfumes for men should have scent and not colour; for women should have colour and not scent." (Mishkát al-Masábíh ii. 361.)

RICHARD BURTON

*

RELIEVING CRAMP

Now the old hag was lean-bodied and hollow-eyed, and she bound her legs tightly round with cords just above her feet, till she drew near the Moslem camp, when she unwound them, leaving their marks deeply embedded in her ankles.

These are the "Hibás" or thin cords of wool which the Badawi binds round his legs, I believe to keep off cramp. (Pilgrimage iii. 78).

*

HEAVEN, HELL, AND PURGATORY

I.E. MEN, ANGELS and devils, the "Triloka" (triple people) of the Hindus. Alamín (plur.), never Alamayn (dual), is the Triregno denoted by the papal Tiara, the three Christian kingdoms being Heaven, Hell and Purgatory.

*

MIRACULOUS SIGN

KIRÁMAT, A SIGN, a prodigy, opposed to Mu'ujizah, a miracle wrought by a prophet. The Súfis explain this thaumaturgy by Allah changing something of Nature's ordinary course in

favour of an especial worshipper; and, after a fashion, this is
Catholic doctrine (See Dabistan, iii. 173).

*

WATERS OF PARADISE

KORAN, II. 149. Hence the vulgar idea that Martyrs are still
alive in the flesh. See my Pilgrimage (ii. 110 and elsewhere)
for the romantic and picturesque consequences of that belief.
The Commentators (Jalál al-Dín, etc.) play tricks with the
Koranic words, "they (martyrs) are not dead but living" (iii.
179) by placing the happy souls in the crops of green birds
which eat of the fruits and drink of the waters of Paradise;
whereas the reprobates and the (very) wicked are deposited
in black birds which drain the sanies and the boiling waters
of Hell. Amongst the Greeks a body remaining entire long
after death suggests Anathema Maranatha: it is the contrary
with Catholic Christians (Boccaccio iv. 5, of the Pot of Basil).
Concerning this creed see Maundrell, Letter of 1698.

*

THE TRUE MOUNT SINAI

TOR IS "MOUNT Sinai" in the Koran (xcv. I). I have only to
repeat my opinion concerning the present site so called: "It
is evident that Jebel Serbal dates only from the early days
of Coptic Christianity; that Jebel Musa, its Greek rival, rose

after the visions of Helena in the fourth century; whilst the building of the Convent by Justinian belongs to A.D. 527. Ras Safsáfah, its rival to the north, is an affair of yesterday, and may be called the invention of Robinson; and Jebel Katerina, to the South is the property of Rüppell" (Midian Revisited i., 237.). I would therefore call the "Sinaitic" Peninsula, Peninsula of Paran in old days and Peninsula of Tor (from its chief port) in our time. It is still my conviction that the true Mount Sinai will be found in Jabal Aráif, or some such unimportant height to the north of the modern Hajj-road from Suez to Akabah. Even about the name (which the Koran writes "Sainá" and "Sínín") there is a dispute: It is usually derived from the root "Sanah" = sentis, a bush; but this is not satisfactory. Our eminent Assyriologist, Professor Sayce, would connect it with "Sin," the Assyrian Moon-god, as Mount Nebo with the Sun-god and he expects to find there the ruins of a Lunar temple as a Solar fane stands on Ba'al Zapuna (Baal Zephon) or the classical Mount Casius.

*

TWISTED MAGIC

Our Fort is Tor, and flames the fire of fight:
Moses art thou and this is time for aid:
Cast down thy rod, 'twill swallow all they wrought,
Nor dread for men their ropes be vipers made:
For Chapters read on fight-day lines of foes,
And on their necks 'grave versets wi' thy blade!

Alluding to the miracle of Aaron's rod (the gift of Jethro) as related in the Koran (chapts. vii. I., xx., etc.), where the Egyptian sorcerers threw down thick ropes which by their magic twisted and coiled like serpents.

*

CARRIER-PIGEONS

Now the witch had written a letter to the King of Constantinople and despatched it on the wings of a bird, acquainting him with what had passed and ending...

Carrier-pigeons were extensively used at this time. The Caliph Al-Násir li-Díni 'llah (regn. A. H. 575 = 1180) was, according to Ibn Khaldún, very fond of them. The moderns of Damascus still affect them. My successor, Mr. Consul Kirby Green, wrote an excellent report on pigeon-fancying at Damascus. The so-called Maundeville or Mandeville in A.D. 1322 speaks of carrier-pigeons in Syria as a well-known mode of intercourse between lord and lord.

*

SMOKING OUT

"Up and at them, for there remain of them but five-and-twenty men! If we cannot prevail on them to fight, let us light a fire upon them; and if they submit themselves and yield

149

to us, we will take them prisoners; but if they refuse we will leave them for fuel to the fire, so shall they become to men of foreseeing mind a warning dire..."

The "smoking out" practice is common amongst the Arabs: hence Marshal Pelissier's so-called "barbarity." The Public is apt to forget that on a campaign the general's first duty is to save his own men by any practice which the laws of fair warfare do not absolutely forbid.

*

INFIDELITY

...with their standards and ensigns of the Faith of Unity under the dust-clouds and lo! they were like a flight of locusts or rain clouds *raining rain; and the voices of the Moslems chanting the Koran and glorifying the Compassionate One, struck their ears. Now the Infidels knew of the approach of this host through Zat al-Dawahi with her craft and whoredom, calumny and contrivance.*

Arab. "Ahr" or "ihr," fornication or adultery, *i.e.*, irreligion, infidelity as amongst the Hebrews. (Isaiah xxiii. 17).

*

KILL-HUNGER

But like grim lion turning made them flee,
And left on valley-sole my foemen, drunk
Not with old wine but Death-cup's revelry…

Here "Kahwah" (coffee) is used in its original sense of strong old wine. The derivation is "Akhá" = fastidire fecit, causing disinclination for food, the Matambre (kill-hunger) of the Iberians. In old days the scrupulous called coffee "Kihwah" in order to distinguish it from "Kahwah," wine.

*

EYBITTEN

"…I am Afridun the overwhelmed by the well-omened Shawáhi, Zat alDawahi." But he had not ended speaking ere Sharrkan, the Champion of the Moslems, fared forth to meet him, mounted on a sorrel horse worth a thousand pieces of red gold…

From the root "Shauh" = having a fascinating eye, terrifying. The Irish call the fascinater "eybitter" and the victim (who is also rhymed to death) "eybitten."

*

RICHARD BURTON

ZEMZEM

But when Zau al-Makan fared forth into the field, there came with him the Wazir Dandan and the Chamberlain and Bahram, saying, "We will be thy sacrifice." He replied, "By the Holy House and Zemzem and the Place!..."

i.e., of Abraham. For the Well Zemzem and the Place of Abraham, see my Pilgrimage (iii. 171-175, etc.), where I described the water as of salt-bitter taste, like that of Epsom (iii. 203). Sir William Muir (in his excellent life of Mahomet, I. cclviii.) remarks that "the flavour of stale water bottled up for months would not be a criterion of the same water freshly drawn;" but soldered tins-full of water drawn a fortnight before are to be had in Calcutta and elsewhere after Pilgrimage time; and analysis would at once detect the salt.

*

HIPPOMANISTS

Whose neigh sounds glad to the hearer's ears
Like thunders rolling in thund'rous boom:
If he race the wind he will lead the way,
And the lightning-flash will behind him loom.

Racing was and is a favourite pastime with those hippomanists, the Arabs; but it contrasts strongly with our civilised form being a trial of endurance rather than of speed.

CONGRESS WITH A CROCODILE

The Prophet is said to have limited betting in these words, "There shall be no wagering save on the Khuff (camel's foot), the Hafir (hoof of horse, ass, etc.) or the Nasal (arrow-pile or lance head)."

*

LITTERS

Arab. "Azghán" = the camel-litters in which women travel.

*

WHITE EYES

Replied the Wazir: — With love and gladness! Know, O auspicious King, that there reached my ears a relation of a lover and a loved one and of the discourse between them and what befel them of things rare and fair, a story such as repelleth care from the heart and dispelleth sorrow like unto that of the patriarch Jacob…

Whose eyes became white (*i.e.* went blind) with mourning for his son Joseph (Koran, chapt. xii. 84). He recovered his sight when his face was covered with the shirt which Gabriel had given to the youth after his brethren had thrown him into the well.

*

RICHARD BURTON

ADMIRING THE HIPS

*When she draweth nigh she seduceth and when she turneth
her back she slayeth; she ravisheth heart and view and she
looketh even as saith of her the poet...*

A delicate allusion to the size of her hips and back parts, in
which volume is, I have said, greatly admired for the best of
reasons.

*

NIGHT-MARCH

"Travel by Night," said the Prophet, "when the plagues of
earth (scorpions, serpents, etc.) afflict ye not." Yet the night-
march in Arabia is detestable (Pilgrimage iii.)

*

VITALS OF POLITENESS

*...but when morning shone and the sun rose upon hill
and down, of a sudden he saw King Zahr Shah's Wazir
approaching him, with his Chamberlains and high Lords
and Chief Officers of the kingdom; and the two parties joined
company at some parasangs' distance from the city.*

This form of ceremony is called "Istikbál" (coming forth to
greet) and is regulated by the severest laws of etiquette. As

a rule the greater the distance (which may be a minimum of one step) the higher the honour. Easterns infinitely despise strangers who ignore these vitals of politeness.

*

LOSS OF THEIR CHARMS

He is Caliph of Beauty in Yúsufs lieu,
And all lovers fear when they sight his grace:
Pause and gaze with me; on his cheek thou'lt sight
The Caliphate's banner of sable hue.

Allusion to the well-known black banners of the house of Abbas. The Persians describe the growth of hair on a fair young face by, "His cheeks went into mourning for the loss of their charms."

*

BLACK AS A CHEEK-MOLE

"Káfir" a Koranic word meaning Infidel, the active participle of Kufr = Infidelity *i.e.* rejecting the mission of Mohammed. It is insulting and in Turkish has been degraded to "Giaour." Here it means black, as Hafiz of Shiraz terms a cheek-mole "Hindu" *i.e.* dark-skinned and idolatrous.

*

RICHARD BURTON

CONTINUAL YOUTH

I marvel hearing people questioning of
The Fount of Life and in what land 'tis found:
I see it sprung from lips of dainty fawn,
Sweet rosy mouth with green mustachio down'd:
And wondrous wonder 'tis when Moses viewed
That Fount, he rested not from weary round.

Alluding to the travel of Moses (Koran chapt. xviii.) with Al-Khizr (the "evergreen Prophet") who had drunk of the Fountain of Life and enjoyed flourishing and continual youth. Moses is represented as the external and superficial religionist; the man of outsight; Al-Khizr as the spiritual and illuminated man of insight.

*

LYNX

The lynx was used like the lion in Ancient Egypt and the Chita-leopard in India: I have never seen or heard of it in these days.

*

RESPECT

When Taj al-Muluk saw them, he said to one of his companions, "Bring me news of yonder men and question them why they have halted in this place…"

It was not respectful to pitch their camp within dog-bark.

*

GOOD VERSUS BAD

EASTERNS ATTACH GREAT importance to softness and smoothness of skin and they are right: a harsh rough epidermis spoils sport with the handsomest woman.

*

EXQUISITE ETYMOLOGY

ARAB. "TASWIF" = SAYING "Sauf," I will do it soon. It is a beautiful word — etymologically.

*

MOONRISE

Now blame him not; for blame brings only irk and pain!
Indeed, I spake him sooth but ne'er his ear could gain:

157

May Allah guard my moon which riseth in the vale
Beside our camp, from loosed robe like skyey plain...

A very far-fetched allusion. The face of the beloved springing from an unbuttoned robe is the moon rising over the camp in the hollow (*bat' há*).

*

WOMANLY DEVOTION

TALE OF AZIZ AND AZIZAH

Both words (masc. and fem.) mean "dear, excellent, highly-prized." The tale is the Arab form of the European "Patient Griselda" and shows a higher conception of womanly devotion, because Azizah, despite her wearisome weeping, is a girl of high intelligence and Aziz is a vicious zany, weak as water and wilful as wind. The phenomenon (not rare in life) is explained by the couplet: —

I love my love with an S —

Because he is stupid and not intellectual.

This fond affection of clever women for fools can be explained only by the law of unlikeness which mostly governs sexual unions in physical matters; and its appearance in the story gives novelty and point. Aziz can plead only the violence of his passion which distinguished him as a lover among the mob of men who cannot love anything beyond themselves.

And none can pity him for losing a member which he so much abused.

*

MUSK

Musk is one of the perfumes of the Moslem Heaven; and "musky" is much used in verse to signify scented and dark-brown.

*

SHARP WITS

Lane (i. 608) has a valuable note on the language of signs, from M. du Vigneau's "Secretaire Turc," etc. (Paris, 1688), Baron von Hammer-Purgstall ("Mines de l'Orient," No. 1, Vienna, 1809) and Marcel's "Contes du Cheykh El-Mohdy" (Paris, 1833). It is practised in Africa as well as in Asia. At Abeokuta in Yoruba a man will send a symbolical letter in the shape of cowries, palm-nuts and other kernels strung on rice-straw; and sharp wits readily interpret the meaning. A specimen is given in p. 262 of Miss Tucker's "Abbeokuta; or Sunrise within the Tropics."

*

RICHARD BURTON

EYE-LOVE

MR. PAYNE (II. 227) translates "Hawá al-'Uzrí" by "the love of the Beni Udhra, an Arabian tribe famous for the passion and devotion with which love was practised among them." See Night dclxxxiii. I understand it as "excusable love" which, for want of a better term, is here translated "platonic." It is, however, more like the old "bundling" of Wales and Northern England; and allows all the pleasures but one, the toyings which the French call *les plaisirs de la petite oie*; a term my dear old friend Fred. Hankey derived from *la petite voie*. The Afghans know it as "Námzad-bází" or betrothed-play (Pilgrimage, ii. 56); the Abyssinians as eye-love; and the Kafirs as Slambuka a Shlabonka, for which see the traveller Delegorgue.

*

HEART IN HAND

"TURK" IN ARABIC and Persian poetry means a plunderer, a robber. Thus Hafiz: "Agar án Turk-i-Shirázi ba-dast árad dil-i-márá," If that Shirazi (ah, the Turk!) would deign to take my heart in hand, etc.

*

DOG-LAPS

*Quoth she, "O my cousin, as for her sign to thee with her palm
and five fingers its interpretation is, Return after five days;
and the putting forth of her head out of the window, and her
gestures with the mirror and the letting down and raising up
and wringing out of the red kerchief, signify, Sit in the dyer's
shop till my messenger come to thee."*

This gesture speaks for itself: it is that of a dyer staining a
cloth. The "Sabbágh's" shop is the usual small recess, open
to the street and showing pans of various dyes sunk like
"dog-laps" in the floor.

*

SATURN'S DAY

THE ARAB. SABT (from sabata, he kept Sabt) and the Heb.
"Sabbath" both mean Saturn's day, Saturday, transferred
by some unknown process throughout Christendom to
Sunday. The change is one of the most curious in the history
of religions. If there be a single command stronger than all
others it is "Keep the Saturday holy." It was so kept by the
Founder of Christianity; the order was never abrogated
and yet most Christians are not aware that Sabbath, or
"Sawbath," means Saturn's day, the "Shiyár" of the older
Arabs. And to complete its degradation "Sabbat" in French
and German means a *criaillerie*, a "row," a disorder, an

abominable festival of Hexen (witches). This monstrous absurdity can be explained only by aberrations of sectarian zeal, of party spirit in religion.

*

POMPELMOOSE

ARAB. "KUBÁD" = SHADDOCK (citrus decumana): the huge orange which Captain Shaddock brought from the West Indies; it is the Anglo-Indian pompelmoose, vulg. pummelo. An excellent bitter is made out of the rind steeped in spirits. Citronworts came from India whence they spread throughout the tropics: they were first introduced into Europe by the heroic Joam de Castro and planted in his garden at Cintra where their descendants are still seen.

*

PASTRIES

ARAB. BAKLÁWAH, TURK. Baklává, a kind of pastry with blanched almonds bruised small between layers of dough, baked in the oven and cut into lozenges. It is still common.

*

CURSES

"...As for the charcoal, it means Allah blacken thy face for thou makest a lying pretence of love, whereas thou art naught but a child and hast no object in life other than eating and drinking and sleeping! such is the interpretation of her signs, and may Allah Almighty deliver thee from her!"

The curse is pregnant with meaning. On Judgement-day the righteous shall arise with their faces shining gloriously: hence the blessing, "Bayyaz' Allaho wajh-ak" (= Allah whiten thy countenance!). But the wicked shall appear with faces scorched black and deformed by horror (Koran xxiv.): hence "God blacken thy brow!" I may observe that Easterns curse, the curse being everywhere the language of excited destructiveness; but only Westerns, and these chiefly English, swear, a practice utterly meaningless. "Damn *it*" without specifying what the "it" is, sounds like the speech of a naughty child anxious only to use a "wicked word." "Damn *you*!" is intelligible all the world over. It has given rise to "les goddams" in France; "Godámes" in the Brazil and "Gotáma" amongst the Somal of Eastern Africa, who learn it in Aden.

*

LAXATIVE

ARAB. "BALAH," THE unripened date, which is considered a laxative and eaten in hot weather.

RICHARD BURTON

*

SEVERANCE

LANE (I. 611), QUOTING Al-Kazwíní, notes that the date-stone is called "Nawá" (dim. "Nawáyah") which also means distance, absence, severance. Thus the lady threatens to cast off her greedy and sleepy lover.

*

INSIPID FRUIT

Then she made me drink jujube-sherbet and sugar and washed my hands and dried them with a kerchief; after which she sprinkled me with rose-water, and I sat with her awhile in the best of spirits.

Probably fermented to a kind of wine. The insipid fruit (Unnáb) which looks like an apple in miniature, is much used in stews, etc. It is the fruit (Nabak classically Nabik) of Rhamnus Nabeca (or Sidrat) also termed Zizyphus Jujuba, seu Spina Christi because fabled to have formed the crown of thorns: in the English market this plum is called Chinese Japonica. I have described it in Pilgrimage ii. 205, and have noticed the infusion of the leaves for washing the dead (ibid. ii. 105): this is especially the use of the "Ber" in India, where the leaves are superstitiously held peculiarly pure. Our dictionaries translate "Sidr" by "Lote-tree"; and no wonder that believers in Homeric writ feel their bile aroused by so poor a realisation of the glorious myth. The Homerids probably alluded to Hashish or Bhang.

*

BUTTON-HOLES

ARAB. "AZRÁR": THE open collar of the Saub ("Tobe") or long loose dress is symptomatic. The Eastern button is on the same principle as ours (both having taken the place of the classical fibula); but the Moslem affects a loop (like those to which we attach our "frogs") and utterly ignores a button-hole.

*

CROWN OF GLORY

Sweetest of nights the world can show to me, that night
When cups went round and round as fed by ceaseless spring:
There utter severance made I 'twixt mine eyes and sleep,
And joined, rejoined mine ear-drop with the anklet-ring.

The ear-drop is the penis and the anklet its crown of glory.

*

165

RICHARD BURTON

LUMP IN THE THROAT

"Show it me," cried I: but she would not. Then I gave myself up to love-delights and thought no more of my cousin's death: for my mind was unsettled and fain would I have been with my lover the livelong day and night.

The death of Azizah is told with true Arab pathos and simplicity: it still draws tears from the eyes of the Badawi, and I never read it without a "lump in the throat."

*

HORROR OF TRAVELLERS

ARAB. "INSHALLAH BUKRA!" a universal saying which is the horror of travellers.

*

URINARY ETIQUETTE

MOSLEMS NEVER STAND up at such times, for a spray of urine would make their clothes ceremonially impure: hence the scrupulous will break up with stick or knife the hard ground in front of them. A certain pilgrim was reported to have made this blunder which is hardly possible in Moslem dress. A high personage once asked me if it was true that he killed a man who caught him in a standing position;

166

and I found to my surprise that the absurd scandal was already twenty years old. After urining the Moslem wipes the *os penis* with one to three bits of stone, clay or handfuls of earth, and he must perform Wuzu before he can pray. Tournefort (Voyage au Levant iii. 335) tells a pleasant story of certain Christians at Constantinople who powdered with *"Poivre-d'Inde"* the stones in a wall where the Moslems were in the habit of rubbing the *os penis* by way of wiping. The same author (ii. 336) strongly recommends a translation of Rabelais' *Torcheculative* chapter (Lib. i., chapt. 13) for the benefit of Mohammedans.

*

CUP OF THE CROTCH

O thou who barest leg-calf, better to suggest
For passion-madded amourist better things above!
Towards its lover doth the bowl go round and run;
Cup and cup-bearer only drive us daft with love.

The cup is that between the lady's legs.

*

BALL GAMES

"Bat and ball," or hockey on horseback (Polo) is one of the earliest Persian games as shown by every illustrated copy of Firdausi's "Shahnámeh." This game was played with a Kurrah or small hand-ball and a long thin bat crooked at the end called in Persian Chaugán and in Arabic Saulaján. Another sense of the word is given in the Burhán-i-Káti, translated by Vullers (Lex. Persico-Latinum), a large bandy with bent head to which is hung an iron ball, also called Kaukabah (our "morning-star") and like the umbrella it denotes the grandees of the court. The same Kaukabah particularly distinguished one of the Marquesses of Waterford. This Polo corresponds with the folliculus, the pallone, the baloun-game (moyen âge) of Europe, where the horse is not such a companion of man; and whereof the classics sang: —

Folle decet pueros ludere, folle senes.

In these days we should spell otherwise the "folle" of seniors playing at the ball or lawn-tennis.

*

GOOSEBUMPS

Then she wept with sore weeping and waxed wroth and shuddered in my face with skin bristling and looked at me with furious eyes.

This "horripilation," for which we have the poetical term "goosebumps," is often mentioned in Hindu as in Arab literature.

*

FAMILIAR

Then said she, "Thou art of no use to me, now thou art married and hast a child; nor art thou any longer fit for my company; I care only for bachelors and not for married men: these profit us nothing...."

How often we have heard this in England!

*

LEAVING NO MARK

They did her bidding, upon which she arose and fetched a pan of copper and hung it over the brazier and poured into it oil of sesame, in which she fried cheese.

As a styptic. The scene in the text has often been enacted in Egypt when a favourite feminine mode of murdering men is by beating and bruising the testicles. The Fellahs are exceedingly clever in inventing methods of manslaughter. For some years bodies were found that bore no outer mark of violence, and only Frankish inquisitiveness discovered that the barrel of a pistol had been passed up the anus and the weapon discharged internally. Murders of this description are known in English history; but never became popular practice.

RICHARD BURTON

*

GELDING

ARAB. "ZAKAR," THAT which betokens masculinity. At the end of the tale we learn that she also gelded him; thus he was a "Sandali," a *rasé*.

*

JOHNNY RAWS

Luck to the Rubber, whose deft hand o'erflies
A frame begotten twixt the lymph and light:
He shows the thaumaturgy of his craft,
And gathers musk in form of camphor dight.

The rolls of white (camphor-like) scarf-skin and sordes which come off under the bath-man's glove become by miracle of Beauty, as brown musk. The Rubber or Shampooer is called in Egypt "Mukayyis" (vulgarly "Mukayyisáti") or "bagman," from his "Kís," a bag-glove of coarse woollen stuff. To "Johnny Raws" he never fails to show the little rolls which come off the body and prove to them how unclean they are; but the material is mostly dead scarf-skin.

*

CONAL CONGRESS

SED VITAM FACIUNT balnea, vina, Venus! The Hammam to Easterns is a luxury as well as a necessity; men sit there for hours talking chiefly of money and their prowess with the fair; and women pass half the day in it complaining of their husbands' over-amativeness and contrasting their own chaste and modest aversion to carnal congress.

*

MORNING POTATIONS

LANE (I. 616), SAYS "of wine, milk, sherbet, or any other beverage." Here it is wine, a practice famed in Persian poetry, especially by Hafiz, but most distasteful to a European stomach. We find the Mu allakah of Imr al-Kays noticing "our morning draught." Nott (Hafiz) says a "cheerful cup of wine in the morning was a favourite indulgence with the more luxurious Persians. And it was not uncommon among the Easterns, to salute a friend by saying: — May your morning potation be agreeable to you!" In the present day this practice is confined to regular debauchees.

*

RICHARD BURTON

LOVE-LETTERS

Then he folded the letter and sealed it with his signet-ring and gave it to the old woman, saying, "Carry it to the Lady Dunya."

Such letters are generally written on a full-sized sheet of paper ("notes" are held slighting in the East) and folded till the breadth is reduced to about one inch. The edges are gummed; the ink, much like our Indian ink, is smeared with the finger upon the signet-ring; the place where it is to be applied is slightly wetted with the tongue and the seal is stamped across the line of junction to secure privacy. I have given a specimen of an original love-letter of the kind in "Scinde, or the Unhappy Valley," chapt. iv.

*

CRUCIFIXION

ARAB. "SALB" WHICH may also mean hanging, but the usual term for the latter in The Nights is "shanak." Crucifixion, abolished by the superstitious Constantine, was practised as a servile punishment as late as the days of Mohammed Ali Pasha the Great. The malefactors were nailed and tied to the patibulum or cross-piece, without any suppedaneum or foot-rest and left to suffer tortures from flies and sun, thirst and hunger. They often lived three days and died of the wounds mortifying and the nervous exhaustion brought on by cramps and convulsions. In many cases the corpses were

172

left to feed the kites and crows; and this added horror to the death. Moslems care little for mere hanging. Whenever a fanatical atrocity is to be punished, the malefactor should be hung in pig-skin, his body burnt and the ashes publicly thrown into a common cesspool.

*

LOVE-SICKNESS

ACCORDING TO THE Hindus there are ten stages of love-sickness: (1) Love of the eyes; (2) Attraction of the Manas or mind; (3) Birth of desire; (4) Loss of sleep; (5) Loss of flesh; (6) Indifference to objects of sense; (7) Loss of shame; (8) Distraction of thought; (9) Loss of consciousness; and (10) Death.

*

WRIGGLE-WALK

Then she went to Taj al-Muluk and dressing him in woman's clothes, said to him, "Follow me and sway from side to side as thou steppest, and hasten not thy pace nor take heed of any who speaketh to thee."

We should call this walk of "Arab ladies" a waddle: I have never seen it in Europe except amongst the trading classes of Trieste, who have a "wriggle" of their own.

RICHARD BURTON

*

AMOROUSNESS

Asked she, "What then wouldst thou have, O light of my eyes and fruit of my vitals? If thou desire aught beside kissing and embracing and entwining of legs with legs, do what pleaseth thee; for, by Allah, no partner hath any part in us."

The lady proposing extreme measures is characteristic: Egyptians hold, and justly enough, that their women are more amorous than men.

*

STANDING ON ITS HEEL

Then she went forth and fled for her life. Such was her case; but as regards the Epicene he, seeing her alarm, lifted the door off its hinge-pins, and entering found the Lady Dunya with her arms round the neck of Taj al-Muluk and both fast asleep.

i.e. which fit into sockets in the threshold and lintel and act as hinges. These hinges have caused many disputes about how they were fixed, for instance in caverns without moveable lintel or threshold. But one may observe that the upper projections are longer than the lower and that the door never fits close above; so by lifting it up the inferior pins are taken out of the holes. It is the oldest form and the only form known to the Ancients. In Egyptian the hinge is

called Akab = the heel, hence the proverb Wakaf' al-báb
alá 'akabih; the door standeth on its heel; *i.e.* every thing in
proper place.

*

TAKING A TUMBLE

*At this sight he was confounded and was preparing to return
to the King, when the Princess awoke, and seeing him, was
terrified and changed colour and waxed pale, and said to
him, "O Kafur, veil thou what Allah hath veiled!"*

Hence the addresses to the Deity: Yá Sátir and Yá Sattár —
O Thou who veilest the sins of Thy Servants! said *e.g.*, when
a woman is falling from her donkey, etc.

*

CASTRATION

ARAB. "KHASSAT HU" = removed his testicles, gelded him.

*

GINGER POP

*And she was indeed the fairest of maids who are modestly
veiled, lovely-faced with smooth cheeks graced, and slender
waist on heavy hips based; and her shape was the shaft's thin*

line and her lips were sweeter than old wine and the nectar of
her mouth as it were the fountain Salsabíl;

One of the fountains of Paradise (Koran, chapt. lxxvi.): the
word lit. means "water flowing pleasantly down the throat."
The same chapter mentions "Zanjabíl," or the Ginger-fount,
which to the Infidel mind unpleasantly suggests "ginger pop."

*

HELL OF JEALOUSY

His lovers' souls have drawn upon his cheek
An ant that perfected its rosy light:

I marvel at such martyrs Lazá-pent
Who yet with greeny robes of Heaven are dight.

The allusions are far-fetched and obscure as in Scandinavian
poetry. Mr. Payne (ii. 314) translates "Naml" by "net."
I understand the ant (swarm) creeping up the cheeks, a
common simile for a young beard. The lovers are in the Lazá
(hell) of jealousy, etc., yet feel in the Na'ím (heaven) of love
and robe in green, the hue of hope, each expecting to be the
favoured one.

*

REUNION

IN NOMADIC LIFE the parting of lovers happens so frequently that it becomes a stock topic in poetry and often, as here, the lover complains of parting when he is not parted. But the gravamen lies in the word "Wasl" which may mean union, meeting, reunion or coition. As Ka'ab ibn Zuhayr began his famous poem with "Su'ád hath departed," 900 imitators (says Al-Siyuti) adopted the Násib or address to the beloved and Su'ad came to signify a cruel, capricious mistress.

*

HEROIC TREATMENT

As MIGHT BE expected from a nation of camel-breeders actual cautery which can cause only counter-irritation, is a favourite nostrum; and the Hadis or prophetic saying is "Akhir al-dawá (or al-tibb) al-Kayy" = cautery is the end of medicine-cure; and "Fire and sickness cannot cohabit." Most of the Badawi bear upon their bodies grisly marks of this heroic treatment, whose abuse not unfrequently brings on gangrene. The Hadis (Burckhardt, Proverbs, No. 30) also means "if nothing else avail, take violent measures."

*

177

RICHARD BURTON

PINK LEGS

IN TIMES OF mourning Moslem women do not use perfumes or dyes, like the Henna here alluded to in the pink legs and feet of the dove.

*

VENICE TREACLE

Arab. "Tiryák" from Gr. Θηριακόν φάρμακον a drug against venomous bites. It was compounded mainly of treacle, and that of Baghdad and Irák was long held sovereign. The European equivalent, "Venice treacle," (Theriaca Andromachi) is an electuary containing many elements. Badawin eat for counter-poison three heads of garlic in clarified butter for forty days. (Pilgrimage iii. 77.)

*

CHASING PELICANS

When Kanmakan heard this verse again spoken by the same voice yet saw no one, he knew that the speaker was a lover like unto himself, debarred from union with her who loved him; and he said to himself, "'Twere fitting that this man should lay his head to my head and become my comrade in this my strangerhood."

Could Cervantes have read this? In Algiers he might easily have heard it recited by the tale-tellers. Kanmakan is the typical Arab Knight, gentle and valiant as Don Quixote; Sabbáh is the *Grazioso*, a "Beduin" Sancho Panza. In the "Romance of Antar" we have a similar contrast with Ocab who says: "Indeed I am no fighter: the sword in my hand-palm chases only pelicans;" and, "whenever you kill a satrap, I'll plunder him."

*

CAMEL KNOW-HOW

ARAB. "USHÁRI." OLD Purchas (vi., i. 9) says there are three kinds of camels (1) *Huguin* (= Hejin) of tall stature and able to carry 1,000 lbs. (2) *Bechete* (= Bukhti) the two-humped Bactrian before mentioned and, (3) the *Raguahill* (Rahíl) small dromedaries unfit for burden but able to cover a hundred miles in a day. The "King of Timbukhtu" (not "Bukhtu's well" pop. Timbuctoo) had camels which reach Segelmesse (Sijalmas) or Darha, nine hundred miles in eight days at most. Lyon makes the Maherry (also called El-Heirie = Mahri) trot nine miles an hour for a long time. Other travellers in North Africa report the *Sabayee* (Saba'i = seven days wonder) as able to get over six hundred and thirty miles (or thirty-five caravan stages = each eighteen miles) in five to seven days. One of the dromedaries in the "hamlah" or caravan of Mr. Ensor (Journey through Nubia and Darfoor — a charming book) travelled one thousand one hundred

179

and ten miles in twenty-seven days. He notes that his beasts were better with water every five to seven days, but in the cold season could do without drink for sixteen. I found in Al-Hijaz at the end of August that the camels suffered much after ninety hours without drink (Pilgrimage iii. 14). But these were "Júdi" fine-haired animals as opposed to "Khawár" (the Khowás of Chesney, p. 333), coarse-haired, heavy, slow brutes which will not stand great heat.

*

MINARETS

But the Badawi found that the other had the better of him and weighed him down, as the quintal downweighs the dinar; and he looked at his legs firmly planted on the ground, and saw that they were as two minarets strongly based, or two tent-poles in earth encased, or two mountains which may not be displaced.

The "minaret" being feminine is usually compared with a fair young girl. The oldest minaret proper is supposed to have been built in Damascus by the Ommiade Caliph (No. X.) Al-Walid A.H. 86-96 (= 705-715). According to Ainsworth (ii. 113) the second was at Kuch Hisar in Chaldea.

*

CAT AND WOLF

THE BASER SORT of Badawi is never to be trusted: he is a traitor born, and looks upon fair play as folly or cowardice. Neither oath nor kindness can bind him: he unites the cruelty of the cat with the wildness of the wolf. How many Englishmen have lost their lives by not knowing these elementary truths! The race has not changed from the days of Mandeville (A.D. 1322) whose "Arabians, who are called Bedouins and Ascopards (?), are right felonious and foul, and of a cursed nature." In his day they "carried but one shield and one spear, without other arm:" now, unhappily for travellers, they have matchlocks and most tribes can manufacture a something called by courtesy gunpowder.

*

HORSE TALK

IN ARAB. "KHAYL" is = horse; Husan, a stallion; Hudúd, a brood stallion; Faras, a mare (but sometimes used as a horse and meaning "that tears over the ground"); Jiyád a steed (noble); Kadísh, a nag (ignoble); Mohr a colt and Mohrah, a filly. There are dozens of other names but these suffice for conversation.

*

RICHARD BURTON

THE SLAYER

I am a horse-thief and I have busied myself with lifting and snatching horses all my life, night and day, and my name is Ghassán, the plague of every stable and stallion. I heard tell of this horse, that he was in the land of Roum, with King Afridun, where they had named him Al-Katúl and surnamed him Al-Majnún.

Al-Katúl, the slayer; Al-Majnún, the mad; both high compliments in the style inverted.

*

SENSING DANGER

When the robbers heard this, they came out on me and surrounded me on all sides and shot arrows and cast spears at me, whilst I stuck fast on his back and he fended me with hoofs and forehand, till at last he bolted out with me from amongst them like unerring shaft or shooting star.

This is a true and life-like description of horse-stealing in the Desert: Antar and Burckhardt will confirm every word. A noble Arab stallion is supposed to fight for his rider and to wake him at night if he see any sign of danger. The owner generally sleeps under the belly of the beast which keeps eyes and ears alert till dawn.

*

SEMANTICS

Arab. "Bilád al-Súdán" = the Land of the Blacks, negro-land, whence the slaves came, a word now fatally familiar to English ears. There are, however, two regions of the same name, the Eastern upon the Upper Nile and the Western which contains the Niger-Valley; and each considers itself *the* Sudan. And the reader must not confound the Berber of the Upper Nile, the *Berberino* who acts servant in Lower Egypt, with the Berber of Barbary: the former speaks an African language; the latter a "Semitic" (Arabic) tongue.

*

SUMMER-QUARTERS

Arab. "Marba'." In early spring the Badawi tribes leave the Rasm or wintering-place (the Turco-Persian "Kishlák") in the desert, where winter-rains supply them, and make for the Yaylák, or summer-quarters, where they find grass and water. Thus the great Ruwala tribe appears regularly every year on the eastern slopes of the Anti-Libanus (Unexplored Syria, i. 117), and hence the frequent "partings."

*

RICHARD BURTON

THE DUELLO

This "renowning it" and boasting of one's tribe (and oneself) before battle is as natural as the war-cry: both are intended to frighten the foe and have often succeeded. Every classical reader knows that the former practice dates from the earliest ages. It is still customary in Arabia during the furious tribal fights, the duello on a magnificent scale, which often ends in half the combatants on either side being placed hors-de-combat. A fair specimen of "renowning it" is Amrú's Suspended Poem with its extravagant panegyric of the Taghlab tribe (p. 64, "Arabian Poetry for English Readers," etc., by W. A. Clouston, Glasgow: privately printed MDCCCLXXXI.; and transcribed from Sir William Jones's translation).

*

THY HEART'S DESIRE

The "Turk" appeared soon amongst the Abbaside Caliphs. Mohammed was made to prophecy of them under the title Banú Kantúrah, the latter being a slave-girl of Abraham. The Imam Al-Shafi'i (A.H. 195 = A.D. 810) is said to have foretold their rule in Egypt where an Ottoman defended him against a donkey-boy. (For details see Pilgrimage i. 216.) The Caliph Al-Mu'atasim bi'llah (A.D. 833-842) had more than 10,000 Turkish slaves and was the first to entrust them with high office; so his Arab subjects wrote of him: —

184

CONGRESS WITH A CROCODILE

A wretched Turk is thy heart's desire;
And to them thou showest thee dam and sire.

His successor Al-Wásik (Vathek, of the terrible eyes) was
the first to appoint a Turk his Sultan or regent. After his
reign they became prætorians and led to the downfall of the
Abbasides.

*

A LAYER OF THE EARTH

The courser chargeth on battling foe,
Mixing heaven on high with the earth down low:
As though the Morning had blazed his brow,
And he rends her vitals as quid pro quo.

Firdausi, the Homer of Persia, affects the same magnificent
exaggeration. The trampling of men and horses raises such
a dust that it takes one layer (of the seven) from earth and
adds it to the (seven of the) Heavens. The "blaze" on the
stallion's forehead (Arab. "Ghurrah") is the white gleam of
the morning.

*

HAHISH-ORGIE

THE PERS. "BANG"; Indian "Bhang"; Maroccan "Fasúkh"
and S. African "Dakhá." (Pilgrimage i. 64). I heard of

a "Hashish-orgie" in London which ended in half the experimentalists being on their sofas for a week. The drug is useful for stokers, having the curious property of making men insensible to heat. Easterns also use it for "Imsák" prolonging coition, of which I speak presently.

*

DELIRIUM PHANTISTICUM

ARAB. "HASHSHÁSHÍN;" WHENCE De Sacy derived "Assassin." A notable effect of the Hashish preparation is wildly to excite the imagination, a kind of delirium imaginans sive phantasticum.

*

HIGH PRAISE

At this he laughed and said to himself, "As Allah willeth, O Hashish!"

Meaning "Well done!" Mashallah (Má sháa 'llah) is an exclamation of many uses, especially affected when praising man or beast for fear lest flattering words induce the evil eye.

*

THE SITTING

ARAB. "MAJLIS" = SITTING. The postures of coition, ethnologically curious and interesting, are subjects so extensive that they require a volume rather than a note. Full information can be found in the Ananga-ranga, or Stage of the Bodiless One, a treatise in Sanskrit verse vulgarly known as Koka Pandit from the supposed author, a Wazir of the great Rajah Bhoj or, according to others, of the Maharajah of Kanoj. Under the title Lizzat al-Nisá (The Pleasures — or enjoying — of Women) it has been translated into all the languages of the Moslem East, from Hindustani to Arabic. It divides postures into five great divisions: (1) the woman lying supine, of which there are eleven subdivisions; (2) lying on her side, right or left, with three varieties; (3) sitting, which has ten; (4) standing, with three subdivisions, and (5) lying prone, with two. This total of twenty-nine, with three forms of "Purusháyit," when the man lies supine (see the Abbot in Boccaccio i. 4), becomes thirty-two, approaching the French *quarante façons*. The Upavishta, majlis, or sitting postures, when one or both "sit at squat" somewhat like birds, appear utterly impossible to Europeans who lack the pliability of the Eastern's limbs. Their object in congress is to avoid tension of the muscles which would shorten the period of enjoyment. In the text the woman lies supine and the man sits at squat between her legs: it is a favourite from Marocco to China. A literal translation of the Ananga-ranga appeared in 1873 under the name of Káma-Shástra; or the Hindoo Art of Love (Ars Amoris Indica); but of this only

187

six copies were printed. It was re-issued (printed but not published) in 1885. The curious in such matters will consult the Index Librorum Prohibitorum (London, privately printed, 1879) by Pisanus Fraxi (H. S. Ashbee).

*

GLORIOUS HIGHWAYMEN

THE KARDOUKHOI (CARDUCHI) of Xenophon; also called (Strabo xv.) "Kárdakís, from a Persian word signifying manliness," which would be "Kardak" = a doer (of derring-do). They also named the Montes Gordæi the original Ararat of Xisisthrus-Noah's Ark. The Kurds are of Persian race, speaking an old and barbarous Iranian tongue and often of the Shi'ah sect. They are born bandits, highwaymen, cattle-lifters; yet they have spread extensively over Syria and Egypt and have produced some glorious men, witness Sultan Saláh al-Din (Saladin) the Great. They claim affinity with the English in the East, because both races always inhabit the highest grounds they can find.

*

BANDITRY

So the hundred horsemen fell upon them and surrounded them on all sides, and King Rumzan shouted his war cry, and thus also did his nephew Kanmakan, and ere long they made prize of them all, to the number of near three hundred horsemen, banded together of the refuse of rascality.

These irregular bands who belong to no tribe are the most dangerous bandits in Arabia, especially upon the northern frontier. Burckhardt, who suffered from them, gives a long account of their treachery and utter absence of that Arab "pundonor" which is supposed to characterise Arab thieves.

*

EYE OF THE BEHOLDER

ARAB. "KHIZÁB" A paste of quicklime and lamp-black kneaded with linseed oil which turns the Henna to a dark olive. It is hideously ugly to unaccustomed eyes and held to be remarkably beautiful in Egypt.

*

JOBS FOR THE BLIND

"Tell me thy name and thy father's name, for I am under an oath not to slay any whose name tallies with mine and whose father's name is that of my father; and if this be the case with thee, I will give thee up the maid." Quoth the horseman, "My name is Bilál…"

i.e. "benefits"; also the name of Mohammed's Mu'ezzin, or crier to prayer, who is buried outside the Jábiah gate of Damascus. Hence amongst Moslems Abyssinians were preferred as mosque-criers in the early ages of Al-Islam. Egypt chose blind men because they were abundant and cheap; moreover they cannot take note of what is doing on the adjoining roof-terraces where women and children love to pass the cool hours that begin and end the day. Stories are told of men who counterfeited blindness for years in order to keep the employment. In Moslem cities the stranger required to be careful how he appeared at a window or on the gallery of a minaret: the people hate to be overlooked and the whizzing of a bullet was the warning to be off. Pilgrimage iii. 185.

*

CAP-À-PIE

ARAB. "DARA'" OR "Dira'," a habergeon, a coat of ring-mail, sometimes worn in pairs. During the wretched "Sudan" campaigns much naïve astonishment was expressed by the English Press to hear of warriors armed cap-à-pie in this armour like medieval knights. They did not know that every great tribe has preserved, possibly from Crusading times, a number of hauberks, even to hundreds. I have heard of only one English traveller who had a mail-jacket made by Wilkinson of Pall Mall, imitating in this point Napoleon III. and (according to the Banker-poet, Rogers) the Duke of

Wellington. That of Napoleon is said to have been made of platinum-wire, the work of a Pole who received his money and an order to quit Paris. The late Sir Robert Clifton (they say) tried its value with a Colt after placing it upon one of his coat-models or mannequins. It is easy to make these hauberks arrow-proof or sword-proof, even bullet-proof if Arab gunpowder be used: but against a modern rifle-cone they are worse than worthless as the fragments would be carried into the wound. The British serjeant was right in saying that he would prefer to enter battle in his shirt: and he might even doff that to advantage and return to the primitive custom of man-gymnomachy.

*

COUNTING HUMPS

ARAB. "JAMAL" (BY Badawin pronounced "Gamal" like the Hebrew) is the generic term for "Camel" through the Gr.κάμηλος: "Ibl" is also the camel-species but not so commonly used. "Hajín" is the dromedary (in Egypt, "Dalúl" in Arabia), not the one-humped camel of the zoologist (*C. dromedarius*) as opposed to the two-humped (*C. Bactrianus*), but a running *i.e.* a riding camel. The feminine is Nákah, for like mules females are preferred. "Bakr" (masc.) and "Bakrah" (fem.) are camel-colts. There are hosts of special names besides those which are general. Mr. Ensor is singular when he states (p. 40) "the male (of the camel) is much the safer animal to choose;" and the custom of the universal East disproves his assertion. Mr. McCoan ("Egypt as it is") tells his readers that the Egyptian camel has two humps; in fact, he describes the camel as it is not.

*

GOADING

...a thing called Crupper which he putteth under my tail, and a thing called Bit which he placeth in my mouth: and he fashioneth me a goad and goadeth me with it and maketh me run more than my strength.

The goad still used by the rascally Egyptian donkey-boy is a sharp nail at the end of a stick; and claims the special attention of societies for the protection of animals.

*

SIGHT OF THE DEVIL

"THE MOST UNGRATEFUL of all voices surely is the voice of asses" (Koran xxxi. 18); and hence the "braying of hell" (Koran lxvii. 7). The vulgar still believe that the donkey brays when seeing the Devil. "The last animal which entered the Ark with Noah was the Ass to whose tail Iblis was clinging. At the threshold the ass seemed troubled and could enter no further when Noah said to him: — Fie upon thee! come in. But as the ass was still troubled and did not advance Noah cried: — Come in, though the Devil be with thee!; so the ass entered and with him Iblis. Thereupon Noah asked: — O enemy of Allah who brought thee into the Ark?; and Iblis answered: — Thou art the man, for thou saidest to the ass, come in though the Devil be with thee!" (Kitáb al-Unwán fi Makáid al-Niswán quoted by Lane ii. 54).

*

DEAD DONKEYS

ARAB. "RIHL," A wooden saddle stuffed with straw and matting. In Europe the ass might complain that his latter end is the sausage. In England they say no man sees a dead donkey: I have seen dozens and, unfortunately, my own.

*

ILL-OMENS

After a while the dust lifted and discovered a black steed finely dight with a blaze on the forehead like a dirham round and bright; handsomely marked about the hoof with white and with firm strong legs pleasing to sight and he neighed with affright.

This is one of the lucky signs and adds to the value of the beast. There are some fifty of these marks, some of them (like a spiral of hair in the breast which denotes that the rider is a cuckold) so ill-omened that the animal can be bought for almost nothing. Of course great attention is paid to colours, the best being the dark rich bay ("red" of Arabs) with black points, or the flea-bitten grey (termed Azrak = blue or Akhzar = green) which whitens with age. The worst are dun, cream coloured, piebald and black, which last are very rare. Yet according to the Mishkát al-Masábih (Lane 2, 54) Mohammed said, "The best horses are black (dark brown?) with white blazes (Arab. "Ghurrah") and upper lips; next, black with blaze and three white legs (bad, because white-hoofs are brittle): next, bay with white blaze and white fore and hind legs." He also said, "Prosperity is with sorrel horses;" and praised a sorrel with white forehead and legs; but he dispraised the "Shikál" which has white stockings (Arab. "Muhajjil") on alternate hoofs (*e.g.* right hind and left fore). The curious reader will consult Lady Anne Blunt's "Bedouin Tribes of the Euphrates, with some Account of the Arabs and their Horses" (1879); but he must remember that it treats of the frontier tribes. The late Major Upton also left a book, "Gleanings from the Desert of Arabia" (1881); but it is a marvellous production deriving *e.g.* Khayl (a horse generically) from Kohl or antimony (p. 275). What the Editor was dreaming of I cannot imagine. I have given some details concerning the Arab horse especially in Al-Yaman, among the Zú Mohammed, the Zú Husayn and the Banu Yam in Pilgrimage iii. 270. As late as Marco Polo's day they supplied the Indian market *viâ* Aden; but the "Eye of Al-Yaman" has totally lost the habit of exporting horses.

*

IT IS WRITTEN

Said the peahen, "That which is on our foreheads we must indeed fulfil, and when our doomed day draweth near, who shall deliver us? But not a soul departeth except it have accomplished its predestined livelihood and term."

The vulgar belief is that man's fate is written upon his skull, the sutures being the writing.

*

ROSARY

ARAB "TASBÍH" = SAYING, "Subhán' Allah." It also means a rosary (Egypt. Sebhah for Subhah) a string of 99 beads divided by a longer item into sets of three and much fingered by the would-appear pious. The professional devotee carries a string of wooden balls the size of pigeons' eggs.

*

PIGEON-LORE

Now they resorted only to that mountain where the hermit was, and the reason of their foregathering with the holy man was their assiduity in repeating "Praised be Allah!" for it is recounted that the pigeon sayeth in praise, "Praised be the

RICHARD BURTON

Creator of all Creatures, the Distributor of daily bread, the Builder of the heavens and Dispreader of the earths!"

The pigeon is usually made to say, "Wahhidú Rabba-kumu 'llazi khalaka-kum, yaghfiru lakum zamba-kum" = "Unify (Assert the Unity of) your Lord who created you; so shall He forgive your sin!" As might be expected this "language" is differently interpreted. Pigeon-superstitions are found in all religions and I have noted (Pilgrimage iii. 218) how the Hindu deity of Destruction-reproduction, the third Person of their Triad, Shiva and his Spouse (or active Energy), are supposed to have dwelt at Meccah under the titles of Kapoteshwara (Pigeon-god) and Kapoteshí (Pigeon-goddess).

*

DAY OF DOOM

"Verily my tarrying here this day hath wronged these animals, and what excuse have I towards my Creator and the Creator of these birds and beasts for that I was the cause of their flight from their drink and their daily food and their place of pasturage? Alas for my shame before my Lord on the day when He shall avenge the hornless sheep on the sheep with horns!"

After the Day of Doom, when men's actions are registered, that of mutual retaliation will follow and all creatures (brutes included) will take vengeance on one another.

*

CAVE OF THE SLEEPERS

THE COMRADES OF the Cave, famous in the Middle Ages of Christianity (Gibbon chapt. xxxiii.), is an article of faith with Moslems, being part subject of chapter xviii., the Koranic Surah termed the Cave. These Ripp Van Winkle-tales begin with Endymion so famous amongst the Classics and Epimenides of Crete who slept fifty-seven years; and they extend to modern days as La Belle au Bois dormant. The Seven Sleepers are as many youths of Ephesus (six royal councillors and a shepherd, whose names are given on the authority of Ali); and, accompanied by their dog, they fled the persecutions of Dakianús (the Emperor Decius) to a cave near Tarsús in Natolia where they slept for centuries. The Caliph Mu'awiyah when passing the cave sent into it some explorers who were all killed by a burning wind. The number of the sleepers remains uncertain, according to the Koran (ibid. v. 21) three, five or seven; and their sleep lasted either three hundred or three hundred and nine years. The dog (ibid. v. 17) slept at the cave-entrance with paws outstretched and, according to the general, was called "Katmir" or "Kitmir;" but Al-Rakím (v. 8) is also applied to it by some. Others hold this to be the name of the valley or mountain and others of a stone or leaden tablet on which their names were engraved by their countrymen who built a chapel on the spot (v. 20). Others again make the Men of Al-Rakím distinct from the Cave-men, and believe (with

Bayzáwi) that they were three youths who were shut up in a grotto by a rock-slip. Each prayed for help through the merits of some good deed: when the first had adjured Allah the mountain cracked till light appeared; at the second petition it split so that they saw one another and after the third it opened. However that may be, Kitmir is one of the seven favoured animals; the others being the Hudhud (hoopoe) of Solomon (Koran xxii. 20); the she-camel of Sálih (chapt. lxxxvii.); the cow of Moses which named the Second Surah; the fish of Jonah; the serpent of Eve; and the peacock of Paradise. For Koranic revelations of the Cave see the late Thomas Chenery (p. 414 The Assemblies of Al-Hariri: Williams and Norgate, 1870) who borrows from the historian Tabari.

*

WOLF WICKED

THE WOLF (TRULY enough to nature) is the wicked man without redeeming traits; the fox of Arab folk-lore is the cunning man who can do good on occasion. Here the latter is called "Sa'alab" which may, I have noted, mean the jackal; but further on "Father of a Fortlet" refers especially to the fox. Herodotus refers to the gregarious Canis Aureus when he describes Egyptian wolves as being "not much bigger than foxes" (ii. 67). Canon Rawlinson, in his unhappy version, does not perceive that the Halicarnassian means the jackal and blunders about the hyena.

*

ROYAL BIRD

Arab. "Bází," Pers. "Báz" (here Richardson is wrong *s. v.*); a term to a certain extent generic, but specially used for the noble Peregrine (*F. Peregrinator*) whose tiercel is the Sháhín (or "Royal Bird"). It is sometimes applied to the goshawk (*Astur palumbarius*) whose proper title, however, is Shah-báz (King-hawk). The Peregrine extends from the Himalayas to Cape Comorin and the best come from the colder parts: in Iceland I found that the splendid white bird was sometimes trapped for sending to India. In Egypt "Bazi" is applied to the kite or buzzard and "Hidyah" (a kite) to the falcon (Burckhardt's Prov. 159, 581 and 602). Burckhardt translates "Hidáyah," the Egyptian corruption, by "an ash-grey falcon of the smaller species common throughout Egypt and Syria."

*

SUFI

Arab. "Súf;" hence "Súfi," = (etymologically) one who wears woollen garments, a devotee, a Santon; from σοφὸς = wise; from σαφής = pure, or from Safá = he was pure. This is not the place to enter upon such a subject as "Tasawwuf," or Sufism; that singular reaction from arid Moslem realism and materialism, that immense development of gnostic and Neo-platonic transcendentalism which is found only germinating in the Jewish and Christian creeds. The poetry of Omar-i-Khayyám, now familiar to English readers, is a fair specimen; and the student will consult the last chapter of the Dabistan "On the religion of the Sufiahs." The first Moslem Sufi was Abu Háshim of Kufah, ob. A. H. 150 = 767, and the first Convent of Sufis called "Takiyah" (Pilgrimage i. 124) was founded in Egypt by Saladin the Great.

*

IN A CROWD

"...And death in company is the best of things; wherefore I will certainly and assuredly hasten to slay thee ere thou see me slain."

The Persian proverb is "Marg-i-amboh jashni dárad" — death in a crowd is as good as a feast.

*

ENSORCELLED SNAKE

ARAB. "HÁWÍ" = A juggler who plays tricks with snakes: he is mostly a Gypsy. The "recompense" the man expects is the golden treasure which the ensorcelled snake is supposed to guard. This idea is as old as the Dragon in the Garden of the Hesperides — and older.

*

MONGOOSE

ARAB. BINT 'ARÚS = daughter of the bridegroom, the Hindustani Mungus (vulg. Mongoose); a well-known weasel-like rodent often kept tame in the house to clear it of vermin. It is supposed to know an antidote against snake-poison, as the weasel eats rue before battle (Pliny x. 84; xx. 13). In Modern Egypt this viverra is called "Kitt (or Katt) Far'aun" = Pharaoh's cat: so the Percnopter becomes Pharaoh's hen and the unfortunate (?) King has named a host of things, alive and dead. It was worshipped and mummified in parts of Ancient Egypt *e.g.* Heracleopolis, on account of its antipathy to serpents and because it was supposed to destroy the crocodile, a feat which Ælian and others have overloaded with fable. It has also a distinct antipathy to cats. The ichneumon as a pet becomes too tame and will not leave its master: when enraged it emits an offensive stench. I brought home for the Zoological Gardens a Central African specimen prettily barred. Burckhardt (Prov. 455) quotes a line: —

Rakas 'Ibn Irsin wa zamzama 'l-Nimsu,

(Danceth Ibn Irs whileas Nims doth sing)

and explains Nims by ichneumon and Ibn Irs as a "species of small weasel, or ferret, very common in Egypt: it comes into the houses, feeds upon meat, is of gentle disposition, although not domesticated and full of gambols and frolic."

RICHARD BURTON

*

CATUS

ARAB. "SINNAUR" (ALSO meaning a prince). The common name is Kitt which is pronounced Katt or Gatt; and which Ibn Dorayd pronounces a foreign word (Syriac?). Hence, despite Freitag, Catus (which Isidore derives from catare, to look for) Κάττα or Τάτα, gatto, chat, cat, an animal unknown to the Classics of Europe who used the *mustela* or *putorius vulgaris* and different species of viverræ. The Egyptians, who kept the cat to destroy vermin, especially snakes, called it Mau, Mai, Miao (onomatopoetic): this descendant of the *Felis maniculata* originated in Nubia; and we know from the mummy pits and Herodotus that it was the same in species as ours. The first portraits of the cat are on the monuments of "Beni Hasan," B.C. 2500. I have ventured to derive the familiar "Puss" from the Arab. "Biss" (fem. "Bissah"), which is a congener of Pasht (Diana), the cat-faced goddess of Bubastis (Pi-Pasht), now Zagázig. Lastly "tabby (brindled)-cat" is derived from the Attábi (Prince Attab's) quarter at Baghdad where watered silks were made. It is usually attributed to the Tibbie, Tibalt, Tybalt, Thibert or Tybert (who is also executioner), various forms of Theobald in the old Beast Epic; as opposed to Gilbert the gib-cat, either a tom-cat or a gibbed (castrated) cat.

*

SECRET FRATERNITY

ARAB. "IKHWÁN AL-SAFÁ," a popular term for virtuous friends who perfectly love each other in all purity: it has also a mystic meaning. Some translate it "Brethren of Sincerity," and hold this brotherhood to be Moslem Freemasons, a mere fancy (see the Mesnevi of Mr. Redhouse, Trubner 1881). There is a well-known Hindustani book of this name printed by Prof. Forbes in Persian character and translated by Platts and Eastwick.

*

MAKING BROTHERHOOD

AMONG EASTERN MEN there are especial forms for "making brotherhood." The "Munh-bolá-bhái" (mouth-named brother) of India is well-known. The intense "associativeness" of these races renders isolation terrible to them, and being defenceless in a wild state of society has special horrors. Hence the origin of Caste for which see Pilgrimage (i. 52). Moslems, however, cannot practise the African rite of drinking a few drops of each other's blood. This, by the by, was also affected in Europe, as we see in the Gesta Romanorum, Tale lxvii., of the wise and foolish knights who "drew blood (to drink) from the right arm."

*

203

RICHARD BURTON

DRAWING VENOM

THE SERPENT DOES not "sting" nor does it "bite;" it strikes with the poison-teeth like a downward stab with a dagger. These fangs are always drawn by the jugglers but they grow again and thus many lives are lost. The popular way of extracting the crochets is to grasp the snake firmly behind the neck with one hand and with the other to tantalise it by offering and withdrawing a red rag. At last the animal is allowed to strike it and a sharp jerk tears out both eye-teeth as rustics used to do by slamming a door. The head is then held downwards and the venom drains from its bag in the shape of a few drops of slightly yellowish fluid which, as conjurers know, may be drunk without danger. The patient looks faint and dazed, but recovers after a few hours and feeds as if nothing had happened. In India I took lessons from a snake-charmer but soon gave up the practice as too dangerous.

*

FATHER OF COOLNESS

Replied Abu al-Hasan, "O my brother, I meant thee naught but good; but I feared to tell thee this, lest such transport should betide thee as might hinder thee from foregathering with her, and be a stumbling-block between thee and her. But be of good cheer and keep thine eyes cool and clear; for she to thee inclineth and to favour thee designeth."

CONGRESS WITH A CROCODILE

By a similar image the chamæleon is called Abú Kurrat =
Father of coolness; because it is said to have the "coldest"
eye of all animals and insensible to heat and light, since it
always looks at the sun.

*

TRUE SEDUCER

And if thou crave for more
Take all that satisfies.

Thou donn'st me sickness-dress
Thee with health's weed I bless.

These naïve offers in Eastern tales mostly come from the true
seducer — Eve. Europe, and England especially, still talks
endless absurdity upon the subject. A man of the world may
"seduce" an utterly innocent (which means an ignorant)
girl. But to "seduce" a married woman! What a farce!

*

APPETITE

THE EASTERN HEROINE always has a good appetite and
eats well. The sensible Oriental would infinitely despise
that *maladive* Parisienne in whom our neighbours delight,
and whom I long to send to the Hospital.

205

RICHARD BURTON

*

IMPATIENT

Quoth they, "Maybe that Patience lend thee ease!"
Quoth I, "Since fared he where is Patience' place?"
Covenant he made 'twixt me and him, to cut
The cords of Patience at our last embrace!

Meaning to let Patience run away like an untethered camel.

*

FORBIDDEN WORDS

She split my casque of courage with eye-swords that sorely
smite;
She pierced my patience' ring-mail with her shape like cane-
spear light:
Patched by the musky mole on cheek was to our sight displayed
Camphor set round with ambergris, light dawning through
the night.

i.e. her fair face shining through the black hair. "Camphor"
is a favourite with Arab poets; the Persians hate it because
connected in their minds with death; being used for
purifying the corpse. We read in Burckhardt (Prov. 464)
"Singing without siller is like a corpse without Hanút" —
this being a mixture of camphor and rose-water sprinkled

over the face of the dead before shrouded. Similarly Persians avoid speaking of coffee, because they drink it at funerals and use tea at other times.

*

THE POSSESSED

ARAB. MAJNÚN (*I.E.* one possessed by a Jinni) the well-known model lover of Layla, a fictitious personage for whom see D'Herbelot (*s. v.* Megnoun). She was celebrated by Abu Mohammed Nizam al-Din of Ganjah (ob. A.H. 597 = 1200) pop. known as Nizámi, the caustic and austere poet who wrote: —

The weals of this world are the ass's meed!
Would Nizámi were of the ass's breed.

The series in the East begins chronologically with Yúsuf and Zulaykhá (Potiphar's wife) sung by Jámi (nat. A.H. 817 = 1414); the next in date is Khusraw and Shirin (also by Nizami); Farhad and Shirin; and Layla and Majnun (the Night-black maid and the Maniac-man) are the last. We are obliged to compare the lovers with "Romeo and Juliet," having no corresponding instances in modern days: the classics of Europe supply a host as Hero and Leander, Theagenes and Charicleia, etc. etc.

*

RICHARD BURTON

RASCAL JEWELLERS

Now Abu al-Hasan's friend was a jeweller, and when she was gone, he found a place for speech and said to Ali bin Bakkar, "Doubtless and assuredly the Caliph's household have some demand upon thee or thou hast dealings therewith?"

The jeweller of Eastern tales from Marocco to Calcutta, is almost invariably a rascal: here we have an exception.

*

SEALING-WAX

Then she took leave and repaired to Ali bin Bakkar, whom she found waiting, and gave him the letter. He read it and writing a paper by way of reply, gave it to her; and she carried it to the jeweller, who tore asunder the seal...

This must not be understood of sealing-wax, which, however, is of ancient date. The Egyptians (Herod. ii. 38) used "sealing earth" (γῆ σημαντρίς) probably clay, impressed with a signet (δακτύλιον); the Greeks mud-clay (πηλός); and the Romans first cretula and then wax (Beckmann). Mediæval Europe had bees-wax tempered with Venice turpentine and coloured with cinnabar or similar material. The modern sealing-wax, whose distinctive is shell-lac, was brought by the Dutch from India to Europe; and the earliest seals date from about A.D. 1560. They called it Ziegel-lak, whence the German Siegel-lack, the French preferring *cire-à-cacheter*, as distinguished from *cire-à-sceller*, the softer material. The use of sealing-wax in India dates from old times and the material, though coarse and unsightly, is still preferred by Anglo-Indians because it resists heat whereas the best English softens like pitch.

*

TAKING PRECAUTIONS

AN UNMARRIED MAN is not allowed to live in a respectable quarter of a Moslem city unless he takes such precaution. Lane (Mod. Egypt. *passim*) has much to say on this point; and my excellent friend the late Professor Spitta at Cairo found the native prejudice very troublesome.

*

PIED HORSE

ARAB. "RITÁNAH," FROM "Ratan," speaking any tongue not Arabic, the allusion being to foreign mercenaries, probably Turks. In later days Turkish was called Muwalla', a pied horse, from its mixture of languages.

*

RICHARD BURTON

DESCENDANTS OF THE NORTHMEN

The "topothesia" is worthy of Shakespeare's day. "Khálidán" is evidently a corruption of "Khálidatáni" (for Khálidát), the Eternal, as Ibn Wardi calls the Fortunate Islands, or Canaries, which owe both their modern names to the classics of Europe. Their present history dates from A.D. 1385, unless we accept the Dieppe-Rouen legend of Labat which would place the discovery in A.D. 1326. I for one thoroughly believe in the priority, on the West African Coast, of the gallant descendants of the Northmen.

*

FOUR ARE COMPANY

Four wives are allowed by Moslem law and for this reason. If you marry one wife she holds herself your equal, answers you and "gives herself airs"; two are always quarrelling and making a hell of the house; three are "no company" and two of them always combine against the nicest to make her hours bitter. Four *are* company; they can quarrel and "make it up" amongst themselves, and the husband enjoys comparative peace. But the Moslem is bound by his law to deal equally with the four; each must have her dresses, her establishment and her night, like her sister wives. The number is taken from the Jews (Arbah Turim Ev. Hazaer, i.) "the wise men have given good advice that a man should not marry more than four wives." Europeans, knowing that

Moslem women are cloistered and appear veiled in public, begin with believing them to be mere articles of luxury; and only after long residence they find out that nowhere has the sex so much real liberty and power as in the Moslem East. They can possess property and will it away without the husband's leave: they can absent themselves from the house for a month without his having a right to complain; and they assist in all his counsels for the best of reasons: a man can rely only on his wives and children, being surrounded by rivals who hope to rise by his ruin. As regards political matters the Circassian women of Constantinople really rule the Sultanate and there *soignez la femme!* is the first lesson of getting on in the official world.

*

FALLEN ANGELS

Indeed Allah had clad him in the cloak of comeliness and had crowned him with the crown of completion: his eye-glance was more bewitching than Hárút and Marút and the play of his luring looks more misleading than Tághút…

Two fallen angels who taught men the art of magic. They are mentioned in the Koran (chapt. ii.); and the commentators have extensively embroidered the simple text. Popularly they are supposed to be hanging by their feet in a well in the territory of Babel hence the frequent allusions to "Babylonian sorcery" in Moslem writings; and those who

211

would study the black art at head-quarters are supposed to go there. They are counterparts of the Egyptian Jamnes and Mambres, the Jannes and Jambres of St. Paul (2 Tim. iii. 8).

*

SLEEP VEIL

LANE (II. 222) FIRST read "Múroozee" and referred it to the Murúz tribe near Herat: he afterwards (iii. 748) corrected it to "Marwazee," of the fabric of Marw (Margiana), the place now famed for "Mervousness." As a man of Rayy (Rhages) becomes Rází (*e.g.* Ibn Fáris al-Rází), so a man of Marw is Marázi, not Murúzi nor Márwazi. The "Mikna'" was a veil forming a kind of "respirator," defending from flies by day and from mosquitos, dews and draughts by night. Easterns are too sensible to sleep with bodies kept warm by bedding, and heads bared to catch every blast. Our grandfathers and grandmothers did well to wear bonnets-de-nuit, however ridiculous they may have looked.

*

THE DESPAIRER

IBLIS, MEANING THE Despairer, is called in the Koran (chapt. xviii. 48) "One of the genii (Jinnis) who departed from the command of his Lord." Mr. Rodwell (*in loco*) notes that the Satans and Jinnis represent in the Koran (ii. 32, etc.) the

evil-principle and finds an admixture of the Semitic Satans
and demons with the "Genii from the Persian (Babylonian?)
and Indian (Egyptian?) mythologies."

*

DARK EYES

I kissed him: darker grew those pupils, which
Seduce my soul, and cheeks flushed rosier hue;
O heart, if slanderers dare to deem there be
His like in charms; Say "Bring him hither, you!"

The eyes are supposed to grow darker under the influence
of wine and sexual passion.

*

FIT FOR A JINN

Tell me without leasing and think not to escape from my
hand with falses, for I swear to thee by the letters graven upon
the bezel of the seal-ring of Solomon David-son (on both of
whom be peace!), except thy speech be true, I will pluck out
thy feathers with mine own hand and strip off thy skin and
break thy bones!" Quoth the Ifrit Dahnash son of Shamhúrish
the Flyer, "I accept, O my lady, these conditions." — And
Shahrazad perceived the dawn of day and ceased to say her
permitted say.

Like Dahnash this is a fanciful P. N., fit only for a Jinni. As a rule the appellatives of Moslem "genii" end in — ús (oos), as Tarnús, Húliyánus; the Jewish in — nas, as Jattunas; those of the Tarsá (the "funkers" *i.e.* Christians) in — dús, as Sidús; and the Hindus in — tús, as Naktús (who entered the service of the Prophet Shays, or Seth, and was converted to the Faith). The King of the Genii is Malik Katshán who inhabits Mount Kaf; and to the west of him lives his son-in-law, Abd al-Rahman with 33,000 domestics: these names were given by the Apostle Mohammed. "Baktanús" is lord of three Moslem troops of the wandering Jinns, which number a total of twelve bands and extend from Sind to Europe. The Jinns, Divs, Peris ("fairies") and other pre-Adamitic creatures were governed by seventy-two Sultans all known as Sulayman and the last I have said was Ján bin Ján. The angel Háris was sent from Heaven to chastise him, but in the pride of victory he also revolted with his followers the Jinns whilst the Peris held aloof. When he refused to bow down before Adam he and his chiefs were eternally imprisoned but the other Jinns are allowed to range over earth as a security for man's obedience. The text gives the three orders, flyers, walkers and divers.

*

LEAN HIPS

NOTHING IS MORE "anti-pathetic" to Easterns than lean hips and flat hinder-cheeks in women and they are right in insisting upon the characteristic difference of the male and female figure. Our modern sculptors and painters, whose study of the nude is usually most perfunctory, have often scandalised me by the lank and greyhound-like fining off of the frame, which thus becomes rather simian than human.

*

FINE FOOT

THE SMALL FINE foot is a favourite with Easterns as well as Westerns. Ovid (A. A.) is not ashamed "ad teneros Oscula (not basia or suavia) ferre pedes." Ariosto ends the august person in
Il breve, asciutto, e ritondetto piede,
(The short-sized, clean-cut, roundly-moulded foot).
And all the world over it is a sign of "blood," *i.e.* the fine nervous temperament.

*

SPLASHING

AS HAS BEEN said a single drop of urine renders the clothes ceremoniously impure, hence a stone or a handful of earth must be used after the manner of the torche-cul. Scrupulous Moslems, when squatting to make water, will prod the ground before them with the point of stick or umbrella, so as to loosen it and prevent the spraying of the urine.

RICHARD BURTON

*

SATAN'S WIFE

It is not generally known to Christians that Satan has a wife called Awwá ("Hawwá" being the Moslem Eve) and, as Adam had three sons, the Tempter has nine, viz., Zu 'lbaysun who rules in bazars; Wassin who prevails in times of trouble; Awan who counsels kings; Haffan patron of wine-bibbers; Marrah of musicians and dancers; Masbut of newspreaders (and newspapers?); Dulhán who frequents places of worship and interferes with devotion; Dasim, lord of mansions and dinner tables, who prevents the Faithful saying "Bismillah" and "Inshallah," as commanded in the Koran (xviii. 23), and Lakís, lord of Fire-worshippers (Herklots, chap. xxix. sect. 4).

*

THE SCENT OF DEATH

Strong perfumes, such as musk (which we Europeans dislike and suspect), are always insisted upon in Eastern poetry; and Mohammed's predilection for them is well known. Moreover the young and the beautiful are held (justly enough) to exhale a natural fragrance which is compared with that of the blessed in Paradise. Hence in the Mu'allakah of Imr al-Kays: —

Breathes the scent of musk when they rise to rove,
As the Zephyr's breath with the flavour o' clove.

CONGRESS WITH A CROCODILE

It is made evident by dogs and other fine-nosed animals that every human being has his, or her, peculiar scent which varies according to age and health. Hence animals often detect the approach of death.

*

PEOPLE OF THE TENT

ARAB. "HÁZIR" (ALSO Ahl al-hazar, townsmen) and Bádi, a Badawi, also called "Ahl al-Wabar," people of the camel's hair (tent) and A'aráb (Nomadic) as opposed to Arab (Arab settled or not). They still boast with Ibn Abbas, cousin of Mohammed, that they have kerchiefs (not turbands) for crowns, tents for houses, loops for walls, swords for scarves and poems for registers or written laws.

*

LIVER LOVE

LIT. "MY LIVER;" which viscus, and not the heart, is held the seat of passion; a fancy dating from the oldest days. Theocritus says of Hercules, "In his liver Love had fixed a wound" (Idyl. xiii). In the Anthologia "Cease, Love, to wound my liver and my heart" (lib. vii.) So Horace (Odes, i. 2); his Latin Jecur and the Persian "Jigar" being evident congeners. The idea was long prevalent and we find in Shakespeare: —

217

RICHARD BURTON

Alas, then Love may be called appetite,
o motion of the liver but the palate.

*

TOUCH OF NATURE

Continued she, "Alas! Alas! thou art insolent in thy beauty and comeliness and grace and loving looks! But if thou art handsome, so am I handsome; what then is this thou dost? Have they taught thee to flout me or hath my father, the wretched old fellow, made thee swear not to speak to me to-night?"

A marvellous touch of nature, love ousting affection; the same trait will appear in the lover and both illustrate the deep Italian saying, "Amor discende, non ascende." "The further it goes down the stronger it becomes as of grand-parent for grand-child and *vice versâ.*"

*

POWERS OF PASSION

Then she thrust her hand into his breast and, because of the smoothness of his body, it slipped down to his waist and thence to his navel and thence to his yard, whereupon her heart ached and her vitals quivered and lust was sore upon her, for that the desire of women is fiercer than the desire of men, and she was ashamed of her own shamelessness.

218

This tenet of the universal East is at once fact and unfact. As a generalism asserting that women's passion is ten times greater than man's (Pilgrimage, ii. 282), it is unfact. The world shows that while women have more philoprogenitiveness, men have more amativeness; otherwise the latter would not propose and would nurse the doll and baby. Fact, however, in low-lying lands, like Persian Mazanderan versus the Plateau; Indian Malabar compared with Marátha-land; California as opposed to Utah and especially Egypt contrasted with Arabia. In these hot-damp climates the venereal requirements and reproductive powers of the female greatly exceed those of the male; and hence the dissoluteness of morals would be phenomenal, were it not obviated by seclusion, the sabre and the revolver. In cold-dry or hot-dry mountainous lands the reverse is the case; hence polygamy there prevails whilst the low countries require polyandry in either form, legal or illegal (*i.e.* prostitution). I have discussed this curious point of "geographical morality" (for all morality is, like conscience, both geographical and chronological), a subject so interesting to the lawgiver, the student of ethics and the anthropologist, in "The City of the Saints." But strange and unpleasant truths progress slowly, especially in England.

*

MORNING EVACUATIONS

Then he called out to the eunuch who slept at the door, saying, "Woe to thee, O damned one, arise at once!" So the eunuch rose, bemused with sleep, and brought him basin and ewer, whereupon Kamar al-Zaman entered the water-closet and did his need; then, coming out made the Wuzuablution and prayed the dawn-prayer, after which he sat telling on his beads the ninety-and-nine names of Almighty Allah.

This morning evacuation is considered, in the East, a *sine quâ non* of health; and old Anglo-Indians are unanimous in their opinion of the "bari fajar" (as they mispronounce the dawn-clearance). The natives of India, Hindús (pagans) and Hindís (Moslems), unlike Europeans, accustom themselves to evacuate twice a day, evening as well as morning. This may, perhaps, partly account for their mildness and effeminacy; for: —

C'est la constipation qui rend l'homme rigoureux.

The English, since the first invasion of cholera, in October, 1831, are a different race from their costive grandparents who could not dine without a "dinner-pill." Curious to say the clyster is almost unknown to the people of Hindostan although the barbarous West Africans use it daily to "wash 'um belly," as the Bonney-men say. And, as Sonnini notes, to propose the process in Egypt under the Beys might have cost a Frankish medico his life.

*

BEARD CRAFT

"Long beard and little wits," is a saying throughout the East where the Kausaj (= man with thin, short beard) is looked upon as cunning and tricksy. There is a venerable Joe Miller about a schoolmaster who, wishing to singe his long beard short, burnt it off and his face to boot: — which reminded him of the saying. A thick beard is defined as one which wholly conceals the skin; and in ceremonial ablution it must be combed out with the fingers till the water reach the roots. The Sunnat, or practice of the Prophet, was to wear the beard not longer than one hand and two fingers' breadth. In Persian "Kúseh" (thin-beard) is an insulting term opposed to "Khush-rísh," a well-bearded man. The Iranian growth is perhaps the finest in the world, often extending to the waist; but it gives infinite trouble, requiring, for instance, a bag when travelling. The Arab beard is often composed of two tufts on the chin-sides and straggling hairs upon the cheeks; and this is a severe mortification, especially to Shaykhs and elders, who not only look upon the beard as one of man's characteristics, but attach a religious importance to the appendage. Hence the enormity of Kamar al-Zaman's behaviour. The Persian festival of the vernal equinox was called Kuseh-nishín (Thin-beard sitting). An old man with one eye paraded the streets on an ass with a crow in one hand and a scourge and fan in the other, cooling himself, flogging the bystanders and crying heat! heat! (garmá! garmá!). For other particulars see Richardson (Dissertation, p. lii.). This is the Italian Giorno delle Vecchie, Thursday in Mid-Lent,

RICHARD BURTON

March 12 (1885), celebrating the death of Winter and the birth of Spring.

*

NAME OF DAYS

MOSLEMS HAVE ONLY two names for week days, Friday, Al-Jum'ah or meeting-day, and Al-Sabt, Sabbath-day, that is Saturday. The others are known by numbers after Quaker fashion with us, the usage of Portugal and Scandinavia.

*

HAUNTINGS

ARAB. "TAYF" = PHANTOM, the nearest approach to our "ghost," that queer remnant of Fetishism imbedded in Christianity; the phantasma, the shade (not the soul) of the dead. Hence the accurate Niebuhr declares, "apparitions (*i.e.*, of the departed) are unknown in Arabia." Haunted houses are there tenanted by Ghuls, Jinns and a host of supernatural creatures; but not by ghosts proper; and a man may live years in Arabia before he ever hears of the "Tayf." With the Hindus it is otherwise (Pilgrimage iii. 144.) Yet the ghost, the embodied fear of the dead and of death is common, in a greater or less degree, to all peoples; and, as modern Spiritualism proves, that ghost is not yet laid.

*

TREATING THE INSANE

When her sire saw this, he bade the women lay hands on her; so they seized her and manacled her, then putting a chain of iron about her neck, made her fast to one of the palace-windows and there left her.

This is still the popular Eastern treatment of the insane.

*

DRAGON'S BLOOD

ARAB. "ANDAM," A term applied to Brazil-wood (also called "Bakkam") and to "dragon's blood," but not, I think, to tragacanth, the "goat's thorn," which does not dye. Andam is often mentioned in The Nights.

*

DARKENING THE GROUND

ARAB. "SHAKHS" = A person, primarily a dark spot. So "Sawád" = blackness, in Al-Hariri means a group of people who darken the ground by their shade.

*

RICHARD BURTON

WASHING OF HEALTH

And he ceased not to comfort and solace and encourage Kamar al-Zaman and urge him to eat and drink till he ate food and drank wine, and life returned to him and he was saved from his ill case; and Marzawan cheered him and diverted him with talk and songs and stories, and in good time he became free of his disorder and stood up and sought to go to the Hammam.

The first bath after sickness, I have said, is called "Ghusl al-Sihhah," — the Washing of Health.

*

MAGIC CARPET

SOLOMON'S CARPET OF green silk which carried him and all his host through the air is a Talmudic legend generally accepted in Al-Islam though not countenanced by the Koran, chapt. xxvii. When the "gnat's wing" is mentioned, the reference is to Nimrod who, for boasting that he was lord of all, was tortured during four hundred years by a gnat sent by Allah up his ear or nostril.

*

CRIME OF PASSION

Quoth Kamar al-Zaman, "By Allah, this be indeed a rare device! Thou hast done right well."

The absolute want of morality and filial affection in the chaste young man are supposed to be caused by the violence of his passion, and he would be pardoned because he "loved much."

*

STRIKE OF SAND

I HAVE NOTICED the geomantic process in my "History of Sindh" (chapt. vii.). It is called "Zarb al-Raml" (strike of sand, the French say "frapper le sable") because the rudest form is to make on the ground dots at haphazard, usually in four lines one above the other: these are counted and, if even-numbered, two are taken (* *); if odd one (*); and thus the four lines will form a scheme say

* *
*
*
* *

This is repeated three times, producing the same number of figures; and then the combination is sought in an explanatory table or, if the practitioner be expert, he pronounces off-hand. The Nights speak of a "Takht Raml" or a board, like

225

a schoolboy's slate, upon which the dots are inked instead of points in sand. The moderns use a "Kura'h," or oblong die, upon whose sides the dots, odd and even, are marked; and these dice are hand-thrown to form the figure. By way of complication Geomancy is mixed up with astrology and then it becomes a most complicated kind of ariolation and an endless study. "Napoleon's Book of Fate," a chap-book which appeared some years ago, was Geomancy in its simplest and most ignorant shape. For the rude African form see my Mission to Dahome, i. 332; and for that of Darfour, pp. 360-69 of Shaykh Mohammed's Voyage before quoted.

*

TOOTHPICK ETIQUETTE

ARAB. "ARÁK" = TOOTH-STICK of the wild caper-tree; "Ará-ka" lit. = I see thee. The *capparis spinosa* is a common desert-growth and the sticks about a span long (usually called Miswák), are sold in quantities at Meccah after being dipped in Zemzem water. In India many other woods are used, date-tree, Salvadora, Achyrantes, phyllanthus, etc. Amongst Arabs peculiar efficacy accompanies the tooth-stick of olive, "the tree springing from Mount Sinai" (Koran xxiii. 20); and Mohammed would use no other, because it prevents decay and scents the mouth. Hence Koran, chapt. xcv. 1. The "Miswák" is held with the unused end between the ring-finger and minimus, the two others grasp the middle and the thumb is pressed against the back close to the lips. These articles have long been sold at the Medical Hall near the "Egyptian Hall," Piccadilly. They are better than our unclean tooth-brushes because each tooth gets its own especial rubbing, not a general sweep; at the same time the operation is longer and more troublesome. In parts of Africa as well as Asia many men walk about with the tooth-stick hanging by a string from the neck.

*

STALLIONS OF THE JINNS

THE "MEHARI," OF which the Algerine-French speak, are the dromedaries bred by the Mahrah tribe of Al-Yaman, the descendants of Mahrat ibn Haydán. They are covered by small wild camels (?) called Al-Húsh, found between Oman and Al-Shihr: others explain the word to mean "stallions of the Jinns," and term those savage and supernatural animals, "Najáib al-Mahriyah" — nobles of the Mahrah.

*

ADMIRED FORM

AS THE NIGHTS show, Arabs admire slender forms; but the hips and hinder cheeks must be highly developed and the stomach fleshy rather than lean. The reasons are obvious. The Persians who exaggerate everything say *e.g.* (Husayn Váiz in the Anvár-i-Suhayli): —

How paint her hips and waist? Who saw
A mountain (Koh) dangling to a straw (káh)?
In Antar his beloved Abla is a tamarisk (*T. Orientalis*).
Others compare with the palm-tree (Solomon), the Cypress
(Persian, esp. Hafiz and Firdausi) and the Arák or wild
Capparis (Arab.).

*

SIGN OF MAN

UBI AVES IBI angeli. All African travellers know that a few
birds flying about the bush, and a few palm-trees waving in
the wind, denote the neighbourhood of a village or a camp
(where angels are scarce). The reason is not any friendship
for man but because food, animal and vegetable, is more
plentiful. Hence Albatrosses, Mother Carey's (Mater Cara,
the Virgin) chickens, and Cape pigeons follow ships.

*

IN AND OUT

MOSLEM PORT TOWNS usually have (or had) only two gates.
Such was the case with Bayrut, Tyre, Sidon and a host of
others; the faubourg-growth of modern days has made these
obselete. The portals much resemble the entrances of old
Norman castles — Arques for instance. Pilgrimage, i. 185.

CONGRESS WITH A CROCODILE

*

TOTAL ABLUTION

Then Queen Budur stood up and wiped away her tears and, making the lesser ablution, applied her to pray: nor did she give over praying till drowsiness overcame the Lady Hayat al-Nufus and she slept, whereupon the Lady Budur came and lay by her till the morning.

Showing that there had been no consummation of the marriage which would have demanded "Ghusl", or total ablution, at home or in the Hammam.

*

NUPTIALS

THE BELIEF THAT young pigeon's blood resembles the virginal discharge is universal; but the blood most resembling man's is that of the pig which in other points is so very human. In our day Arabs and Hindus rarely submit to inspection the nuptial sheet as practised by the Israelites and Persians. The bride takes to bed a white kerchief with which she staunches the blood and next morning the stains are displayed in the Harem. In Darfour this is done by the bridegroom. "Prima Venus debet esse cruenta," say the Easterns with much truth, and they have no faith in our complaisant creed which allows the hymen-membrane to disappear by any but one accident.

229

RICHARD BURTON

*

LIMBO ZONE

ARAB. "IDDAT," ALLUDING to the months of celibacy which, according to Moslem law, must be passed by a divorced woman before she can re-marry.

*

TRIPLE DIVORCE

ARAB. "TALÁK BI'L-SALÁSAH" = a triple divorce which cannot be revoked; nor can the divorcer re-marry the same woman till after consummation with another husband. This subject will continually recur.

*

BLOOD OR BRAIN

Then they rent his belly and tearing out his entrails, poured the blood on the grave of the slain: moreover, they stripped off his skin and tare his flesh in pieces and, pulling out the rest of the bowels, scattered them hither and thither.

An allusion to a custom of the pagan Arabs in the days of ignorant Heathenism. The blood or brain, soul or personality of the murdered man formed a bird called Sady or Hámah (not the Humá or Humái, usually translated

230

"phœnix") which sprang from the head, where four of the five senses have their seat, and haunted his tomb, crying continually, "Uskúni!" = Give me drink (of the slayer's blood)! and which disappeared only when the vendetta was accomplished. Mohammed forbade the belief. Amongst the Southern Slavs the cuckoo is supposed to be the sister of a murdered man ever calling for vengeance.

*

FLEETNESS

ARAB. "ASÁFÍRÍ," so called because they attract sparrows (asáfír) a bird very fond of the ripe oily fruit. In the Romance of "Antar" Asáfír camels are beasts that fly like birds in fleetness. The reader must not confound the olives of the text with the hard unripe berries ("little plums pickled in stale") which appear at English tables; nor wonder that bread and olives are the beef-steak and potatoes of many Mediterranean peoples. It is an excellent diet, the highly oleaginous fruit supplying the necessary carbon.

*

NO NATIVE NONSENSE

ARAB. "TAMAR AL-HINDI" = the "Indian-date," whence our word "Tamarind." A sherbet of the pods, being slightly laxative, is much drunk during the great heats; and the dried fruit, made into small round cakes, is sold in the bazars. The traveller is advised not to sleep under the tamarind's shade, which is infamous for causing ague and fever. In Sind I derided the "native nonsense," passed the night under an "Indian date-tree" and awoke with a fine specimen of ague which lasted me a week.

*

FINAL JUDGEMENT

MOSLEMS ARE NOT agreed upon the length of the Day of Doom when all created things, marshalled by the angels, await final judgement; the different periods named are 40 years, 70, 300 and 50,000. Yet the trial itself will last no longer than while one may milk an ewe, or than "the space between two milkings of a she-camel." This is bringing down Heaven to Earth with a witness; but, after all, the Heaven of all faiths, including "Spiritualism," the latest development, is only an earth more or less glorified even as the Deity is humanity more or less perfected.

*

FIGS

ARAB. "JAMÍZ" (IN Egypt "Jammayz") = the fruit of the true sycomore (F. Sycomorus) a magnificent tree which produces a small tasteless fig, eaten by the poorer classes in Egypt and by monkeys. The "Tín" or real fig here is the woman's parts; the "mulberry-fig," the anus. Martial (i. 65) makes the following distinction: —

Dicemus ficus, quas scimus in arbore nasci,
Dicemus ficos, Cæciliane, tuos.

And Modern Italian preserves a difference between *fico* and *fica*.

*

THE FOURTH CLASS

Arab. "Khunsa" flexible or flaccid, from Khans = bending inwards, *i.e.* the mouth of a water-skin before drinking. Like Mukhannas, it is also used for an effeminate man, a passive sodomite and even for a eunuch. Easterns still believe in what Westerns know to be an impossibility, human beings with the parts and proportions of both sexes equally developed and capable of reproduction; and Al-Islam even provides special rules for them (Pilgrimage iii. 237). We hold them to be Buffon's fourth class of (duplicate) monsters, belonging essentially to one or the other sex, and related to its opposite only by some few characteristics. The old Greeks dreamed, after their fashion, a beautiful poetic dream of a human animal uniting the contradictory beauties of man and woman. The duality of the generative organs seems an old Egyptian tradition; at least we find it in Genesis (i. 27), where the image of the Deity is created male and female, before man was formed out of the dust of the ground (ii. 7). The old tradition found its way to India (if the Hindus did not borrow the idea from the Greeks); and one of the forms of Mahadeva, the third person of their triad, is entitled "Ardhanárí" = the Half-woman, which has suggested to them some charming pictures. Europeans, seeing the left breast conspicuously feminine, have indulged in silly surmises about the "Amazons."

*

DYING OF LAUGHTER

Then loudly laughed Queen Budur till she fell on her back, and said, "O my dearling, how quickly thou hast forgotten the nights we have lain together!"

This is a mere phrase for our "dying of laughter": the queen *was* on her back. And as Easterns sit on carpets, their falling back is very different from the same movement off a chair.

*

JOINING THE LOCKS

Then Queen Budur perfumed the letter-paper with a profusion of odoriferous musk and, winding it in her hair-strings which were of Iráki silk, with pendants of oblong emeralds, set with pearls and stones of price, delivered it to the old woman, bidding her carry it to Prince As'ad.

The reader will note in the narration concerning the two Queens the parallelism of the Arab's style which recalls that of the Hebrew poets. Strings of black silk are plaited into the long locks (an "idiot-fringe" being worn over the brow) because a woman is cursed "who joineth her own hair to the hair of another" (especially human hair). Sending the bands is a sign of affectionate submission; and, in extremest cases the hair itself is sent.

*

SWEAT OF THE STONE

ABDULLAH IBN AL-ZUBAYR a nephew of Ayishah, who had rebuilt the Ka'abah in A.H. 64 (A.D. 683), revolted (A.D. 680) against Yezid and was proclaimed Caliph at Meccah. He was afterwards killed (A.D. 692) by the famous or infamous Hajjáj general of Abd al-Malik bin Marwan, the fifth Ommiade, surnamed "Sweat of a stone" (skin-flint) and "Father of Flies," from his foul breath. See my Pilgrimage, etc. iii., 192-194, where are explained the allusions to the Ka'abah and the holy Black Stone.

*

RICHARD BURTON

SECTARIAN WARS

Ere this Zubayr-son felt their spiteful hate,
Who fled for refuge to the House and Stone:
Would that when Khárijah was for Amru slain
They had ransomed Ali with all men they own.

These lines are part of an elegy on the downfall of one of
the Moslem dynasties in Spain, composed in the twelfth
century by Ibn Abdun al-Andalúsi. The allusion is to the
famous conspiracy of the Khárijites (the first sectarians in
Mohammedanism) to kill Ali, Mu'awiyah and Amru (so
written but pronounced "Amr") al-As, in order to abate
intestine feuds in Al-Islam. Ali was slain with a sword-cut
by Ibn Muljam a name ever damnable amongst the Persians;
Mu'awiyah escaped with a wound and Kharijah, the Chief
of Police at Fustat or old Cairo was murdered by mistake for
Amru. After this the sectarian wars began.

*

PAINTED EYE AND SWORD

ARAB. "SARÁB" = (KORAN, chapt. xxiv.) the reek of the Desert,
before explained. It is called "Lama," the shine, the loom,
in Al-Hariri. The world is compared with the mirage, the
painted eye and the sword that breaks in the sworder's hand.

UPON THE MOUNTAIN

They took the way trending to the top and gave not over following it five days, but saw no end to it and were overcome with weariness, being unused to walking upon the mountains or elsewhere.

A proceeding fit only for thieves and paupers: "Alpinism" was then unknown. "You come from the mountain" (al-Jabal) means, "You are a clod-hopper"; and "I will sit upon the mountain" = turn anchorite or magician. (Pilgrimage i. 106).

*

PAWS OF THE SPHINX

Amjad took him in his arms and walked on with him, bytimes sitting down to rest till break of day, when they came to the mountain-top and found there a stream of running water and by it a pomegranate-tree and a prayer-niche.

Corresponding with wayside chapels in Catholic countries. The Moslem form would be either a wall with a prayer-niche (Mihráb) fronting Meccah-wards or a small domed room. These little oratories are often found near fountains, streams or tree-clumps where travellers would be likely to alight. I have described one in Sind ("Scinde or the Unhappy

Valley" i. 79); and have noted that scrawling on the walls is even more common in the East than in the West; witness the monuments of old Egypt bescribbled by the Greeks and Romans. Even the paws of the Sphinx are covered with such *graffiti*; and those of Ipsambul or Abu Simbal have proved treasures to epigraphists.

*

SUN AND FIRE

THE PARSIS, WHO are the representatives of the old Guebres, turn towards the sun and the fire as their Kiblah or point of prayer; all deny that they worship it. But, as in the case of saints' images, while the educated would pray before them for edification (Latria), the ignorant would adore them (Dulia); and would make scanty difference between the "reverence of a servant" and the "reverence of a slave." The human sacrifice was quite contrary to Guebre, although not to Hindu, custom; although hate and vengeance might prompt an occasional murder.

*

SECRET DUNGEONS

So the black carried him out at another door and, raising a flag in the floor, discovered a flight of twenty steps leading to a chamber under the earth, into which he descended with him

*and, laying his feet in irons, gave him over to the slave-girl
and went away.*

These *oubliettes* are common in old eastern houses as in the
medieval Castles of Europe, and many a stranger has met his
death in them. They are often so well concealed that even
the modern inmates are not aware of their existence.

*

THE BRAVE

A SERVILE NAME in Persian, meaning "the brave," and a title
of honour at the Court of Delhi when following the name.
Many English officers have made themselves ridiculous
(myself amongst the number) by having it engraved on their
seal-rings, *e.g.* Brown Sáhib Bahádur. To write the word
"Behadir" or "Bahádir" is to adopt the wretched Turkish
corruption.

*

THE THREE FORBIDDENS

ARAB. "JALLÁB," ONE of the three muharramát or forbiddens;
the Hárik al-hajar (burner of stone), the Káti' al-shajar (cutter
of trees, without reference to Hawarden N. B.) and the Báyi'
al-bashar (seller of men, vulg. Jalláb). The two former worked,
like the Italian Carbonari, in desert places where they had

especial opportunities for crime. (Pilgrimage iii. 140). None of these things must be practised during Pilgrimage on the holy soil of Al-Hijaz — not including Jeddah.

*

MIRACLES

Then she questioned him of the religion of Al-Islam and he told her that it was the true and right Faith and that our lord Mohammed had approved himself by surpassing miracles and signs manifest, and that fire-worship is harmful and not profitable; and he went on to expound to her the tenets of Al-Islam till she was persuaded and the love of the True Faith entered her heart.

This is the vulgar belief, although Mohammed expressly disclaimed the power in the Koran (chapt. xiii. 8), "Thou art commissioned to be a preacher only and not a worker of miracles." "Signs" (Arab. Ayát) may here also mean verses of the Koran, which the Apostle of Allah held to be his standing miracles. He despised the common miracula which in the East are of everyday occurrence and are held to be easy for any holy man. Hume does not believe in miracles because he never saw one. Had he travelled in the East he would have seen (and heard of) so many that his scepticism (more likely that testimony should be false than miracles be true) would have been based on a firmer foundation. It is one of the marvels of our age that whilst two-thirds of Christendom (the

Catholics and the "Orthodox" Greeks) believe in "miracles" occurring not only in ancient but even in our present days, the influential and intelligent third (Protestant) absolutely "denies the fact."

*

TOM, DICK, OR HARRY

While thou'rt my lord whose bounty's my estate,
A sword whereby my woes to annihilate,
Recourse I never need to Amru or Zayd,
Nor aught save thee if way to me grow strait!

i.e. "to Tom, Dick or Harry:" the names like John Doe and Richard Roe are used indefinitely in Arab. Grammar and Syntax. I have noted that Amru is written and pronounced Amr: hence Amru, the Conqueror of Egypt, when told by an astrologer that Jerusalem would be taken only by a *trium literarum homo*, with three letters in his name, sent for the Caliph Omar (Omr), to whom the so-called Holy City at once capitulated. Hence also most probably, the tale of Bhurtpore and the Lord Alligator (Kumbhir), who however did not change from Cotton to Combermore for some time after the successful siege.

*

RICHARD BURTON

AN IRON HAND

And Ni'amah exclaimed, "Heaven favoured art thou, O Naomi!" But whilst they led thus the most joyous life, behold! Al-Hajjáj, [6] the Viceroy of Cufa said to himself, "Needs must I contrive to take this girl named Naomi and send her to the Commander of the Faithful, Abd al-Malik bin Marwán, for he hath not in his palace her like for beauty and sweet singing."

Bin Yúsuf al-Sakafi, a statesman and soldier of the seventh and eighth centuries (A.D.). He was Governor of Al-Hijaz and Al-Irak under the fifth and sixth Ommiades, and I have noticed his vigorous rule of the Moslems' Holy Land in my Pilgrimage (iii. 194, etc.). He pulled down the Ka'abah and restored it to the condition in which it now is. Al-Siyuti (p. 219) accuses him of having suborned a man to murder Ibn Omar with a poisoned javelin, and of humiliating the Prophet's companions by "sealing them in the necks and hands," that is he tied a thong upon the neck of each and sealed the knot with lead. In Irak he showed himself equally masterful; but an iron hand was required by the revolutionists of Kufah and Basrah. He behaved like a good Knight in rescuing the Moslem women who called upon his name when taken prisoners by Dahir of Debal (Tathá in Sind). Al-Hajjaj was not the kind of man the Caliph would have chosen for a pander; but the Shi'ahs hated him and have given him a lasting bad name. In the East men respect manly measures, not the hysterical, philanthropic pseudo-humanitarianism of our modern government which is really the cruellest of all. When Ziyád bin Abihi was sent by Caliph Mu'awiyah to reform Bassorah, a den of thieves, he informed the lieges that he intended to rule by the sword and advised all evil-doers to quit the city. The people were forbidden, under pain of death, to walk the streets after prayers; on the first night two hundred suffered; on the second five and none afterwards. Compare this with our civilised rule in Egypt where even bands of brigands, a phenomenon perfectly new and unknown to this century, have started up, where crime has doubled in quantity and quality, and where "Christian rule" has thoroughly scandalised a Moslem land.

*

IN GRATIUDE

EASTERNS, I HAVE observed, have no way of saying "Thank you;" they express it by a blessing or a short prayer. They have a right to your surplus: daily bread is divided, they say and, eating yours, they consider it their own. I have discussed this matter in Pilgrimage i. 75-77, in opposition to those who declare that "gratitude" is unknown to Moslems.

*

DIFFERENT WANTS

ABD AL-MALIK has been before mentioned as the "Sweat of a Stone," etc. He died recommending Al-Hajjaj to his son,

Al-Walid, and one of his sayings is still remembered. "He who desireth to take a female slave for carnal enjoyment, let him take a native of Barbary; if he need one for the sake of children, let him have a Persian; and whoso desireth one for service, let him take a Greek." Moderns say, "If you want a brother (in arms) try a Nubian; one to get you wealth an Abyssinian and if you want an ass (for labour) a Sáwahíli, or Zanzibar negroid."

*

WATER-DOCTOR

ARAB. "KÁRÚRAH": THE "water-doctor" has always been an institution in the East and he has lately revived in Europe — especially at the German baths and in London.

*

THE FAIRER SEX

EASTERNS, I HAVE remarked, mostly recognise the artistic truth that the animal man is handsomer than woman; and that "fair sex" is truly only of skin-colour. The same is the general rule throughout creation, for instance the stallion compared with the mare, the cock with the hen; while there are sundry exceptions such as the Falconidæ.

CONGRESS WITH A CROCODILE

*

GAIT

THE BADAWI (WHO is nothing if not horsey) compares the gait of a woman who walks well (in Europe rarely seen out of Spain) with the slightly swinging walk of a thoroughbred mare, bending her graceful neck and looking from side to side at objects as she passes.

*

SEALING RING

THE EASTERN RING is rarely plain; and, its use being that of a signet, it is always in intaglio: the Egyptians invented engraving hieroglyphics on wooden stamps for marking bricks and applied the process to the ring. Moses B.C. 1491 (Exod. xxviii. 9) took two onyx-stones, and graved on them the names of the children of Israel. From this the signet ring was but a step. Herodotus mentions an emerald seal set in gold, that of Polycrates, the work of Theodorus son of Telecles the Samian (iii. 141). The Egyptians also were perfectly acquainted with working in cameo (anaglyph) and rilievo, as may be seen in the cavo rilievo of the finest of their hieroglyphs. The Greeks borrowed from them the cameo and applied it to gems (*e.g.* Tryphon's in the Marlborough collection), and they bequeathed the art to the Romans. We read in a modern book "Cameo means an onyx, and the most famous cameo in the world is the onyx containing the Apotheosis of Augustus." The ring is given in marriage because it was a seal by which orders were signed (Gen. xxxviii. 18 and Esther iii. 10-12). I may note that the seal-ring of Cheops (Khufu), found in the Greatest Pyramid, was in the possession of my old friend, Doctor Abbott, of Auburn (U.S.), and was sold with his collection. It is the oldest ring in the world, and settles the Cheops-question.

*

WEEPING IN JOY

THIS HABIT OF weeping when friends meet after long parting is customary, I have noted, amongst the American "Indians," the Badawin of the New World; they shed tears thinking of the friends they have lost. Like most primitive people they are ever ready to weep as was Æneas or Shakespeare's saline personage: —

This would make a man, a man of salt
To use his eyes for garden waterpots.
(King Lear, iv. 6.)

*

INTOXICANTS

ARAB. "BARSH" OR "Bars," the commonest kind. In India it is called Ma'jún (= electuary, generally): it is made of Ganja or young leaves, buds, capsules and florets of hemp (*C. sativa*), poppy-seed and flowers of the thorn-apple (*datura*) with milk and sugar-candy, nutmegs, cloves, mace and saffron, all boiled to the consistency of treacle which hardens when cold. Several recipes are given by Herklots (Glossary *s. v.* Majoon). These electuaries are usually prepared with "Charas," or gum of hemp, collected by hand or by passing a blanket over the plant in early morning, and it is highly intoxicating. Another intoxicant is "Sabzi," dried hemp-leaves, poppy-seed, cucumber-seed, black pepper and cardamoms rubbed down in a mortar with a wooden pestle, and made drinkable by adding milk, ice-cream, etc. The Hashish of Arabia is the Hindustani Bhang, usually drunk and made as follows. Take of hemp-leaves, well washed, 3 drams; black pepper 45 grains and of cloves, nutmeg and mace (which add to the intoxication) each 12 grains. Triturate in 8 ounces of water or the juice of watermelon or cucumber, strain and drink. The Egyptian Zabíbah is a preparation of hemp-florets, opium and honey, much affected by the lower orders, whence the proverb: "Temper thy sorrow with Zabibah,." In Al-Hijaz it is mixed with raisins (Zabíb) and smoked in the water-pipe. (Burckhardt No. 73). Besides these there is (1) "Post" poppy-seed prepared in various ways but especially in sugared sherbets; (2) Datura (*stramonium*) seed, the produce of the thorn-apple, bleached and put into sweetmeats by dishonest confectioners; it is a dangerous intoxicant, producing spectral visions, delirium tremens, etc.; and (3) various preparations of opium especially the "Madad," pills made up with toasted betel-leaf and smoked. Opium, however, is usually drunk in the shape of "Kusumba," a pill placed in wet cotton and squeezed in order to strain and clean it of the cowdung and other filth with which it is adulterated.

*

QUACKS, LIZARDS, AND CERTAIN FISH

Arab. "Sikankúr" (Gr. Σκίγκος, Lat. Scincus) a lizard (*S. officinalis*) which, held in the hand, still acts as an aphrodisiac in the East, and which in the Middle Ages was considered a universal medicine. In the "Adja'ib al-Hind" (Les Merveilles de l'Inde) we find a notice of a bald-headed old man who was compelled to know his wife twice a day and twice a night in consequence of having eaten a certain fish. (Chapt. lxxviii. of the translation by M. L. Marcel Devic, from a manuscript of the tenth century; Paris, Lemaire, 1878). Europeans deride these prescriptions, but Easterns know better: they affect the fancy, that is, the brain; and often succeed in temporarily relieving impotence. The recipes for this evil, which is incurable only when it comes from heart-affections, are innumerable in the East; and about half of every medical work is devoted to them. Many a quack has made his fortune with a few bottles of tincture of cantharides, and a man who could discover a specific would become a millionaire in India only. The curious reader will consult for specimens the Ananga-Ranga Shastra by Koka Pandit; or the "Rujú 'al-Shaykh ila 'l-Sabáh fi Kuwwati 'l-Báh" (the Return of the Old Man to Youth in power of Procreation) by Ahmad bin Sulaymán known as Ibn Kamál Báshá in 139 chapters lithographed at Cairo. Of these aphrodisiacs I shall have more to say.

*

GLORY OF THE FAITH

ALÁ AL-DIN (OUR old friend Aladdin) = Glory of the Faith, a name of which Mohammed, who preferred the simplest, like his own, would have highly disapproved. The most grateful names to Allah are Abdallah (Allah's Slave) and Abd al-Rahmán (Slave of the Compassionate); the truest are Al-Hárith (the gainer, "bread-winner") and Al-Hammám (the griever); and the hatefullest are Al-Harb (witch) and Al-Murrah (bitterness, Abu Murrah being a kunyat or by-name of the Devil). Abu al-Shámát (pronounced Abush-shámát) = Father of Moles, concerning which I have already given details. These names ending in -Din (faith) began with the Caliph Al-Muktadi bi-Amri 'llah (regn. A.H. 467 = 1075), who entitled his Wazir "Zahír al-Din" (Backer or Defender of the Faith) and this gave rise to the practice. It may be observed that the superstition of naming by omens is in no way obsolete.

*

RICHARD BURTON

AVERTION

Rejoined the Deputy, "Never in our born days have we seen thee with a son," and Shams al-Din answered, "When thou gavest me the seed-thickener, my wife conceived and bare this youth; but I reared him in a souterrain for fear of the evil eye, nor was it my purpose that he should come forth, till he could take his beard in his hand.

i.e. when the evil eye has less effect than upon children. Strangers in Cairo often wonder to see a woman richly dressed leading by the hand a filthy little boy (rarely a girl) in rags, which at home will be changed to cloth of gold.

*

LOADING THE BEASTS

ARAB. "AKKÁM," ONE who loads camels and has charge of the luggage. He also corresponds with the modern Mukharrij or camel-hirer (Pilgrimage i. 339); and hence the word Moucre (Moucres) which, first used by La Brocquière (A.D. 1432), is still the only term known to the French.

*

ANCIENT ORDERS

A MYSTIC OF the twelfth century A.D. who founded the Kádirí order (the oldest and chiefest of the four universally recognised), to which I have the honour to belong, teste my diploma (Pilgrimage, Appendix i.). Visitation is still made to his tomb at Baghdad. The Arabs (who have no hard g-letter) alter to "Jílán" the name of his birth-place "Gilan," a tract between the Caspian and the Black Seas.

*

OBJECTIONS

And when he ended his verses he said to Mahmud of Balkh, "Verily this merchandise is a trust from Allah and may not be sold..."

i.e. his chastity: this fashion of objecting to infamous proposals is very characteristic: ruder races would use their fists.

*

FOOLS OF DESPAIR

ARAB. "MUSTAHALL," "MUSTAHILL" and vulg. "Muhallil" (= one who renders lawful). It means a man hired for the purpose who marries *pro formâ* and after wedding, and bedding with actual consummation, at once divorces the woman. He is held the reverse of respectable and no wonder. Hence, probably, Mandeville's story of the Islanders who, on the marriage-night, "make another man to lie by their wives, to have their maidenhead, for which they give great hire and much thanks. And there are certain men in every town that serve for no other thing; and they call them cadeberiz, that is to say, the fools of despair, because they believe their occupation is a dangerous one." Burckhardt gives the proverb (No. 79), "A thousand lovers rather than one Mustahall," the latter being generally some ugly fellow picked up in the streets and disgusting to the wife who must permit his embraces.

*

LEPROSY

The lady listened to him and found his voice as melodious as the psalms of David sung by David himself, which when she heard, she exclaimed, "Allah disappoint the old hag who told me that he was affected with leprosy! Surely this is not the voice of one who hath such a disease; and all was a lie against him."

There is a peculiar thickening of the voice in leprosy which at once betrays the hideous disease.

*

FATHER OF OMENS

Arab. "Ghuráb al-*Bayn*" = raven of the waste or the parting: hence the bird of Odin symbolises separation (which is also called Al-bayn). The Raven (Ghurab = Heb. Oreb and Lat. Corvus, one of the prehistoric words) is supposed to be seen abroad earlier than any other bird; and it is entitled "Abu Zájir," father of omens, because lucky when flying towards the right and *v.v.* It is opposed in poetry to the (white) pigeon, the emblem of union, peace and happiness. The vulgar declare that when Mohammed hid in the cave the crow kept calling to his pursuers, "Ghár! Ghár!" (cavern, cavern): hence the Prophet condemned him to wear eternal mourning and ever to repeat the traitorous words. This is the old tale of Coronis and Apollo (Ovid, lib. ii.)

— who blacked the raven o'er
And bid him prate in his white plumes no more.

*

FATHER OF THE SIDE-LOCKS

Now these four Dervishes were none other than the Caliph Harun al-Rashid, his Wazir Ja'afar the Barmecide, Abu al-Nowás al-Hasan son of Háni and Masrur the sworder; and the reason of their coming to the house was that the Caliph, being heavy at heart, had summoned his Minister and said, "O Wazir! it is our will to go down to the city and pace its streets, for my breast is sore straitened."

Lit. "The father of side-locks," a nickname of one of the Tobba Kings. This "Hasan of the ringlets" who wore two long pig-tails hanging to his shoulders was the Rochester or Piron of his age: his name is still famous for brilliant wit, extempore verse and the wildest debauchery. D'Herbelot's sketch of his life is very meagre. "His poetry has survived to the present day and (unhappily) we shall hear more of Abu Nowás." On the subject of these patronymics Lane (Mod. Egypt, chapt. iv.) has a strange remark that "Abu Dáúd is not the Father of Dáúd or Abu Ali the Father of Ali, but whose Father is (or was) Dáúd or Ali." Here, however, he simply confounds Abu = father of (followed by a genitive), with Abu-h (for Abu-hu) = he, whose father.

*

SWEETMEAT OF SAFETY

Arab. "Haláwah" = sweetmeat; meaning an entertainment such as men give to their friends after sickness or a journey: it is technically called as above, "The Sweetmeat of Safety."

*

PROTUBERANCE OF THE CORPSE

ARAB. "HADBÁ," LIT. "hump-backed;" alluding to the Badawi bier; a pole to which the corpse is slung (Lane). It seems to denote the protuberance of the corpse when placed upon the bier which before was flat. The quotation is from Ka'ab's Mantle-Poem (Burdah v. 37) "Every son of a female, long though his safety may be, is a day borne upon a *ridged implement*," says Mr. Redhouse, explaining the latter as a "bier with a ridged lid." Here we differ: the Janázah with a lid is not a Badawi article: the wildlings use the simplest stretcher; and I would translate the lines: —

> The son of woman, whatso his career,
> One day is borne upon the gibbous bier.

*

HEMPING

"Tabannuj" literally "hemping" (drugging with hemp or henbane) is the equivalent in Arab medicine of our "anæsthetics." These have been used in surgery throughout the East for centuries before ether and chloroform became the fashion in the civilised West.

*

BLOOD-RED DRESS

Then he put his hand to the chair and found neither dress nor signet nor rosary nor dagger-sword nor kerchief nor lanthorn; whereat he was exceeding wroth and donning the dress of anger, which was a scarlet suit, sat down in the Divan.

This till very late years was the custom in Persia; and Fath Ali Shah never appeared in scarlet without ordering some horrible cruelties. In Dar-For wearing a red cashmere turban was a sign of wrath and sending a blood-red dress to a subject meant that he would be slain.

*

MUST AND VINEGAR

Cried he, "Thou liest!" "How so, O Prince of True Believers?" asked the Emir. So he told him the case and added, "I charge thee to bring me back all the stolen things." Replied the Emir, "O Commander of the Faithful, the vinegar worm is of and in the vinegar, and no stranger can get at this place."

That is, this robbery was committed in the palace by some one belonging to it. References to vinegar are frequent; that of Egypt being famous in those days. "Optimum et laudatissimum acetum a Romanis habebatur Ægyptum" (Facciolati); and possibly it was sweetened: the Gesta (Tale xvii.) mentions "must and vinegar." In Arab Proverbs, "One mind by vinegar and another by wine" = each mind goes its own way. (Arab. Prov. ii. 628); or, "with good and bad," vinegar being spoilt wine.

*

VARYING EFFECTS

THE SIGHT OF running water makes a Persian long for strong drink as the sight of a fine view makes the Turk feel hungry.

*

DEATH BY DECREE

THE POPULAR TALE of Burckhardt's death in Cairo was that the names of the three first Caliphs were found written upon his slipper-soles and that he was put to death by decree of the Olema. It is the merest nonsense, as the great traveller died of dysentery in the house of my old friend John Thurburn and was buried outside the Bab al-Nasr of Cairo, where his tomb was restored by the late Rogers Bay (Pilgrimage i. 123).

*

FORBIDDEN DRINKS

ARAB. "KHAMMÁRAH"; STILL the popular term throughout Egypt for a European Hotel. It is not always intended to be insulting but it is, meaning the place where Franks meet to drink forbidden drinks.

*

RICHARD BURTON

THE NAME OF HATIM

A NOBLE TRIBE of Badawin that migrated from Al-Yaman and settled in Al-Najd. Their Chief, who died a few years before Mohammed's birth, was Al-Halim (the "black crow"), a model of Arab manliness and munificence; and although born in the Ignorance he will enter Heaven with the Moslems. Hatim was buried on the hill called Owárid: I have already noted this favourite practice of the wilder Arabs and the affecting idea that the Dead may still look upon his kith and kin. There is not an Arab book nor, indeed, a book upon Arabia which does not contain the name of Hatim: he is mentioned as unpleasantly often as Aristides.

*

LORD OF CATTLE-FEET

At the foot of the hill was a stream of running water, and when wayfarers camped there, they heard loud crying and keening in the night, from dark till daybreak; but when they arose in the morning, they found nothing but the girls carved in stone. Now when Zú 'l-Kurá'a, King of Himyar, going forth of his tribe, came to that valley, he halted to pass the night there —— And Shahrazad perceived the dawn of day and ceased saying her permitted say.

Lord of "Cattle-feet," this King's name is unknown; but the Kámús mentions two Kings called Zu 'l Kalá'a, the

258

Greater and the Less. Lane's Shaykh (ii. 333) opined that the man who demanded Hatim's hospitality was one Abu 'l-Khaybari.

*

METHODS OF SLAUGHTER

THE CAMEL'S THROAT, I repeat, is not cut as in the case of other animals; the muscles being too strong: it is slaughtered by the "nahr," *i.e.* thrusting a knife into the hollow at the commissure of the chest. (Pilgrimage iii. 303.)

*

NOTHING BEHIND ME

A RIVAL IN generosity to Hatim: a Persian poet praising his patron's generosity says that it buried that of Hatim and dimmed that of Ma'an (D'Herbelot). He was a high official under the last Ommiade, Marwán al-Himár (the "Ass," or the "Century," the duration of Ommiade rule) who was routed and slain in A.H. 132 = 750. Ma'an continued to serve under the Abbasides and was a favourite with Al-Mansúr. "More generous or bountiful than Ka'ab" is another saying (A. P., i. 325); Ka'ab ibn Mámah was a man who, somewhat like Sir Philip Sidney at Zutphen, gave his own portion of drink while he was dying of thirst to a man who looked wistfully at him, whence the saying "Give drink to thy brother the Námiri" (A. P., i. 608). Ka'ab could not mount, so they put garments over him to scare away the wild beasts and left him in the desert to die. "Scatterer of blessings" (Náshir al-Ni'am) was a title of King Malik of Al-Yaman, son of Sharhabil, eminent for his liberality. He set up the statue in the Western Desert, inscribed "Nothing behind me," as a warner to others.

*

NO REPEATS

From that liberal hand on his foes he rains
Shafts aureate-headed and manifold:
Wherewith the hurt shall chirurgeon pay,
And for slain the shrouds round their corpses roll'd.

The first girl calls gold "Tibr" (pure, unalloyed metal); the second "Asjad" (gold generally) and the third "Ibríz" (virgin ore, the Greek ὄβρυζον). This is a law of Arab rhetoric never to repeat the word except for a purpose and, as the language *can* produce 1,200,000 (to 100,000 in English) the copiousness is somewhat painful to readers.

*

TRUTH TELLING

So they laid hands on him; and when he saw the multitude
of Chamberlains and Wazirs and Lords of State, he was in

nowise concerned and questioned not of them, but let his chin drop on his breast and looked where his feet fell, till they brought him to the Caliph when he stood before him, with head bowed groundwards and saluted him not and spoke him not.

i.e. in the palace when the hunt was over. The bluntness and plain-speaking of the Badawi, which caused the revelation of the Koranic chapter "Inner Apartments" (No. xlix.) have always been favourite themes with Arab tale-tellers as a contrast with citizen suavity and servility. Moreover the Badawi, besides saying what he thinks, always tells the truth (unless corrupted by commerce with foreigners); and this is a startling contrast with the townsfolk. To ride out of Damascus and have a chat with the Ruwalá is much like being suddenly transferred from amongst the trickiest of Mediterranean people to the bluff society of the Scandinavian North. And the reason why the Turk will never govern the Arab in peace is that the former is always trying to finesse and to succeed by falsehood, when the truth, the whole truth and nothing but the truth is wanted.

*

AMPLE SLEEVES

ARAB. "KUMM;" THE Moslem sleeve is mostly (like his trousers) of ample dimensions and easily converted into a kind of carpet-bag by depositing small articles in the middle and gathering up the edge in the hand. In this way carried the weight would be less irksome than hanging to the waist. The English of Queen Anne's day had regular sleeve-pockets for memoranda, etc., hence the saying, to have in one's sleeve.

*

ATMOSPHERE OF 1850

DONE IN HOT weather throughout the city, a dry line for camels being left in mid-street to prevent the awkward beasts slipping. The watering of the Cairo streets of late years has been excessive; they are now lines of mud in summer as well as in winter and the effluvia from the droppings of animals have, combined with other causes, seriously deteriorated the once charming climate. The only place in Lower Egypt, which has preserved the atmosphere of 1850, is Suez.

*

SILENT AND SAFE

THE KATÁ (SAND-GROUSE) always enters into Arab poetry because it is essentially a desert bird; and here the comparison is good because it lays its eggs in the waste far from water which it must drink morning and evening. Its cry is interpreted "man sakat, salam" (silent and safe), but it does not practice that precept, for it is usually betrayed by its piping Kata! Kata! Hence the proverb, "More veracious than the sand-grouse;" and "Speak not falsely, for the Kata sayeth sooth," is Komayt's saying. It is an emblem of swiftness: when the brigand-poet Shanfara boasts, "The ash-coloured Katas can drink only my leavings, after hastening all night to slake their thirst in the morning," it is a hyperbole boasting of his speed. In Sind it is called the "rock pigeon" and it is not unlike a grey partridge when on the wing.

*

APPROPRIATE FOR A NIGHTMAN

I HAVE NOTICED how the left hand is used in the East. In the second couplet we have "Istinjá" = washing the fundament after stool. The lines are highly appropriate for a nightman. Easterns have many foul but most emphatic expressions like those in the text: I have heard a mother say to her brat, "I would eat thy merde!" (*i.e.* how I love thee!)

*

SOMETHING ROUND

ARAB. "MUDAWWARAH," WHICH generally means a small round cushion, of the Marocco-work well known in England. But one does not strike a cushion for a signal; so we must revert to the original sense of the word "something round," as a circular plate of wood or metal, a gong, a "bell" like that of the Eastern Christians.

RICHARD BURTON

*

FOOT FIRST

So I entered and, going up to the couch, found that my wife had come back from the bath and was lying asleep there. Seeing this I sat down at her feet and rubbed them; whereupon she opened her eyes and seeing me, drew up both her feet and gave me a kick that threw me off the couch, saying, "O traitor, thou hast been false to thine oath and hast perjured thyself..."

In the East cloth of frieze that mates with cloth of gold must expect this treatment. Fath Ali Shah's daughters always made their husbands enter the nuptial bed by the foot end.

*

NUTS AND BEANS

ARAB. "FÚL AL-HÁRR" = beans like horsebeans soaked and boiled as opposed to the "Fúl Mudammas" (esp. of Egypt) = unshelled beans steamed and boiled all night and eaten with linseed oil as "kitchen" or relish. Lane (M. E., chapt. v.) calls them after the debased Cairene pronunciation, Mudemmes. A legend says that, before the days of Pharaoh (always he of Moses), the Egyptians lived on pistachios which made them a witty, lively race. But the tyrant remarking that the domestic ass, which eats beans, is degenerate from the wild ass, uprooted the pistachio-trees and compelled the lieges

264

to feed on beans which made them a heavy, gross, cowardly people fit only for burdens. Badawis deride "bean-eaters" although they do not loathe the pulse like onions. The principal result of a bean diet is an extraordinary development of flatulence both in stomach and intestines: hence, possibly, Pythagoras who had studied ceremonial purity in Egypt, forbade the use, unless he referred to venery or political business. I was once sitting in the Greek quarter of Cairo dressed as a Moslem when arose a prodigious hubbub of lads and boys, surrounding a couple of Fellahs. These men had been working in the fields about a mile east of Cairo; and, when returning home, one had said to the other, "If thou wilt carry the hoes I will break wind once for every step we take." He was as good as his word and when they were to part he cried, "And now for thy bakhshish!" which consisted of a volley of fifty, greatly to the delight of the boys.

*

POTTERY

NO PORCELAIN WAS ever, as far as we can discover, made in Egypt or Syria of the olden day; but, as has been said, there was a regular caravan-intercourse with China. At Damascus I dug into the huge rubbish-heaps and found quantities of pottery, but no China. The same has lately been done at Clysma, the artificial mound near Suez, and the glass and pottery prove it to have been a Roman work which defended the mouth of the old classical sweet-water canal.

RICHARD BURTON

*

THE GREEN PROPHET

But, as we flew, behold, One clad in green raiment, with streaming tresses and radiant face, holding in his hand a javelin whence flew sparks of fire, accosted me, saying, "O Abu Mohammed, say: — There is no god but the God and Mohammed is the Apostle of God; or I will smite thee with this javelin."

This must be the ubiquitous Khizr, the Green Prophet; when Ali appears, as a rule he is on horseback.

*

JINN-LAND

Thereupon I asked him the name of the city, and he replied, "It is called Hanád and is in the land of China."

The name is apparently imaginary; and a little below we find that it was close to Jinn-land. China was very convenient for this purpose: the medieval Moslems, who settled in considerable numbers at Canton and elsewhere, knew just enough of it to know their own ignorance of the vast empire. Hence the Druzes of the Libanus still hold that part of their nation is in the depths of the Celestial Empire.

*

CITY OF BRASS

Then the horseman took me up behind him and rode on with me to a desert place, when he said, "Dismount now and walk on between these two mountains, till thou seest the City of Brass; then halt afar off and enter it not, ere I return to thee and tell thee how thou shalt do." "To hear is to obey," replied I and, dismounting from behind him, walked on till I came to the city, the walls whereof I found of brass.

I am unwilling to alter the old title to "City of Copper" as it should be; the pure metal having been technologically used long before the alloy of copper and zinc. But the Maroccan City (Night dlxvi. *et seq.*) was of brass (not copper). The Hindus of Upper India have an Iram which they call Hari Chand's city (Colonel Tod); and I need hardly mention the Fata Morgana, Island of Saint Borondon; Cape Fly-away; the Flying Dutchman, etc. etc., all the effect of "looming."

*

CLOAK OF INVISIBILITY

Then I began to pace round about it, hoping to find a gate, but found none; and presently as I persevered behold, the serpent's brother rejoined me and gave me a charmed sword which should hinder any from seeing me, then went his way.

This sword which makes men invisible and which takes place of Siegfried's Tarnkappe (invisible cloak) and of "Fortunatus' cap" is common in Moslem folk-lore. The idea probably arose from the venerable practice of inscribing the blades with sentences, verses and magic figures.

*

MOON-FACED

"MOON-FACED" NOW SOUNDS sufficiently absurd to us, but it was not always so. Solomon (Cant. vi. 10) does not disdain the image "fair as the moon, clear as the sun;" and those who have seen a moon in the sky of Arabia will thoroughly appreciate it. We find it amongst the Hindus, the Persians, the Afghans, the Turks and all the nations of Europe. We have, finally, the grand example of Spenser: —

Her spacious forehead, like the clearest moon, etc.

*

FIERCE-EYED

BLUE EYES HAVE a bad name in Arabia as in India: the witch Zarká of Al-Yamamah was noted for them; and "blue-eyed" often means "fierce-eyed," alluding to the Greeks and Daylamites, mortal enemies to Ishmael. The Arabs say "ruddy of mustachio, blue of eye and black of heart."

*

FILLING THE MOUTH

*She proudly turned away from me, showed shoulders, cried
aloud: —
'No! no! by Him,whose hest mankind from nothingness hath
made,
For hoary head and grizzled chin I've no especial love:
What! stuff my mouth with cotton ere in sepulchre I'm laid?'"*

Before explained as used with camphor to fill the dead
man's mouth.

*

BOXING THE NECK

As HAS BEEN seen, slapping on the neck is equivalent to our
"boxing ears," but much less barbarous and likely to injure
the child. The most insulting blow is that with shoe, sandal
or slipper because it brings foot in contact with head. Of this
I have spoken before.

*

OBSCENE SPEAK

ARAB. "KHIYÁL"; AFTERWARDS called Kara Gyuz (= "black
eyes," from the celebrated Turkish Wazir). The *mise-en-*

269

scène was like that of Punch, but of transparent cloth, lamp-lit inside and showing silhouettes worked by hand. Nothing could be more Fescennine than Kara Gyuz, who appeared with a phallus longer than himself and made all the Consuls-General periodically complain of its abuse; while the dialogue, mostly in Turkish, was even more obscene. Most ingenious were Kara Gyuz's little ways of driving on an obstinate donkey and of tackling a huge Anatolian pilgrim. He mounted the Neddy's back, face to tail, and inserting his left thumb like a clyster, hammered it with his right, when the donkey started at speed. For the huge pilgrim he used a ladder. These shows, now obsolete, used to enliven the Ezbekiyah Gardens every evening and explain Ovid's words. Delicias videam, *Nile jocose*, tuas!

*

TIME TO WEAR WHITE

Mohammed (Mishkát al-Masábih ii. 360-62) says, "Change the whiteness of your hair but not with anything black." Abu Bakr, who was two years and some months older than the Prophet, used tincture of Henna and Katam. Old Turkish officers justify black dyes because these make them look younger and fiercer. Henna stains white hair orange red; and the Persians apply after it a paste of indigo leaves; the result is successively leek-green, emerald-green, bottle-green and lastly lamp-black. There is a stage in life (the youth of old age) when man uses dyes: presently he finds that the whole

270

face wants dye; that the contrast between juvenile coloured hair and ancient skin is ridiculous and that it is time to wear white.

*

THIRST OF THE DESERT

THIRST IS THE strongest of all pleas to an Eastern, especially to a Persian who never forgets the sufferings of his Imam, Husayn, at Kerbela: he would hardly withhold it from the murderer of his father. There is also a Hadis, "Thou shalt not refuse water to him who thirsteth in the desert."

*

SAVOURS OF IDOLATRY

ARAB. "SIFR": I have warned readers that whistling is considered a kind of devilish speech by the Arabs, especially the Badawin; and that the traveller must avoid it. It savours of idolatry: in the Koran we find (chapt. viii. 35), "Their prayer at the House of God (Ka'abah) is none other than whistling and hand-clapping;" and tradition says that they whistled through their fingers. Besides many of the Jinn have only round holes by way of mouths and their speech is whistling — a kind of bird-language like sibilant English.

*

271

RICHARD BURTON

GREETING THE MEAT

EASTERNS HAVE A superstitious belief in the powers of food:
I knew a learned man who never sat down to eat without a
ceremonious salam to his meat.

*

SLAVE OF THE SLAVE

THE RULE IN Turkey where catamites rise to the highest
rank: *C'est un homme de bonne famille* (said a Turkish
officer in Egypt) *il a été acheté*. Hence "Alfi" (one who costs
a thousand) is a well-known cognomen. The Pasha of the
Syrian caravan, with which I travelled, had been the slave of
a slave and he was not a solitary instance (Pilgrimage i. 90).

*

USE AND MISUSE

IN PAST DAYS before Egypt was "frankified" many overlanders
used to wash away the traces of travel by a Turkish bath
which mostly ended in the appearance of a rump-wriggling
little lad who offered to shampoo them. Many accepted his
offices without dreaming of his usual use or misuse.

*

CONGRESS WITH A CROCODILE
MUSCLES OF THE HOLDER

ARAB "FI ZAMAN-HI," alluding to a peculiarity highly prized by Egyptians; the use of the constrictor vaginæ muscles, the sphincter for which Abyssinian women are famous. The "Kabbázah" (= holder), as she is called, can sit astraddle upon a man and can provoke the venereal orgasm, not by wriggling and moving but by tightening and loosing the male member with the muscles of her privities, milking it as it were. Consequently the *casse-noisette* costs treble the money of other concubines (Ananga-Ranga, p. 127).

*

AGREEABLE VACILLATION

LANE (II. 494) RELATES from Al-Makrizi, that when Khamárawayh, Governor of the Egypt (ninth century), suffered from insomnia his physician ordered a pool of quicksilver, 50 by 50 cubits, to be laid out in front of his palace, now the Rumaylah square. "At the corners of the pool were silver pegs to which were attached by silver rings, strong bands of silk, and a bed of skins, inflated with air, being thrown upon the pool and secured by the bands remained in a continual state of agreeable vacillation." We are not told that the Prince was thereby salivated like the late Colonel Sykes when boiling his mercury for thermometric experiments.

RICHARD BURTON

*

ALWAYS MORE JEALOUS

WEALTHY HAREMS, I have said, are hot-beds of Sapphism and
Tribadism. Every woman past her first youth has a girl whom
she calls her "Myrtle" (in Damascus). At Agbome, capital of
Dahome, I found that a troop of women was kept for the use
of the "Amazons" (Mission to Gelele, ii. 73). Amongst the
wild Arabs, who ignore Socratic and Sapphic perversions,
the lover is always more jealous of his beloved's girl-friends
than of men rivals. In England we content ourselves with
saying that women corrupt women more than men do.

*

NIGHT TALK

ARAB. "MUSÁMIRAH" = CHATTING at night. Easterns are
inordinately fond of the practice and the wild Arabs often
sit up till dawn, talking over the affairs of the tribe, indeed a
Shaykh is expected to do so. "Early to bed and early to rise"
is a civilised not a savage or a barbarous saying. Samír is a
companion in night talk; Rafík of the road; Rahíb in riding
horse or camel; Ká'id in sitting; Sharíb and Rafís at drink,
and Nadím at table: Ahíd is an ally, and Sharík a partner —
all on the model of "Fa'íl."

*

274

IN NO RUSH

Then I sat down and presently, behold, Jubayr and his beloved came out of the bath in the house, and I saw them both wringing their locks.

Showing that consummation had taken place. It was a sign of good breeding to avoid all "indecent hurry" when going to bed. In some Moslem countries the bridegroom does not consummate the marriage for seven nights; out of respect for (1) father (2) mother (3) brother and so forth. If he hurry matters he will be hooted as an "impatient man" and the wise will quote, "Man is created of precipitation" (Koran chapt. xxi. 38), meaning hasty and inconsiderate. I remark with pleasure that the whole of this tale is told with commendable delicacy. O si sic omnia!

*

COOL-SKINNED

WOMEN WITH WHITE skins are supposed to be heating and unwholesome: hence the Hindu Rajahs slept with dark girls in the hot season.

*

RICHARD BURTON

HELL: COLD OR HOT

MOSLEMS SENSIBLY HAVE a cold as well as a hot Hell, the former called Zamharir (lit. "intense cold") or Al-Barahút, after a well in Hazramaut; as Gehenna (Arab. Jahannam) from the furnace-like ravine East of Jerusalem (Night cccxxv). The icy Hell is necessary *in terrorem* for peoples who inhabit cold regions and who in a hot Hell only look forward to an eternity of "coals and candles" gratis. The sensible missionaries preached it in Iceland till foolishly forbidden by Papal Bull.

*

AT SPEED

Farewell thy love, for see, the Cafilah's on the move:
O man, canst bear to say adieu and leave thy love?
'Tis as her going were to seek her neighbour's tent, The gait of
fat fair maid, whom hearts shall all approve.

Arab "Rakb," usually applied to a fast-going caravan of dromedary riders (Pilgrimage ii. 329). The "Cafilah" is Arab.: "Caravan" is a corruption of the Pers. Karwán.

*

CONGRESS WITH A CROCODILE

WALKING TUN-BUTT

ALTHOUGH THE ARAB's ideal of beauty, as has been seen and said, corresponds with ours, the Egyptians (Modern) the Maroccans and other negrofied races like "walking tun-butts" as Clapperton called his amorous widow.

*

VEIL OF NATURE

When thou pissest thou swishest; if thou turd thou gruntest like a bursten wine-skin or an elephant transmogrified. If thou go to the water-closet, thou needest one to wash thy gap and pluck out the hairs which overgrow it; and this is the extreme of sluggishness and the sign, outward and visible, of stupidity.

This is the popular idea of a bushy "veil of nature" in women: it is always removed by depilatories and vellication. When Bilkis Queen of Sheba discovered her legs by lifting her robe (Koran xxvii.), Solomon was minded to marry her, but would not do so till the devils had by a depilatory removed the hair. The popular preparation (called Núrah) consists of quicklime 7 parts, and Zirník or orpiment, 3 parts: it is applied in the Hammam to a perspiring skin, and it must be washed off immediately the hair is loosened or it burns and discolours. The rest of the body-pile (Sha'arat opp. to Sha'ar = hair) is eradicated by applying a mixture of boiled honey with turpentine or other gum, and rolling it with the hand till the hair comes off. Men I have said remove the pubes by shaving, and pluck the hair of the armpits, one of the vestages of pre-Adamite man. A good depilatory is still a desideratum, the best perfumers of London and Paris have none which they can recommend. The reason is plain: the hair-bulb can be eradicated only by destroying the skin.

*

CLOTHING DOGS

IN ALL HOT-DAMP countries it is necessary to clothe dogs, morning and evening especially: otherwise they soon die of rheumatism and loin disease.

*

A JEALOUS GOD

THE MOSLEMS BORROWED the horrible idea of a "jealous God" from their kinsmen, the Jews. Every race creates its own Deity after the fashion of itself: Jehovah is distinctly a Hebrew; the Christian Theos is originally a Judæo-Greek and Allah a half-Badawi Arab. In this tale Allah, despotic and unjust, brings a generous and noble-minded man to beggary, simply because he fed his dogs off gold plate. Wisdom and morality have their infancy and youth: the great value of such tales as these is to show and enable us to measure man's development.

*

NATURAL PENCHANT

Arab. "Kird" (pron. in Egypt "Gird"). It is usually the hideous Abyssinian cynocephalus which is tamed by the ape-leader popularly called Kuraydati (Lane, M. E., chapt. xx.). The beast has a natural penchant for women; I heard of one which attempted to rape a girl in the public street and was prevented only by a sentinel's bayonet. They are powerful animals and bite like greyhounds.

*

GERM-THEORY

Easterns, attribute many complaints (such as toothache) to worms, visible as well as microscopic; which may be held a fair prolepsis of the "germ-theory" the bacterium, the bacillus, the microbe. Nymphomania, the disease alluded to in these two tales is always attributed to worms in the vagina.

*

CONGRESS WITH A CROCODILE

Bestiality, very rare in Arabia is fatally common amongst those most debauched of debauched races, the Egyptian proper and the Sindis. Hence the Pentateuch, whose object was to breed a larger population of fighting men, made death the penalty for lying with a beast (Deut. xxvii. 21). C. S. Sonnini (Travels, English translation, p. 663) gives a curious account of Fellah lewdness. "The female crocodile during congress is turned upon her back (?) and cannot rise without difficulty. Will it be believed that there are men who take advantage of the helpless situation of the female, drive off the male, and supplant him in this frightful intercourse? Horrible embraces, the knowledge of which was wanting to complete the disgusting history of human perversity!" The French traveller forgets to add the superstitious explanation of this congress which is the sovereignest charm for rising to rank and riches. The Ajáib al-Hind tells a tale (chapt. xxxix.) of a certain Mohammed bin Bullishad who had issue by a she-ape: the young ones were hairless of body and wore quasi-human faces; and the father's sight had become dim by his bestial practice.

*

THE MAGIC HORSE

THE MAGIC HORSE may have originated with the Hindu tale of a wooden Garuda (the bird of Vishnu) built by a youth for the purpose of a vehicle. It came with the "Moors" to Spain and appears in "Le Cheval de Fust," a French poem of the thirteenth Century. Thence it passed over to England as shown by Chaucer's "Half-told tale of Cambuscan (Janghíz Khan?) bold," as

The wondrous steed of brass

On which the Tartar King did ride;
And Leland (Itinerary) derives "Rutlandshire" from "a man named Rutter who rode round it on a wooden horse constructed by art magic." Lane (ii. 548) quotes the parallel story of Cleomades and Claremond which Mr. Keightley (Tales and Popular Fictions, chapt. ii) dates from our thirteenth century. See Vol. i., p. 160.

*

GRAVEN IMAGES

ALL MOSLEMS, EXCEPT those of the Máliki school, hold that the maker of an image representing anything of life will be commanded on the Judgement Day to animate it, and failing will be duly sent to the Fire. This severity arose apparently from the necessity of putting down idol-worship and, perhaps, for the same reason the Greek Church admits pictures but not statues. Of course the command has been honoured with extensive breaching: for instance all the Sultans of Stambul have had their portraits drawn and painted.

*

NIGHT-WEAR

EASTERN WOMEN IN hot weather, lie mother-nude under a sheet here represented by the hair. The Greeks and Romans also slept stripped and in mediæval England the most modest women saw nothing indelicate in sleeping naked by their naked husbands. The "night-cap" and the "night-gown" are comparatively modern inventions.

*

AMBITION OF A SLAVE

THE DEAREST AMBITION of a slave is not liberty but to have a slave of his own. This was systematised by the servile rulers known in history as the Mameluke Beys and to the Egyptians as the Ghuzz. Each had his household of servile pages and squires, who looked forward to filling the master's place as knight or baron.

*

ARABIA FELIX

THE WELL-KNOWN CAPITAL of Al-Yaman, a true Arabia Felix, a Paradise inhabited by demons in the shape of Turkish soldiery and Arab caterans. According to Moslem writers Sana'a was founded by Shem son of Noah who, wandering southward with his posterity after his father's death, and finding the site delightful, dug a well and founded the citadel, Ghamdán, which afterwards contained a *Maison Carrée* rivalling (or attempting to rival) the Meccan Ka'abah. The builder was Surahbíl who, says M. C. de Perceval coloured its four faces red, white, golden and green; the central quadrangle had seven stories (the planets) each forty cubits high, and the lowest was a marble hall ceiling'd with a single slab. At the four corners stood hollow lions through whose mouths the winds roared. This palatial citadel-temple was destroyed by order of Caliph Omar. The city's ancient name was Azal or Uzal whom some identify with one of the thirteen sons of Joktan (Genesis xi. 27): it took its present name from the Ethiopian conquerors (they say) who, seeing it for the first time, cried "Hazá Sana'ah!" meaning in their tongue, this is commodious, etc. I may note that the word is Kisawahili (Zanzibarian) *e.g.* "Yámbo *sáná* — is the state *good*?" Sana'a was the capital of the Tabábi'ah or Tobba Kings who judaized; and the Abyssinians with their Negush made it Christian while the Persians under Anushirwán converted it to Guebrism. It is now easily visited but to little purpose; excursions in the neighbourhood being deadly dangerous. Moreover the Turkish garrison would probably murder a stranger who sympathised with the Arabs, and the Arabs kill one who took part with their hated and hateful conquerors. The late Mr. Shapira of Jerusalem declared that he had visited it and Jews have great advantages in such travel. But his friends doubted him.

*

PURGATIVES

ARAB. "HANZAL" = COLOQUINTIDA, an article often mentioned by Arabs in verse and prose; the bright coloured little gourd attracts every eye by its golden glance when travelling through the brown-yellow waste of sand and clay. A favourite purgative (enough for a horse) is made by filling the inside with sour milk which is drunk after a night's soaking: it is as active as the croton-nut of the Gold Coast.

*

FIRST MOVES

Quoth she, "And how may one come by enjoyment?" Quoth the other, "By letters and messages, my lady; by whispered words of compliment and by greetings before the world; all this bringeth lovers together and makes hard matters easy.

This is done by the man passing his fingers over the brow as if to wipe off perspiration; the woman acknowledges it by adjusting her head-veil with both hands. As a rule in the Moslem East women make the first advances; and it is truly absurd to see a great bearded fellow blushing at being ogled. During the Crimean war the fair sex of Constantinople began by these allurements but found them so readily accepted by the Giaours that they were obliged to desist.

*

KEEPING SECRETS

THE GREATEST OF all explorers and discoverers of the world will be he who finds a woman confessing inability to keep a secret.

*

LION-TALES

Still the belief of the Badawi who tries to work upon the beast's compassion: "O great King I am a poor man, with wife and family, so spare me that Allah spare thee!" and so forth. If not famished the lion will often stalk off looking behind him as he goes; but the man will never return by the same path; "for," says he, "haply the Father of Roaring may repent him of a wasted opportunity." These lion-tales are very common, witness that of Androcles at Rome and a host of others. Una and her lion is another phase. It remained for M. Jules Gérard, first the *chasseur* and then the *tueur, du lion,* to assail the reputation of the lion and the honour of the lioness.

*

MIGHTY APPARATUS

Arab. "Khilál," as an emblem of attenuation occurring in Al-Hariri (Ass. of Alexandria, etc.); also thin as a spindle (Maghzal), as a reed, and dry as a pair of shears. In the Ass. of Barka'id the toothpick is described as a beautiful girl. The use of this cleanly article was enjoined by Mohammed: "Cleanse your mouths with toothpicks; for your mouths are the abode of the guardian angels; whose pens are the tongues, and whose ink is the spittle of men; and to whom naught is more unbearable than remains of food in the mouth." A mighty apparatus for a small matter; but in very hot lands cleanliness must rank before godliness.

*

SUBSTITUTE TO A SPONGE

ARAB. "LÍF" (NOT "fibres which grow at the top of the trunk," Lane ii. 577); but the fibre of the fronds worked like the cocoa-nut fibre which forms the now well-known Indian "coir." This "líf" is also called "filfil" or "fulfil" which Dr. Jonathan Scott renders "pepper" (Lane i. 8) and it forms a clean succedaneum for one of the uncleanest articles of civilisation, the sponge. It is used in every Hammam and is (or should be) thrown away after use.

*

MAKING A CASTRATO

Whereupon the eunuch wept and embraced him, saying, "Allah preserve thee, O thou friendly face! Ispahan is mine own country and I have there a cousin, the daughter of my father's brother, whom I loved from my childhood and cherished with fond affection; but a people stronger than we fell upon us in foray and taking me among other booty, cut off my yard and sold me for a castrato, whilst I was yet a lad; and this is how I came to be in such case." —— And Shahrazad perceived the dawn of day and ceased to say her permitted say.

CONGRESS WITH A CROCODILE

The eunuch tells him that he is not a "Sandalí" = one whose penis and testes are removed; and consequently the highest valued. There are many ways of making the castrato; in some (as here) only the penis is removed, in others the testes are bruised or cut off; but in all cases the animal passion remains, for in man, unlike other animals, the *fons veneris* is the brain. The story of Abelard proves this. Juvenal derided the idea of married eunuchs and yet almost all these neutrals have wives with whom they practise the manifold *plaisirs de la petite oie* (masturbation, tribadism, irrumation, tête-bêche, feuille-de-rose, etc.), till they induce the venereal orgasm. Such was the account once given to me by a eunuch's wife; and I need hardly say that she, like her confrerie was to be pitied. At the critical moment she held up a little pillow for her husband to bite who otherwise would have torn her cheeks or breasts.

*

EUNUCH TALES

She said, It hath reached me, O auspicious King, that the eunuch who came forth from the castle, where Rose-in-Hood was confined, told Uns al-Wujud all his tale and said: — "The raiders who captured me cut off my yard and sold me for a castrato; and this is how I came to be in such case."

In real life the eunuch, as a rule, avoids all allusion to his misfortune, although the slave will often describe his being sold merrily enough.

RICHARD BURTON

*

BIRD TALK

ALL PRIMITIVE PEOPLES translate the songs of birds with
human language; but, as I have noticed, the versions differ
widely. The pigeon cries, "Allah! Allah!" The dove "Karim,
Tawwá" (Bountiful, Pardoner!) the Katá or sand-grouse
"Man sakat salam" (who is silent is safe) yet always betrays
itself by its lay of "Kat-ta" and lastly the cock "Uzkurú
'llah ya gháfilún" (Remember, or take the name of Allah, ye
careless!)

*

CONTEMPLATION OF THE SUFIS

ARAB. "MAJZUB" = DRAWN, attracted (literally); the popular
term for one absorbed in the contemplation of the Deity.
During this process the soul is supposed to quit the body
leaving the latter irresponsible for its actions. I remember a
scandal being caused in a village near Tunis by one of these
men who suddenly started up from his seat in a dusty corner
and, in presence of a small crowd of people, had connection
with a she-donkey. The supporters of the holy man declared
that the deed was proof positive of his exceptional holiness;
but there were lewd fellows, Moslems Voltaireans, who had
their doubts and held that the reverend man had so acted
"for the gallery." A similar story is told with due reserve by

288

the late Abbe Hamilton in his book on the Cyrenaic. There are three grand divisions of the Sufis; (1) Mukímán, the stationaries; (2) Sálikán, the travellers, or progressives, and (3) Wásilán, those who reach the desired end. And No. 2 has two classes: the Sálik-i-majzúb, one progressing in Divine Love; and the other, who has made greater progress, is the Majzúb-i-Sálik (Dabistan iii. 251).

*

HONEY-MOON

In Egypt the shorter "honey-moon" lasts a week; and on the seventh day (pop. called Al-Subú'a) bride and bridegroom receive visits with all ceremony, of course in separate apartments. The seventh day (like the fortieth, the end of six months and the anniversary) is kept for births and deaths with Khatmahs (perlections) of the Koran, "Saylah" family gatherings and so forth. The fortieth day ends the real honey-moon. See Night dccxcii.

*

FREAK OF THE BRIDE

Then they went forth and distributed to the folk alms and presents of money and raiment and rare gifts and other tokens of generosity; after which Rose-in-Hood bade clear the bath for her and, turning to Uns al-Wujud said to him, "O

289

coolth of my eyes, I have a mind to see thee in the Hammam, and therein we will be alone together."

I have noted the popular practice, amongst men as well as women, of hiring the Hammam for private parties and picnicking in it during the greater part of the day. In this tale the bath would belong to the public and it was a mere freak of the bride to bathe with her bridegroom. "Respectable" people do not.

*

ALISH TAKISH

Then eat of these and drink of those
Old wines that bring you jollity:
And have each other, turn by turn,
Shampooing this my tool you see.

Mr. Payne omits the last line. It refers to what Persian boys call, in half-Turkish phrase, "Alish Takish," each acting woman after he has acted man. The best wine is still made in monasteries and the so-called Sinai convent is world-famous for its "Ráki" distilled from raisins.

*

CONGRESS WITH A CROCODILE

OVERACTING

When he heard this, he planned to enter the house amongst the mob of women and saw the twain seated on the bridal couch.

On this occasion, and in presence of the women only, the groom first sees or is supposed to see the face of his wife. It is, I have said, the fashion for both to be greatly overcome and to appear as if about to faint: the groom looks especially ridiculous when so attitudinising.

*

RETAINING THE SEED

And seen me she had hidden it
But 'twas too plump for fingers fine.
Would Heaven that I were on it,
An hour, or better two hours, li'en.

This leisurely operation of the "deed of kind" was sure to be noticed; but we do not find in The Nights any allusion to that systematic *prolongatio veneris* which is so much cultivated by Moslems under the name Imsák = retention, withholding *i.e.* the semen. Yet Eastern books on domestic medicine consist mostly of two parts; the first of general prescriptions and the second of aphrodisiacs especially those *qui prolongent le plaisir* as did the Gaul by thinking of *sa pauvre mère*. The Ananga-Ranga, by the Reverend Koka Pandit before quoted, gives a host of recipes which are used, either externally or internally, to hasten the paroxysm of the woman and delay the orgasm of the man (p.27). Some of these are curious in the extreme. I heard of a Hindi who made a candle of frogs' fat and fibre warranted to retain the seed till it burned out: it failed notably because, relying upon it, he worked too vigorously. The essence of the "retaining art" is to avoid over-tension of the muscles and to pre-occupy the brain: hence in coition Hindus will drink sherbet, chew betel-nut and even smoke. Europeans ignoring the science and practice, are contemptuously compared with village-cocks by Hindu women who cannot be satisfied, such is their natural coldness, increased doubtless by vegetable diet and unuse of stimulants, with less than twenty minutes. Hence too while thousands of Europeans have cohabited for years with and have had families by "native women," they are never loved by them: — at least I never heard of a case.

*

BLANDISHMENT

THE CALC. EDIT. by mistake reads "Izzah." Torrens (notes i.-xi.) remarks "The word *Ghoonj* is applied to this sort of blandishment" (*i.e.* an affected gait), and says Burckhardt (Prov. No. 685), "The women of Cairo flatter themselves that their *Ghoonj* is superior to that of all other females in the Levant." But Torrens did not understand and Burckhardt would not explain "Ghunj" except by "assumed airs" (see No. 714). It here means the art of moving in coition, which is especially affected, even by modest women, throughout the East and they have many books teaching the genial art. In China there are professors, mostly old women, who instruct young girls in this branch of the gymnastic.

*

ROYAL FRIVOLITY

Now Mohammed al-Amín, son of Zubaydah, heard of her and was urgent with Ja'afar to sell her to him; but he replied, "Thou knowest it beseemeth not one of my rank to sell slave-girls nor set prices on concubines; but were she not a rearling I would send her to thee, as a gift, nor grudge her to thee."

Immediate successor of Harun al-Rashid. Al-Amin is an imposing physical figure, fair, tall, handsome and of immense strength; according to Al-Mas'údi, he killed a lion with his own hands; but his mind and judgement were weak. He was fond of fishing; and his reply to the courtier bringing important news, "Confound thee! leave me! for Kausar (an eunuch whom he loved) hath caught two fish and I none," reminds one of royal frivolity in France.

*

RICHARD BURTON

FREE TO ROAM

Meanwhile in came her friend who bade her to a wedding at his house; so she agreed and laying the fish in a jar of water, went off with him and was absent a whole week till the Friday following; whilst her husband sought her from house to house and enquired after her; but none could give him any tidings of her.

Moslem women have this advantage over their Western sisterhood: they can always leave the house of father or husband and, without asking permission, pay a week or ten days' visit to their friends. But they are not expected to meet their lovers.

*

THE GORDIAN KNOT

ACCORDING TO MOSLEM law, laid down by Mohammed on a delicate occasion and evidently for a purpose, four credible witnesses are required to prove fornication, adultery, sodomy and so forth; and they must swear that they actually saw *rem in re*, the "Kohl-needle in the Kohl-étui," as the Arabs have it. This practically prevents conviction and the sabre cuts the Gordian knot.

*

SECRET CHAMBERS

It has always been my opinion founded upon considerations too long to detail, that the larger Pyramids contain many unopened chambers. Dr. Grant Bey of Cairo proposed boring through the blocks as Artesian wells are driven. I cannot divine why Lane (ii. 592) chose to omit this tale, which is founded on historic facts and interests us by suggesting a comparison between Mediæval Moslem superstitions and those of our xixth Century, which to our descendants will appear as wild, if not as picturesque, as those of The Nights. The "inspired British inch" and the building by Melchisedek (the Shaykh of some petty Syrian village) will compare not unaptly with the enchanted swords, flexible glass and guardian spirits. But the Pyramidennarren is a race which will not speedily die out: it is based on Nature, the Pyramids themselves.

*

TRUE KNOWLEDGE

Arab. "Taríkah" = the path trodden by ascetics and mystics in order to attain true knowledge (Ma'rifat in Pers. Dánish). These are extensive subjects: for the present I must refer readers to the Dabistan, iii. 35 and iii. 29, 36–7.

*

RICHARD BURTON

SQUEEZING THE TOMB

He was wont to go out to the grave-yards and say, "Ye once ruled the world, but that saved you not from death, and now are ye come to your sepulchres! Would Heaven I knew what ye said and what is said to you!"

Alluding to the Fishár or "Squeeze of the tomb." This is the Jewish Hibbut hak-keber which all must endure, save those who lived in the Holy Land or died on the Sabbath-eve (Friday night). Then comes the questioning by the Angels Munkar and Nakir (vulgarly called Nákir and Nakír) for which see Lane (M. E. chapt. xviii.). In Egypt a "Mulakkin" (intelligencer) is hired to prompt and instruct the dead. Moslems are beginning to question these facts of their faith: a Persian acquaintance of mine filled his dead father's mouth with flour and finding it *in loco* on opening the grave, publicly derided the belief. But the Mullahs had him on the hip, after the fashion of reverends, declaring that the answers were made through the whole body, not only by the mouth. At last the Voltairean had to quit Shiraz.

*

BIG HEADWEAR

Then he greatened his turband and sat down at the door of the school; and when the people, who passed by, saw his huge head-gear and tablets and scrolls, they thought he must be a very learned pedagogue; so they brought him their children; and he would say to this, "Write," and to that "Read"; and thus the little ones taught one another.

The custom (growing obsolete in Egypt) is preserved in Afghanistan where the learned wear turbans equal to the canoe-hats of the Spanish cardinals.

*

ROC FEATHERS

THE OLDER "ROC" which may be written "Rukh" or "Rukhkh." Colonel Yule, the learned translator of Marco Polo, has shown that "Roc's" feathers were not uncommon curiosities in mediæval ages; and holds that they were mostly fronds of the palm Raphia vinifera, which has the largest leaf in the vegetable kingdom and which the Moslems of Zanzibar call "Satan's date-tree." I need hardly quote "Frate Cipolla and the Angel Gabriel's Feather." (Decameron vi. 10.)

*

FRANTIC VENGEFULNESS

The whole house was thrown open to feasting: there were rices of five several colours, and sherbets of as many more; and kids stuffed with walnuts and almonds and pistachios and a camel-colt roasted whole.

This is a favourite Badawi dish, but too expensive unless some accident happen to the animal. Old camel is much like bull-beef, but the young meat is excellent, although not relished by Europeans because, like strange fish, it has no recognised flavour. I have noticed it in my "First Footsteps" (p. 68, etc.). There is an old idea in Europe that the maniacal vengeance of the Arab is increased by eating this flesh; the beast is certainly vindictive enough; but a furious and frantic vengefulness characterises the North American Indian who never saw a camel. Mercy and pardon belong to the elect, not to the miserables who make up "humanity."

*

SWISS OF ARABIA

Here he met with many Arabs, especially Hazramís, who recommended him to the King; and this King (who was a Kafir) trusted him and advanced him to the captain-ship of his body-guard.

i.e., of the Province Hazramaut, the Biblical Hazarmaveth (Gen. x. 26). The people are the Swiss of Arabia and noted for thrift and hard bargains; hence the saying, If you meet a serpent and a Hazrami, slay the Hazrami. To prove how ubiquitous they are it is related that a man, flying from their society, reached the uttermost parts of China where he thought himself safe. But, as he was about to pass the night in some ruin, he heard a voice hard by him exclaim, O

'Imád al-Din! (the name of the patron-saint of Hazramaut). Thereupon he arose and fled and he is, they say, flying still.

*

POINT OF HONOUR

And he ceased not travelling and voyaging and returned to India; and there abode in self-exile till he died; and the mercy of Allah be upon him!

This story is curious and ethnologically valuable. The Badawi who eructates as a civility, has a mortal hatred to a *crepitus ventris*; and were a by-stander to laugh at its accidental occurrence, he would at once be cut down as a "pundonor." The same is the custom amongst the Highlanders of Afghanistan, and its artificial nature suggests direct derivation; for the two regions are separated by a host of tribes, Persians and Baloch, Sindis and Panjábis who utterly ignore the point of honour and behave like Europeans. The raids of the pre-Islamitic Arabs over the lands lying to the north-east of them are almost forgotten; still there are traces, and this may be one of them.

*

RICHARD BURTON

CURING THE MAD

TILL LATELY IT was the custom to confine madmen in Syrian monasteries, hoping a cure from the patron Saint; and a terrible time they had of it. Every guide book relates the healing process as formerly pursued at the Maronite Convent Koshaya not far from Bayrut. The idiot or maniac was thrust headlong by the monks into a dismal cavern with a heavy chain round his neck, and was tied up within a span of the wall to await the arrival of Saint Anthony who especially affects this holy place. In very few weeks the patient was effectually cured or killed by cold, solitude and starvation.

*

FORBIDDEN SINS

WITHIN THE HUDÚD al-Haram (bounds of the Holy Places), at Al-Medinah as well as Meccah, all "Muharramát" (forbidden sins) are doubly unlawful, such as drinking spirits, immoral life, etc. The Imam Malik forbids slaying animals without, however, specifying any penalty. The felling of trees is a disputed point; and no man can be put to death except invaders, infidels and desecraters (Pilgrimage ii. 167).

*

THE WHALE'S BELLY

IN ARAB. = A fawn beginning to walk; also the 28th lunar mansion or station, usually known as Batn al-Hut or Whale's belly. These mansions or houses, the constellations through which the moon passes in her course along her orbit, are much used in Moslem astrology and meteorology.

*

BREAKING THE SEAL

EASTERNS DURING PURGATION are most careful and deride the want of precaution in Europeans. They do not leave the house till all is passed off, and avoid baths, wine and women, which they afterwards resume with double zest. Here "breaking the seal" is taking the girl's maidenhead.

*

SILK-MAN AND SEANCES

THE "SILK-MAN" AND the celebrated author of the Makámát, assemblies or seances, translated (or attempted) into all the languages of Europe. We have two in English, the first by Theodore Preston, M.A. (London, Madden, 1850); but it contains only twenty of the fifty pieces. The second by the late Mr. Chenery (before alluded to) ends with the twenty-sixth assembly: one volume in fact, the other never having

301

been finished. English readers, therefore, are driven to the grand edition of the Makámát in folio by Baron Silvestre de Sacy.

*

SWORD OF THE EYE

THE SWORD OF the eye has a Hamáil (baldrick worn over right shoulder, Pilgrimage i. 352) to support the "Ghimd" (vulg. Ghamad) or scabbard (of wood or leather): and this baldrick is the young whisker.

*

SEEKING PROOF

THE DETECTED SODOMITE is punished with death according to Moslem law, but again comes the difficulty of proof. At Shiraz I have heard of a pious Moslem publicly executing his son.

Arab. "Lúti," (plur. Lawáti), much used in Persian as a buffoon, a debauchee, a rascal. The orig. sig. is "One of (the people of) Lot." The old English was Ingle or Yngle (a bardachio, a catamite, a boy kept for sodomy), which Minsheu says is, "Vox hispanica et significat Latinè Inguen" (the groin). Our vulgar modern word like the Italian bugiardo is pop. derived from Fr. Bougre, alias Bulgarus, a Bulgarian, a heretic: hence

Boulgrin (Rabelais i. chapt. ii.) is popularly applied to the Albigeois (Albigenses, whose persecution began shortly after A.D. 1200) and the Lutherans. I cannot but think that "bougre" took its especial modern signification after the French became acquainted with the Brazil, where the Huguenots (in A.D. 1555) were founding a Nouvelle France, alias Equinoctiale, alias Antarctique, and whence the savages were carried as curiosities to Paris. Their generic name was "Bugre" (properly a tribe in Southern Brazil, but applied to all the redskins) and they were all born Sodomites. More of this in the terminal Essay.

*

IMPERIAL CYPHERS

The Kazi wrote the act and made it binding on all men, after they had sworn in a body the oath of fealty to Hasan.

By affixing his own seal and that of the King. This in later times was supplanted by the "Tughrá," the imperial cypher or counter-mark (much like a writing master's flourish), with which Europe has now been made familiar through the agency of Turkish tobacco.

*

RICHARD BURTON

EATING THE DEAD

THE SENSIBLE CREED of Al-Islam freely allow anthropophagy when it saves life; a contrast to the sentimentalism of the West which brings a "charge of cannibalism" against unfortunate expeditionists. I particularly allude to the scandalous pulings of the English Press over the gallant and unfortunate Greely voyage (The Academy, Sept. 25, 1884).

*

MAKING HASTE

AS IN MOST hot climates so in Egypt the dead are buried at once despite the risk of vivisepulture. This seems an instinct with the Semitic (Arabian) race *teste* Abraham, as with the Gypsy. Hence the Moslems have invoked religious aid. The Mishkát al-Masábih (i. 387) makes Mohammed say, "When any one of you dieth you may not keep him in the house but bear him quickly to his grave"; and again, "Be quick in raising up the bier: for if the dead have been a good man, it is good to bear him gravewards without delay; and if bad, it is frowardness ye put from your necks."

*

BITING THE HAND

So he ate and drank and made merry and took his pleasure and gave gifts of gear and coin and was profuse with gold and addrest himself up to eating fowls and breaking the seals of wine-flasks and listening to the giggle of the daughter of the vine, as she gurgled from the flagon and enjoying the jingle of the singinggirls; nor did he give over this way of life, till his wealth was wasted and the case worsened and all his goods went from him and he bit his hands in bitter penitence.

This biting of the hand in Al-Haríri expresses bitterness of repentance and he uses more than once the Koranic phrase (chapter vii., 148) "Sukita fï aydíhim," lit. where it (the biting) was fallen upon their hands; *i.e.* when it repented them; "sukita" being here not a passive verb as it appears, but an impersonal form uncommon in Arabic. The action is instinctive, a survival of the days when man was a snarling and snapping animal (physically) armed only with claws and teeth.

*

MONKEYS AND CHRISTIANS

ARAB WRITERS OFTEN mention the smile of beauty, but rarely, after European fashion, the laugh, which they look upon as undignified. A Moslem will say "Don't guffaw (Kahkahah) in that way; leave giggling and grinning to monkeys and

Christians." The Spaniards, a grave people, remark that Christ never laughed. I would draw the reader's attention to a theory of mine that the open-hearted laugh has the sound of the vowels *a* and *o*; while *e*, *i*, and *u* belong to what may be roughly classed as the rogue order.

*

GIVING THE LOOK

In a little while they arrived at the palace of the Caliphate, knowing not what was to be done, and the Caliph sent for them to his sitting-chamber and ordered them to be seated. So they sat down and he bade bring the damsel Tawaddud, who came and unveiling, showed herself, as she were a sparkling star.

She unveiled being a slave-girl and for sale. If a free woman show her face to a Moslem, he breaks out into violent abuse, because the act is intended to let him know that he is looked upon as a small boy or an eunuch or a Christian — in fact not a man.

*

HIND PARTS TO HEAVEN

As FAR AS I know Christians are the only worshippers who kneel as if their lower legs were cut off and who "join hands" like the captive offering his wrists to be bound (dare manus).

The posture, however, is not so ignoble as that of the Moslem "Sijdah" (prostration) which made certain North African tribes reject Al-Islam, saying, "These men show their hind parts to heaven."

*

SNUFFING WATER

ARAB. "ISTINSHÁK" = SNUFFING up water from the palm of the right hand so as to clean thoroughly the nostrils. This "function" is unreasonably neglected in Europe, to the detriment of the mucous membrane and the olfactory nerves.

*

ABLUTIONS

COMPLETE ABLUTION IS rendered necessary chiefly by the emission of semen either in copulation or in nocturnal pollution. The water must be pure and not less than a certain quantity, and it must touch every part of the skin beginning with the right half of the person and ending with the left. Hence a plunge-bath is generally preferred.

*

RICHARD BURTON

WATER-BANDAGES

ARABS HAVE A prejudice against the hydropathic treatment of wounds, holding that water poisons them: and, as the native produce usually contains salt, soda and magnesia, they are justified by many cases. I once tried water-bandages in Arabia and failed dismally.

*

WHITE THREAD, BLACK THREAD

The traditional ordinances of fasting are, hastening to break the fast at sundown; deferring the fore dawn meal, and abstaining from speech, save for good works and for calling on the name of Allah and reciting the Koran.

The meal must be finished before the faster can plainly distinguish the white thread from the black thread (Koran ii. 183); some understand this literally, others apply it to the dark and silvery streak of zodiacal light which appears over the Eastern horizon an hour or so before sunrise. The fast then begins and ends with the disappearance of the sun. I have noticed its pains and penalties in my Pilgrimage, i. 110, etc.

*

DANCING WITH JOY

"Under what conditions is the Hajj or Pilgrimage obligatory?"—Manhood, and understanding and being a Moslem and practicability…"

The word is the Heb. גח Hagg whose primary meaning is circularity of form or movement. Hence it applied to religious festivals in which dancing round the idol played a prime part; and Lucian of "saltation" says, dancing was from the beginning and coeval with the ancient god, Love. But man danced with joy before he worshipped, and, when he invented a systematic saltation, he made it represent two things, and only two things, love and war, in most primitive form, courtship and fighting.

*

EXPIATING SINS

THE PARTITION-WALL between Heaven and Hell which others call Al-'Urf (in the sing. from the verb meaning he separated or parted). The Jeus borrowed from the Guebres the idea of a partition between Heaven and Hell and made it so thin that the blessed and damned can speak together. There is much dispute about the population of Al-A'aráf, the general idea being that they are men who do not deserve reward in Heaven or punishment in Hell. But it is not a "Purgatory" or place of expiating sins.

RICHARD BURTON

*

LOOK OF AGE

THE JEWISH KORAH (Numbers xvi.) fabled by the Koran (xxviii. 76), following a Talmudic tradition, to have been a man of immense wealth. The notion that lying with an old woman, after the menses have ceased, is unwholesome, dates from great antiquity; and the benefits of the reverse process were well known to *good* King David. The faces of children who sleep with their grandparents (a bad practice now waxing obsolete in England), of a young wife married to an old man and of a young man married to an old woman, show a peculiar wizened appearance, a look of age overlaying youth which cannot be mistaken.

*

BAT-BLOOD WAXING

ARAB. "KHUFFÁSH" AND "Watwát": in Egypt a woman is called "Watwátíyah" when the hair of her privities has been removed by applying bats' blood. I have often heard of this; but cannot understand how such an application can act depilatory.

*

CALCULATIONS

As a RULE Moslems are absurdly ignorant of arithmetic and apparently cannot master it. Hence in Egypt they used Copts for calculating-machines and further East Hindús. The mildest numerical puzzle, like the above, is sure of success.

*

PARADISAL TREE

THE PARADISAL TREE which supplied every want. Mohammed borrowed it from the Christians (Rev. xxi. 10–21 and xxii. 1–2) who placed in their paradise the Tree of Life which bears twelve sorts of fruits and leaves of healing virtue. (See also the 3rd book of Hermas, his Similitudes.) The Hebrews borrowed it from the Persians. Amongst the Hindus it appears as "Kalpavriksha;" amongst the Scandinavians as Yggdrasil. The curious reader will consult Mr. James Fergusson's learned work, "Tree and Serpent Worship," etc. London, 1873.

*

WHERE TO DIE

THE STRICTER KIND of Eastern Jew prefers to die on the floor not in bed, as was the case with the late Mr. Emmanuel

Deutsch, who in his well-known article on the Talmud had the courage to speak of "Our Saviour." But as a rule the Israelite, though he mostly appears as a Deist, a Unitarian, has a fund of fanatical feelings which crop up in old age and near death. The "converts" in Syria and elsewhere, whose Judaism is intensified by "conversion," when offers are made to them by the missionaries repair to the Khákhám (scribe) and, after abundant wrangling determine upon a *modus vivendi*. They are to pay a proportion of their wages, to keep careful watch in the cause of Israel and to die orthodox. In Istria there is a legend of a Jew Prior in a convent who was not discovered till he announced himself most unpleasantly on his death-bed. For a contrary reason to Jewish humility the Roman Emperors preferred to die standing.

*

SUPREME INTELLIGENCE

ARAB. "LA'AN" = curse. The word is in every mouth though strongly forbidden by religion. Even of the enemies of Al-Islam the learned say, "Ila'an Yezíd wa lá tazíd" = curse Yezid but do not exceed (*i.e.* refrain from cursing the others). This, however, is in the Shafi'í school and the Hanafís do not allow it (Pilgrimage i. 198). Hence the Moslem when scrupulous uses na'al (shoe) for la'an (curse) as Ina'al abúk (for Ila'an abu'-k) or, *drat* (instead of *damn*) your father. Men must hold Supreme Intelligence to be of feeble kind if put off by such miserable pretences.

CONGRESS WITH A CROCODILE

*

LORD OF THE TWO HORNS

I.E. THE KORANIC and our mediæval Alexander, Lord of the two Horns (East and West) much "Matagrobolized" and very different from him of Macedon. The title is variously explained, from two protuberances on his head or helm, from two long locks and, possibly, from the ram-horns of Jupiter Ammon. The anecdote in the text seems suggested by the famous interview (probably a *canard*) with Diogenes: see in the Gesta, Tale cxlvi. "The answer of Diomedes the Pirate to Alexander." Iskandar was originally called Marzbán (Lord of the Marches), son of Marzabah; and, though descended from Yunán, son of Japhet, the eponymus of the Greeks, was born obscure, the son of an old woman. According to the Persians he was the son of the Elder Dáráb (Darius Codomannus of the Kayanian or Second dynasty), by a daughter of Philip of Macedon; and was brought up by his grandfather. When Abraham and Isaac had rebuilt the Ka'abah they foregathered with him and Allah sent him forth against the four quarters of the earth to convert men to the faith of the Friend or to cut their throats; thus he became one of the four world-conquerors with Nimrod, Solomon, Bukht al-Nasr (Nabochodonosor); and he lived down two generations of men. His Wazir was Aristú (the Greek Aristotle) and he carried a couple of flags, white and black, which made day and night for him and facilitated his conquests. At the end of Persia, where he was invited by the people, on account of the cruelty of his half brother Darab II., he came upon two huge mountains on the same line, behind which dwelt a host of abominable pygmies, two spans high, with curious eyes, ears which served as mattresses and coverlets, huge fanged mouths, lions' claws and hairy hind quarters. They ate men, destroyed everything, copulated in public and had swarms of children. These were Yájúj and Májúj (Gog and Magog) descendants of Japhet. Sikandar built against them the famous wall with stones cemented and riveted by iron and copper. The "Great Wall" of China, the famous bulwark against the Tartars dates from B.C. 320; (Alexander of Macedon died B.C. 324) and as the Arabs knew Canton well before Mohammed's day, they may have built their romance upon it. The Guebres consigned Sikandar to hell for burning the Nusks or sections of the Zendavesta.

*

WHERE THE SUN GOES DOWN

"And why so?" asked Iskandar, and the King answered, "Because all men are thy foes by reason of the wealth and the worlds thou hast won: while all men are my true friends, because of my contentment and pauperdom, for that I possess nothing, neither covet aught of the goods of life; I have no desire to them nor wish for them, neither reck I aught save contentment." So Iskandar pressed him to his breast and kissed him between the eyes and went his way.

These terrific preachments to Eastern despots (who utterly ignore them) are a staple produce of Oriental tale-literature and form the chiaro-oscuro, as it were, of a picture whose lights are brilliant touches of profanity and indelicate humour. It certainly has the charm of contrast. Much of the above is taken from the Sikandar-nameh (Alexander Book) of the great Persian poet, Nizámi, who flourished A.H. 515–597, between the days of Firdausi (ob. A.D. 1021) and Sa'adi (ob. A.D. 1291). In that romance Sikandar builds, "where the sun goes down," a castle of glittering stone which kills men by causing excessive laughter and surrounds it with yellow earth like gold. Hence the City of Brass. He also converts, instead of being converted by, the savages of the text. He finds a stone of special excellence which he calls Almás (diamond); and he obtains it from the Valley of Serpents by throwing down flesh to the eagles. Lastly he is accompanied by "Bilínás" or "Bilínús," who is apparently Apollonius of Tyana.

*

ETERNAL TRUTH

At this Anushirwan rejoiced and rendered thanks to the Lord, saying, "I was but minded to try my kingdom and prove mine empire, that I might know if any place therein remained ruined and deserted, so I might rebuild and repeople it; but, since there be no place in it but is inhabited, the affairs of the reign are best-conditioned and its ordinance is excellent; and its populousness hath reached the pitch of perfection."

Here we find an eternal truth, of which Malthusians ever want reminding; that the power of a nation simply consists in its numbers of fighting men and in their brute bodily force. The conquering race is that which raises most foot-pounds: hence the North conquers the South in the Northern hemisphere and *vice versâ*.

*

MAN OF THE PEN

As a rule (much disputed) the Sayyid is a descendant from Mohammed through his grandchild Hasan, and is a man of the pen; whereas the Sharif derives from Husayn and is a man of the sword. The Najíb al-taraf is the son of a common Moslemah by a Sayyid, as opposed to the "Najib al-tarafayn," when both parents are of Apostolic blood. The distinction is not noticed in Lane's "Modern Egyptians." The Sharif is a fanatic and often dangerous, as I have instanced in Pilgrimage iii. 132.

*

FOOD SUPERSTITIONS

Except on the two great Festivals when fasting is forbidden. The only religion which has shown common sense in this matter is that of the Guebres or Parsis: they consider fasting neither meritorious nor lawful; and they honour Hormuzd by good living "because it keeps the soul stronger." Yet even they have their food superstitions, *e.g.* in Gate No. xxiv.: "Beware of sin specially on the day thou eatest flesh, for flesh is the diet of Ahrimán." And in India the Guebres have copied the Hindus in not slaughtering horned cattle for the table.

*

NO SHAME IN IT

A SAYING OF Mohammed is recorded "Al-fakru fakhrí" (poverty is my pride!), intelligible in a man who never wanted for anything. Here he is diametrically opposed to Ali who honestly abused poverty; and the Prophet seems to have borrowed from Christendom, whose "Lazarus and Dives" shows a man sent to Hell because he enjoyed a very modified Heaven in this life and which suggested that one of the man's greatest miseries is an ecclesiastical virtue — "Holy Poverty" — represented in the Church as a bride young and lovely. If a "rich man can hardly enter the kingdom" what must it be with a poor man whose conditions are far more unfavourable? Going to the other extreme we may say that Poverty is the root of all evil and the more so as it curtails man's power of benefiting others. Practically I observe that those who preach and praise it the most, practise it the least willingly: the ecclesiastic has always some special reasons, a church or a school is wanted; but not the less he wishes for more money. In Syria this Holy Poverty leads to strange abuses. At Bayrut I recognised in most impudent beggars well-to-do peasants from the Kasrawán district, and presently found out that whilst their fields were under snow they came down to the coast, enjoyed a genial climate and lived on alms. When I asked them if they were not ashamed to beg, they asked me if I was ashamed of following in the footsteps of the Saviour and Apostles. How much wiser was Zoroaster who found in the Supreme Paradise (Minuwán-minu) "many persons, rich in gold and silver who had worshipped the Lord and had been grateful to Him." (Dabistan i. 265.)

*

PORTABLE PILLORY

ARAB. "AL-BAYT" = THE house. The Arabs had probably learned this pleasant mode of confinement from the Chinese whose *Kea* or Cangue is well known. The Arabian form of it is "Ghull," or portable pillory, which reprobates will wear on Judgement Day.

*

FGM

MOSLEMS LIKE THE Classics (Aristotle and others) hold the clitoris (*Zambúr*) to be the sedes et scaturigo veneris which, says Sonnini, is mere profanity. In the babe it protrudes beyond the labiæ and snipping off the head forms female circumcision. This rite is supposed by Moslems to have been invented by Sarah who so mutilated Hagar for jealousy and was afterwards ordered by Allah to have herself circumcised at the same time as Abraham. It is now (or should be) universal in Al-Islam and no Arab would marry a girl "unpurified" by it. Son of an "uncircumcised" mother (Ibn al-bazrá) is a sore insult. As regards the popular idea that Jewish women were circumcised till the days of Rabbi Gershom (A.D. 1000) who denounced it as a scandal to the Gentiles, the learned Prof. H. Graetz informs me, with some indignation, that the rite was never practised and that the great Rabbi contended only against polygamy. Female circumcision, however, is I believe the rule amongst some outlying tribes of Jews. The rite is the proper complement of male circumcision, evening the sensitiveness of the genitories by reducing it equally in both sexes: an uncircumcised woman has the venereal orgasm much sooner and oftener than a circumcised man, and frequent coitus would injure her health; hence I believe, despite the learned historian, that it is practised by some Eastern Jews. "Excision" is universal amongst the negroids of the Upper Nile (Werne), the Somál and other adjacent tribes. The operator, an old woman, takes up the instrument, a knife or razor-blade fixed into a wooden handle, and with three sweeps cuts off the labia and the head of the clitoris. The parts are then sewn up with a pack-needle and a thread of sheepskin; and in Dar-For a tin tube is inserted for the passage of urine. Before marriage the bridegroom trains himself for a month on beef, honey and milk; and, if he can open his bride with the natural weapon, he is a sworder to whom no woman in the tribe can deny herself. If he fail, he tries penetration with his fingers and by way of last resort whips out his whittle and cuts the parts open. The sufferings of the first few nights must be severe. The few Somáli prostitutes who practised at Aden always had the labiæ and clitoris excised and the skin showing the scars of coarse sewing. The moral effect of female circumcision is peculiar. While it diminishes the heat of passion it increases licentiousness, and breeds a debauchery of mind far worse than bodily unchastity, because accompanied by a peculiar cold cruelty and a taste for artificial stimulants to "luxury." It is the sexlessness of a spayed canine imitated by the suggestive brain of humanity.

*

SEEDY BOY

Sídi (CONTRACTED FROM Sayyidí = my lord) is a title still applied to holy men in Marocco and the Maghrib; on the East African coast it is assumed by negro and negroid Moslems, *e.g.* Sidi Mubárak Bombay; and "Seedy boy" is the Anglo-Indian term for a Zanzibar-man. "Khawwás" is one who weaves palm-leaves (Khos) into baskets, mats, etc.: here, however, it may be an inherited name.

*

GOD-SPEED

THE MOSLEM IS still unwilling to address Salám (Peace be with you) to the Christian, as it is obligatory (Farz) to a Moslem (Koran, chapt. iv. and lxviii.). He usually evades the difficulty by saluting the nearest Moslem or by a change of words Allah Yahdí-k (Allah direct thee to the right way) or "Peace be upon us and the righteous worshippers of Allah" (not you) or Al-Samm (for Salam) alayka = poison to thee. The idea is old: Alexander of Alexandria in his circular letter describes the Arian heretics as "men whom it is not lawful to salute or to bid God-speed."

*

REASON WANTS TO KNOW

IN SUFISTICAL PARLANCE, the creature is the lover and the Creator the Beloved: worldly existence is Disunion, parting, severance; and the life to come is Reunion. The basis of the idea is the human soul being a divinæ particula auræ, a disjoined molecule from the Great Spirit, imprisoned in a jail of flesh; and it is so far valuable that it has produced a grand and pathetic poetry; but Common Sense asks, Where is the proof? And Reason wants to know, What does it all mean?

*

RICHARD BURTON

LEPROSY: WHITE AND BLACK

ARABS NOTE TWO kinds of leprosy, "Bahak" or "Baras" the common or white, and "Juzám" the black leprosy; the leprosy of the joints, mal rouge. Both are attributed to undue diet as eating fish and drinking milk; and both are treated with tonics, especially arsenic. Leprosy is regarded by Moslems as a Scriptural malady on account of its prevalence amongst the Israelites who, as Manetho tells us, were expelled from Egypt because they infected and polluted the population. In mediæval Christendom an idea prevailed that the Saviour was a leper; hence the term "morbus sacer"; the honours paid to the sufferers by certain Saints and the Papal address (Clement III. A.D. 1189) dilectis filiis leprosis. (Farrar's Life of Christ, i. 149.) For the "disgusting and impetuous lust" caused by leprosy, see Sonnini (p. 560) who visited the lepers at Canea in Candia. He is one of many who describes this symptom; but in the Brazil, where the foul malady still prevails, I never heard of it.

*

LACTATION

THE USUAL TERM of lactation in the East, prolonged to two years and a-half, which is considered the rule laid down by the Shara' or precepts of the Prophet. But it is not unusual to see children of three and even four years hanging to their mothers' breasts. During this period the mother does not

322

cohabit with her husband; the separation beginning with her pregnancy. Such is the habit, not only of the "lower animals," but of all ancient peoples, the Egyptians (from whom the Hebrews borrowed it), the Assyrians and the Chinese. I have discussed its bearing upon pregnancy in my "City of the Saints": the Mormons insist upon this law of purity being observed; and the beauty, strength and good health of the younger generation are proofs of their wisdom.

*

GUARDING THE EARTH-TREASURES

THE STUDENT OF Hinduism will remember the Nága-Kings and Queens (Melusines and Echidnæ) who guard the earth-treasures in Naga-land. The first appearance of the snake in literature is in Egyptian hieroglyphs, where he forms the letters f and t, and acts as a determinative in the shape of a Cobra di Capello (Coluber Naja) with expanded hood.

*

END OF TIME

"AKHIR AL-ZAMÁN." As old men praise past times, so prophets prefer to represent themselves as the last. The early Christians caused much scandal amongst the orderly law-loving Romans by their wild and mistaken predictions of the end of the world being at hand. The catastrophe is a fact for each man under the form of death; but the world has endured for untold ages and there is no apparent cause why it should not endure as many more. The "latter days," as the religious dicta of most "revelations" assure us, will be richer in sinners than in sanctity: hence "End of Time" is a facetious Arab title for a villain of superior quality. My Somali escort applied it to one thus distinguished: in 1875, I heard at Aden that he ended life by the spear as we had all predicted.

*

THE SECOND HELL

The first stage he named Jahannam and appointed the same for the punishment of the transgressors of the True-believers, who die unrepentant; the second he named Lazá and appointed for Unbelievers: the name of the third is Jahím and is appointed for Gog and Magog.

Vulgarly pronounced "Jahannum." The second hell is usually assigned to Christians. As there are seven Heavens (the planetary orbits) so, to satisfy Moslem love of symmetry, there must be as many earths and hells under the earth. The Egyptians invented these grim abodes, and the marvellous Persian fancy worked them into poem.

*

SPLIT MAN

THE ARABS CALL "Shikk" (split man) and the Persians "Nímchahrah" (half-face) a kind of demon like a man divided longitudinally: this gruesome creature runs with amazing speed and is very cruel and dangerous. For the celebrated soothsayers Shikk and Sátih see Chenery's Al-Hariri, p. 371.

*

SAFE FROM SERPENT

ARAB. "LA'AL." AND "Yákút," the latter also applied to the garnet and to a variety of inferior stones. The ruby is supposed by Moslems to be a common mineral thoroughly "cooked" by the sun, and produced only on the summits of mountains inaccessible even to Alpinists. The idea may have originated from exaggerated legends of the Badakhshán country (supposed to be the home of the ruby) and its terrors of break-neck foot-paths, jagged peaks and horrid ravines: hence our "*balass*-ruby" through the Spanish corruption "Balaxe." Epiphanius, archbishop of Salamis in Cyprus, who died A.D. 403, gives, in a little treatise (De duodecim gemmis rationalis summi sacerdotis Hebræorum Liber, opera Fogginii, Romæ, 1743, p. 30), a precisely similar description of the mode of finding jacinths in Scythia. "In a wilderness in the interior of Great Scythia," he writes, "there is a valley begirt with stony mountains

325

as with walls. It is inaccessible to man, and so excessively deep that the bottom of the valley is invisible from the top of the surrounding mountains. So great is the darkness that it has the effect of a kind of chaos. To this place certain criminals are condemned, whose task it is to throw down into the valley slaughtered lambs, from which the skin has been first taken off. The little stones adhere to these pieces of flesh. Thereupon the eagles, which live on the summits of the mountains, fly down following the scent of the flesh, and carry away the lambs with the stones adhering to them. They, then, who are condemned to this place, watch until the eagles have finished their meal, and run and take away the stones." Epiphanius, who wrote this, is spoken of in terms of great respect by many ecclesiastical writers, and St. Jerome styles the treatise here quoted, "Egregium volumen, quod si legere volueris, plenissimam scientiam consequeris;" and, indeed, it is by no means improbable that it was from the account of Epiphanius that this story was first translated into Arabic. A similar account is given by Marco Polo and by Nicolò de Conti, as of a usage which they had heard was practised in India, and the position ascribed to the mountain by Conti, namely, fifteen days' journey north of Vijanagar, renders it highly probable that Golconda was alluded to. He calls the mountain Albenigaras, and says that it was infested with serpents. Marco Polo also speaks of these serpents, and while his account agrees with that of Sindbad, inasmuch as the serpents, which are the prey of Sindbad's Rukh, are devoured by the Venetian's eagles, that of Conti makes the vultures and eagles fly away with the meat to places where they may be safe from the serpents. (Introd. p. xlii., India in the Fifteenth Century, etc., R. H. Major, London, Hakluyt Soc. MDCCCLVII.)

*

SWAN-MAIDENS

Then they put off their feathers and became three maidens, as they were moons, that had not their like in the whole world.

These are the "Swan-maidens" of whom Europe in late years has heard more than enough. It appears to me that we go much too far for an explanation of the legend; a high-bred girl is so like a swan in many points that the idea readily suggests itself. And it is also aided by the old Egyptian (and Platonic) belief in pre-existence and by the Rabbinic and Buddhistic doctrine of ante-natal sin, to say nothing of metempsychosis (Joseph Ant. xvii. 153).

*

ROSE-WATER TEA

IT MAYBE NOTED that rose-water is sprinkled on the faces of the "nobility and gentry," common water being good enough for the commonalty. I have had to drink tea made in compliment with rose-water and did not enjoy it.

*

327

RICHARD BURTON

THE GREEN ONE

LIT. "THE GREEN" (Prophet), a mysterious personage confounded with Elijah, St. George and others. He was a Moslem, *i.e.* a true believer in the Islam of his day and Wazir to Kaykobad, founder of the Kayanian dynasty, sixth century B.C. We have before seen him as a contemporary of Moses. My learned friend Ch. Clermont-Ganneau traces him back, with a multitude of his similars (Proteus, Perseus, etc.), to the son of Osiris (p. 45, Horus et Saint Georges).

*

THE RIGHT CUT

THE MOSLEM RITUAL for slaughtering (by cutting the throat) is not so strict as that of the Jews; but it requires some practice; and any failure in the conditions renders the meat impure, mere carrion (fatís).

*

SETTING IT STRAIGHT

ARAB. "HABASH": THE word means more than "Abyssinia" as it includes the Dankali Country and the sea-board, a fact unknown to the late Lord Stratford de Redcliffe when he disputed with the Porte. I ventured to set him right and suffered accordingly.

*

HAWKING AN ELEPHANT

She said, It hath reached me, O auspicious King, that Sindbad the Seaman continued in these words: — My wonder redoubled and I remembered a story I had heard aforetime of pilgrims and travellers, how in a certain island dwelleth a huge bird, called the "Rukh" which feedeth its young on elephants; and I was certified that the dome which caught my sight was none other than a Rukh's egg.

The older "roc." The word is Persian, with many meanings, *e.g.* a cheek (Lalla "Rookh"); a "rook" (hero) at chess; a rhinoceros, etc. The fable world-wide of the *wundervogel* is, as usual, founded upon fact: man remembers and combines but does not create. The Egyptian Bennu (Ti-bennu = phœnix) may have been a reminiscence of gigantic pterodactyls and other winged monsters. From the Nile the legend fabled by these Oriental "putters out or five for one" overspread the world and gave birth to the Eorosh of the Zend, whence the Pers. "Símurgh" (= the "thirty-fowl-like"), the "Bar Yuchre" of the Rabbis, the "Garuda" of the Hindus; the "Anká" ("longneck") of the Arabs; the Hathilinga bird, of Buddhagosha's Parables, which had the strength of five elephants; the Kerkes of the Turks; the Gryps of the Greeks; the Russian "Norka"; the sacred dragon of the Chinese; the Japanese "Pheng" and "Kirni"; the "wise and ancient Bird" which sits upon the ash-tree Yggdrasil, and the dragons, griffins, basilisks, etc. of the Middle Ages. A second basis wanting only a superstructure of exaggeration (M. Polo's Ruch had wing-feathers twelve paces long) would be the huge birds but lately killed out. Sindbad may allude to the Æpyornus of Madagascar, a gigantic ostrich whose egg contains 2.35 gallons. The late Herr Hildebrand discovered on the African coast, facing Madagascar, traces of another huge bird. Bochart (Hierozoicon ii. 854) notices the Avium Avis Ruch and taking the *pulli* was followed by lapidation on the part of the parent bird. A Persian illustration in Lane (iii. 90) shows the Rukh carrying off three elephants in beak and pounces with the proportions of a hawk and field mice: and the Rukh hawking at an elephant is a favourite Persian subject. It is possible that the "Twelve Knights of the Round Table" were the twelve Rukhs of Persian story. We need not go, with Faber, to the Cherubim which guarded the Paradise-gate. The curious reader will consult Dr. H. H. Wilson's Essays, edited by my learned correspondent, Dr. Rost, Librarian of the India House, vol. i. pp. 192–3.

*

DIAMOND FOLKLORE

However, I took courage and walking along the Wady found that its soil was of diamond, the stone wherewith they pierce minerals and precious stones and porcelain and the onyx, for that it is a dense stone and a dure, whereon neither iron nor

*hardhead hath effect, neither can we cut off aught therefrom
nor break it, save by means of lead-stone.*

It is not easy to explain this passage unless it be a garbled allusion
to the steel-plate of the diamond-cutter. Nor can we account
for the wide diffusion of this tale of perils unless to enhance
the value of the gem. Diamonds occur in alluvial lands mostly
open and comparatively level, as in India, the Brazil and the
Cape. Archbishop Epiphanius of Salamis (ob. A.D. 403)
tells this story about the jacinth or ruby (Epiphanii Opera, a
Petaio, Coloniæ 1682); and it was transferred to the diamond
by Marco Polo (iii. 29, "of Eagles bring up diamonds") and
Nicolò de Conti, whose "mountain Albenigaras" must be
Vijayanagar in the kingdom of Golconda. Major Rennel
places the famous mines of Pauna or Purna in a mountain-
tract of more than 200 miles square to the south-west of the
Jumna. Al-Kazwini locates the "Chaos" in the "Valley of the
Moon amongst the mountains of Serendib" (Ceylon); the
Chinese tell the same tale in the campaigns of Hulaku; and it
is known in Armenia. Col. Yule (M. P. ii. 349) suggests that
all these are ramifications of the legend told by Herodotus
concerning the Arabs and their cinnamon (iii. 3). But
whence did Herodotus borrow the tale?

*

RICHARD BURTON

CAMPHOR-LAND

When the folk have a mind to get camphor, they bore into the upper part of the bole with a long iron; whereupon the liquid camphor, which is the sap of the tree, floweth out and they catch it in vessels, where it concreteth like gum; but, after this, the tree dieth and becometh firewood.

Sindbad correctly describes the primitive way of extracting camphor, a drug unknown to the Greeks and Romans, introduced by the Arabs and ruined in reputation by M. Raspail. The best Laurus Camphora grows in the Malay Peninsula, Sumatra and Borneo: although Marsden (Marco Polo) declares that the tree is not found South of the Equator. In the Calc. Edit. of two hundred Nights the camphor-island (or peninsula) is called "Al-Rîhah" which is the Arab name for Jericho-town.

*

WHITE HORN

In Bul. Edit. Kazkazan: Calc. Karkaddan and others Karkand and Karkadan; the word being Persian, Karg or Kargadan; the καρτάζυνον of Ælian (Hist. Anim. xvi. 21). The length of the horn (greatly exaggerated) shows that the white species is meant; and it supplies only walking-sticks. Cups are made of the black horn (a bundle of fibres) which, like Venetian glass, sweat at the touch of poison. A

332

section of the horn is supposed to show white lines in the figure of a man, and sundry likenesses of birds; but these I never saw. The rhinoceros gives splendid sport and the African is perhaps the most dangerous of noble game. It has served to explain away and abolish the unicorn among the Scientists of Europe. But Central Africa with one voice assures us that a horse-like animal with a single erectile horn on the forehead exists. The late Dr. Baikic, of Niger fame, thoroughly believed in it and those curious on the subject will read about Abu Karn (Father of a Horn) in Preface (pp. xvi.-xviii.) of the Voyage au Darfour, by Mohammed ibn Omar al-Tounsy (Al-Tunisi), Paris, Duprat, 1845.

*

LEGEND OF THE PYGMIES

IBN AL-WARDI MENTIONS an "Isle of Apes" in the Sea of China and Al-Idrísi places it two days' sail from Sukutra (Dwipa Sukhatra, Socotra). It is a popular error to explain the Homeric and Herodotean legend of the Pygmies by anthropoid apes. The Pygmy fable (Pygmæi Spithamai = 1 cubit = 3 spans) was, as usual, based upon fact, as the explorations of late years have proved: the dwarfs are homunculi of various tribes, the Akka, Doko, Tiki-Tiki, Wambilikimo ("two-cubit men"), the stunted race that share the central regions of Intertropical Africa with the abnormally tall peoples who speak dialects of the Great South African tongue, miscalled the "Bantu." Hole makes the Pygmies "monkeys," a word we have borrowed from the Italians (monichio à mono = ape) and quotes Ptolemy, Νῆσοι τῶν Σατυρῶν (Ape-islands) East of Sunda.

*

GIANTS

Moreover, he had long loose lips like camel's, hanging down upon his breast, and ears like two Jarms falling over his shoulder-blades and the nails of his hands were like the claws of a lion.

This giant is distinctly Polyphemus; but the East had giants and cyclopes of her own (Hierozoicon ii. 845). The Ajáib al-Hind (chapt. cxxii.) makes Polyphemus copulate with the sheep. Sir John Mandeville (if such person ever existed) mentions men fifty feet high in the Indian Islands; and Al-Kazwini and Al-Idrisi transfer them to the Sea of China, a Botany Bay for monsters in general.

*

SON OF A BURNT FATHER

FIRE IS FORBIDDEN as a punishment amongst Moslems, the idea being that it should be reserved for the next world. Hence the sailors fear the roasting more than the eating: with ours it would probably be the reverse. The Persian insult "Pidar-sokhtah" = (son of a) burnt father, is well known. I have noted the advisability of burning the Moslem's corpse under certain circumstances: otherwise the murderer may come to be canonised.

*

THE BREATH OF CROCODILES

"LIKE A CLOSET," in the Calc. Edit. The serpent is an exaggeration of the python which grows to an enormous size. Monstrous Ophidia are mentioned in sober history, *e.g.* that which delayed the army of Regulus. Dr. de Lacerda, a sober and sensible Brazilian traveller, mentions his servants sitting down upon a tree-trunk in the Captaincy of Sam Paulo (Brazil), which began to move and proved to be a huge snake. F. M. Pinto (the Sindbad of Portugal though not so respectable) when in Sumatra takes refuge in a tree from "tigers, crocodiles, copped adders and serpents which slay men with their breath." Father Lobo in Tigre (chapt. x.) was nearly killed by the poison-breath of a huge snake, and healed himself with a bezoar carried *ad hoc*. Maffæus makes the breath of crocodiles suavissimus, but that of the Malabar serpents and vipers "adeo teter ac noxius ut afflatu ipso necare perhibeantur."

*

RICHARD BURTON

THE BEAUTY OF A MIRACLE

We ceased not to buy and sell at the several islands till we came to the land of Hind, where we bought cloves and ginger and all manner spices; and thence we fared on to the land of Sind, where also we bought and sold. In these Indian seas, I saw wonders without number or count, amongst others a fish like a cow which bringeth forth its young and suckleth them like human beings; and of its skin bucklers are made.

Evidently the hippopotamus (Pliny, viii. 25; ix. 3 and xxiii. 11). It can hardly be the Mulaccan Tapir, as shields are not made of the hide. Hole suggests the buffalo which found its way to Egypt from India *viâ* Persia; but this would not be a speciosum miraculum.

*

ASS-HEADED

There were eke fishes like asses and camels and tortoises twenty cubits wide.

The ass-headed fish is from Pliny (ix. cap. 3): all those tales are founded upon the manatee (whose dorsal protuberance may have suggested the camel), the seal and the dugong or sea-calf. I have noticed (Zanzibar i. 205) legends of ichthyological marvels current on the East African seaboard; and even the monsters of the Scottish waters are not all

336

known: witness the mysterious "brigdie." See Bochart De Cetis i. 7; and Purchas iii. 930.

*

MONSTROUS DIMENSIONS

THE COLOSSAL TORTOISE is noticed by Ælian (De Nat. Animal. xvi. 17), by Strabo (Lib. xv.), by Pliny (ix. 10) and Diodorus Siculus (iv. 1) who had heard of a tribe of Chelonophagi. Ælian makes them 16 cubits long near Taprobane and serving as house-roofs; and others turn the shell into boats and coracles. A colossochelys was first found on the Scwalik Hills by Dr. Falconer and Major (afterwards Sir Proby) Cantley. In 1867 M. Emile Blanchard exhibited to the Académie des Sciences a monster crab from Japan 1.20 metres long (or 2.50 including legs); and other travellers have reported 4 metres. These crustacea seem never to cease growing and attain great dimensions under favourable circumstances, *i.e.* when not troubled by man.

*

WILD TRADITIONS

And I saw also a bird that cometh out of a sea-shell and layeth eggs and hatcheth her chicks on the surface of the water, never coming up from the sea to the land.

Lane suggests (iii. 97), and with some probability, that the "bird" was a nautilus; but the wild traditions concerning the barnacle-goose may perhaps have been the base of the fable. The albatross also was long supposed never to touch land. Possibly the barnacle, like the barometz or Tartarean lamb, may be a survivor of the day when the animal and vegetable kingdoms had not yet branched off into different directions.

*

THE INSANE HERB

So we sat down and they set food before us such as we knew not and whose like we had never seen in all our lives.

This is the "insane herb." Davis, who visited Sumatra in 1599 (Purchas i. 120) speaks "of a kind of seed, whereof a little being eaten, maketh a man to turn foole, all things seeming to him to be metamorphosed." Linschoten's "Dutroa" was a poppy-like bud containing small kernels like melons which stamped and administered as a drink make a man "as if he were foolish, or out of his wits." This is Father Lobo's "Vanguini" of the Cafres, called by the Portuguese *dutro* (*Datura Stramonium*) still used by dishonest confectioners. It may be Dampier's Ganga (Ganjah) or Bang (Bhang) which he justly describes as acting differently "according to different constitutions; for some it stupefies, others it makes sleepy, others merry and some quite mad." (Harris, Collect. ii. 900). Dr. Fryer also mentions Duty, Bung and Post, the Poust of Bernier, an infusion of poppy-seed.

*

RELIGION OF COMMON SENSE

When I saw this, I was confounded and concerned for them, nor was I less anxious about myself, for fear of the naked folk. So I watched them narrowly, and it was not long before I discovered them to be a tribe of Magian cannibals whose King was a Ghul.

Arab. "Ghul," here an ogre, a cannibal. I cannot but regard the "Ghul of the waste" as an embodiment of the natural fear and horror which a man feels when he faces a really dangerous desert. As regards cannibalism, Al-Islam's religion of common sense freely allows it when necessary to save life, and unlike our mawkish modern sensibility, never blames those who
Alimentis talibus usi
Produxere animos.

*

DOG-DESCENDED RACE

FOR CANNIBALS, SEE the Massagetæ of Herod (i.), the Padæi of India (iii.), and the Essedones near Mæotis (iv.);

Strabo (lib. iv.) of the Luci; Pomponius Mela (iii. 7) and St. Jerome (ad Jovinum) of Scoti. M. Polo locates them in Dragvia, a kingdom of Sumatra (iii. 17), and in Angaman (the Andamanian Isles?), possibly the ten Maniolai which Ptolemy (vii.), confusing with the Nicobars, places on the Eastern side of the Bay of Bengal; and thence derives the Heraklian stone (magnet) which attracts the iron of ships (See Serapion, De Magnete, fol. 6, Edit. of 1479, and Brown's Vulgar Errors, p. 74, 6th Edit.). Mandeville finds his cannibals in Lamaray (Sumatra) and Barthema in the "Isle of Gyava" (Java). Ibn Al-Wardi and Al-Kazwini notice them in the Isle Saksar, in the Sea of the Zanj (Zanzibar): the name is corrupted Persian "Sag-Sar" (Dogs'-heads) hence the dog-descended race of Camoens in Pegu (The Lus. x. 122). The Bresl. Edit. (iv. 52) calls them "Khawárij" = certain sectarians in Eastern Arabia. Needless to say that cocoa-nut oil would have no stupefying effect unless mixed with opium or datura, hemp or henbane.

*

GRAINS OF PARADISE

BLACK PEPPER IS produced in the Goanese but we must go south to find the "Bilád al-Filfil" (home of pepper) *i.e.* Malabar. The exorbitant prices demanded by Venice for this spice led directly to the discovery of The Cape route by the Portuguese; as the "Grains of Paradise" (Amomum Granum Paradisi) induced the English to explore the West African Coast.

340

*

BIRD LEGENDS

Then the she-Rukh let fall her rock, which was bigger than that of her mate, and as Destiny had decreed, it fell on the poop of the ship and crushed it, the rudder flying into twenty pieces; whereupon the vessel foundered and all and everything on board were cast into the main.

This tale is borrowed from Ibn Al-Wardi, who adds that the greybeards awoke in the morning after eating the young Rukh with black hair which never turned white. The same legend is recounted by Al-Dimiri (ob. A.H. 808 = 1405–6) who was translated into Latin by Bochart (Hierozoicon ii. p. 854) and quoted by Hole and Lane (iii. 103). An excellent study of Marco Polo's Rukh was made by my learned friend the late Prof. G. G. Bianconi of Bologna, "Dell'Uccello Ruc," Bologna, Gamberini, 1868. Prof. Bianconi predicted that other giant birds would be found in Madagascar on the East African Coast opposite; but he died before hearing of Hildebrand's discovery.

*

MAN OF THE WOODS

THE PERSIANS HAVE a Plinian monster called "Tasmeh-pá" = Strap-legs without bones. The "Old Man" is not an ourang-outang nor an Ifrít as in Sayf al-Mulúk, Night dcclxxi., but a jocose exaggeration of a custom prevailing in parts of Asia and especially in the African interior where the Tsetse-fly prevents the breeding of burden-beasts. Ibn Batútah tells us that in Malabar everything was borne upon men's backs. In Central Africa the kinglet rides a slave, and on ceremonious occasions mounts his Prime Minister. I have often been reduced to this style of conveyance and found man the worst imaginable riding: there is no hold and the sharpness of the shoulder-ridge soon makes the legs ache intolerably. The classicists of course find the Shaykh of the Sea in the Tritons and Nereus, and Bochart (Hiero. ii. 858, 880) notices the homo aquaticus, Senex Judæus and Senex Marinus. Hole (p. 151) suggests the inevitable ourang-outang (man o' wood), one of "our humiliating copyists," and quotes "Destiny" in Scarron's comical romance (Part ii. chapt. 1) and "Jealousy" enfolding Rinaldo (O.F. lib. 42).

*

I AM THINE EVIL DEEDS

I told them all that had betided me, whereat they marvelled with exceeding marvel and said, "He who rode on thy shoulder is called the 'Shaykh al-Bahr' or Old Man of the Sea, and none ever felt his legs on neck and came off alive but thou; and those who die under him he eateth: so praised be Allah for thy safety!"

More literally "The Chief of the Sea (-Coast)," Shaykh being here a chief rather than an elder (eoldermann, alderman). So the "Old Man of the Mountain," famous in crusading days, was the Chief who lived on the Nusayriyah or Ansári range, a northern prolongation of the Libanus. Our "old man" of the text may have been suggested by the Koranic commentators on chapt. vi. When an Infidel rises from the grave, a hideous figure meets him and says, Why wonderest thou at my loathsomeness? I am thine Evil Deeds: thou didst ride upon me in the world and now I will ride upon thee (suiting the action to the words).

*

IN GORILLA-LAND

IN PARTS OF West Africa and especially in Gorilla-land there are many stories of women and children being carried off by apes, and all believe that the former bear issue to them. It is certain that the anthropoid ape is lustfully excited by the presence of women and I have related how at Cairo (1856) a huge cynocephalus would have raped a girl had it not been bayonetted. Young ladies who visited the Demidoff Gardens and menagerie at Florence were often scandalised by the vicious exposure of the baboons' parti-coloured persons. The female monkey equally solicits the attentions of man and I heard in India from my late friend, Mirza Ali Akbar of Bombay, that to his knowledge connection had taken place. Whether there would be issue and whether such issue would be viable are still disputed points: the produce would add another difficulty to the pseudo-science called psychology, as such mule would have only half a soul and issue by a congener would have a quarter-soul. A traveller well known to me once proposed to breed pithecoid men who might be useful as hewers of wood and drawers of water: his idea was to put the highest races of apes to the lowest of humanity. I never heard what became of his "breeding stables."

*

ON PEARLS

I NEED HARDLY trouble the reader with a note on pearl-fisheries: the descriptions of travellers are continuous from the days of Pliny (ix. 35), Solinus (cap. 56) and Marco Polo (iii. 23). Maximilian of Transylvania, in his narrative of Magellan's voyage (Novus Orbis, p. 532) says that the Celebes produce pearls big as turtle-doves' eggs; and the King of Porne (Borneo) had two unions as great as goose's eggs. Pigafetta (in Purchas) reduces this to hen's eggs and Sir Thomas Herbert to dove's eggs.

*

AMBROSIA

ARAB. "ANBAR" PRONOUNCED "Ambar;" wherein I would derive "Ambrosia." Ambergris was long supposed to be a fossil, a vegetable which grew upon the sea-bottom or rose in springs; or a "substance produced in the water like naphtha or bitumen"(!): now it is known to be the egesta of a whale. It is found in lumps weighing several pounds upon the Zanzibar Coast and is sold at a high price, being held a potent aphrodisiac. A small hollow is drilled in the bottom of the cup and the coffee is poured upon the bit of ambergris it contains; when the oleaginous matter shows in dots amidst the "Kaymagh" (coffee-cream), the bubbly froth which floats upon the surface and which an expert "coffee servant" distributes equally among the guests. Argensola mentions in Ceylon, "springs of liquid bitumen thicker than our oil and some of pure balsam."

*

STOLEN SHROUD

She said, It hath reached me, O auspicious King, that Sindbad the Seaman continued in these words: — Now after I had buried the last of my party and abode alone on the island, I arose and dug me a deep grave on the sea-shore, saying to myself, "Whenas I grow weak and know that death cometh to me, I will cast myself into the grave and die there, so the wind may drift the sand over me and cover me and I be buried therein."

This custom is alluded to by Lane (Mod. Egypt, ch. xv.): it is the rule of pilgrims to Meccah when too ill to walk or ride (Pilgrimage i. 180). Hence all men carry their shrouds:

345

mine, after being dipped in the Holy Water of Zemzem, was stolen from me by the rascally Somal of Berberah.

*

UNDERGROUND RIVERS

My boat-raft drifted with the stream, I pondering the issue of my affair; and the drifting ceased not till I came to the place where it disappeared beneath the mountain. I rowed my conveyance into the place which was intensely dark; and the current carried the raft with it down the underground channel.

These underground rivers (which Dr. Livingstone derided) are familiar to every geographer from Spenser's "Mole" to the Poika of Adelberg and the Timavo near Trieste. Hence "Peter Wilkins" borrowed his cavern which led him to Grandevolet. I have some experience of Sindbad's sorrows, having once attempted to descend the Poika on foot. The Classics had the Alpheus (Pliny v. 31; and Seneca, Nat. Quæ. vi.), and the Tigris-Euphrates supposed to flow underground: and the Mediævals knew the Abana of Damascus and the Zenderúd of Isfahan.

*

WHITE-SKINNED ARROGANCE

ABYSSINIANS CAN HARDLY be called "blackamoors," but the arrogance of the white skin shows itself in Easterns (*e.g.* Turks and Brahmans) as much as, if not more than, amongst Europeans. Southern India at the time it was explored by Vasco da Gama was crowded with Abyssinian slaves imported by the Arabs.

*

TUSKS NOT TEETH

"Tusks" not "teeth" which are not valued. As Hole remarks, the elephants of Pliny and Sindbad are equally conscious of the value of ivory. Pliny (viii. 3) quotes Herodotus about the buying of ivories and relates how elephants, when hunted, break their "cornua" (as Juba called them) against a tree trunk by way of ransom. Ælian, Plutarch, and Philostratus speak of the linguistic intelligence and religious worship of the "half-reason with the hand," which the Hindus term "Háthí" = unimanus. Finally, Topsell's Gesner (p. 152) makes elephants bury their tusks, "which commonly drop out every tenth year." In Arabian literature the elephant is always connected with India.

*

DREAMS OF A CAMEL

Of my friends and of my neighbours had power to mend my plight:
Through my life I was wearied in journeying to death

347

RICHARD BURTON

In stress or in solace, in joyance or despight:
So when money-bags are bloated, and dinar unto dinar
Thou addest, all may leave thee with fleeting of the night...

The camel carries the Badawi's corpse to the cemetery which is often distant: hence to dream of a camel is an omen of death.

*

QUADRILLIONS

The Arabs have no word for million; so Messer Marco Miglione could not have learned it from them. On the other hand the Hindus have more quadrillions than modern Europe.

*

COLOUR NAMES

THE NAMES OF colours are as loosely used by the Arabs as by the Classics of Europe; for instance, a light grey is called a "blue or a green horse." Much nonsense has been written upon the colours in Homer by men who imagine that the semi-civilised determine tints as we do. They see them but they do not name them, having no occasion for the words. As I have noticed, however, the Arabs have a complete terminology for the varieties of horse-hues. In our day we have witnessed the birth of colours, named by the dozen, because required by women's dress.

*

RAISING THE SKIRTS

Passing onwards they came to a saloon builded all of polished marble, inlaid with jewels, which seemed to the beholder as though the floor were flowing water and whoso walked thereon slipped.

Alluding to the trick played upon Bilkís by Solomon who had heard that her legs were hairy like those of an ass: he laid down a pavement of glass over flowing water in which fish were swimming and thus she raised her skirts as she approached him and he saw that the report was true. Hence, as I have said, the depilatory (Koran xxvii.).

*

CONTRIVER OF THE STAKES

PHARAOH, SO CALLED in Koran (xxxviii. 11) because he tortured men by fastening them to four stakes driven into the ground. Sale translates "the contriver of the stakes" and adds, "Some understand the word figuratively, of the firm establishment of Pharaoh's kingdom, because the Arabs fix their tents with stakes; but they may possibly intend that prince's obstinacy and hardness of heart." I may note that in "Tasawwuf," or Moslem Gnosticism, Pharaoh represents, like Prometheus and Job, the typical creature who upholds his own dignity and rights in presence and despight of the Creator. Sáhib the Súfí declares that the secret of man's soul (*i.e.* its emanation) was first revealed when Pharaoh declared himself god; and Al-Ghazálí sees in his claim the most noble aspiration to the divine, innate in the human spirit (Dabistan, vol. iii.).

*

WILD WOMEN OF HANNO

MANKIND, WHICH SEES itself everywhere and in everything, must create its own analogues in all the elements, air (Sylphs), fire (Jinns), water (Mermen and Mermaids) and earth (Kobolds). These merwomen were of course seals or manatees, as the wild women of Hanno were gorillas.

*

HOUSE THAT JACK BUILT

ARAB HISTORY IS full of petty wars caused by trifles. In Egypt the clans Sa'ad and Harám and in Syria the Kays and Yaman (which remain to the present day) were as pugnacious as Highland Caterans. The tale bears some likeness to the accumulative nursery rhymes in "The House that Jack

Built," and "The Old Woman and the Crooked Sixpence;" which find their indirect original in an allegorical Talmudic hymn.

*

WOMEN CORRUPTING WOMEN

EASTERNS, I HAVE said, are perfectly aware of the fact that women corrupt women much more than men do. The tale is the "Story of the Libertine Husband" in the Book of Sindibad; blended with the "Story of the Go-between and the Bitch" in the Book of Sindibad. It is related in the "Disciplina Clericalis" of Alphonsus (A.D. 1106); the fabliau of *La vieille qui séduisit la jeune fille*; the Gesta Romanorum (thirteenth century) and the "Cunning Siddhikari" in the Kathá-Sarit-Ságara.

*

TREACHEROUS

THE KASHMÍR PEOPLE, men and women, have a very bad name in Eastern tales, the former for treachery and the latter for unchastity. A Persian distich says:

If folk be scarce as food in dearth ne'er let three lots come near ye:

First Sindi, second Jat, and third a rascally Kashmeeree.

The women have fair skins and handsome features but, like all living in that zone, Persians, Sindis, Afghans, etc., their bosoms fall after the first child and become like udders. This is not the case with Hindú women, Rajpúts, Maráthís, etc.

*

FATE AND FORTUNE

EASTERN TALE-TELLERS ALWAYS harp upon this theme, the cunning precautions taken by mankind and their utter confusion by "Fate and Fortune." In such matters the West remarks, "Ce que femme veut, Dieu veut."

*

PLEASING THE MISTRESS

At last he caught sight of a charming lady looking and leaning out of one of the windows, and being smitten with amazement at her grace and charms, cast about for a means of getting to her, but could find none.

As favourite an occupation in Oriental lands as in Southern Europe and the Brazil, where the Quinta or country villa must be built by the road-side to please the mistress.

*

SIGN OF THE SCRIBE

So he called up one of his pages, who brought him ink-case and paper and wrote her a letter, setting forth his condition for love of her. Then he set it on the pile-point of an arrow and shot it at the pavilion, and it fell in the garden, where the lady was then walking with her maidens.

The ink-case would contain the pens; hence called in India Kalamdán = reed (pen) box. I have advised travellers to prefer the strong Egyptian article of brass to the Persian, which is of wood or papier-mâché, prettily varnished, but not to wear it in the waist-belt, as this is a sign of being a scribe (Pilgrimage i. 353).

*

ROBED WITH THE SUN

THE VULGAR EASTERN idea is that women are quite knowing enough without learning to read and write: and at all events they should not be taught anything beyond reading the Koran, or some clearly-written book. The contrast with modern Europe is great; greater still in Anglo-America of our day, and greatest with the new sects which propose "biunes" and "bisexuals" and "women robed with the sun."

*

RICHARD BURTON

OF CURSED LIFE

THE CROW IS an ill-omened bird in Al-Islam and in Eastern Christendom. "The crow of cursed life and foul odour," says the Book of Kalilah and Dimna (p. 44). The Hindus are its only protectors, and in this matter they follow suit with the Guebres. I may note that the word belongs to the days before "Aryan" and "Semitic" speech had parted; we find it in Heb. Oreb; Arab. Ghuráb; Lat. Corvus; Engl. Crow, etc.

*

DRESSED TO DRINK

WHEN EASTERNS SIT down to a drinking bout, which means to get drunk as speedily and pleasantly as possible, they put off dresses of dull colours and robe themselves in clothes supplied by the host, of the brightest he may have, especially yellow, green and red of different shades. So the lady's proceeding was not likely to breed suspicion; although her tastes were somewhat fantastic and like Miss Julia's — peculiar.

*

OFFENSIVE MUCUS

ARAB. "NAJÁSAH," MEANING anything unclean which requires ablution before prayer. Unfortunately mucus is not of the

354

number, so the common Moslem is very offensive in the matter of nose.

*

THREE WISHES

THE MAC. EDIT. is here very concise; better the Bresl. Edit. (xii. 326). Here we have the Eastern form of the Three Wishes which dates from the earliest ages and which amongst us has been degraded to a matter of "black pudding." It is the grossest and most brutal satire on the sex, suggesting that a woman would prefer an additional inch of penis to anything this world or the next can offer her. In the Book of Sindibad it is the story of the Peri and Religious Man; his learning the Great Name; and his consulting with his wife. See also La Fontaine's "Trois Souhaits," Prior's "Ladle," and "Les quatre Souhaits de Saint-Martin."

*

NIGHT OF POWER

ARAB. "LAYLAT AL-KADR" = Night of Power or of Divine Decrees. It is "better than a thousand months" (Koran xcvii. 3), but unhappily the exact time is not known although all agree that it is one of the last ten in Ramazan. The latter when named by Kiláb ibn Murrah, ancestor of Mohammed, about two centuries before Al-Islam, corresponded with July-August and took its name from "Ramzá" or intense heat. But the Prophet, in the tenth Hijrah year, most unwisely forbade "Nasy" = triennial intercalation (Koran ix. 36) and thus the lunar month went round all the seasons. On the Night of Power the Koran was sent down from the Preserved Tablet by Allah's throne, to the first or lunar Heaven whence Gabriel brought it for opportunest revelation to the Apostle (Koran xcvii.). Also during this night all Divine Decrees for the ensuing year are taken from the Tablet and are given to the angels for execution whilst, the gates of Heaven being open, prayer (as in the text) is sure of success. This mass of absurdity has engendered a host of superstitions everywhere varying. Lane (Mod. Egypt, chapt. xxv.) describes how some of the Faithful keep tasting a cup of salt water which should become sweet in the Night of Nights. In (Moslem) India not only the sea becomes sweet, but all the vegetable creation bows down before Allah. The exact time is known only to Prophets; but the pious sit through the Night of Ramazan 27th (our 26th) praying and burning incense-pastilles. In Stambul this is officially held to be the Night of Power. So in mediæval Europe on Christmas Eve the cattle worshipped God in their stalls and I have met peasants in France and Italy who firmly believed that brute beasts on that night not only speak but predict the events of the coming year.

*

KISSING BREAD

One day as he sat upon the bench before his door, there came up a grizzled crone, as she were a snake speckled white and black, calling aloud on the name of Allah, magnifying Him inordinately and, at the same time, putting away the stones and other obstacles from the path.

This is done only by the very pious: if they see a bit of bread they kiss it, place it upon their heads and deposit it upon a wall or some place where it will not be trodden on. She also removed the stones lest haply they prove stumbling-blocks to some Moslem foot.

*

PEEKING BENEATH

ARAB. "KINÁ'," A true veil, not the "Burka'" or "nose-bag" with the peepholes. It is opposed to the "Tarkah" or "head-veil." Europeans inveigh against the veil which represents the *loup* of Louis Quatorze's day: it is on the contrary the most coquettish of contrivances, hiding coarse skins, fleshy noses, wide mouths and vanishing chins; and showing only lustrous and liquid black eyes. Moreover a pretty woman, when she wishes, will always let you see something under the veil. (Pilgrimage i. 337).

*

RICHARD BURTON

SEA-FLEAS

Asked the other, "How can that be?"; and the Shaykh answered, "What if he say, I will take the measure full of gold or silver, wilt thou give it to him?" "Yes," replied the other, "I will give it to him and still be the gainer." And the Shaykh answered, "And if he say, I will take the measure full of fleas, half male and half female, what wilt thou do?" So the sharper knew that he was worsted.

The idea would readily occur in Egypt where the pulex is still a plague although the Sultan is said to hold his court at Tiberias. "Male and female" says the rogue, otherwise it would be easy to fill a bushel with fleas. The insect was unknown to older India according to some and was introduced by strangers. This immigration is quite possible. In 1863 the jigger (*P. penetrans*) was not found in Western Africa; when I returned there in 1882 it had passed over from the Brazil and had become naturalised on the equatorial African seaboard. The Arabs call shrimps and prawns "sea-fleas" (bargúth al-bahr) showing an inland race. (See Pilgrimage i. 322.)

*

IMPROBABLE TALES

THE USUAL FORMULA when telling an improbable tale. But here it is hardly called for: the same story is told (on weak authority) of the Alewife, the Three Graziers and Attorney-General Nay (temp. James II. 1577–1634) when five years old (Journ. Asiat. Soc. N.S. xxx. 280). The same feat had been credited to Thomas Egerton, Lord Chancellor in A.D. 1540–1617 (Chalmers, Biographical Dictionary xxiii. 267–68). But the story had already found its way into the popular jest-books such as "Tales and Quick Answers, very Mery and Pleasant to Rede" (1530); "Jacke of Dover's Quest of Inquirie for the Foole of all Fooles" (1604) under the title "The Foole of Westchester", and in "Witty and Entertaining Exploits of George Buchanan, commonly called the King's Fool." The banker-bard Rogers (in Italy) was told a similar story concerning a widow of the Lambertini house (xiv[th] century). Thomas Wright (Introduction to the Seven Sages) says he had met the tale in Latin (xiii[th]-xiv[th] centuries) and a variant in the "Nouveaux Contes à rire" (Amsterdam 1737), under the title "Jugement Subtil du Duc d'Ossone contre Deux Marchands." Its origin is evidently the old Sindibád-namah translated from Syriac into Greek ("Syntipas," xi[th] century); into Hebrew (Mishlé Sandabar, xii[th] century), and from the Arabian version into old Castilian, "Libro de los Engannos et los Asayamientos de las Mugeres" (A.D. 1255), whereof a translation is appended to Professor Comparetti's "Ricerche intorne al Libro di Sindibad," translated by Mr. H. C. Coote for the Folk-Lore Society. The Persian metrical form (an elaboration of one much older) dates from 1375; and gave rise to a host of imitations such as the Turkish Tales of the Forty Wazirs and the Canarese "Kathá Manjari," where four persons contend about a purse. See also Gladwin's "Persian

Moonshee," No. vi. of "Pleasing Stories;" and Mr. Clouston's paper, "The Lost Purse," in the *Glasgow Evening Times*. All are the Eastern form of Gavarni's "Enfants Terribles," showing the portentous precocity for which some children (infant phenomena, calculating boys, etc. etc.) have been famous.

*

PEOPLE OF MAGIC

PLUR. OF MAGHRIBÍ, a Western man, a Moor. I have already derived the word through the Lat. "Maurus" from Maghribiyún. Europeans being unable to pronounce the Ghayn (or gh like the modern Cairenes) would turn it into "Ma'ariyún." They are mostly of the Maliki school (for which see Sale) and are famous as magicians and treasure-finders. Amongst the suite of the late Amir Abd al-Kadir, who lived many years and died in Damascus, I found several men profoundly versed in Eastern spiritualism and occultism.

*

THE HATCHET

ARAB. "FÁS AND Miknás" which the writer evidently regards as one city. "Fás" means a hatchet, from the tradition of one having been found, says Ibn Sa'id, when digging the base under the founder Idrís bin Idrís (A.D. 808). His sword was placed on the pinnacle of the minaret built by the Imám Abu

Ahmad bin Abi Bakr enclosed in a golden étui studded with pearls and precious stones. From the local pronunciation "Fes" is derived the red cap of the nearer Moslem East (see Ibn Batutah p. 230).

*

SPICED CLOTH

ARAB. "BUKJAH," FROM the Persian Bukcheh: a favourite way of keeping fine clothes in the East is to lay them folded in a piece of rough long-cloth with pepper and spices to drive away moths.

*

FOOT-BACK

So he rose and they went afoot without the city, where they found two slaves, each holding a she-mule.

This is always specified, for respectable men go out of town on horse-back, never on "foot-back," as our friends the Boers say. I have seen a Syrian put to sore shame when compelled by politeness to walk with me, and every acquaintance he met addressed him, "Anta Zalamah!" — What! afoot!

*

RICHARD BURTON

GENDER OF LANGUAGE

*But she thought he was laughing at her and making mock of
her; so she said to him, "Yauh! Yauh! [284] what is come to
thee? Dost thou dream or art thou daft?"*

Equivalent to our Alas! It is woman's word never used by
men; and foreigners must be most careful of this distinction
under pain of incurring something worse than ridicule.
I remember an officer in the Bombay Army who, having
learned Hindostani from women, always spoke of himself in
the feminine and hugely scandalised the Sepoys.

*

NO PARADISE

A MOSLEM PRISON is like those of Europe a century ago; to
think of it gives goose-bumps. Easterns laugh at our idea of
penitentiary and the Arabs of Bombay call it "Al-Bistán" (the
Garden) because the court contains a few trees and shrubs.
And with them a garden always suggests an idea of Paradise.
There are indeed only two efficacious forms of punishment
all the world over, corporal for the poor and fines for the
rich, the latter being the severer form.

*

362

TYPES OF THIEVERY

Eastern thieves count four modes of housebreaking; (1) picking out burnt bricks; (2) cutting through unbaked bricks; (3) wetting a mud wall and (4) boring through a wooden wall (Vikram and the Vampire p. 172).

*

MACES

Arab. "Dabbús." The Eastern mace is well known to English collectors; it is always of metal, and mostly of steel, with a short handle like our facetiously called "life-preserver." The head is in various forms, the simplest a ball, smooth and round, or broken into sundry high and angular ridges like a melon, and in select weapons shaped like the head of some animal, bull, etc. See Night dcxlvi.

*

WHITE DEATH

So the Wazir laid down his arms and donning a white habit, took a rosary in his hand and set out afoot alone and unattended.

The red habit is a sign of wrath and vengeance and the Persian Kings like Fath Ali Shah, used to wear it when about to order some horrid punishment, such as the "Shakk";

in this a man was hung up by his heels and cut in two from the fork downwards to the neck, when a turn of the chopper left that untouched. White robes denoted peace and mercy as well as joy. The "white" hand and "black" hand have been explained. A "white death" is quiet and natural, with forgiveness of sins. A "black death" is violent and dreadful, as by strangulation: a "green death" is robing in rags and patches like a dervish; and a "red death" is by war or bloodshed (A. P. ii. 670). Among the mystics it is the resistance of man to his passions.

*

ARTISTIC EFFECT

I HAVE NOTED that as a rule in The Nights poetical justice is administered with much rigour and exactitude. Here, however, the tale-teller allows the good brother to be slain by the two wicked brothers as he permitted the adulterous queens to escape the sword of Kamar al-Zaman. Dr. Steingass brings to my notice that I have failed to do justice to the story of Sharrkán (vol. ii., p. 172), where I note that the interest is injured by the gratuitous incest. But this has a deeper meaning and a grander artistic effect. Sharrkán begins with most unbrotherly feelings towards his father's children by a second wife. But Allah's decree forces him to love his half-sister despite himself, and awe and repentance convert the savage, who joys at the news of his brother's reported death, to a loyal and devoted subject of the same brother. But Judar with all his goodness proved himself an arrant softy and was no match for two atrocious villains. And there may be overmuch of forgiveness as of every other good thing.

*

WHAT IS TO COME

VON HAMMER HOLDS this story to be a satire on Arab superstition and the compulsory propagation, the *compelle intrare*, of Al-Islam. Lane (iii. 235) omits it altogether for reasons of his own. I differ with great diffidence from the learned Baron whose Oriental reading was extensive; but the tale does not seem to justify his explanations. It appears to me simply one of the wilder romances, full of purposeful anachronisms (*e.g.* dated between Abraham and Moses, yet quoting the Koran) and written by someone familiar with the history of Oman. The style too is peculiar, in many places so abrupt that much manipulation is required to make it presentable: it suits, however, the rollicking, violent, brigand-like life which it depicts. There is only one incident about the end which justifies Von Hammer's suspicion.

*

LYNXING

Now behold, one day, there came horsemen and footmen into the forest with hawks and hounds and horses laden with

partridges and cranes and wild geese and divers and other
waterfowl; and young ostriches and hares and gazelles and
wild oxen and lynxes and wolves and lions.

The game is much mixed up after Arab fashion. The "Tufat"
is the Siyáhgosh = Black-ears, of India (*Felis caracal*), the
Persian lynx, which gives very good sport with Dachshunds.
Lynxes still abound in the thickets near Cairo.

*

SONS OF THE SAND

THE BADAWI USE javelins or throw-spears of many kinds,
especially the prettily worked Mizrák (Pilgrimage i. 349);
spears for footmen (Shalfah, a bamboo or palm-stick with
a head about a hand broad), and the knightly lance, a male
bamboo some 12 feet long with iron heel and a long tapering
point often of open work or damascened steel, under which
are tufts of black ostrich feathers, one or two. I never saw a
crescent-shaped head as the text suggests. It is a "Pundonor"
not to sell these weapons: you say, "Give me that article and
I will satisfy thee!" After which the Sons of the Sand will
haggle over each copper as if you were cheapening a sheep
(Ibid. iii. 73).

*

MARE'S SKIN

So CALLED FROM the flavour of the kernel: it is well-known at Damascus where a favourite fruit is the dried apricot with an almond by way of kernel. There are many preparations of apricots, especially the "Mare's skin" (Jild al-faras or Kamar al-din) a paste folded into sheets and exactly resembling the article from which it takes a name. When wanted it is dissolved in water and eaten as a relish with bread or biscuit (Pilgrimage i. 289).

*

PRETEND CANNIBALS

Thereupon Sa'adan cried to his slaves, saying, "Take this fatted calf and roast him quickly." So they hastened to skin the Infidel and roasted him and brought him to the Ghul, who ate his flesh and crunched his bones.

This manœuvre has often been practised; especially by the first Crusaders under Bohemond (Gibbon) and in late years by the Arab slavers in Eastern Intertropical Africa. After their skirmishes with the natives they quartered and "brittled" the dead like game, roasted and boiled the choice pieces and pretended to eat the flesh. The enemy, who was not afraid of death, was struck with terror by the idea of being devoured; and this seems instinctive to the undeveloped mind.

RICHARD BURTON

*

HUNG BY THE HEELS

As has been seen, acids have ever been and are still administered as counter-inebriants, while hot spices and sweets greatly increase the effect of Bhang, opium, henbane, datura, &c. The Persians have a most unpleasant form of treating men when dead-drunk with wine or spirits. They hang them up by the heels, as we used to do with the drowned, and stuff their mouths with human ordure which is sure to produce emesis.

*

RIVER OF BLOOD

The battle waxed fierce and fell, the blood ran in rills, nor did they cease to wage war with lunge of lance and sway of sword in lustiest way, till the day darkened and the night starkened, when the drums beat the retreat and the two hosts drew asunder.

Compare with this and other Arab battle-pieces the Pandit's description in the Kathá Sarit Sagara, *e.g.* "Then a confused battle arose with dint of arrow, javelin, lance, mace and axe, costing the lives of countless soldiers (N.B. — Millions are nothing to him); rivers of blood flowed with the bodies of elephants and horses for alligators, with the pearls from the heads of elephants for sands and with the heads of heroes for stones. That feast of battle delighted the flesh-loving demons who, drunk with blood instead of wine, were dancing with the palpitating trunks," etc., etc. Fasc. xii. 526.

*

OF THE ANTELOPES

Now the Moslems were evilly entreated that day by reason of the riders on elephants and giraffes, and many of them were killed and most of the rest were wounded.

The giraffe is here mal-placé: it is, I repeat, one of the most timid of the antelope tribe. Nothing can be more graceful than this huge game as it stands under a tree extending its long and slender neck to the foliage above it; but when in flight all the limbs seem loose and the head is carried almost on a level with the back.

*

BESTIAL ARMS

THE FIRE-ARMS may have been inserted by the copier; the cross-bow (Arcubalista) is of unknown antiquity. I have remarked in my book of the Sword (p. 19) that the bow is the first crucial evidence of the distinction between the human weapon and the bestial arm, and like the hymen or membrane of virginity proves a difference of degree if not of kind between man and the so-called lower animals. I note from Yule's Marco Polo (ii., 143) "that the crossbow was re-introduced into European warfare during the twelfth century"; but the arbalest was well known to the *bon roi* Charlemagne (Regnier Sat. X).

*

PARROT-SEEDS

ARAB. "AL-WARS," WITH two meanings. The Alfáz Adwiyah gives it = Kurkum, curcuma, turmeric, safran d'Inde; but popular usage assigns it to Usfur, Kurtum or safflower (*carthamus tinctorius*). I saw the shrub growing all about Harar which exports it, and it is plentiful in Al-Yaman (Niebuhr, p. 133), where women affect it to stain the skin a light yellow and remove freckles: it is also an internal remedy in leprosy. But the main use is that of a dye, and the Tob stained with Wars is almost universal in some parts of Arabia. Sonnini (p. 510) describes it at length and says that Europeans in Egypt call it "Parrot-seeds" because the bird loves it, and the Levant trader "Saffrenum."

*

CONGRESS WITH A CROCODILE

THE GARDEN

EVERY EASTERN CITY has its special title. Al-Medinah is entitled "Al-Munawwarah" (the Illumined) from the blinding light which surrounds the Prophet's tomb and which does not show to eyes profane (Pilgrimage ii. 3). I presume that the idea arose from the huge lamps of "The Garden." I have noted that Mohammed's coffin suspended by magnets is an idea unknown to Moslems, but we find the fancy in Al-Harawi related of St. Peter, "Simon Cephas (the rock) is in the City of Great Rome, in its largest church within a silver ark hanging by chains from the ceiling." (Lee, Ibn Batutah, p. 161).

*

TRANSFERENCE

So I repaired thither, and, behold, over the grave was a tall tree, on which hung fillets of red and green and yellow stuffs.

Here the fillets are hung instead of the normal rag-strips to denote an honoured tomb. Lane (iii. 242) and many others are puzzled about the use of these articles. In many cases they are suspended to trees in order to transfer sickness from the body to the tree and whoever shall touch it. The Sawáhílí people term such articles a Keti (seat or vehicle) for the mysterious haunter of the tree who prefers occupying it to the patient's person. Briefly the custom still popular throughout Arabia, is African and Fetish.

371

RICHARD BURTON

*

TENT ARCHITECTURE

THE TENTS OF black wool woven by the Badawi women are generally supported by three parallel rows of poles lengthways and crossways (the highest line being the central) and the covering is pegged down. Thus the outline of the roofs forms two or more hanging curves, and these characterise the architecture of the Tartars and Chinese; they are still preserved in the Turkish (and sometimes in the European) "Kiosque," and they have extended to the Brazil where the upturned eaves, often painted vermilion below, at once attract the traveller's notice.

*

FATHER OF BITTERNESS

They replied, "What old man? By Allah, no one hath gone in to thee this day!" So I returned pondering the matter, when, behold, there arose from one of the corners of the house, a Vox et præterea nihil, saying, "O Abu Ishak, no harm shall befal thee. 'Tis I, Abú Murrah, who have been thy cup-companion this day, so fear nothing!"

i.e. Father of Bitterness = the Devil. This legend of the Foul Fiend appearing to Ibrahim of Mosul (and also to Isam, N. dcxcv.) seems to have been accepted by contemporaries and

372

reminds us of similar visitations in Europe — notably to Dr. Faust. One can only exclaim, "Lor, papa, what nonsense you are talking!" the words of a small girl whose father thought proper to indoctrinate her into certain Biblical stories. I once began to write a biography of the Devil; but I found that European folk-lore had made such an unmitigated fool of the grand old Typhon-Ahriman as to take away from him all human interest.

*

HOBBLING

TYING UP THE near foreleg just above the knee; and even with this a camel can hop over sundry miles of ground in the course of a night. The hobbling is shown in Lane (Nights vol. ii., p. 46).

*

WHEN AND HOW TO DRINK

WE DRINK (OR drank) after dinner; Easterns before the meal and half-Easterns (like the Russians) before and after. We talk of liquor being unwholesome on an empty stomach; but the truth is that all is purely habit. And as the Russian accompanies his Vodki with caviare, etc., so the Oriental drinks his Raki or Mahayá (Ma al-hayát — aqua vitæ) alternately with a Salátah, for whose composition see

Pilgrimage i. 198. The Eastern practice has its advantages: it awakens the appetite, stimulates digestion and, what Easterns greatly regard, it is economical; half a bottle doing the work of a whole. Bhang and Kusumbá (opium dissolved and strained through a pledget of cotton) are always drunk before dinner and thus the "jolly" time is the preprandial, not the postprandial.

*

THE JOY OF RAIN

THOSE WHO LIVE in the wet climates of the Northern temperates can hardly understand the delight of a shower in rainless lands, like Arabia and Nubia. In Sind we used to strip and stand in the downfall and raise faces sky-wards to get the full benefit of the douche. In Southern Persia food is hastily cooked at such times, wine strained, Kaliuns made ready and horses saddled for a ride to the nearest gardens and a happy drinking-bout under the cypresses. If a man refused, his friends would say of him, "See how he turns his back upon the blessing of Allah!" (like an ass which presents its tail to the weather).

*

IN REVERENCE

HE WAS WAZIR to the Great "Saladin" (Saláh al-Din = one conforming with the Faith): see vol. iv. 271, where Saladin is

also entitled al-Malik al-Nasir = the Conquering King. He
was a Kurd and therefore fond of boys (like Virgil, Horace,
etc.), but that perversion did not prevent his being one of
the noblest of men. He lies in the Great Amawi Mosque of
Damascus and I never visited a tomb with more reverence.

*

REFERENCING

*Then she walked on and Khatun after her, followed by the
young merchant, till she came to a dyery, kept by a master
dyer, by name Hajj Mohammed, a man of ill-repute; like the
colocasia seller's knife cutting male and female, and loving to
eat both figs and pomegranates.*

See vol. iii. 302. The figs refer to the anus and the
pomegranates, like the sycomore, to the female parts. Me
nec fæmina nec puer, &c., says Horace in pensive mood.

*

WHORES BY THE HEELS

BURCKHARDT NOTES THAT the Wali, or chief police officer
at Cairo, was exclusively termed Al-Agha and quotes the
proverb (No. 156) "One night the whore repented and
cried: — What! no Wali (Al-Aghá) to lay whores by the
heels?" Some of these Egyptian by-words are most amusing

and characteristic; but they require literal translation, not the timid touch of the last generation. I am preparing, for the use of my friend, Bernard Quaritch, a bonâ fide version which awaits only the promised volume of Herr Landberg.

*

PLUNDERING

Answered the old woman, "O my lady, an hundred of them are thine, under the sherbet-gugglet whereof thou drinkest, and the other hundred do thou keep for me against I come back," presently adding, "Now let me out by the private door."

A delicate way of offering a fee. When officers commanding regiments in India contracted for clothing the men, they found these douceurs under their dinner-napkins. All that is now changed; but I doubt the change being an improvement: the public is plundered by a "Board" instead of an individual.

*

CEREMONY AND ETIQUETTE

So IN THE Brazil you are invited to drink a *copa d'agua* and find a splendid banquet. There is a smack of Chinese ceremony in this practice which lingers throughout southern Europe; but the less advanced society is, the more it is fettered by ceremony and "etiquette."

*

STRAW-DEATH

Arab. Ghandúr for which the Dictionaries give only "fat, thick." It applies in Arabia especially to a Harámi, brigand or freebooter, most honourable of professions, slain in foray or fray, opposed to "Fatís" or carrion (the *corps créé* of the Klephts), the man who dies the straw-death. Pilgrimage iii. 66.

*

FLIRTATION

To whom dost thou belong?"; and quoth she, "To the gallant like thee;" and he said, "Art thou wife or spinster?" "Married," said she. Asked Ali, "Shall it be in my lodging or thine?" and she answered, "I am a merchant's daughter and a merchant's wife and in all my life I have never been out of doors till to-day, and my only reason was that when I made ready food and thought to eat, I had no mind thereto without company.

My fair readers will note with surprise how such matters are hurried in the East. The picture is, however, true to life in lands where "flirtation" is utterly unknown and, indeed, impossible.

*

RICHARD BURTON

TOTAL ABLUTION

ARAB. "IHTILÁM," THE sign of puberty in boy or girl; this, like all emissions of semen, voluntary or involuntary, requires the Ghuzl or total ablution before prayers can be said, etc. See vol. v. 199, in the Tale of Tawaddud.

*

DIFFERING HUES

THE CONJUNCTIVA IN Africans is seldom white; often it is red and more frequently yellow.

*

TENSIONS

THE SLIGHTEST MOVEMENT causes a fight at a funeral or a wedding-procession in the East; even amongst the "mild Hindus."

*

FRENCH LETTERS

ARAB. "AL-MUSRÁN" (PLUR. of "Masír") properly the intestines which contain the chyle. The bag made by Ali was, in fact, a "Cundum" (so called from the inventor, Colonel Cundum of the Guards in the days of Charles Second) or "French letter"; une capote anglaise, a "check upon child." Captain Grose says (Class. Dict. etc. s.v. Cundum) "The dried gut of a sheep worn by a man in the act of coition to prevent venereal infection. These machines were long prepared and sold by a matron of the name of Philips at the Green Canister in Half Moon Street in the Strand * * * Also a false scabbard over a sword and the oilskin case for the colours of a regiment." Another account is given in the Guide Pratique des Maladies Secrètes, Dr. G. Harris, Bruxelles. Librairie Populaire. He calls these petits sachets de baudruche "Candoms, from the doctor who invented them." (Littré ignores the word) and declares that the famous Ricord compared them with a bad umbrella which a storm can break or burst, while others term them cuirasses against pleasure and cobwebs against infection. They were much used in the last century. "Those pretended stolen goods were Mr. Wilkes's Papers, many of which tended to prove his authorship of the North Briton, No. 45, April 23, 1763, and some *Cundums* enclosed in an envelope" (Records of C. of King's Bench, London, 1763). "Pour finir l'inventaire de ces curiosités du cabinet de Madame Gourdan, il ne faut pas omettre une multitude de *redingottes* appelées *d'Angleterre*, je ne sais pourquois. Vous connoissez, au surplus, ces espèces de boucliers qu'on oppose aux traits empoisonnés de l'amour; et qui n'emoussent que ceux du plaisir." (L'Observateur Anglois, Londres 1778, iii. 69). Again we read: —

"Les capotes mélancoliques
Qui pendent chez les gros Millan (?)
S'enflent d'elles-mêmes, lubriques,

Et dechargent en se gonflant."
Passage Satyrique.

Also in Louis Prolat: —
"Il fuyait, me laissant une capote au cul."
The articles are now of two kinds mostly of baudruche
(sheep's gut) and a few of caoutchouc. They are made almost
exclusively in the faubourgs of Paris, giving employment
to many women and young girls; Grenelle turns out
the baudruche and Grenelle and Lilas the India-rubber
article; and of the three or four makers M. Deschamps is
best known. The sheep's gut is not joined in any way but
of single piece as it comes from the animal after, of course,
much manipulation to make it thin and supple; the inferior
qualities are stuck together at the sides. Prices vary from 4½
to 36 francs per gross. Those of India-rubber are always
joined at the side with a solution especially prepared for
the purpose. I have also heard of fish-bladders but can
give no details on the subject. The Cundum was unknown
to the ancients of Europe although syphilis was not: even
prehistoric skeletons show traces of its ravages.

*

BUFFOONS

ARAB. "KHALBÚS," PROP. the servant of the Almah-girls who
acts buffoon as well as pimp. The "Maskharah" (whence
our "mask") corresponds with the fool or jester of mediæval

CONGRESS WITH A CROCODILE

Europe: amongst the Arnauts he is called "Suttari" and is known by his fox's tails: he mounts a mare, tom-toms on the kettle-drum and is generally one of the bravest of the corps. These buffoons are noted for extreme indecency: they generally appear in the ring provided with an enormous phallus of whip-cord and with this they charge man, woman and child, to the infinite delight of the public.

*

CUSTOMS OF DOGS

EVERY TRAVELLER DESCRIBES the manners and customs of dogs in Eastern cities where they furiously attack all canine intruders. I have noticed the subject in writing of Al-Medinah where the beasts are confined to the suburbs (Pilgrimage ii. 52–54).

*

ARK OF THE COVENANT

ARAB. "TÁBÚT," A term applied to the Ark of the Covenant (Koran ii. 349), which contained Moses' rod and shoes, Aaron's mitre, the manna-pot, the broken Tables of the Law, and the portraits of all the prophets which are to appear till the end of time — an extensive list for a box measuring 3 by cubits. Europeans often translate it coffin, but it is properly the wooden case placed over an honoured grave. "Irán" is the Ark of Moses' exposure, also the large hearse on which tribal chiefs were carried to earth.

*

ANNOUNCING SEPARATION

ARAB. TÁIR AL-BAYN, any bird, not only the Hátim or black crow, which announces separation. Crows and ravens flock for food to the camps broken up for the springtide and autumnal marches, and thus become emblems of desertion and desolation. The same birds are also connected with Abel's burial in the Koran (v. 34), a Jewish tradition borrowed by Mohammed. Lastly, here is a paronomasia in the words "Ghuráb al-Bayn" = Raven of the Wold (the black bird with white breast and red beak and legs): "Ghuráb" (Heb. Oreb) connects with Cuba = strangerhood, exile, and "Bayn" with distance, interval, disunion, the desert (between the cultivated spots). There is another and a similar pun anent the Bán-tree; the first word meaning "he fared, he left."

*

BROKEN HEART OF APPLE-FLAVOUR

ARAB. "KAANNAHU HUWA"; lit. = as he (was) he. This reminds us of the great grammarian, Sibawayh, whose name the Persians derive from "Apple-flavour" (Sib + BA). He was disputing, in presence of Harun al-Rashid with a rival Al-Kiss, and advocated the Bastian form, "Fa-izá huwa hú" (behold, it was he) against the Ku fan, "Fa-izá huwa IA" (behold, it was him). The enemy overcame him by appealing to Badawin, who spoke impurely, whereupon Sibawayh left the court, retired to Khorasan and died, it is said of a broken heart.

*

MEDICINAL OILS

IN DICTIONARIES "BÁN" (Anglice ben-tree) is the myrobalan which produces gum benzoin. It resembles the tamarisk. Mr. Lyall (p. 74 Translations of Ancient Arab Poetry, Williams and Norgate, 1885), calls it a species of Moringa, tall, with plentiful and intensely green foliage used for comparisons on account of its straightness and graceful shape of its branches. The nut supplies a medicinal oil.

*

POWERFUL ODOURS

Then she stripped him and painted him with Henna...

The same traveller notes a singular property in the Henna-flower that when smelt closely it exhales a "very powerful spermatic odour," hence it became a favourite with women as the tea-rose with us. He finds it on the nails of mummies, and identifies it with the Kupros of the ancient Greeks (the moderns call it Kene or Kena) and the Βότρυς τῆς κύπρου (Botrus cypri) of Solomon's Song (i. 14). The Hebr. is "Copher," a well-known word which the A. V. translates by "a cluster of camphire (?) in the vineyards of En-gedi"; and a note on iv. 13 ineptly adds, "or, cypress." The Revised Edit. amends it to "a cluster of henna-flowers." The Solomonic (?) description is very correct; the shrub affects vineyards, and about Bombay forms fine hedges which can be smelt from a distance.

*

PAINTING PATCHES

...from his nails to his shoulders and from his insteps to his thighs and tattooed him about the body, till he was like red roses upon alabaster slabs.

Hardly the equivalent of the Arab. "Kataba" (which includes true tattooing with needles) and is applied to painting "patches" of blue or green colour, with sprigs and arabesques upon the arms and especially the breasts of women. "Kataba" would also be applied to striping the fingers with Henna which becomes a shining black under a paste of honey, lime and sal-ammoniac. This "patching" is alluded to by Strabo and Galen (Lane M. E. chapt ii.); and we may note that savages and barbarians can leave nothing of beauty unadorned; they seem to hate a plain surface like the Hindu silversmith, whose art is shown only in chasing.

CONGRESS WITH A CROCODILE

*

PECULIAR LEATHER

A VIOLENT TEMPER, accompanied with *voies de fait* and personal violence, is by no means rare amongst Eastern princesses; and terrible tales are told in Persia concerning the daughters of Fath Ali Shah. Few men and no woman can resist the temptations of absolute command. The daughter of a certain Dictator all-powerful in the Argentine Republic was once seen on horseback with a white bridle of peculiar leather; it was made of the skin of a man who had boasted of her favours. The slave-girls suffer first from these masterful young persons and then it is the turn of the eunuchry.

*

SLAVE-GIRLS

She said, It hath reached me, O auspicious King, that the King after taking the maiden, committed her to the tire-women bidding them amend her case and set her in a bower, and ordered his chamberlains to shut all the doors upon her when they had lodged her in a chamber whose latticed casements overlooked the main. Then Shahriman went in to her; but she spake not to him neither took any note of him.

These pretentious and curious displays of coquetry are not uncommon in handsome slave-girls when newly bought;

and it is a kind of pundonor to humour them. They may also refuse their favours and a master who took possession of their persons by brute force would be blamed by his friends, men and women. Even the most despotic of despots, Fath Ali Shah of Persia, put up with refusals from his slave-girls and did not, as would the mean-minded, marry them to the grooms or cooks of the palace.

*

LOST VALUE

So he loved her with exceeding love and falling upon her, took her maidenhead and found her a pure virgin; whereat he rejoiced with excessive joy and said in himself, "By Allah, 'tis a wonder that a girl so fair of form and face should have been left by the merchants a clean maid as she is!"

Such continence is rarely shown by the young Jallabs or slave-traders; when older they learn how much money is lost with the chattel's virginity.

*

DIVINATIONS

MIDWIVES IN THE East, as in the less civilised parts of the West, have many nostrums for divining the sex of the unborn child.

*

A PRIME GLORY OF RACE

ARABIC (WHICH HAS no written "g") from Pers. Gulnár (Gul-i-anár) pomegranate-flower, the "Gulnare" of Byron who learnt his Orientalism at the Mekhitarist (Armenian) Convent, Venice. I regret to see the little honour now paid to the gallant poet in the land where he should be honoured the most. The systematic depreciation was begun by the late Mr. Thackeray, perhaps the last man to value the noble independence of Byron's spirit; and it has been perpetuated, I regret to see, by better judges. These critics seem wholly to ignore the fact that Byron founded a school which covered Europe from Russia to Spain, from Norway to Sicily, and which from England passed over to the two Americas. This exceptional success, which has not yet fallen even to Shakespeare's lot, was due to genius only, for the poet almost ignored study and poetic art. His great misfortune was being born in England under the Georgium Sidus. Any Continental people would have regarded him as one of the prime glories of his race.

*

HURCULEAN LABOURS

I HAVE ALREADY noted that the heroes and heroines of Eastern love-tales are always *bonnes fourchettes*: they eat and drink hard enough to scandalise the sentimental amourist of the West; but it is understood that this abundant diet is necessary to qualify them for the Herculean labours of the love night

*

SOLOMON'S RING

THE OATH BY the Seal-ring of Solomon was the Stygian "swear" in Fairy-land. The signet consisted of four jewels, presented by as many angels, representing the Winds, the Birds, Earth (including sea) and Spirits, and the gems were inscribed with as many sentences (1) To Allah belong Majesty and Might; (2) All created things praise the Lord; (3) Heaven and Earth are Allah's slaves and (4) There is no god but *the* God and Mohammed is His messenger. For Sakhr and his theft of the signet see Dr. Weil's, "The Bible, the Koran, and the Talmud."

*

EATING FIRST

So they obeyed him and the Wazir Faris and some of his intimates sat down, whilst certain of the lesser sort remained afoot to wait on him. When they had sat awhile, the servants spread the tables and they all, men and beasts, ate their sufficiency.

This is in accordance with Eastern etiquette; the guest must be fed before his errand is asked. The Porte, in the days of its pride, managed in this way sorely to insult the Ambassadors of the most powerful European kingdoms and the first French Republic had the honour of abating the barbarians' nuisance. So the old Scottish Highlanders never asked the name or clan of a chance guest, lest he prove a foe before he had eaten their food.

*

ONIONS

ARAB. "TAKLIYAH" FROM kaly, a fry: Lane's Shaykh explained it as "onions cooked in clarified butter, after which they are put upon other cooked food." The mention of onions points to Egypt as the origin of this tale and certainly not to Arabia, where the strong-smelling root is hated.

*

REAL DANGER

The apes came down and surrounded him; then they forewent him, signing to him to follow them, and walked on, and he too, till he came to a castle, tall of base and strong of build whose ordinance was one brick of gold and one of silver.

He had ample reason to be frightened. The large Cynocephalus is exceedingly dangerous. When travelling on the Gold Coast with my late friend Colonel De Ruvignes, we suddenly came in the grey of the morning upon a herd of these beasts. We dismounted, hobbled our nags and sat down, sword and revolver in hand. Luckily it was feeding time for the vicious brutes, which scowled at us but did not attack us. During my four years' service on the West African Coast I heard enough to satisfy me that these powerful beasts often kill men and rape women; but I could not convince myself that they ever kept the women as concubines.

*

TRANSFORMED INTO MONKEYS

Quoth the youth, "This is their custom. Every Sabbath, all the apes in the island come hither, some from two and three days' distance, and stand here till I awake from sleep and put forth my head from this lattice, when they kiss ground before me and go about their business.

As Trébutien shows (ii. 155) these apes were a remnant of some ancient tribe possibly those of Ád who had gone to Meccah to pray for rain and thus escaped the general destruction. See vol. i. 65. Perhaps they were the Jews of Aylah who in David's day were transformed into monkeys for fishing on the Sabbath (Saturday). Koran ii. 61.

*

PLUCKING THE EYES

We believed him so fared on, as he bade us, till we came to the cavern, where we found many guests, Sons of Adam like ourselves, but they were all blinded; and when we entered, one said, "I'm sick"; and another, "I'm weak."

Probably alluding to the most barbarous Persian practice of plucking or tearing out the eyes from their sockets. See Sir John Malcolm's description of the capture of Kirmán and Morier (in Zohrab, the hostage) for the wholesale blinding of the Asterabadian by the Eunuch-King Agha Mohammed Shah. I may note that the mediæval Italian practice called *bacinare*, or scorching with red-hot basins, came from Persia.

*

OF EASTERN ORIGIN

In Trébutien (ii. 168) the cannibal is called "Goul Eli-Fenioun" and Von Hammer remarks, "There is no need of such likeness of name to prove that all this episode is a manifest imitation of the adventures of Ulysses in Polyphemus' cave; * * * and this induces the belief that the Arabs have been acquainted with the poems of Homer." Living intimately with the Greeks they could not have ignored the Iliad and the Odyssey: indeed we know by tradition that they had translations, now apparently lost. I

391

cannot however, accept Lane's conjecture that "the story of Ulysses and Polyphemus may have been of Eastern origin." Possibly the myth came from Egypt, for I have shown that the opening of the Iliad bears a suspicious likeness to the proem of Pentaur's Epic.

*

ALCHEMY

So she questioned him and he told her what had passed between himself and the Persian, which when she heard, her heart fluttered and she strained him to her bosom, saying, "O my son, beware of hearkening to the talk of the folk, and especially of the Persians, and obey them not in aught; for they are sharpers and tricksters, who profess the art of alchemy and swindle people and take their money and devour it in vain."

Arab. Kímiyá, (see vol. i. 305) properly the substance which transmutes metals, the "philosopher's stone" which, by the by, is not a stone; and comes from χυμεία, χυμός = a fluid, a wet drug, as opposed to Iksír (Al-) ξηρόν, ξήριον, a dry drug. Those who care to see how it is still studied will consult my History of Sindh (chapt. vii) and my experience which pointed only to the use made of it in base coinage. Hence in mod. tongue Kímiyáwi, an alchemist, means a coiner, a smasher. The reader must not suppose that the transmutation of metals is a dead study: I calculate that there are about one hundred workers in London alone.

*

COITION SUPERSTITION

ARAB. "BARAS AU Juzám," the two common forms of leprosy. See vol. iv. 51). Popular superstition in Syria holds that coition during the menses breeds the Juzám, Dáa al-Kabír (Great Evil) or Dáa al-Fíl (Elephantine Evil), *i.e.* Elephantiasis and that the days between the beginning of the flow (Sabíl) to that of coition shows the age when the progeny will be attacked; for instance if it take place on the first day, the disease will appear in the tenth year, on the fourth the fortieth and so on. The only diseases really dreaded by the Badawin are leprosy and small-pox. Coition during the menses is forbidden by all Eastern faiths under the severest penalties. Al-Mas'údi relates how a man thus begotten became a determined enemy of Ali; and the ancient Jews attributed the magical powers of Joshua Nazarenus to this accident of his birth, the popular idea being that sorcerers are thus impurely engendered.

*

FORBIDDEN CLOSET

THE FORBIDDEN CLOSET occurs also in Sayf Zú al-Yazan, who enters it and finds the bird-girls. Trébutien ii, 208 says, "Il est assez remarquable qu'il existe en Allemagne une tradition à peu près semblable, et qui a fourni le sujet d'un des contes de Musaeus, entitulé *le voile enlevé*." Here

Hasan is artfully left alone in a large palace without other companions but his thoughts and the reader is left to divine the train of ideas which drove him to open the door.

*

CHOOSERS OF THE SLAIN

HERE AGAIN ARE the "Swan-maidens" (See vol. v. 346) "one of the primitive myths, the common heritage of the whole Aryan (Iranian) race." In Persia Bahram-i-Gúr when carried off by the Dív Sapíd seizes the Peri's dove-coat: in Santháli folk-lore Torica, the Goatherd, steals the garment doffed by one of the daughters of the sun; and hence the twelve birds of Russian Story. To the same cycle belong the Seal-tales of the Faroe Islands (Thorpe's Northern Mythology) and the wise women or mermaids of Shetland (Hibbert). Wayland the smith captures a wife by seizing a mermaid's raiment and so did Sir Hagán by annexing the wardrobe of a Danubian water-nymph. Lettsom, the translator, mixes up this swan-raiment with that of the Valkyries or Choosers of the Slain. In real life stealing women's clothes is an old trick and has often induced them, after having been seen naked, to offer their persons spontaneously. Of this I knew two cases in India, where the theft is justified by divine example. The blue god Krishna, a barbarous and grotesque Hindu Apollo, robbed the raiment of the pretty Gopálís (cowherdesses) who were bathing in the Arjun River and carried them to the top of a Kunduna tree; nor would he restore them till he had reviewed the naked girls and taken one of them to wife. See also Imr al-Kays (of the Mu'allakah) with "Onaiza" at the port of Daratjuljul (Clouston's Arabian Poetry, p. 4). A critic has complained of my tracing the origin of the Swan-maiden legend to the physical resemblance between the bird and a high-bred girl (vol. v. 346). I should have explained my theory which is shortly, that we must seek a material basis for all so-called supernaturalisms, and that anthropomorphism satisfactorily explains the Swan-maiden, as it does the angel and the devil. There is much to say on the subject; but this is not the place for long discussion.

*

WÁK-WÁK

AFTERWARDS CALLED WÁK Wák, and in the Bresl. Edit. Wák al-Wák. See Lane's notes upon these Islands. Arab Geographers evidently speak of two Wak Waks. Ibn al-Fakih and Al-Mas'údi (Fr. Transl., vol. iii. 6-7) locate one of them in East Africa beyond Zanzibar and Sofala. "Le territoire des Zendjes (Zanzibar-Negroids) commence au canal (Al-Khalij) dérivé du haut Nil (the Juln River?) et se prolonge jusqu'au pays de Sofalah et des Wak-Wak." It is simply the peninsula of Guardafui (Jard Hafun.) occupied by the Gallas, pagans and Christians, before these were ousted by the Moslem Somal; and the former perpetually ejaculated "Wak" (God) as Moslems cry upon Allah. This identification explains a host of other myths such as the

Amazons, who as Marco Polo tells us held the "Female Island" Socotra (Yule ii. 396). The fruit which resembled a woman's head (whence the puellæ Wakwakienses hanging by the hair from trees), and which when ripe called out "Wak Wak" and "Allah al-Khallák" (the Creator) refers to the Calabash-tree (*Adausonia digitata*), that grotesque growth, a vegetable elephant, whose gourds, something larger than a man's head, hang by a slender filament. Similarly the "cocoa" got its name, in Port. = Goblin, from the fancied face at one end. The other Wak Wak has been identified in turns with the Seychelles, Madagascar, Malacca, Sunda or Java (this by Langlès), China and Japan. The learned Prof. de Goeje (Arabishe Berichten over Japan, Amsterdam Muller, 1880) informs us that in Canton the name of Japan is Wo-Kwok, possibly a corruption of Koku-tan, the ebony-tree (*Diospyros ebenum*) which Ibn Khordábah and others find together with gold in an island 4,500 parasangs from Suez and East of China. And we must remember that Basrah was the chief starting-place for the Celestial Empire during the rule of the Tang dynasty (seventh and ninth centuries). Colonel J. W. Watson of Bombay suggests New Guinea or the adjacent islands where the Bird of Paradise is said to cry "Wak Wak!" Mr. W. F. Kirby in the Preface (p. ix.) to his neat little book "The New Arabian Nights," says: "The Islands of Wak-Wak, seven years' journey from Bagdad, in the story of Hasan, have receded to a distance of a hundred and fifty years' journey in that of Majin (of Khorasan). There is no doubt (?) that the Cora Islands, near New Guinea, are intended; for the wonderful fruits which grow there are

Birds of Paradise, which settle in flocks on the trees at sunset and sunrise, uttering this very cry." Thus, like Ophir, Wak Wak has wandered all over the world and has been found even in Peru by the Turkish work Tárikh al-Hind al-Gharbi = History of the West Indies (Orient. Coll. ii. 189).

*

AGE AND UGLINESS

So Hasan did the like and looking at his companion, saw her to be a grizzled old woman, blue-eyed and big-nosed, a calamity of calamities, the foulest of all created things, with face pock-marked and eyebrows bald, gap-toothed and chap-fallen, with hair hoary, nose running and mouth slavering;

The author neglects to mention the ugliest part of old-womanhood in the East, long empty breasts like tobacco-pouches. In youth the bosom is beautifully high, arched and rounded, firm as stone to the touch, with the nipples erect and pointing outwards. But after the girl-mother's first child (in Europe *le premier embellit*) all changes. Nature and bodily power have been overtasked; then comes the long suckling at the mother's expense: the extension of the skin and the enlargement of its vessels are too sudden and rapid for the diminished ability of contraction and the bad food aids in the continual consumption of vitality. Hence, among Eastern women age and ugliness are synonymous. It is only in the highest civilisation that we find the handsome old woman.

RICHARD BURTON

*

IN WAK-LAND

And thou must know, O my son, that these troops are all virgin girls, and that the ruler over us is a woman of the Archipelago of Wak. On the bank of the river aforesaid is another mountain, called Mount Wak, and it is thus named by reason of a tree which beareth fruits like heads of the Sons of Adam.

These are the Puellæ Wakwakienses of whom Ibn Al-Wardi relates after an ocular witness, "Here too is a tree which bears fruits like women who have fair faces and are hung by their hair. They come forth from integuments like large leathern bags (calabash-gourds?) and when they sense air and sun they cry "Wak! Wak!" (God! God!) till their hair is cut, and when it is cut they die; and the islanders understand this cry wherefrom they augur ill." The Ajáib al-Hind (chapt. xv.) places in Wak-land the Samandal, a bird which enters the fire without being burnt evidently the Egyptian "Pi-Benni," which the Greeks metamorphised to "Phœnix." It also mentions a hare-like animal, now male then female; and the Somal behind Cape Guardafui tell the same tale of their Cynhyænas.

*

398

CONGRESS WITH A CROCODILE

THE SEVEN HEAVENS

ONE OF THE Hells (see vol. iv. 143). Here it may be advisable to give the names of the Seven Heavens (which are evidently based upon Ptolemaic astronomy) and which correspond with the Seven Hells after the fashion of Arabian system-mania. (1) Dár al-Jalál (House of Glory), made of pearls; (2) Dár al-Salám (of Rest), rubies and jacinths; (3) Jannat al-Maawá (Garden of Mansions, not "of mirrors," as Herklots has it, p. 98), made of yellow copper; (4) Jannat al-Khuld (of Eternity), yellow coral; (5) Jannat al-Na'ím (of Delights), white diamond; (6) Jannat al-Firdaus (of Paradise), red gold; and (7) Jannat al-'Adn (of Eden, or Al-Karár = of everlasting abode, which some make No. 8), of red pearls or pure musk. The seven Hells are given in vol. v. 241; they are intended for Moslems (Jahannam); Christians (Lazà); Jews (Hutamah); Sabians (Sa'ír); Guebres (Sakar); Pagans or idolaters (Jahím); and Hypocrites (Háwiyah).

*

BASTARDY

AMONGST MOSLEMS BASTARDY is a sore offence and a love-child is exceedingly rare. The girl is not only carefully guarded but she also guards herself knowing that otherwise she will not find a husband. Hence seduction is all but unknown. The wife is equally well guarded and lacks opportunities hence adultery is found difficult except in books. Of the Ibn (or Walad) Harám (bastard as opposed to the Ibn Halál) the proverb says, "This child is not thine, so the madder he be the more is thy glee!" Yet strange to say public prostitution has never been wholly abolished in Al-Islam. Al-Mas'údi tell us that in Arabia were public prostitutes (Bagháyá), even before the days of the Apostle, who affected certain quarters as in our day the Tartúshah of Alexandria and the Hosh Bardak of Cairo. Here says Herr Carlo Landberg (p. 57, Syrian Proverbs) "Elles parlent une langue toute à elle." So pretentious and dogmatic a writer as the author of Proverbes et Dictons de la Province de Syrie, ought surely to have known that the Hosh Bardak is the head-quarters of the Cairene Gypsies. This author, who seems to write in order to learn, reminds me of an acute Oxonian undergraduate of my day who, when advised to take a "coach," became a "coach" himself.

*

BLOOD-WIT

THE OLD WOMAN, in the East as in the West, being the most vindictive of her kind. I have noted (Pilgrimage iii. 70) that a Badawi will sometimes though in shame take the blood-wit; but that if it be offered to an old woman she will dash it to the ground and clutch her knife and fiercely swear by Allah that she will not eat her son's blood.

*

CRIPPLE, CROW, OR CYCLOPS

Then, going up to the first ape, who was still tied to the tree, he said to him, "See, O unlucky, how fulsome was the counsel thou gavest me! None but thou made me light on this second ape: and for that thou gavest me good-morrow with thy one eye and thy lameness, I am become distressed and weary, without dirham or dinar."

Alluding to the well-known superstition, which has often appeared in The Nights, that the first object seen in the morning, such as a crow, a cripple, or a cyclops determines the fortunes of the day. Notices in Eastern literature are as old as the days of the Hitopadesa; and there is a something instinctive in the idea to a race of early risers. At an hour when the senses are most impressionable the aspect of unpleasant spectacles has double effect.

*

THOU ART A MAN

If I give it him, it will be no light matter to me, and if I give it not, he will torment me; but torture is easier to me than the giving up of the cash.

This is the true Fellah idea. A peasant will go up to his proprietor with the "rint" in gold pieces behind his teeth and undergo an immense amount of flogging before he spits them out. Then he will return to his wife and boast of the number of sticks he has eaten instead of paying at once and his spouse will say, "Verily thou art a man." Europeans know nothing of the Fellah. Napoleon Buonaparte, for political reasons, affected great pity for him and horror of his oppressors, the Beys and Pashas; and this affectation gradually became public opinion. The Fellah must either tyrannise or be tyrannised over; he is never happier than under a strong-handed despotism and he has never been more miserable than under British rule or rather misrule. Our attempts to constitutionalise him have made us the laughing-stock of Europe.

*

CHAMPIONS

THE EGYPTIAN FELLAH knows nothing of boxing like the Hausá man; but he is fond of wrestling after a rude and uncultivated fashion, which would cause shouts of laughter in Cumberland and Cornwall. And there are champions in this line. See vol. iii. 93.

*

CLOTHING THE REED

ANGLICÈ, "FINE FEATHERS make fine birds"; and in Eastern parlance, "Clothe the reed and it will become a bride." (Labbis al-Búsah tabkí 'Arúsah, Spitta Bey, No. 275.) I must allow myself a few words of regret for the loss of this Savant, one of the most single-minded men known to me. He was vilely treated by the Egyptian Government, under the rule of the Jew-Moslem Riyáz; and, his health not allowing him to live in Austria, he died shortly after return home.

*

THIN AS A TOOTHPICK

ARAB. "KHILÁL." THE toothpick, more esteemed by the Arabs than by us, is, I have said, often used by the poets as an emblem of attenuation without offending good taste. Nizami (Layla u Majnún) describes a lover as "thin as a toothpick." The "elegant" Hariri (Ass. of Barkaid) describes a toothpick with feminine attributes, "shapely of shape, attractive, provocative of appetite, delicate as the leanest of lovers, polished as a poniard and bending as a green bough."

Until she had done every work of hers; And with sweet milk had filled the porringers.

*

ORANGES

THE ORANGE I have said is the growth of India and the golden apples of the Hesperides were not oranges but probably golden nuggets. Captain Rolleston (*Globe*, Feb. 5, '84, on

"Morocco-Lixus") identifies the Garden with the mouth of the Lixus River while M. Antichan would transfer it to the hideous and unwholesome Bissagos Archipelago.

*

STRONG OLD WINE

Then coffee was served up and each drank what he would, after which they sat talking, till presently the garden-keeper who was young went away and returning with a basket full of roses, said to them, "What say ye, O my masters, to flowers?" Quoth one of them, "There is no harm in them, especially roses, which are not to be resisted."

"Coffee" is here evidently an anachronism and was probably inserted by the copyist. See vol. v. 169, for its first mention. But "Kahwah" may have preserved its original meaning = strong old wine (vol. ii. 261); and the amount of wine-drinking and drunkenness proves that the coffee movement had not set in.

*

SPANGLES OF METAL

IT IS THE custom for fast youths, in Egypt, Syria, and elsewhere to stick small gold pieces, mere spangles of metal on the brows, cheeks and lips of the singing and dancing girls and the perspiration and mask of cosmetics make them adhere for a time till fresh movement shakes them off.

*

PROHIBITIONS AND EXCUSES

"THEY WILL ASK thee concerning wine and casting of lots; say: — In both are great sin and great advantages to mankind; but the sin of them both is greater than their advantage." See Koran ii. 216. Mohammed seems to have made up his mind about drinking by slow degrees; and the Koranic law is by no means so strict as the Mullahs have made it. The prohibitions, revealed at widely different periods and varying in import and distinction, have been discussed by Al-Bayzáwi in his commentary on the above chapter. He says that the first revelation was in chapt. xvi. 69 but, as the passage was disregarded, Omar and others consulted the Apostle who replied to them in chapt. ii. 216. Then, as this also was unnoticed, came the final decision in chapt. v. 92, making wine and lots the work of Satan. Yet excuses are never wanting to the Moslem, he can drink Champagne and Cognac, both unknown in Mohammed's day and he can use wine and spirits medicinally, like sundry of ourselves, who turn up the nose of contempt at the idea of drinking for pleasure.

*

RICHARD BURTON

THE FEMALE SCREW

The girl took the bag from him and opening it shook it,
whereupon there fell thereout two-and-thirty pieces of wood,
which she fitted one into other, male into female and female into
male till they became a polished lute of Indian workmanship.

So we speak of a "female screw." The allusion is to the dove-
tailing of the pieces. This personification of the lute has
occurred before: but I solicit the reader's attention to it; it
has a fulness of Oriental flavour all its own.

*

ZEAL EXCEEDING KNOWLEDGE

EVERY WHERE IN the Moslem East the slave holds himself
superior to the menial freeman, a fact which I would impress
upon the several Anti-slavery Societies, honest men whose
zeal mostly exceeds their knowledge, and whose energy
their discretion.

*

TUNING THE LUTE

"MOST OF THE great Arab musicians had their own peculiar
fashion of tuning the lute, for the purpose of extending
its register or facilitating the accompaniment of songs

composed in uncommon keys and rhythms or possibly of increasing its sonority, and it appears to have been a common test of the skill of a great musician, such as Ishac el-Mausili or his father Ibrahim, to require him to accompany a difficult song on a lute purposely untuned. As a (partial) modern instance of the practice referred to in the text, may be cited Paganini's custom of lowering or raising the G string of the violin in playing certain of his own compositions. According to the Kitab el-Aghani, Ishac el-Mausili is said to have familiarized himself, by incessant practice, with the exact sounds produced by each division of the strings of the four course lute of his day, under every imaginable circumstance of tuning." It is regrettable that Mr. Payne does not give us more of such notes.

*

EATEN ATOM BY ATOM

THE INHABITANTS OF temperate climates have no idea what ants can do in the tropics. The Kafirs of South Africa used to stake down their prisoners (among them a poor friend of mine) upon an ant-hill and they were eaten atom after atom in a few hours. The death must be the slowest form of torture; but probably the nervous system soon becomes insensible. The same has happened to more than one hapless invalid, helplessly bedridden, in Western Africa. I have described an invasion of ants in my "Zanzibar," vol. ii. 169; and have suffered from such attacks in many places between that and Dahomey.

*

LESSONS IN SNAKE-CATCHING

Arab. "Háwi" from "Hayyah," a serpent. See vol. iii 145. Most of the Egyptian snake-charmers are Gypsies, but they do not like to be told of their origin. At Baroda in Guzerat I took lessons in snake-catching, but found the sport too dangerous; when the animal flies, the tail is caught by the left hand and the right is slipped up to the neck, a delicate process, as a few inches too far or not far enough would be followed by certain death in catching a Cobra. At last certain of my messmates killed one of the captives and the snake-charmer would have no more to do with me.

*

THE GNAWING

Whoso doeth the work appointed unto him, the steward bringeth him forth of that straitness; but whoso doeth it not within the stablished term is punished. After awhile, behold, they find honey exuding from the chinks of the house and when they have eaten thereof and tasted its sweetness of savour, they slacken in their ordered task and cast it behind their backs.

CONGRESS WITH A CROCODILE

This is a Moslem *lieu commun*; usually man is likened to one suspended in a bottomless well by a thin rope at which a rodent is continually gnawing and who amuses himself in licking a few drops of honey left by bees on the revetement.

*

RIDING WITH A LADY'S HAND

ARAB. "LIJÁM SHADÍD:" the ring-bit of the Arabs is perhaps the severest form known: it is required by the Eastern practice of pulling up the horse when going at full speed and it is too well known to require description. As a rule the Arab rides with a "lady's hand" and the barbarous habit of "hanging on by the curb" is unknown to him. I never pass by Rotten Row or see a regiment of English Cavalry without wishing to leave riders nothing but their snaffles.

*

AFTERLIFE

IT IS THE innate craving in the "Aryan" (Iranian, not the Turanian) mind, this longing to know what follows Death, or if nothing follow it, which accounts for the marvellous diffusion of the so-called Spiritualism which is only Swedenborgianism systematised and carried out into action, amongst nervous and impressionable races like the Anglo-American. In England it is the reverse; the obtuse sensitiveness of a people bred on beef and beer has made the "Religion of the Nineteenth Century" a manner of harmless magic, whose miracles are table-turning and ghost seeing whilst the prodigious rascality of its prophets (the so-called Mediums) has brought it into universal disrepute. It has been said that Catholicism must be true to co-exist with the priest and it is the same with Spiritualism proper, by which I understand the belief in a life beyond the grave, a mere continuation of this life; it flourishes (despite the Medium) chiefly because it has laid before man the only possible and intelligible idea of a future state.

*

EUTHANASIA

THE ARABS WHO had a variety of anæsthetics never seem to have studied the subject of "euthanasia." They preferred seeing a man expire in horrible agonies to relieving him by means of soporifics and other drugs: so I have heard Christians exult in saying that the sufferer "kept his senses to the last." Of course superstition is at the bottom of this barbarity; the same which a generation ago made the silly accoucheur refuse to give ether because of the divine (?) saying "In sorrow shalt thou bring forth children." (Gen. iii. 16). In the Bosnia-Herzegovina campaign many of the Austrian officers carried with them doses of poison to be used in case of being taken prisoners by the ferocious savages against whom they were fighting. As many anecdotes about

"Easing off the poor dear" testify, the Euthanasia-system is by no means unknown to the lower classes in England. I shall have more to say on this subject.

*

DEMOCRACY OF DESPOTISM

So the Wazir went out from him and told the lieges all he had said to him; and, when morning morrowed, the King came forth of his privacy and bade admit the people, to whom he excused himself, promising them that thenceforward he would deal with them as they wished, wherewith they were content and departed each to his own dwelling.

Another instance, and true to life, of the democracy of despotism in which the express and combined will of the people is the only absolute law. Hence Russian autocracy is forced into repeated wars for the possession of Constantinople which, in the present condition of the Empire, would be an unmitigated evil to her and would be only too glad to see a Principality of Byzantium placed under the united protection of the European Powers. I have treated of this in my paper on the "Partition of Turkey," which first appeared, headed the "Future of Turkey," in the *Daily Telegraph*, of March 7, 1880, and subsequently by its own name in the *Manchester Examiner*, January 3, 1881. The main reason why the project is not carried out appears to be that the "politicals" would thereby find their

411

occupation gone and they naturally object to losing so fine a field of action. So Turkey still plays the rôle of the pretty young lady being courted by a rabble of valets.

*

VIGILANCE COMMITTEES

So he arose and lay with her, which when the young men aforesaid saw, they ran upon them and seized them, saying, "We will not let you go, for ye are adulterers, and except we have carnal knowledge of the woman, we will report you to the police."

Good Moslems are bound to abate such scandals; and in a case of the kind even neighbours are expected to complain before the Chief of Police. This practice forms "Vigilance Committees" all over the Mahommedan East: and we may take a leaf out of their books if dynamite-outrages continue.

*

STRANGE POISON

THE STRANGEST POISON is mentioned by Sonnini who, as a rule, is a trustworthy writer. Noticing the malignity of Egyptian women he declares (p. 628, English trans.) that they prepare a draught containing a quant. suff. of menstruous discharge at certain phases of the moon,

412

which produces symptoms of scurvy; the gums decay, the teeth, beard and hair fall off, the body dries, the limbs lose strength and death follows within a year. He also asserts that no counterpoison is known and if this be true he confers a boon upon the Locustæ and Brinvilliers of modern Europe. In Morocco "Ta'am" is the vulgar name for a mixture of dead men's bones, eyes, hair and similar ingredients made by old wives and supposed to cause a wasting disease for which the pharmacopœia has no cure. Dogs are killed by needles cunningly inserted into meat-balls; and this process is known throughout the Moslem world.

*

BOUNTY OF HEAVEN

ARAB. "MUUNAH" WHICH in Morocco applies to the provisions furnished gratis by the unfortunate village-people to travellers who have a passport from the Sultan: its root is Maun = supplying necessaries. "The name is supposed to have its origin in that of *Manna*, the miraculous provision bestowed by the bounty of Heaven on the Israelites while wandering in the deserts of Arabia." Such is the marvellous information we find in p. 40, "Morocco and the Moors" by John Drummond Hay (Murray, 1861).

*

RICHARD BURTON

HIGHER NUMERALS

ARABIC HAS NO single word for million although the Moroccans have adopted "Milyún" from the Spaniards (see p. 100 of the Rudimentos del Árabe vulgar que se habla en el imperio de Marruccos por El P. Fr. Josè de Lerchundi, Madrid 1872). This lack of the higher numerals, the reverse of the Hindu languages, makes Arabic "arithmology" very primitive and almost as cumbrous as the Chinese.

*

MAMBRINO'S HELMET

THE PATIENT IS usually lathered in a big basin of tinned brass, a "Mambrino's helmet" with a break in the rim to fit the throat; but the poorer classes carry only a small cup with water instead of soap and water ignoring the Italian proverb, "Barba ben saponata mezza fatta" = well lathered is half shaved. A napkin fringed at either end is usually thrown over the Figaro's shoulder and used to wipe the razor.

*

STATE OF PERSPIRATION

On the fourth day the barber invited the King, who took horse with his Grandees and rode to the Baths, where he put off his clothes and entered; then Abu Sir came in to him and rubbed

414

his body with the bag-gloves, peeling from his skin dirt-rolls like lamp-wicks and showing them to the King, who rejoiced therein, and clapping his hand upon his limbs heard them ring again for very smoothness and cleanliness; after which thorough washing Abu Sir mingled rose-water with the water of the tank and the King went down therein.

Men are often seen doing this in the Hammam. The idea is that the skin when free from sebaceous exudation sounds louder under the clapping. Easterns judge much by the state of the perspiration, especially in horse-training, which consists of hand-gallops for many successive miles. The sweat must not taste over salt and when held between thumb and forefinger and the two are drawn apart must not adhere in filaments.

*

ABSURD APPELLATIONS

IN THE FIRST room of the Hammam, called the Maslakh or stripping-place, the keeper sits by a large chest in which he deposits the purses and valuables of his customers and also makes it the *caisse* for the pay. Something of the kind is now done in the absurdly called "Turkish Baths" of London.

*

RICHARD BURTON

PASSING FOR CASTRATOS

Then he seated himself by the pay-chest and customers flocked in upon him, each putting down that which was easy to him, nor had eventide evened ere the chest was full of the good gifts of Allah the Most High. Presently the Queen desired to go to the Hammam, and when this came to Abu Sir's knowledge, he divided the day on her account into two parts, appointing that between dawn and noon to men and that between midday and sundown to women.

This is the rule in Egypt and Syria and a clout hung over the door shows that women are bathing. I have heard, but only heard, that in times and places when eunuchs went in with the women youths managed by long practice to retract the testicles so as to pass for castratos. It is hard to say what perseverance may not effect in this line; witness Orsini and his abnormal development of hearing, by exercising muscles which are usually left idle.

*

DIGIT NAMES

ARAB. "KHINSIR" OR "Khinsar," the little finger or the middle finger. In Arabic each has its own name or names which is also that of the corresponding toe *e.g.* Ibhám (thumb); Sabbábah, Musabbah or Da"áah (forefinger); Wastá (medius); Binsir (annularis, ring-finger) and Khinsar (minimus). There are

416

also names for the several spaces between the fingers. See the English Arabic Dictionary (London, Kegan Paul and Co., 1881) by the Revd. Dr. Badger, a work of immense labour and research but which I fear has been to the learned author a labour of love not of profit.

*

EMPIRE OF OPINION

ARAB. "NAFAKAH"; FOR its conditions see Pilgrimage iii. 224. I have again and again insisted upon the Anglo-Indian Government enforcing the regulations of the Faith upon pauper Hindi pilgrims who go to the Moslem Holy Land as beggars and die of hunger in the streets. To an "Empire of Opinion" this is an unmitigated evil (Pilgrimage iii. 256); and now, after some thirty-four years, there are signs that the suggestions of common sense are to be adopted. England has heard of the extraordinary recklessness and inconsequence of the British-Indian "fellow subject."

*

ACCIDENTAL EXPOSURE

Easterns wear as a rule little clothing but it suffices for the essential purposes of decency and travellers will live amongst them for years without once seeing an accidental "exposure of the person." In some cases, as with the Nubian thong-apron, this demand of modesty requires not a little practice of the muscles; and we all know the difference in a Scotch kilt worn by a Highlander and a cockney sportsman.

*

CALLITRIS QUADRIVALVIS

Then I went up to the end of the roof and beheld there, behind a goodly curtain, a little chamber in whose midst stood a couch of juniper-wood plated with shimmering gold and covered with a handsome carpet.

This "'Ar'ar" is probably the Callitris quadrivalvis whose resin ("Sandarac") is imported as varnish from African Mogador to England. Also called the Thuja, it is of cypress shape, slow growing and finely veined in the lower part of the base. Most travellers are agreed that it is the Citrus-tree of Roman Mauritania, concerning which Pliny (xiii. 29) gives curious details, a single table costing from a million sesterces (£900) to 1,400,000. For other details see p. 95. "Morocco and the Moors," by my late friend Dr. Leared (London: Sampson Low, 1876).

*

AMULETS AND TALISMANS

I sold and bought a whole year, at the end of which I took the amulet and said, "This hath been with me some while, and I know not what it is nor what may be its value."

Arab. "Ta'wíz" = the Arab Tilasm, our Talisman, a charm, an amulet; and in India mostly a magic square. The subject is complicated and occupies in Herklots some sixty pages, 222–284.

*

DEATH BY SNEEZING

To SPIT OR blow the nose in good society is "vulgar." Sneezing (Al-'Atsah) is a complicated affair. For Talmudic traditions of death by sneezing see Lane (M. E. chapt. viii). Amongst Hindus sneezing and yawning are caused by evil spirits whom they drive away by snapping thumb and forefinger as loudly as possible. The pagan Arabs held sneezing a bad omen, which often stopped their journeys. Moslems believe that when Allah placed the Soul (life?) in Adam, the dry clay became flesh and bone and the First Man, waking to life, sneezed and ejaculated "Alhamdolillah;" whereto Gabriel replied, "Allah have mercy upon thee, O Adam!" Mohammed, who liked sneezing because accompanied by lightness of body and openness of pores, said of it, "If a man sneeze or eructate and say 'Alhamdolillah' he averts seventy diseases of which the least is leprosy" (Juzám); also, "If one of you sneeze, let him exclaim, 'Alhamdolillah,' and let those around salute him in return with, 'Allah have mercy upon thee!' and lastly let him say, 'Allah direct you and strengthen your condition.'" Moderns prefer, "Allah avert what may joy thy foe!" = (our God bless you!) to which the answer is "Alhamdolillah!" Mohammed disliked yawning (Suabá or Thuabá), because not beneficial as a sneeze and said, "If one of you gape and cover not his mouth, a devil leaps into it." This is still a popular superstition from Baghdad to Morocco.

*

BALLROOM FLIRTATIONS

KAMAR AL-ZAMAN AND THE JEWELLER'S WIFE

Lane rejects this tale because it is "extremely objectionable; far more so than the title might lead me to expect." But he quotes the following marginal note by his Shaykh: — "Many persons (women) reckon marrying a second time amongst the most disgraceful of actions. This opinion is commonest in the country-towns and villages; and my mother's relations are thus distinguished; so that a woman of them, when her husband dieth or divorceth her while she is young, passeth in widowhood her life, however long it may be, and disdaineth to marry a second time." I fear that this state of things belongs to the good old days now utterly gone by; and the loose rule of the stranger, especially the English, in Egypt will renew the scenes which characterised Sind when Sir Charles Napier hanged every husband who cut down an adulterous wife. I have elsewhere noticed the ignorant idea that Moslems deny to women souls and seats in Paradise, whilst Mohammed canonised two women in his own family. The theory arose with the "Fathers" of the Christian Church who simply exaggerated the misogyny of St. Paul. St. Ambrose commenting on Corinthians i. ii., boldly says: — "Feminas ad imaginem Dei factas non esse." St. Thomas Aquinas and his school adopted the Aristotelian view, "Mulier est erratum naturæ, et mas occasionatus, et per accidens generatur; atque idèo est monstrum." For other instances see Bayle s. v. Gediacus (Revd. Simon of Brandebourg) who in 1695 published a "Defensio Sexus muliebris," a refutation of an anti-Socinian satire or squib, "Disputatio perjucunda, Mulieres homines non esse," Parisiis, 1693. But when Islam arose in the seventh century, the Christian learned cleverly affixed the stigma of their own misogyny upon the Moslems ad captandas fœminas and in Southern Europe the calumny still bears fruit. Mohammed (Koran, chapt. xxiv.) commands for the first time, in the sixth year of his mission, the veiling and, by inference, the seclusion of women, which apparently unknown to the Badawin and, if practised in the cities was probably of the laxest. Nor can one but confess that such modified separation of the sexes, which it would be impossible to introduce into European manners, has great and notable advantages. It promotes the freest intercourse between man and man, and thus civilises what we call the "lower orders": in no Moslem land, from Morocco to China, do we find the brutals without manners or morals which are bred by European and especially by English civilisation. For the same reason it enables women to enjoy fullest intimacy and friendship with one another, and we know that the best of both sexes are those who prefer the society of their own as opposed to "quite the lady's man" and "quite the gentleman's woman." It also adds an important item to social decorum by abolishing *e.g.* such indecencies as the "ballroom *flirtation*" — a word which must be borrowed from us, not translated by foreigners. And especially it gives to religious meetings, a tone which the presence of women modifies and not for the better. Perhaps, the best form is that semi-seclusion of the sex, which prevailed in the heroic ages of Greece, Rome, and India (before the Moslem invasion), and which is perpetuated in Christian Armenia and in modern Hellas. It is a something between the conventual strictness of Al-Islam and the liberty, or rather licence, of the "Anglo-Saxon" and the "Anglo-American." And when England shall have cast off that peculiar insularity which makes her differ from all civilised peoples, she will probably abolish three gross abuses, time-honoured scandals, which bear very heavily on women and children. The first is the Briton's right to will property away from his wife and offspring. The second is the action for "breach of promise," salving the broken heart with pounds, shillings, and pence: it should be treated simply as an exaggerated breach of contract. The third is the procedure popularly called "Crim.

Con.," and this is the most scandalous of all: the offence is against the rights of property, like robbery or burglary, and it ought to be treated criminally with fine, imprisonment and in cases with corporal punishment after the sensible procedure of Moslem law.

*

SICILIAN VESPERS

As for the people of Bassorah they are dying of this annoy; for every Friday forenoon they shut up the dogs and cats, to hinder them from going about the market-streets, and all the people of the city enter the cathedral-mosques, where they lock the doors on them, and not one of them can pass about the bazar nor even look out of casement; nor knoweth any the cause of this calamity.

The fiction may have been suggested by the fact that in all Moslem cities from India to Barbary the inner and outer gates are carefully shut during the noontide devotions, *not* "because Friday is the day on which creation was finished and Mohammed entered Al-Medinah;" but because there is a popular idea that in times now approaching the Christians will rise up against the Moslems during prayers and will repeat the "Sicilian Vespers."

*

423

RICHARD BURTON

SPECIES OF HUSBAND

AMONG MOSLEMS HUSBANDS are divided into three species;
(1) of "Bahr" who is married for love; (2) of "Dahr," for
defence against the world, and (3) of "Mahr" for marriage-
settlements (money). Master Obayd was an unhappy
compound of the two latter; but he did not cease to be a
man of honour.

*

IBLIS AND JINN

IBLIS AND HIS connection with Diabolos has been noticed in
vol. i. 13. The word is foreign as well as a P.N. and therefore
is imperfectly declined, although some authorities deduce it
from "ablasa" = he despaired (of Allah's mercy). Others call
him Al-Háris (the Lion) hence Eve's first-born was named
in his honour Abd al-Haris. His angelic name was Azázíl
before he sinned by refusing to prostrate himself to Adam,
as Allah had commanded the heavenly host for a trial of
faith, not to worship the first man, but to make him a Keblah
or direction of prayer addressed to the Almighty. Hence he
was ejected from Heaven and became the arch-enemy of
mankind (Koran xviii. 48). He was an angel but related to
the Jinn: Al-Bayzáwi, however (on Koran ii. 82), opines that
angelic by nature he became a Jinn by act. Ibn Abbas held
that he belonged to an order of angels who are called Jinn
and begot issue as do the nasnás, the Ghúl and the Kutrub

which, however, are male and female, like the pre-Adamite man-woman of Genesis, the "bi-une" of our modern days. For this subject see Terminal Essay.

*

REGARDING ADULTERY

So, if this woman would not consent to replace her dead husband with a Sultan, how shall she be compared with one who replaced her husband, whilst he was yet alive, with a youth of unknown extraction and condition, and especially when this was in lewd carriage and not by way of lawful marriage? So he who deemeth all women alike, there is no remedy for the disease of his insanity.

A popular saying also applied to men. It is usually accompanied with showing the open hand and a reference to the size of the fingers. I find this story most interesting from an anthropological point of view; suggesting how differently various races regard the subject of adultery. In Northern Europe the burden is thrown most unjustly upon the man, the woman who tempts him being a secondary consideration; and in England he is absurdly termed "a seducer." In former times he was "paraded" or "called out," now he is called up for damages, a truly ignoble and shopkeeper-like mode of treating a high offence against private property and public morality. In Anglo-America, where English feeling is exaggerated, the lover is revolver'd and the woman is left unpunished. On the other hand, amongst Eastern and especially Moslem peoples, the woman is cut down and scant reckoning is taken from the man. This more sensible procedure has struck firm root amongst the nations of Southern Europe where the husband kills the lover only when he still loves his wife and lover-like is furious at her affection being alienated.

Practically throughout the civilised world there are only two ways of treating women. Moslems keep them close, defend them from all kinds of temptations and if they go wrong kill them. Christians place them upon a pedestal, the observed of all observers, expose them to every danger and if they fall, accuse and abuse them instead of themselves. And England is so grandly logical that her law, under certain circumstances, holds that Mrs. A. has committed adultery with Mr. B. but Mr. B. has not committed adultery with Mrs. A. Can any absurdity be more absurd? Only "summum jus, summa injuria." See my Terminal Essay. I shall have more to say upon this curious subject, the treatment of women who can be thoroughly guarded only by two things, firstly their hearts and secondly by the "Spanish Padlock."

*

INDEBTEDNESS

A Moslem is bound, not only by honour but by religion, to discharge the debts of his dead father and mother and so save them from punishment on Judgement-day. Mohammed who enjoined mercy to debtors while in the flesh (chapt. ii. 280, etc.) said "Allah covereth all faults except debt; that is to say, there will be punishment therefor." Also "A martyr shall be pardoned every fault but debt." On one occasion he refused to pray for a Moslem who died insolvent. Such harshness is a curious contrast with the leniency which advised the creditor to remit debts by way of alms. And practically this mild view of indebtedness renders it highly unadvisable to oblige a Moslem friend with a loan.

*

WARDING OFF ILLS

KORAN XXIV. MALE CHILDREN are to the Arab as much prized an object of possession as riches, since without them wealth is of no value to him. Mohammed, therefore, couples wealth with children as the two things wherewith one wards off the ills of this world, though they are powerless against those of the world to come.

*

EYE OF THE NEEDLE

THE WICKET OR small doorway, especially by the side of a gate or portal, is called "the eye of the needle" and explains Matt. xix. 24, and Koran vii. 38. In the Rabbinic form of the proverb the camel becomes an elephant. Some have preferred to change the Koranic Jamal (camel) for Habl (cable) and much ingenuity has been wasted by Christian commentators on Mark x. 25, and Luke xviii. 25.

*

SKIN BEAUTY

ORIENTAL WRITERS, INDIAN and Persian, as well as Arab, lay great stress upon the extreme delicacy of the skin of the fair ones celebrated in their works, constantly attributing to their heroines bodies so sensitive as to brook with difficulty the contact of the finest shift. Several instances of this will be found in the present collection and we may fairly assume that the skin of an Eastern beauty, under the influence of constant seclusion and the unremitting use of cosmetics and the bath, would in time attain a pitch of delicacy and sensitiveness such as would in some measure justify the seemingly extravagant statements of their poetical admirers, of which the following anecdote (quoted by Ibn Khellikan from the historian Et Teberi) is a fair specimen. Ardeshir ibn Babek (Artaxerxes I.), the first Sassanian King of Persia (A.D. 226–242), having long unsuccessfully besieged El Hedr, a strong city of Mesopotamia belonging to the petty King Es Satiroun, at last obtained possession of it by the treachery of the owner's daughter Nezireh and married the latter, this having been the price stipulated by her for the betrayal to him of the place. "It happened afterwards that, one night, as she was unable to sleep and turned from side to side in the bed, Ardeshir asked her what prevented her from sleeping. She replied, 'I never yet slept on a rougher bed than this; I feel something irk me.' He ordered the bed to be changed, but she was still unable to sleep. Next morning, she complained of her side, and on examination, a myrtle-leaf was found adhering to a fold of the skin, from which it had drawn blood. Astonished at this circumstance, Ardeshir asked her if it was this that had kept her awake and she replied in the affirmative. 'How then,' asked he, 'did your father bring you up?' She answered, 'He spread me a bed of satin and clad me in silk and fed me with marrow and cream and the honey of virgin bees and gave me pure wine to drink.' Quoth Ardeshir, 'The same return which you made your father for his kindness would be made much more readily to me'; and bade bind her by the hair to the tail of a horse, which galloped off with her and killed her." It will be remembered that the true princess, in the well-known German popular tale, is discovered by a similar incident to that of the myrtle-leaf. I quote this excellent note from Mr. Payne (ix. 148), only regretting that annotation did not enter into his plan of producing The Nights. Amongst Hindu story-tellers a phenomenal softness of the skin is a *lieu commun*: see Vikram and the Vampire (p. 285, "Of the marvellous delicacy of their Queens"); and the Tale of the Sybarite might be referred to in the lines given above.

*

429

RICHARD BURTON

CELESTIAL CONCUBINES

"(55) INDEED JOYOUS on that day are the people of Paradise in their employ; (56) In shades, on bridal couches reclining they and their wives: (57) Fruits have they therein and whatso they desire. (58) 'Peace!' shall be a word from a compassionating Lord." Koran xxxvi. 55–58, the famous Chapt. "Yá Sín;" which most educated Moslems learn by heart. See vol. iii. 19. In addition to the proofs there offered that the Moslem Paradise is not wholly sensual I may quote, "No soul wotteth what coolth of the eyes is reserved (for the good) in recompense of their works" (Koran lxx. 17). The Paradise of eating, drinking, and copulating which Mr. Palgrave (Arabia, i. 368) calls "an everlasting brothel between forty celestial concubines" was preached solely to the baser sort of humanity which can understand and appreciate only the pleasures of the flesh. To talk of spiritual joys before the Badawin would have been a *non-sens*, even as it would be to the roughs of our great cities.

*

DEPLORABLE LENIENCY

So she took it and the Kazi made peace between them, saying, "O wife, obey thy husband; and thou, O man, deal kindly with her."

CONGRESS WITH A CROCODILE

This is a true picture of the leniency with which women were treated in the Kazi's court at Cairo; and the effect was simply deplorable. I have noted that matters have grown even worse since the English occupation, for history repeats herself; and the same was the case in Afghanistan and in Sind. We govern too much in these matters, which should be directed not changed, and too little in other things, especially in exacting respect for the conquerors from the conquered.

*

PLACE OF HONOUR

They gave me what I asked and I went to the merchants' bazar, where, seeing goods, I bought them and sold them next day at a profit of fifty gold pieces and bought others.

This is a true picture of the tact and *savoir faire* of the Cairenes. It was a study to see how, under the late Khedive they managed to take precedence of Europeans who found themselves in the background before they knew it. For instance, every Bey, whose degree is that of a Colonel was made an "Excellency" and ranked accordingly at Court whilst his father, some poor Fellah, was ploughing the ground. Tanfîk Pasha began his ill-omened rule by always placing natives close to him in the place of honour, addressing them first and otherwise snubbing Europeans who, when English, were often too obtuse to notice the petty insults lavished upon them.

RICHARD BURTON

*

CRUELTY OF LOVE

THE VERY CRUELTY of love which hates nothing so much as a rejected lover. The Princess, be it noted, is not supposed to be merely romancing, but speaking with the second sight, the clairvoyance, of perfect affection. Men seem to know very little upon this subject, though every one has at times been more or less startled by the abnormal introvision and divination of things hidden which are the property and prerogative of perfect love.

*

THE SHE-BOY

And going round of youths to whom the world inclines
Ne'er, save in whatso was they please, their hearts wring.
From hand of coynted lass begarbed like yarded lad,
Wencher and Tribe of Lot alike enamouring…

Here Abu Nowas whose name always ushers in some abomination alluded to the "Ghulámiyah" or girl dressed like boy to act cupbearer. Civilisation has everywhere the same devices and the Bordels of London and Paris do not ignore the "she-boy," who often opens the door.

*

432

ANIMATED EGGS

Time-measurers are of very ancient date. The Greeks had clepsydræ and the Romans gnomons, portable and ring-shaped, besides large standing town-dials as at Aquileja and San Sabba near Trieste. The "Saracens" were the perfecters of the clepsydra: Bosseret (p. 16) and the Chronicon Turense (Beckmann ii. 340 *et seq.*) describe the water-clock sent by Al-Rashid to Karl the Great as a kind of "cuckoo-clock." Twelve doors in the dial opened successively and little balls dropping on brazen bells told the hour: at noon a dozen mounted knights paraded the face and closed the portals. Trithonius mentions an horologium presented in A.D. 1232 by Al-Malik al-Kámil the Ayyubite Soldan to the Emperor Frederick II: like the Strasbourg and Padua clocks it struck the hours, told the day, month and year, showed the phases of the moon, and registered the position of the sun and the planets. Towards the end of the fifteenth century Gaspar Visconti mentions in a sonnet the watch proper (certi orologii piccioli e portativi); and the "animated eggs" of Nurembourg became famous. The earliest English watch (Sir Ashton Lever's) dates from 1541: and in 1544 the portable chronometer became common in France.

*

RICHARD BURTON

SYPHYLIS

*Elsewhere it settled as a sporadic and now it appears to be
dying out while gonorrhoea is on the increase.*

I may be allowed to note that syphilis does not confine
itself to man: a charger infected with it was pointed out to
me at Baroda by my late friend, Dr. Arnott (18th Regiment,
Bombay N.I.) and Tangier showed me some noticeable
cases of this hippic syphilis, which has been studied in
Hungary. Eastern peoples have a practice of "passing on"
venereal and other diseases, and transmission is supposed
to cure the patient; for instance a virgin heals (and catches)
gonorrhœa. Syphilis varies greatly with climate. In Persia it
is said to be propagated without contact: in Abyssinia it is
often fatal and in Egypt it is readily cured by sand baths and
sulphur-unguents. Lastly in lands like Unyamwezi, where
mercurials are wholly unknown, I never saw caries of the
nasal or facial bones.

*

COFFEE PROPER

THE FIRST MENTION of coffee proper (not of Kahwah or old
wine in vol. ii. 260) is in Night cdxxvi. vol. v. 169, where
the coffee-maker is called Kahwahjiyyah, a mongrel term
showing the modern date of the passage in Ali the Cairene.
As the work advances notices become thicker, *e.g.* in Night

dccclxvi. where Ali Nur al-Din and the Frank King's daughter seems to be a modernisation of the story "Ala al-Din Abu al-Shámát" (vol. iv. 29); and in Abu Kir and Abu Sir (Nights cmxxx. and cmxxxvi.) where coffee is drunk with sherbet after present fashion. The use culminates in Kamar al-Zaman II. where it is mentioned six times (Nights cmlxvi. cmlxx. cmlxxi. twice; cmlxxiv. and cmlxxvii.), as being drunk after the dawn-breakfast and following the meal as a matter of course. The last notices are in Abdullah bin Fazil, Nights cmlxxviii. and cmlxxix.

*

JAPANESE TOBACCO

IT HAS BEEN suggested that Japanese tobacco is an indigenous growth and sundry modern travellers in China contend that the potato and the maize, both white and yellow, have there been cultivated from time immemorial.

*

EAR, EYES, AND TONGUE

AS LEARNING A language is an affair of pure memory, almost without other exercise of the mental faculties, it should be assisted by the ear and the tongue as well as the eyes. I would invariably make pupils talk, during lessons, Latin and Greek, no matter how badly at first; but unfortunately I should have to begin with teaching the pedants who, as a class, are far more unwilling and unready to learn than are those they teach.

*

SKULLS IN THE CELLAR

CATALOGUE OF PRINTED Books, 1884, p. 159, col. i. I am ashamed to state this default in the British Museum, concerning which Englishmen are apt to boast and which so carefully mulcts modern authors in unpaid copies. But it is only a slight specimen of the sad state of art and literature in England, neglected equally by Conservatives, Liberals and Radicals. What has been done for the endowment of research? What is our equivalent for the Prix de Rome? Since the death of Dr. Birch who can fairly deal with a Demotic papyrus? Contrast the Société Anthropologique and its palace and professors in Paris with our "Institute" *au second* in a corner of Hanover Square and its skulls in the cellar!

*

INCURIOUSNESS AND IGNORANCE

Oppida tota canem venerantur nemo Dianam...

A notable instance of Roman superficiality, incuriousness and ignorance. Every old Egyptian city had its idols (images of metal, stone or wood), in which the Deity became incarnate as in the Catholic host; besides its own symbolic animal used as a Kiblah or prayer-direction (Jerusalem or Meccah), the visible means of fixing and concentrating the thoughts of the vulgar, like the crystal of the hypnotist or the disk of the electro-biologist. And goddess Diana was in no way better than goddess Pasht. For the true view of idolatry see Koran xxxix. 4. I am deeply grateful to Mr. P. le Page Renouf (Soc. of Biblic. Archæology, April 6, 1886) for identifying the Manibogh, Michabo or Great Hare of the American indigenes with Osiris Unnefer ("Hare God"). These are the lines upon which investigation should run. And of late years there is a notable improvement of tone in treating of symbolism or idolatry: the Lingam and the Yoni are now described as "mystical representations, and perhaps the best possible impersonal representatives, of the abstract expressions paternity and maternity" (Prof. Monier Williams in "Folk-lore Record" vol. iii. part i. p. 118).

*

CAMEL US AND CAMEL THYSELF

THERE ARE THREE distinct Lokmans who are carefully confounded in Sale (Koran chapt. xxxi.) and in Smith's Dict. of Biography etc. art. Æsopus. The first or eldest Lokman, entitled Al-Hakím (the Sage) and the hero of the Koranic chapter which bears his name, was son of Bá'úrá of the Children of Azar, sister's son to Job or son of Job's maternal aunt; he witnessed David's miracles of mail-making and when the tribe of 'Ád was destroyed, he became King of the country. The second, also called the Sage, was a slave, an Abyssinian negro, sold to the Israelites during the reign of David or Solomon, synchronous with the Persian Kay Káús and Kay Khusrau, also Pythagoras the Greek(!). His physique is alluded to in the saying, "Thou resemblest Lokman (in black ugliness) but not in wisdom" (Ibn Khallikan i. 145). This negro or negroid, after a godly and edifying life, left a volume of "Amsál," proverbs and exempla (not fables or apologues); and Easterns still say, "One should not pretend to teach Lokmán" — in Persian, "Hikmat ba Lokman ámokhtan." Three of his apothegms dwell in the public memory: "The heart and the tongue are the best and worst parts of the human body." "I learned wisdom from the blind who make sure of things by touching them" (as did St. Thomas); and, when he ate the colocynth offered by his owner, "I have received from thee so many a sweet that 'twould be surprising if I refused this one bitter." He was buried (says the Tárikh Muntakhab) at Ramlah in Judæa, with the seventy Prophets stoned in one day by the Jews. The youngest Lokman "of the vultures" was a prince of the tribe of Ad who lived 3,500 years, the age of seven vultures (Tabari). He could dig a well with his nails; hence the saying, "Stronger than Lokman" (A. P. i. 701); and he loved the arrow-game, hence "More gambling than Lokman" (ibid. ii. 938). "More voracious than Lokman" (ibid. i. 134) alludes to his eating one camel for breakfast and another for supper. His wife Barákish also appears in proverb, *e.g.* "Camel us and camel thyself" (ibid. i. 295) *i.e.* give us camel flesh to eat, said when her son by a former husband brought her a fine joint which she and her husband relished. Also, "Barákish hath sinned against her kin" (ibid. ii. 89). More of this in Chenery's Al-Hariri p. 422; but the three Lokmans are there reduced to two.

*

FOX AND JACKAL

Some of the apologues in The Nights are pointless enough, rien moins qu'amusants; Wolf and the Fox (the but in the best specimens, such as the wicked man and the wily man), both characters are carefully kept distinct and neither action nor dialogue ever flags.

The fox and the jackal are confounded by the Arabic dialects not by the Persian, whose "Rubáh" can never be mistaken for "Shaghál." "Sa'lab" among the Semites is locally applied to either beast and we can distinguish the two only by the fox being solitary and rapacious, and the jackal gregarious and a carrion-eater. In all Hindu tales the jackal seems to be an awkward substitute for the Grecian and classical fox, the Giddar or Kolá (*Canis aureus*) being by no means sly and wily as the Lomri (*Vulpes vulgaris*). This is remarked by Weber (Indische Studien) and Prof. Benfey's retort about "King Nobel" the lion is by no means to the point. See Katha Sarit Sagara, ii. 28.

I may add that in Northern Africa jackal's gall, like jackal's grape (*Solanum nigrum* = black nightshade), ass's milk and melted camel-hump, is used aphrodisiacally as an unguent by both sexes. See p. 239, etc. of Le Jardin parfumé du Cheikh Nefzaoui, of whom more presently.

*

CAPTAIN GULLIVER

Some years ago I was asked by my old landlady if ever in the course of my travels I had come across Captain Gulliver.

*

THE PERFUMED GARDEN

See Le Jardin Parfumé du Cheikh Nefzaoui Manuel d'Erotologie Arabe Traduction revue et corrigée Edition privée, imprimé à deux cent.-vingt exemplaires, par Isidore Liseux et ses Amis, Paris, 1866. The editor has forgotten to note that the celebrated Sidi Mohammed copied some of the tales from The Nights and borrowed others (I am assured by a friend) from Tunisian MSS. of the same work. The book has not been fairly edited: the notes abound in mistakes, the volume lacks an index, &c., &c. Since this was written the Jardin Parfumé has been twice translated into English as "The Perfumed Garden of the Cheikh Nefzaoui, a Manual of Arabian Erotology (sixteenth century). Revised and corrected translation, Cosmopoli: mdccclxxxvi.: for the Kama Shastra Society of London and Benares and for private circulation only." A rival version will be brought out by a bookseller whose Committee, as he calls it, appears to be the model of literary pirates, robbing the author as boldly and as openly as if they picked his pocket before his face.

*

CLOCK AND ELEPHANT

THE PRESENT OF the famous horologium-clepsydra-cuckoo clock, the dog Becerillo and the elephant Abu Lubabah sent by Harun to Charlemagne is not mentioned by Eastern authorities and consequently no reference to it will be found in my late friend Professor Palmer's little volume "Haroun Alraschid," London, Marcus Ward, 1881. We have allusions to many presents, the clock and elephant, tent and linen hangings, silken dresses, perfumes, and candelabra of auricalch brought by the Legati (Abdalla, Georgius Abba et Felix) of Aaron Amiralmumminim Regis Persarum who entered the Port of Pisa (A.D. 801) in (vol. v. 178) Recueil des Histor. des Gaules et de la France, etc., par Dom Martin Bouquet, Paris, mdccxliv. The author also quotes the lines:

Persarum Princeps illi devinctus amore
Præcipuo fuerat, nomen habens Aaron.
Gratia cui Caroli præ cunctis Regibus atque
Illis Principibus tempora cara fuit.

*

RICHARD BURTON

OF CAMELS AND BOOKS

WHEN IBN ABBÁD the Sáhib (Wazir) was invited to visit
one of the Samanides, he refused, one reason being that he
would require 400 camels to carry only his books.

*

MUMMERS

I PREFER THIS derivation to Strutt's adopted by the popular,
"*mumm* is said to be derived from the Danish word *mumme*,
or *momme* in Dutch (Germ. = larva) and signifies disguise in
a mask, hence a mummer." In the Promptorium Parvulorum
we have "Mummynge, mussacio, vel mussatus": if was a
pantomime in dumb show, *e.g.* "I mumme in a mummynge;"
"Let us go mumme (mummer) to nyghte in women's
apparayle." "Mask" and "Mascarade," for persona, larva or
vizard, also derive, I have noticed, from an Arabic word —
Maskharah.

*

PRIVATE CIRCULATION

*Kitáb al'Ízáh fí asrár al'Nikaáh (Book of the Exposition on
the Mysteries of married Fruition).*

It has been translated from the Sanscrit and annotated by A.F.F. and B.F.R. Reprint: Cosmopoli: mdccclxxxv: for the Kama Shastra Society, London and Benares, and for private circulation only. The first print has been exhausted and a reprint will presently appear.

*

DEBASING PUBLIC MORALS

THE LOCAL PRESS has often proposed to abate this nuisance of erotic publication which is most debasing to public morals already perverted enough. But the "Empire of Opinion" cares very little for such matters and, in the matter of the "native press," generally seems to seek only a quiet life. In England if erotic literature were not forbidden by law, few would care to sell or to buy it, and only the legal pains and penalties keep up the phenomenally high prices.

*

GOOD BREEDING

THE SPECTATOR (No. 119) complains of an "infamous piece of good breeding," because "men of the town, and particularly those who have been polished in France, make use of the most coarse and uncivilised words in our language and utter themselves often in such a manner as a clown would blush to hear."

RICHARD BURTON

*

CONTRA NATURAM

SEE THE NOVELLE of Bandello the Bishop (Tome I; Paris, Liseux, 1879, small in 18), where the dying fisherman replies to his confessor "Oh! Oh! your reverence, to amuse myself with boys was natural to me as for man to eat and drink; yet you asked me if I sinned against nature!" Amongst the wiser ancients sinning contra naturam was not marrying and begetting children.

*

A CURE FOR PASSION

"MASCULA," FROM THE priapiscus, the over-development of clitoris (the veretrum muliebre, in Arabic Abu Tartúr, habens cristam) which enabled her to play the man. Sappho (nat. B.C. 612) has been retoillée like Mary Stuart, La Brinvilliers, Marie Antoinette and a host of feminine names which have a savour not of sanctity. Maximus of Tyre (Dissert. xxiv.) declares that the Eros of Sappho was Socratic and that Gyrinna and Atthis were as Alcibiades and Chermides to Socrates: Ovid, who could consult documents now lost, takes the same view in the Letter of Sappho to Phaon and in Tristia ii. 265.

Lesbia quid docuit Sappho nisi amare puellas?

Suidas supports Ovid. Longinus eulogises the ἐρωτικὴ

μανία (a term applied only to carnal love) of the far-famed Ode to Atthis: —

Ille mî par esse Deo videtur * * *

(Heureux! qui près de toi pour toi seule soupire * * *

Blest as th' immortal gods is he, etc.)

By its love symptoms, suggesting that possession is the sole cure for passion, Erasistratus discovered the love of Antiochus for Stratonice. Mure (Hist. of Greek Literature, 1850) speaks of the Ode to Aphrodite (Frag. 1) as "one in which the whole volume of Greek literature offers the most powerful concentration into one brilliant focus of the modes in which amatory concupiscence can display itself." But Bernhardy, Bode, Richter, K. O. Müller and esp. Welcker have made Sappho a model of purity, much like some of our dull wits who have converted Shakespeare, that most debauched genius, into a good British bourgeois.

*

ARTIFICIAL MEANS

THE ARABIC SAHHÁKAH, the Tractatrix or Subigitatrix, who has been noticed in vol. iv. 134. Hence to Lesbianise (λεσβίζειν) and tribassare (τρίβεσθαι); the former applied to the love of woman for woman and the latter to its mécanique: this is either natural, as friction of the labia and insertion of the clitoris when unusually developed; or artificial by means of the fascinum, the artificial penis (the Persian "Mayájang"); the patte de chat, the banana-fruit and a multitude of other succedanea. As this feminine perversion is only glanced at in The Nights I need hardly enlarge upon the subject.

*

THREE SPECIES OF HUMANITY

PLATO (SYMP.) IS probably mystical when he accounts for such passions by there being in the beginning three species of humanity, men, women and men-women or androgynes. When the latter were destroyed by Zeus for rebellion, the two others were individually divided into equal parts. Hence each division seeks its other half in the same sex; the primitive man prefers men and the primitive woman women. C'est beau, but — is it true? The idea was probably derived from Egypt which supplied the Hebrews with androgynic humanity; and thence it passed to extreme India, where Shiva as Ardhanárí was male on one side and female on the other side of the body, combining paternal and maternal qualities and functions. The first creation of humans (Gen. i. 27) was hermaphrodite (= Hermes and Venus) masculum et fœminam creavit eos — male and female created He them — on the sixth day, with the command to increase and multiply (ibid. v. 28) while Eve the woman was created subsequently. Meanwhile, say certain Talmudists, Adam carnally copulated with all races of animals. See L'Anandryne in Mirabeau's Erotika Biblion, where Antoinette Bourgnon laments the undoubling which disfigured the work of God, producing monsters incapable of independent self-reproduction like the vegetable kingdom.

*

LOVE OF INFERNAL GODS

Yet some purity must have sup vived, even amongst the Boeotians who produced the famous Narcissus, described by Ovid (Met. iii. 339)…

The word is from νάρκη, numbness, torpor, narcotism: the flowers, being loved by the infernal gods, were offered to the Furies. Narcissus and Hippolytus are often assumed as types of morosa voluptas, masturbation and clitorisation for nymphomania: certain mediæval writers found in the former a type of the Saviour; and Mirabeau a representation of the androgynous or first Adam: to me Narcissus suggests the Hindu Vishnu absorbed in the contemplation of his own perfections.

*

THREE CLASSES OF PROSTITUTE

THE VENERABLE SOCIETY of prostitutes contained three chief classes. The first and lowest were the Dicteriads, so called from Diete (Crete) who imitated Pasiphaë, wife of Minos, in preferring a bull to a husband; above them was the middle

447

class, the Aleutridæ who were the Almahs or professional musicians, and the aristocracy was represented by the Hetairai, whose wit and learning enabled them to adorn more than one page of Grecian history. The grave Solon, who had studied in Egypt, established a vast Dicterion (Philemon in his Delphica), or bordel, whose proceeds swelled the revenue of the Republic.

*

THREE MOSLEM RACES

In old Mauritania, now Marocco, the Moors proper are notable sodomites; Moslems, even of saintly houses, are permitted openly to keep catamites, nor do their disciples think worse of their sanctity for such licence: in one case the English wife failed to banish from the home "that horrid boy."

This magnificent country which the petty jealousies of Europe condemn, like the glorious regions about Constantinople, to mere barbarism, is tenanted by three Moslem races. The Berbers, who call themselves Tamazight (plur. of Amazigh), are the Gætulian indigenes speaking an Africo-Semitic tongue (see Essai de Grammaire Kabyle, etc. par A. Hanoteau, Paris, Benjamin Duprat). The Arabs, descended from the conquerors in our eighth century, are mostly nomades and camel-breeders. Third and last are the Moors proper, the race dwelling in towns, a mixed breed originally Arabian but modified by six centuries of Spanish residence and showing by thickness of feature and a parchment-coloured skin, resembling the American Octaroon's, a negro innervation of old date. The latter are well described in "Morocco and the Moors," etc. (Sampson Low and Co., 1876), by my late friend Dr. Arthur Leared, whose work I should like to see reprinted.

*

CASTRATION TEXTS

It was practised as a religious rite by the Tympanotribas or Gallus, the castrated votary of Rhea or Bona Mater, in Phrygia called Cybele, self-mutilated but not in memory of Atys; and by a host of other creeds: even Christianity, as sundry texts show, could not altogether cast out the old possession.

The texts justifying or conjoining castration are Matt. xviii. 8–9; Mark ix. 43–47; Luke xxiii. 29 and Col. iii. 5. St. Paul preached (1 Corin. vii. 29) that a man should live with his wife as if he had none. The Abelian heretics of Africa abstained from women because Abel died virginal. Origen mutilated himself after interpreting too rigorously Matth. xix. 12, and was duly excommunicated. But his disciple, the Arab Valerius founded (A.D. 250) the castrated sect called Valerians who, persecuted and dispersed by the Emperors Constantine and Justinian, became the spiritual fathers of the modern Skopzis. These eunuchs first appeared in Russia at the end of the xith century, when two Greeks,

John and Jephrem, were metropolitans of Kiew: the former
was brought thither in A.D. 1089 by Princess Anna
Wassewolodowna and is called by the chronicles Nawjè or
the Corpse. But in the early part of the last century (1715–
1733) a sect arose in the circle of Uglitseh and in Moscow,
at first called Clisti or flagellants which developed into the
modern Skopzi. For this extensive subject see De Stein
(Zeitschrift für Ethn. Berlin, 1875) and Mantegazza, chapt.
vi.

*

LAND OF VENUS

*The site, Apheca, now Wady al'Afik on the route from Bayrut
to the Cedars, is a glen of wild and wondrous beauty, fitting
frame-work for the loves of goddess and demigod: and the
ruins of the temple destroyed by Constantine contrast with
Nature's work, the glorious fountain, splendidior vitro,
which feeds the River Ibrahim and still at times Adonis runs
purple to the sea.*

In this classical land of Venus the worship of Ishtar-Ashtaroth
is by no means obsolete. The Metáwali heretics, a people
of Persian descent and Shiite tenets, and the peasantry of
"Bilád B'sharrah," which I would derive from Bayt Ashirah,
still pilgrimage to the ruins and address their vows to the
Sayyidat al-Kabírah, the Great Lady. Orthodox Moslems
accuse them of abominable orgies and point to the lamps

and rags which they suspend to a tree entitled Shajarat al-Sitt — the Lady's tree — an Acacia Albida which, according to some travellers, is found only here and at Sayda (Sidon) where an avenue exists. The people of Kasrawán, a Christian province in the Libanus, inhabited by a peculiarly prurient race, also hold high festival under the far-famed Cedars and their women sacrifice to Venus like the Kadashah of the Phœnicians. This survival of old superstition is unknown to missionary "Handbooks," but amply deserves the study of the anthropologist.

*

SWAN-DOWN

So AMONGST THE Romans we have the Iatroliptæ, youths or girls who wiped the gymnast's perspiring body with swan-down, a practice renewed by the professors of "Massage"; Unctores who applied perfumes and essences; Fricatrices and Tractatrices or shampooers; Dropacistæ, corn-cutters; Alipilarii who plucked the hair, etc., etc., etc.

*

GRELOTS LASCIFS

THEY MUST NOT be confounded with the *grelots lascifs*, the little bells of gold or silver set by the people of Pegu in the prepuce-skin, and described by Nicolo de Conti who however refused to undergo the operation.

*

OF VESTAL VIRGINS

FASCINUS IS THE Priapus-god to whom the Vestal Virgins of Rome, professed tribades, sacrificed; also the neck-charm in phallus-shape. Fascinum is the male member.

*

COUNTERFEIT HAIR

CAPTAIN GROSE (LEXICON Balatronicum) explains merkin as "counterfeit hair for women's privy parts. See Bailey's Dict." The Bailey of 1764, an "improved edition," does not contain the word which is now generally applied to a cunnus succedaneus.

*

PHENOMENAL CANNIBALISM

I HAVE NOTICED this phenomenal cannibalism in my notes to Mr. Albert Tootle's excellent translation of "The Captivity of Hans Stade of Hesse:" London, Hakluyt Society, mdccclxxiv.

CONGRESS WITH A CROCODILE

*

FAMOUS PEDERASTS

A FRIEND LEARNED in these matters supplies me with the following list of famous pederasts. Those who marvel at the wide diffusion of such erotic perversion, and its being affected by so many celebrities, will bear in mind that the greatest men have been some of the worst: Alexander of Macedon, Julius Cæsar and Napoleon Buonaparte held themselves high above the moral law which obliges commonplace humanity. All three are charged with the Vice. Of Kings we have Henri iii., Louis xiii. and xviii., Frederick ii. of Prussia, Peter the Great, William ii. of Holland and Charles ii. and iii. of Parma. We find also Shakespeare (i., xv., Edit. Francois. Hugo) and Molière, Theodorus Beza, Lully (the Composer), D'Assoucy, Count Zintzendorff, the Grand Condé, Marquis de Villette, Pierre Louis Farnèse, Duc de la Vallière, De Soleinne, Count D'Avaray, Saint Mégrin, D'Epernon, Admiral de la Susse, La Roche-Pouchin Rochfort. S. Louis, Henne (the Spiritualist), Comte Horace de Viel Castel, Lerminin, Fievée, Théodore Leclerc, Archi-Chancellier Cambacèrés, Marquis de Custine, Sainte-Beuve and Count D'Orsay. For others refer to the three Volumes of Pisanus Fraxi; Index Librorum Prohibitorum (London, 1877), Centuria Librorum Absconditorum (before alluded to) and Catena Librorum Tacendorum, London, 1885. The indices will supply the names.

453

RICHARD BURTON

*

BABOON PASSION

The second the grimmest and most earnest phase of the perversion, for instance where Abu Nowas debauches the three youths (vol. v. 64-69); whilst in the third form it is wisely and learnedly discussed, to be severely blamed, by the Shaykhah or Reverend Woman (vol. v. 154).

Of this peculiar character Ibn Khallikan remarks (ii. 43), "There were four poets whose works clearly contraried their character. Abu al-Atahíyah wrote pious poems himself being an atheist; Abú Hukayma's verses proved his impotence, yet he was more salacious than a he-goat; Mohammed ibn Házim praised contentment, yet he was greedier than a dog; and Abú Nowás hymned the joys of sodomy, yet he was more passionate for women than a baboon."

*

COCK-SPEAK

So saying, he went away, whilst Masrur entered, and taking up Abu al-Hasan, shut the door behind him, and made after his master, till he reached with him the palace what while the night drew to an end and the cocks began crowing, and set him down before the Commander of the Faithful, who laughed at him.

A natural clock, called by West Africans Cokkerapeek = Cock-speak. All the world over it is the subject of superstition: see Giles's "Strange Stories from a Chinese Studio" (i. 177), where Miss Li, who is a devil, hears the cock crow and vanishes.

*

BIG TOE

Said she, "At thy service;" and he continued, "I have it in mind to play a trick on the Caliph and thou shalt do the like with the Lady Zubaydah, and we will take of them at once, to begin with, two hundred dinars and two pieces of silk."

"Kalb" here is not heart, but stomach. The big toes of the Moslem corpse are still tied in most countries, and in some a sword is placed upon the body; but I am not aware that a knife and salt (both believed to repel evil spirits) are so used in Cairo.

*

FEET TOWARDS MECCA

THE MOSLEM, WHO may not wear unmixed silk during his lifetime, may be shrouded in it. I have noted that the "Shukkah," or piece, averages six feet in length.

"Kiblah" ("in the direction of the Kiblah") and notes that

some Moslems turn the corpse's head towards Meccah and others the right side, including the face. So the old version reads "feet towards Mecca." But the preposition "Alá" requires the former sig.

*

LED BY THE NOSE

Quoth one of the youths, "I am the son of him to whom all necks abase themselves, alike the nose-pierced of them and the breaker they come to him in their own despite, abject and submissive, and he taketh of their wealth and of their blood."

"Necks" per synecdochen for heads. The passage is a description of a barber-surgeon in a series of double-entendres the "nose-pierced" (Makhzúm) is the subject who is led by the nose like a camel with halter and ring and the "breaker" (háshim) may be a breaker of bread as the word originally meant, or breaker of bones. Lastly the "wealth" (mál) is a recondite allusion to the hair.

*

ON EUNUCHS

"Eunuch," etymologically meaning chamberlain ({eynè échein}), a bed-chamber-servant or slave, was presently confined to castrated men found useful for special purposes, like gelded horses, hounds, and cockerels turned to capons. Some writers hold that the creation of the semivir or apocopus began as a punishment in Egypt and elsewhere; and so under the Romans amputation of the "peccant part" was frequent: others trace the Greek "invalid," i.e., impotent man, to marital jealousy, and not a few to the wife who wished to use the sexless for hard work in the house without danger to the slave-girls. The origin of the mutilation is referred by Ammianus Marcellinus (lib. iv. chap. 17), and the Classics generally, to Semiramis, an "ancient queen" of decidedly doubtful epoch, who thus prevented the propagation of weaklings. But in Genesis (xxxvii. 36; xxxix. 1, margin) we find Potiphar termed a "Sarím" (castrato), an "attenuating circumstance" for Mrs. P. Herodotus (iii. chap. 48) tells us that Periander, tyrant of Corinth, sent three hundred Corcyrean boys to Alyattes for castration {epì êt ektomê}, and that Panionios of Chios sold caponised lads for high prices (viii. 105): he notices (viii. 104 and other places) that eunuchs "of the Sun, of Heaven, of the hand of God," were looked upon as honourable men amongst the Persians whom Stephanus and Brissonius charge with having invented the name (Dabistan i. 171). Ctesias also declares that the Persian kings were under the influence of eunuchs. In the debauched ages of Rome the women found a new use for these effeminates, who had lost only the testes or testiculi = the witnesses (of generative force): it is noticed by Juvenal (i. 22; ii. 365-379; vi. 36

— sunt quos imbelles et mollia semper Oscula delectant.

So Martial,

— vult futui Gallia, non parere,

And Mirabeau knew (see Kadísah) "qu'ils mordent les femmes et les liment avec une précieuse continuité." (Compare my vol. ii. 90; v. 46.) The men also used them as catamites (Horace i. Od. xxxvii.).

"Contaminato cum grege turpium, Morbo virorum."

In religion the intestabilis or intestatus was held ill-omened, and not permitted to become a priest (Seneca Controv. ii. 4), a practice perpetuated in the various Christian churches. The manufacture was forbidden, to the satisfaction of Martial, by Domitian, whose edict Nero confirmed; and was restored by the Byzantine empire, which advanced eunuchs, like Eutropius and Narses, to the highest dignities of the realm. The cruel custom to the eternal disgrace of mediæval Christianity was revived in Rome for providing the choirs in the Sistine Chapel and elsewhere with boys' voices. Isaiah mentions the custom (lvi. 3-6). Mohammed, who notices in the Koran (xxiv. 31), "such men as attend women and have no need of women," i.e. "have no natural force," expressly forbade (iv. 118), "changing Allah's creatures," referring, say the commentators, to superstitious ear-cropping of cattle, tattooing, teeth-sharpening, sodomy, tribadism, and slave-gelding. See also the "Hidáyah," vol. iv. 121; and the famous divine Al-Siyúti, the last of his school, wrote a tractate Fi 'l-Tahrími Khidmati 'l-Khisyán = on the illegality of using eunuchs. Yet the Harem perpetuated the practice throughout AI-Islam and African jealousy made a gross abuse of it. To quote no other instance, the Sultan of Dár-For had a thousand eunuchs under a Malik or king, and all the chief offices of the empire, such as Ab (father) and Báb (door), were monopolised by these neutrals. The centre of supply was the Upper Nile, where the operation was found dangerous after the age of fifteen, and when badly performed only one in four survived. For this reason, during the last century the Coptic monks of Girgah and Zawy al-Dayr, near Assiout, engaged in this scandalous traffic, and declared that it was philanthropic to operate scientifically (Prof. Panuri and many others). Eunuchs are now made in the Sudán, Nubia, Abyssinia, Kordofán, and Dár-For, especially the Messalmiyah district: one of those towns was called "Tawáshah" (eunuchry) from the traffic there conducted by Fukahá or religious teachers. Many are supplied by the district between Majarah (Majarash?) and the port Masawwah; there are also depôts at Mbadr, near Tajurrah-harbour, where Yusuf Bey, Governor in 1880, caponised some forty boys, including the brother of a hostile African chief: here also the well-known Abu Bakr was scandalously active. It is calculated that not less than eight thousand of these unfortunates are annually exported to Arabia, Egypt, and Turkey. Article IV. of the Anglo-Egyptian Convention punishes the offense with death, and no one would object to hanging the murderer under whose mutilating razor a boy dies. Yet this, like most of our modern "improvements" in Egypt, is a mere brutum fulmen. The crime is committed under our very eyes, but we will not see it.

The Romans numbered three kinds of eunuchs: — 1. Castrati, clean-shaved, from Gr. {késtros}; 2. Spadones, from {spáoo}, when the testicles are torn out, not from "Spada,"

459

town of Persia; and, 3. Thlibii, from {thliboo}, to press, squeeze, when the testicles are bruised, &c. In the East also, as I have stated (v. 46), eunuchs are of three kinds: — 1. Sandali, or the clean-shaved, the classical apocopus. The parts are swept off by a single cut of a razor, a tube (tin or wooden) is set in the urethra, the wound is cauterised with boiling oil, and the patient is planted in a fresh dunghill. His diet is milk; and if under puberty, he often survives. This is the eunuque aqueduc, who must pass his water through a tube. 2. The eunuch whose penis is removed: he retains all the power of copulation and procreation without the wherewithal; and this, since the discovery of caoutchouc, has often been supplied. 3. The eunuch, or classical Thlibias and Semivir, who has been rendered sexless by removing the testicles (as the priests of Cybele were castrated with a stone knife), or by bruising (the Greek Thlásias), twisting, searing, or bandaging them. A more humane process has lately been introduced: a horsehair is tied round the neck of the scrotum and tightened by slow degrees till the circulation of the part stops and the bag drops off without pain. This has been adopted in sundry Indian regiments of Irregular Cavalry, and it succeeded admirably: the animals rarely required a day's rest. The practice was known to the ancients. See notes on Kadísah in Mirabeau. The Eunuchata virgo was invented by the Lydians, according to their historian Xanthus. Zachias (Quaest. medico-legal.) declares that the process was one of infibulation or simple sewing up the vulva; but modern experience has suggested an operation like the "spaying" of bitches, or mutilation of the womb, in modern euphuism "baby-house." Dr. Robert ("Journey from Delhi to Bombay, Müller's Archiv. 1843") speaks of a eunuch'd woman who after ovariotomy had no breasts, no pubes, no rotundities, and no desires. The Australians practice exsection of the ovaries systematically to make women barren. Miklucho Maclay learned from the traveller Retsch that about Lake Parapitshurie men's urethras were split, and the girls were spayed: the latter showing two scars in the groin. They have flat bosoms, but feminine forms, and are slightly bearded; they mix with the men, whom they satisfy mechanically, but without enjoyment (?). MacGillivray, of the "Rattlesnake," saw near Cape York a woman with these scars: she was a surdo-mute, and had probably been spayed to prevent increase. The old Scandinavians, from Norway to Iceland, systematically gelded "sturdy vagrants" in order that they might not beget bastards. The Hottentots before marriage used to cut off the left testicle, meaning by such semi-castration to prevent the begetting of twins. This curious custom, mentioned by the Jesuit Tochard, Boeving, and Kolbe, is now apparently obsolete — at least, the traveller Fritsch did not find it.

*

FEAR OF THE EYE

As for one of them, a company of the guards of the king of those parts found him and carried him to their lord, who marvelled at him with exceeding marvel and adopted him, giving out to the folk that he was his own son, whom he had hidden, of his love for him.

i.e. For fear of the "eye"; see vol. i. 123 and passim. In these days the practice is rare; but, whenever you see at Cairo an Egyptian dame daintily dressed and leading by the hand a grimy little boy whose eyes are black with flies and whose dress is torn and unclean, you see what has taken its place. And if you would praise the brat you must not say "Oh, what a pretty boy!" but "Inshallah!" — the Lord doth as he pleaseth.

*

THE LAW OF RETALIATION

Then he asked Arwa, "What wilt thou that I do with them?" and she answered, "Accomplish on them the ordinance of Almighty Allah let the slayer be slain and the transgressor transgressed against, even as he transgressed against us; yea, and to the well-doer weal shall be done even as he did unto us."

i.e. the lex talionis, which is the essence of Moslem, and indeed, of all criminal jurisprudence. We cannot wonder at the judgement of Queen Arwa: even Confucius, the mildest and most humane of lawgivers, would not pardon the man who allowed his father's murderer to live. The Moslem lex talionis (Koran ii. 173) is identical with that of the Jews (Exod. xxi. 24), and the latter probably derives from immemorial usage. But many modern Rabbins explain away the Mosaical command as rather a demand for a pecuniary mulct than literal retaliation. The well-known Isaac Aburbanel cites many arguments in proof of this position: he asks, for instance, supposing the accused have but one eye, should he lose it for having struck out one of another man's two? Moreover, he dwells upon the impossibility of inflicting a punishment the exact equivalent of the injury; like Shylock's pound of flesh without drawing blood. Moslems, however, know nothing of these frivolities, and if retaliation be demanded the judge must grant it. There is a legend in Marocco of an English merchant who was compelled to forfeit tooth for tooth at the instance of an old woman, but a profitable concession gilded the pill.

*

THE DEVIL'S OWN

But she retorted, "There is a thing wherewith we will make her confess, and all that is in her heart shall be discovered to thee."

I have noted that Moslem law is not fully satisfied without such confession which, however, may be obtained by the bastinado. It is curious to compare English procedure with what Moslem would be in such a case as that of the famous Tichborne Claimant. What we did need hardly be noticed. An Arab judge would in a case so suspicious at once have applied the stick and in a quarter of an hour would have settled the whole business; but then what about the "Devil's own," the lawyers and lawyers' fees? And he would have remarked that the truth is not less true because obtained by such compulsory means.

*

HOOPOE

THE HUDHUD, so called from its cry "Hood! Hood!" It is the Lat. upupa, Gr. {épops} from its supposed note epip or upup; the old Egyptian Kukufa; Heb. Dukiphath and Syriac Kikuphá (Bochart Hierozoicon, part ii. 347). The Spaniards call it Gallo de Marzo (March-Cock) from its returning in that month, and our old writers "lapwing" (Deut. xiv. 18). This foul-feeding bird derives her honours from chapt. xxvii. of the Koran (q.v.), the Hudhud was sharp-sighted and sagacious enough to discover water underground which the devils used to draw after she had marked the place by her bill.

*

MASCULINE KISSES

They informed him that a page of the king had committed a mighty great and he was about to do him crime that die; so the Captain of the thieves pressed forward and looking upon the prisoner, knew him, whereupon he went up to him and strained him to his bosom and threw his arms round his neck, and fell to kissing him upon his mouth.

As he would kiss a son. I have never yet seen an Englishman endure these masculine kisses, formerly so common in France and Italy, without showing clearest signs of his disgust.

*

MAKING RUBIES

Quoth she, "I have a bangle sell it and buy seed-pearls with the price then round them and fashion them into great unions and thereby thou shalt gain much money, with the which we may find our way to thy country."

I have often heard of this mysterious art in the East, also of similarly making rubies and branch-coral of the largest size; but, despite all my endeavours, I never was allowed to witness the operation. It was the same with alchemy, which, however, I found very useful to the "smasher." See my History of Sindh, chapt. vii.

*

RICHARD BURTON

FIGHTING RAMS

Now there was in the house a fighting-ram, which the Persian had trained to butting, and when he saw what the woman was doing, he thought she wished to do battle with him so he broke his halter and running at her, butted her and split her skull.

Alluding to the fighting rams which are described by every Anglo-Indian traveller. They strike with great force, amply sufficient to crush the clumsy hand which happens to be caught between the two foreheads. The animals are sometimes used for Fál or consulting futurity: the name of a friend is given to one and that of a foe to the other; and the result of the fight suggests victory or defeat for the men.

*

THE DODGE

IN MY PILGRIMAGE (i. 38), I took from Mr. Galton's Art of Travel, the idea of opening with a lancet the shoulder or other fleshy part of the body and inserting into it a precious stone. This was immensely derided by not a few including one who, then a young man from the country, presently became a Cabinet Minister. Despite their omniscience, however, the "dodge" is frequently practised. See how this device was practised by Jeshua Nazarenus, vol. v. 238.

*

LONG LOCKS

So he went back to the trooper's house and found her sitting as before; whereupon he was abashed in her presence and seating himself in the trooper's sitting-chamber, ate and drank with him and became drunken and abode senseless all that day till nightfall, when the trooper arose and, the fuller's hair being long and flowing, he shaved off a portion of it after the fashion of the Turks, clipped the rest short and clapped a Tarbúsh on his head.

This leaving a long lock upon the shaven poll is a very ancient practice: we find it amongst the old Egyptians. For the Shúshah or top-knot of hair, see vol. i. 308. It is differently worn in the several regions of the Moslem world: the Maroccans of the Ríf country grow it not on the poll but on one side of the head. As a rule, however, it is confined to boys, and is shaved off at puberty.

*

ABOMINABLE WITCHCRAFT

When she grew feeble and decrepit, the townsfolk succoured her not with aught, but thrust her forth of the city, saying, "This old woman shall not neighbour with us, for that we do good to her and she requiteth us with evil."

Suspecting her to be a witch because she was old and poor. The same was the case in Europe when these unfortunates were burned during the early part of the last century and even now the country-folk are often ready to beat or drown them. The abominable witchcraft acts, which arose from bibliolatry and belief in obsolete superstitions, can claim as many victims in "Protestant" countries, England and the Anglo-American States as the Jesuitical Inquisition.

*

IRREVOCABLE DIVORCE

When he saw that he got no profit of him, he said to him, "Swear by the oath of divorce from thy wife that thou hast nothing." So he sware and his wife said to him, "Fie on thee! Wilt thou divorce me? Is not the hoard buried in yonder chamber?"

i.e. The oath of triple divorce which is, I have said, irrevocable, and the divorcée may not be taken again by her husband till her marriage with another man (the Mustahill of The Nights) has been consummated. See vol. iv., 48.

*

WARDING WITH FIRE

When the woman came to her delivery-time, she gave birth to a girl-child in the night and they sought fire of the neighbours.

The fire was intended to defend the mother and babe from Jinns, bad spirits, the evil eye, etc. Romans lit candles in the room of the puerpara; hence the goddess Candelifera, and the term Candelaria applied to the B.V. In Brand's Popular Antiquities (ii. 144) we find, "Gregory mentions an ordinary superstition of the old wives who dare not trust a child in a cradle by itself alone without a candle;" this was for fear of the "night-hag" (Milton, P. L., ii. 662). The same idea prevailed in Scotland and in Germany: see the learned Liebrecht (who translated the Pentamerone) "Zur Volkskunde," p. 31. In Sweden if the candle go out, the child may be carried off by the Trolls (Weckenstedt, Wendische Sagen, p. 446). The custom has been traced to the Malay peninsula, whither it was probably imported by the Hindus or the Moslems, and amongst the Tajiks in Bokhara. For the Hindu practice, see Katha S. S. 305, and Prof. Tawney's learned note analysed above.

*

DUNG BONBONS

Now there was in another city a second sharper, hight Al-Rází, one of its worst, who went out the same day, bearing a load of goat's droppings, anent which he had sworn to himself that he would not sell it but at the price of sun-dried figs.

Normally used for fuel and at times by funny men to be put into sweetmeats by way of practical joke: these are called

"Nukl-i-Pishkil" = goat-dung bonbons. The tale will remind old Anglo-Indians of the two Bengal officers who were great at such "sells" and who "swopped" a spavined horse for a broken-down "buggy."

*

WASH FOR THE CORPSE

Arab. "Hanút," i.e., leaves of the lotus-tree to be infused as a wash for the corpse; camphor used with cotton to close the mouth and other orifices; and, in the case of a wealthy man, rose-water, musk, ambergris, sandal-wood, and lign-aloes for fumigation.

*

THE NICHE

Arab. "Lahd, Luhd," the niche or cell hollowed out in the side of the oblong trench: here the corpse is deposited and covered with palm-fronds etc. to prevent the earth touching it. See my Pilgrimage ii. 304.

*

CONGRESS WITH A CROCODILE

EATING STICK

ARAB. "JARÍDAH" (WHENCE the Jaríd-game) a palm-frond stripped of its leaves and used for a host of purposes besides flogging, chairs, sofas, bedsteads, cages, etc. etc. Tales of heroism in "eating stick" are always highly relished by the lower orders of Egyptians who pride themselves upon preferring the severest bastinado to paying the smallest amount of "rint."

*

TOWER OF SILENCE

ARAB. "NÁWÚS," THE hollow tower of masonry with a grating over the central well upon which the Magian corpse is placed to be torn by birds of prey: it is kept up by the Parsi population of Bombay and is known to Europeans as the "Tower of Silence." Náís and Náwús also mean a Pyrethrum, a fire-temple and have a whimsical resemblance to the Greek.

*

PASSING INTEREST

The man rejoined, "I know naught of this," and words were bandied about between them, whilst the folk who heard them disputed together concerning their sayings and doings, till their voices rose high and the neighbours had knowledge of that which passed between them.

Characteristically Eastern and Moslem is this action of the neighbours and bystanders. A walk through any Oriental city will show a crowd of people screaming and gesticulating, with thundering yells and lightning glances, as if about to close in mortal fight, concerning some matter which in no way concerns them. Our European cockneys and badauds mostly content themselves with staring and mobbing.

*

DARKENED SKIES

MOST ARABS BELIEVE that the black cloud which sometimes produces, besides famine, contagious fevers and pestilence, like that which in 1799 depopulated the cities and country of Barbary, is led by a king locust, the Sultan Jarád.

*

FEROCIOUS HOUNDS

THE BADAWI DOGS are as dangerous as those of Montenegro but not so treacherous: the latter will sneak up to the stranger and suddenly bite him most viciously. I once had a narrow escape from an ignoble death near the slaughter-house of Alexandria-Ramlah, where the beasts were unusually ferocious. A pack assailed me at early dawn and but for an iron stick and a convenient wall I should have been torn to pieces.

*

SUICIDE

SUICIDE IS RARE in Moslem lands, compared with India, China, and similar "pagan" countries; for the Mussulman has the same objection as the Christian "to rush into the presence of his Creator," as if he could do so without the Creator's permission. The Hindu also has some curious prejudices on the subject; he will hang himself, but not by the neck, for fear lest his soul be defiled by exiting through an impure channel. In England hanging is the commonest form for men; then follow in due order drowning, cutting or stabbing, poison, and gun-shot: women prefer drowning (except in the cold months) and poison. India has not yet found a Dr. Ogle to tabulate suicide; but the cases most familiar to old Anglo-Indians are leaping down cliffs (as at Giruar), drowning, and starving to death. And so little is life valued that a mother will make a vow obliging her son to suicide himself at a certain age.

*

RICHARD BURTON

BOBBIES

THE FIRST CONSTABLE'S HISTORY

These policemen's tales present a curious contrast with the detective stories of M. Gaboriau and his host of imitators. In the East the police, like the old Bow Street runners, were and are still recruited principally amongst the criminal classes on the principle of "Set a thief," &c. We have seen that the Barmecide Wazirs of Baghdad "anticipated Fourier's doctrine of the passionel treatment of lawless inclinations," and employed as subordinate officers, under the Wali or Prefect of Police, accomplished villains like Ahmad al-Danaf (vol. iv. 75), Hasan Shuuman and Mercury Ali (ibid.) and even women (Dalilah the Crafty) to coerce and checkmate their former comrades. Moreover a gird at the police is always acceptable, not only to a coffee-house audience, but even to a more educated crowd; witness the treatment of the "Charley" and the "Bobby" in our truly English pantomimes.

*

FLIBBERTIGIBBETS

THESE UNFORTUNATES IN hot climates enjoy nothing so much as throwing off the clothes which burn their feverish skins: see Pilgrimage iii. 385. Hence the boys of Eastern cities, who are perfect imps and flibbertigibbets, always raise the cry "Majnún" when they see a man naked whose sanctity does not account for his nudity.

*

DAMP-HOT

PARTURITION AND DEATH in warm climates, especially the damp-hot like Egypt are easy compared with both processes in the temperates of Europe. This is noticed by every traveller. Hence probably Easterns have never studied the artificial Euthanasia which is now appearing in literature. See p. 143 "My Path to Atheism," by Annie Besant, London: Freethought Publishing Company, 28, Stonecutter Street, E. C., 1877, based upon the Utopia of the highly religious Thomas Moore. Also "Essay on Euthanasia," by P. D. Williams, Jun., and Mr. Tollemache in the "Nineteenth Century."

*

HIDDEN WEAPONS

"By Allah, an thou open not to me, I will slay thee; for am none of those whom thou canst readily cozen ?" "What deemest thou of cozening?"

Being a merchant he wore dagger and sword, a safe practice as it deters attack and far better than carrying hidden weapons, derringers and revolvers which, originating in the

475

United States, have now been adopted by the most civilised nations in Europe.

*

GETTING RELIGION

I HAVE REPEATEDLY noticed that singing and all music are, in religious parlance, "Makrúh," blameable though not actually damnable; and that the first step after "getting religion" is to forswear them.

*

SKULL TALK

THE LOWER ORDERS of Egypt and Syria are addicted to this bear-like attack; so the negroes imitate fighting-rams by butting with their stony heads. Let me remark that when Herodotus (iii. 12), after Psammenitus' battle of Pelusium in B.C. 524, made the remark that the Egyptian crania were hardened by shaving and insolation and the Persians were softened by wearing head-cloths, he tripped in his anthropology. The Iranian skull is naturally thin compared with that of the negroid Egyptian and the negro.

*

WITH WINE

"A madman! A madman!" till I came to my house and knocked at the door; whereupon out came my wife and seeing me naked, tall, bare of head, cried out and ran in again, saying, "This is a maniac, a Satan!"

This habit "torquere mero," was a favourite with the mediæval Arabs. Its effect varies greatly with men's characters, making some open-hearted and communicative, and others more cunning and secretive than in the normal state. So far it is an excellent detection of disposition, and many a man who passes off well when sober has shown himself in liquor a rank snob. Among the lower orders it provokes what the Persians call Bad-mastí (le vin méchant) see Pilgrimage iii. 385.

*

SALTING THE HEAD

In Marocco there is great difficulty about finding an executioner who becomes obnoxious to the Thár, vendetta or blood-revenge. For salting the criminal's head, however, the soldiers seize upon the nearest Jew and compel him to clean out the brain and to prepare it for what is often a long journey. Hence, according to some, the local name of the Ghetto, Al-Malláh, = the salting-ground.

*

RICHARD BURTON

DESTINY

A FAIR FRIEND found the idea of Destiny in The Nights become almost a night-mare. Yet here we suddenly alight upon the true Johnsonian idea that conduct makes fate. Both extremes are as usual false. When one man fights a dozen battles unwounded and another falls at the first shot we cannot but acknowledge the presence of that mysterious "luck" whose laws, now utterly unknown to us, may become familiar with the ages. I may note that the idea of an appointed hour beyond which life may not be prolonged, is as old as Homer (Il. vi. 487).

The reader has been told (vol. vii. 135) that "Kazá" is Fate in a general sense, the universal and eternal Decree of Allah, while "Kadar" is its special and particular application to man's lot, that is Allah's will in bringing forth events at a certain time and place. But the former is popularly held to be of two categories, one Kazá al-Muham which admits of modification and Kazá al-Muhkam, absolute and unchangeable, the doctrine of irresistible predestination preached with so much energy by St. Paul (Romans ix. 15-24); and all the world over men act upon the former while theoretically holding to the latter. Hence "Chinese Gordon" whose loss to England is greater than even his friends suppose, wrote "It is a delightful thing to be a fatalist," meaning that the Divine direction and pre-ordination of all things saved him so much trouble of forethought and afterthought. In this tenet he was not only a Calvinist but also a Moslem whose contradictory ideas of Fate and

478

Freewill (with responsibility) are not only beyond Reason but are contrary to Reason; and although we may admit the argumentum ad verecundiam, suggesting that there are things above (or below) human intelligence, we are not bound so to do in the case of things which are opposed to the common sense of mankind. Practically, however, the Moslem attitude is to be loud in confessing belief of "Fate and Fortune" before an event happens and after it wisely to console himself with the conviction that in no way could he have escaped the occurrence. And the belief that this destiny was in the hands of Allah gives him a certain dignity especially in the presence of disease and death which is wanting in his rival religionist the Christian. At the same time the fanciful picture of the Turk sitting stolidly under a shower of bullets because Fate will not find him out unless it be so written is a freak of fancy rarely found in real life.

There are four great points of dispute amongst the schoolmen in Al-Islam; (1) the Unity and Attributes of Allah, (2) His promises and threats, (3) historical as the office of Imám; and (4) Predestination and the justice thereof. On the latter subject opinions range over the whole cycle of possibilities. For instance, the Mu'tazilites, whom the learned Weil makes the Protestants and Rationalists of Al-Islam, contend that the word of Allah was created in subjecto, ergo, an accident and liable to perish, and one of their school, the Kádiriyah (= having power) denies the existence of Fate and contends that Allah did not create evil but left man an absolutely free agent. On the other hand, the Jabariyah (or Mujabbar = the compelled) is an absolute Fatalist who believes in the

479

omnipotence of Destiny and deems that all wisdom consists in conforming with its decrees. Al-Mas'udi (chapt. cxxvii.) illustrates this by the saying of a Moslem philosopher that chess was the invention of a Mu'tazil, while Nard (backgammon with dice) was that of a Mujabbar proving that play can do nothing against Destiny. Between the two are the Ashariyah; trimmers whose stand-point is hard to define; they would say, "Allah creates the power by which man acts, but man wills the action," and care not to answer the query, "Who created the will ?" (See Pocock, Sale and the Dabistan ii. 352). Thus Sa'adi says in the Gulistan (iii. 2), "The wise have pronounced that though daily bread be allotted, yet it is so conditionally upon using means to acquire it, and although calamity be predestined, yet it is right to secure oneself against the portals by which it may have access." Lastly, not a few doctors of Law and Religion hold that Kaza al-Muhkam, however absolute, regards only man's after or final state; and upon this subject they are of course as wise as other people, and — no wiser. Lane has treated the Moslem faith in Destiny very ably and fully (Arabian Nights, vol. i. pp. 58-61), and he being a man of moderate and orthodox views gives valuable testimony.

*

ANOINTING

Now Ishak had returned to his house on an occasion that called for him; and when he entered the vestibule, he heard a sound of singing, the like whereof he had never heard in the world, for that it was soft as the breeze and more strengthening than oil of almonds.

Arab. "Akwà min dahni 'l-lauz." These unguents have been used in the East from time immemorial whilst the last generation in England knew nothing of anointing with oil for incipient consumption. A late friend of mine, Dr. Stocks of the Bombay Establishment, and I proposed it as long back as 1845; but in those days it was a far cry from Sind to London.

*

IN THE SADDLE

So she mounted and the horse heaved like a wave under her and putting forth wings soared upwards with her, while the Shaykh flew by her side; whereat she was affrighted and clung to the pommel of the saddle; nor was it but an hour ere they came to a fair green meadow, fresh-flowered as if the soil thereof were a fine robe, purfled with all manner bright hues.

Which, in the East, is high and prominent whilst the cantle forms a back to the seat and the rider sits as in a baby's chair. The object is a firm seat when fighting: "across country" it is exceedingly dangerous.

*

RICHARD BURTON

INNER SIGHT

In Swedenborg's "Arcana Cœlestia" we read, "When man's inner sight is opened, which is that of his spirit; then there appear the things of another life which cannot be made visible to the bodily sight." Also "Evil spirits, when seen by eyes other than those of their infernal associates, present themselves by correspondence in the beast (fera) which represents their particular lust and life, in aspect direful and atrocious." These are the Jinns of Northern Europe.

*

NOT FOR INFIDEL EYES

I need hardly note the inscriptions upon the metal trays sold to Europeans. They are usually imitation words so that infidel eyes may not look upon the formulæ of prayer; and the same is the case with table-cloths, etc., showing a fancy Tohgra or Sultanic sign-manual.

*

SENSIBILITY OF THE GLANS

I here propose to consider at some length this curious custom which has prevailed amongst so many widely separated races. Its object has been noted (vol. v. 209), viz. to diminish the sensibility of the glans, no longer lubricated with prostatic lymph; thus the part is hardened against injury and disease and its work in coition is prolonged. On the other hand, "præputium in coitu voluptatem (of the woman) auget, unde femina præputiatis concubitum malunt quam cum Turcis ac Judæis " says Dimerbroeck (Anatomie). I vehemently doubt the fact. Circumcision was doubtless practised from ages immemorial by the peoples of Central Africa, and Welcker found traces of it in a mummy of the xvith century B.C. The Jews borrowed it from the Egyptian priesthood and made it a manner of sacrament, "uncircumcised" being = "unbaptised," that is, barbarian, heretic; it was a seal of reconciliation, a sign of alliance between the Creator and the Chosen People, a token of nationality imposed upon the body politic. Thus it became a cruel and odious protestation against the brotherhood of man, and the cosmopolitan Romans derided the verpæ ac verpi. The Jews also used the term figuratively as the "circumcision of fruits" (Lev. xix. 23), and of the heart (Deut. x. 16); and the old law gives copious historical details of its origin and continuance. Abraham first amputated his horny "calotte" at æt. 99, and did the same for his son and household (Gen. xvii. 24-27). The rite caused a separation between Moses and his wife (Exod. iv. 25). It was suspended during the Desert Wanderings and was resumed by Joshua (v. 3-7), who cut off two tons weight of prepuces. The latter became, like the scalps of the Scythians and the North-American "Indians," trophies of victory; Saul promised his daughter Michol to David for a dowry of one hundred, and the son-in-law brought double tale.

Amongst the early Christians opinions concerning the rite differed. Although the Founder of Christianity was circumcised, St. Paul, who aimed at a cosmopolitan faith discouraged it in the physical phase. St. Augustine still sustained that the rite removed original sin despite the Fathers who preceded and followed him, Justus, Tertullian, Ambrose and others. But it gradually lapsed into desuetude and was preserved only in the outlying regions. Paulus Jovius and Munster found it practised in Abyssinia, but as a mark of nobility confined to the descendants of "Nicaules, queen of Sheba." The Abyssinians still follow the Jews in performing the rite within eight days after the birth and baptise boys after forty and girls after eighty days. When a circumcised man became a Jew he was bled before three witnesses at the place where the prepuce had been cut off and this was called the "Blood of alliance." Apostate Jews effaced the sign of circumcision: so in 1 Matt. i. 16, fecerunt sibi præputia et recesserunt a Testamento Sancto. Thus making prepuces was called by the Hebrews Meshookim = recutiti{s}, and there is an allusion to it in 1 Cor. vii. 18, 19, {mè epispásthai} (Farrar, Paul ii. 70). St. Jerome and others deny the possibility; but Mirabeau (Akropodie) relates how Father Conning by liniments of oil, suspending weights, and wearing the virga in a box gained in 43 days 7¼ lines. The process is still practiced by Armenians and other Christians who, compelled to Islamise, wish to return to Christianity. I cannot however find a similar artifice applied to a circumcised clitoris. The simplest form of circumcision is mere amputation of the prepuce and I have noted (vol. v. 209) the difference between the Moslem and the Jewish rite, the latter according to some being supposed to heal in kindlier way. But the varieties of circumcision are immense. Probably none is more terrible than that practiced in the Province Al-Asír, the old Ophir, lying south of Al-Hijáz, where it is called Salkh, lit. = scarification. The patient, usually from ten to twelve years old, is placed upon raised ground holding m right hand a spear, whose heel rests upon his foot and whose point shows every tremour of the nerves. The tribe stands about him to pass judgement on his fortitude, and the barber performs the operation with the Jumbiyah-dagger, sharp as a razor. First he makes a shallow cut, severing only the skin across the belly immediately below the navel, and similar incisions down each groin; then he tears off the epidermis from the cuts downwards and flays the testicles and the penis, ending with amputation of the foreskin. Meanwhile the spear must not tremble and in some clans the lad holds a dagger over the back of the stooping barber, crying, "Cut and fear not!" When the ordeal is over, he exclaims, "Allaho Akbar!" and attempts to walk towards the tents soon falling for pain and nervous exhaustion, but the more steps he takes the more applause he gains. He is dieted with camel's milk, the wound is treated with salt and turmeric, and the chances in his favour are about ten to one. No body-pile or pecten ever grows upon the excoriated part which preserves through life a livid ashen hue. Whilst Mohammed Ali Pasha occupied the province he forbade "scarification" under pain of impalement, but it was resumed the moment he left Al-Asir. In Africa not only is circumcision indigenous, the operation varies more or less in the different tribes. In Dahome it is termed Addagwibi, and is performed between the twelfth and twentieth year. The rough operation is made peculiar by a double cut above and below; the prepuce being treated in the Moslem, not the Jewish fashion (loc. cit.). Heated sand is applied as a styptic and the patient is dieted with ginger-soup and warm drinks of ginger-water, pork being especially forbidden. The Fantis of the Gold Coast circumcise in sacred places, e.g., at Accra on a Fetish rock rising from the sea. The peoples of Sennaar, Taka, Masawwah and the adjacent regions follow the Abyssinian custom. The barbarous Bissagos and Fellups of North Western Guinea make cuts on the prepuce without amputating it; while the Baquens and Papels circumcise like Moslems. The blacks of Loango are all "verpæ," otherwise they would be rejected by the women. The Bantu or Caffre tribes are circumcised between the ages of fifteen and eighteen; the "Fetish boys," as we call them, are chalked white and wear only grass belts; they live outside the villages in special houses under an old "medicine-man," who teaches them not only virile arts but also to rob and fight. The "man-making" may last five months and ends in fêtes and dances: the patients are washed in the river, they burn down their quarters, take new names, and become adults, donning a kind of straw thimble over the prepuce. In Madagascar three several cuts are made causing much suffering to the children; and the nearest male relative swallows the prepuce. The Polynesians circumcise when childhood ends and thus consecrate the fecundating organ to the Deity. In Tahiti the operation is performed by the priest, and in Tonga only the priest is exempt. The Maories on the other hand fasten the prepuce over the glans, and the women of the Marquesas Islands have shown great cruelty to shipwrecked sailors who expose the glans. Almost all the known Australian tribes circumcise after some fashion: Bennett supposes the rite to have been borrowed from the Malays, while Gason enumerates the "Kurrawellie wonkauna" among the five mutilations of puberty. Leichhardt found circumcision about the Gulf of Carpentaria and in the river-valleys of the Robinson and Macarthur: others observed it on the Southern Coast and among the savages of Perth, where it is noticed by Salvado. James Dawson tells us "Circumciduntur pueri," etc., in Western Victoria. Brough Smyth, who supposes the object is to limit population (?), describes on the Western Coast and in Central Australia the "Corrobery"-dance and the operation performed with a quartz-flake. Teichelmann details the rite in Southern Australia where the assistants — all men, women, and children being driven away — form a "manner of human altar" upon which the youth is laid for circumcision. He then receives the normal two names, public and secret, and is initiated into the mysteries proper for men. The Australians also for Malthusian reasons produce an artificial hypospadias, while the Karens of New Guinea only split the prepuce longitudinally (Cosmos p. 369, Oct. 1876); the indigens of Port Lincoln on the West Coast split the virga: — Fenditur usque ad urethram a parte infera penis between the ages of twelve and fourteen, says E. J. Eyre in 1845. Missionary Schürmann declares that they open the urethra. Gason describes in the Dieyerie tribe the operation 'Kulpi" which is performed when the beard is long enough for tying. The member is placed upon a slab of tree-bark, the urethra is incised with a quartz-flake mounted in a gum handle and a splinter of bark is inserted to keep the cut open. These men may appear naked before women who expect others to clothe themselves. Miklucho Maclay calls it "Mika" in Central Australia: he was told by a squatter that of three hundred men only three or four had the member intact in order to get children, and that in one tribe the female births greatly outnumbered the male. Those mutilated also marry: when making water they sit like women slightly raising the penis, this in coition becomes flat and broad and the semen does not enter the matrix. The explorer believes that the deed of kind is more quickly done (?). Circumcision was also known to the New World. Herrera relates that certain Mexicans cut off the ears and prepuce of the newly born child, causing many to die. The Jews did not adopt the female circumcision of Egypt described by Huet on Origen — "Circumcisio feminarum fit resectione {tês nymphês} (sive clitoridis) quæ pars in Australium mulieribus ita crescit ut ferro est coërcenda." Here we have the normal confusion between excision of the nymphæ (usually for fibulation) and circumcision of the clitoris. Bruce notices this clitoridectomy among the Abyssinians. Werne describes the excision on the Upper White Nile and I have noted the complicated operation among the Somali tribes. Girls in Dahome are circumcised by ancient sages femmes, and a woman in the natural state would be derided by every one (See my Mission to Dahome, ii. 159) The Australians cut out the clitoris, and as I have noted elsewhere extirpate the ovary for Malthusian purposes (Journ Anthrop. Inst., vol. viii. of 1884).

*

IN THE COMPANY OF JINNS

Wuzu-ablution in that basin and pronouncing the Prohibition, prayed the dawn-prayer and what else had escaped her of orisons: after which she went out and walked in that garden among jessamine and lavender and roses and chamomile and gillyflowers and thyme and violets and basil royal, till she came to the door of the pavilion aforesaid.

i.e. the prayers of the last day and night which she had neglected while in company with the Jinns. The Hammam is not a pure place to pray in; but the Farz or Koranic orisons should be recited there if the legal term be hard upon its end.

*

LOOKING BACK

SLAVES, MALE AS well as female, are as fond of talking over their sale as European dames enjoy looking back upon the details of courtship and marriage.

RICHARD BURTON

*

SATAN'S PRESENCE

Then she pulled off her clothes and washed her body and made her Ghusl-ablution of the whole person and prayed that which was due from her of prayer from the evening of the previous day.

She made the Ghusl not because she had slept with a man, but because the impurity of Satan's presence called for the major ablution before prayer.

*

THE HOUSE AND THE HAUNTER

Presently, she heard a blowing behind her; so she turned and behold, a Head without a body and with eyes slit endlong it was of the bigness of an elephant's skull and bigger and had a mouth as it were an oven and projecting canines as they were grapnels, and hair which trailed upon the ground.

A phenomenon well known to spiritualists and to "The House and the Haunter." An old Dutch factory near Hungarian Fiume is famed for this mode of "obsession": the inmates hear the sound of footfalls, etc., behind them, especially upon the stairs; and see nothing.

*

STOP!

ARAB. "ARJA'" LIT. return! but here meaning to stop. It is much used by donkey-boys from Cairo to Fez in the sense of "Get out of the way." Hence the Spanish arre! which gave rise to arriero = a carrier, a muleteer.

*

DIGNITY

Presently up came the kings of the Jinn from every side and kissed ground before the queen and stood in her service and she thanked them for this, but moved not for one of them.

This assertion of dignity, which is permissible in royalty, has been absurdly affected by certain "dames" in Anglo-Egypt who are quite the reverse of queenly; and who degrade "dignity" to the vulgarest affectation.

*

CONFIRMATIONAL CUT

THE ARAB BOY who, unlike the Jew, is circumcised long after infancy and often in his teens, thus making the ceremony conform after a fashion with our "Confirmation," is displayed before being operated upon, to family and friends; and the

491

seat is a couch covered with the richest tapestry. So far it resembles the bride-throne.

*

YOUNG BLOOD

SHOWING THE ANTIQUITY of "Après moi le déluge," the fame of all old politicians and aged statesmen who can expect but a few years of life. These "burning questions" (e.g. the Bulgarian) may be smothered for a time, but the result is that they blaze forth with increased violence. We have to thank Lord Palmerston (an Irish landlord) for ignoring the growth of Fenianism and another aged statesman for a sturdy attempt to disunite the United Kingdom. An old notion wants young blood at its head.

*

THE LONG-NECKED

Thereat Queen Al-Shahba rejoiced and with her all who were present; and they admired her speech and fell to kissing her; and when she had made an end of her song, Queen Kamariyah said to her, "O my sister, ere thou go to thy palace, I would fain bring thee to look upon Al-'Anká, daughter of Bahram Júr, whom Al-'Anká, daughter of the wind, carried off, and her beauty; for that there is not her fellow on earth's face."

CONGRESS WITH A CROCODILE

Lit. "The long-necked (bird)" before noticed with the Rukh (Roc) in vol. v. 122. Here it becomes a Princess, daughter of Bahrám-i-Gúr (Bahram of the Onager, his favourite game), the famous Persian king in the fifth century, a contemporary of Theodosius the younger and Honorius. The "Anká" is evidently the Iranian Símurgh.

*

DAUGHTERS OF LOVE

ARAB. "BANÁT-AL-HAWÁ" LIT. daughters of love, usually meaning an Anonyma, a fille de joie; but here the girl is of good repute, and the offensive term must be modified to a gay, frolicsome lass.

*

BLEMISHES OF THE UNWANTED

...but, when he lifted the head-gear from the bride's head and the veil from her face and looked, he saw a foul face and a favour right fulsome; indeed he beheld somewhat whereof may Allah never show thee the like! loathly, dispensing from description, inasmuch as there were reckoned in her all legal defects.

i.e. All the blemishes which justify returning a slave to the slave-dealer.

493

RICHARD BURTON

*

UNCLEAN

SEE VOL. V. 199. I may remark that the practice of bathing after copulation was kept up by both sexes in ancient Rome. The custom may have originated in days when human senses were more acute. I have seen an Arab horse object to be mounted by the master when the latter had not washed after sleeping with a woman.

*

CARAVANSERAI

THE EGYPTIAN TERM for a khan, called in Persia caravanserai (karwán-serái); and in Marocco funduk, from the Greek; whence the Spanish "fonda." See vol. i. 92.

*

OUTBURST OF OBSCENITY

Presently, Abú Nowás met him. (Now he was those of is of whom it said, "They love fair lads," and indeed there is said what is said concerning him).

As a rule whenever this old villain appears in The Nights, it is a signal for an outburst of obscenity. Here, however, we are quittes pour la peur. See vol. v. 65 for some of his abominations.

CONGRESS WITH A CROCODILE

*

INSTINCTIVE BRUTALITY

The folk flocked to him from all sides and fell to beating and abusing Nur al-Din, whilst he cried out for aidance but none aided him, and Al-Muradi kept saying to him, "But yesterday the Commander of the Faithful released thee and to-day thou robbest!"

The brutality of a Moslem mob on such occasions is phenomenal: no fellow-feeling makes them decently kind. And so at executions even women will take an active part in insulting and tormenting the criminal, tearing his hair, spitting in his face and so forth. It is the instinctive brutality with which wild beasts and birds tear to pieces a wounded companion.

*

BURNING OIL

Accordingly, the hangman took him and bringing out the knife, proceeded to cut off his hand, while Al-Muradi said to him, "Cut and sever the bone and fry not in oil the stump for him, so he may lose all his blood and we be at rest from him."

RICHARD BURTON

The popular way of stopping hemorrhage by plunging the stump into burning oil which continued even in Europe till Ambrose Paré taught men to take up the arteries.

*

ON BURKAS

ARAB. "BURKA'," THE face veil of Egypt, Syria, and Arabia with two holes for the eyes, and the end hanging to the waist, a great contrast with the "Lithám" or coquettish fold of transparent muslin affected by modest women in Stambul.

*

STOMACH TROUBLES

WINE, CARRION AND pork being lawful to the Moslem if used to save life. The former is also the sovereignest thing for inward troubles, flatulence, indigestion, etc. See vol. v. 2, 24.

*

EMBODIED WILL

I HAVE NOTICED that among Arab lovers it was the fashion to be jealous of the mistress's nightly phantom which, as amongst mesmerists, is the lover's embodied will.

*

CONGRESS WITH A CROCODILE

FRISIAN DIALECT

ARAB. "KATL." I have noticed the Hibernian "kilt" which is not a bull but, like most provincialisms and Americanisms, a survival, an archaism. In the old Frisian dialect, which agrees with English in more words than "bread, butter and cheese," we find the primary meaning of terms which with us have survived only in their secondary senses, e.g. killen = to beat and slagen = to strike. Here is its great value to the English philologist. When the Irishman complains that he is "kilt" we know through the Frisian what he really means.

*

SWOOPING JINN-LIKE

Then he rushed upon him, as he were a swooper of the Jinn, and Hodhayfah met him and they wheeled about a long while.

i.e. as he were a flying Jinni, swooping down and pouncing falcon-like upon a mortal from the upper air.

*

TRICKY AS AN OLD LADY

Now the value of the shop was four thousand dinars so they played and Al-Abbas beat him and won his shop, with whatso was therein; upon which the other arose, shaking his clothes, and said to him, "Up, O youth, and take thy shop."

In sign of quitting possession. Chess in Europe is rarely played for money, with the exception of public matches: this, however, is not the case amongst Easterns, who are also for the most part as tricky as an old lady at cribbage rightly named.

*

VISITS RARE

The Prince did this and the merchant rejoiced in his neighbourhood and left him not night nor day, so Al-Abbas said to him, "By the Lord, we distract thee from thy livelihood."

This most wearisome form of politeness is common in the Moslem world, where men fondly think that the more you see of them the more you like of them. Yet their Proverbial Philosophy ("the wisdom of many and the wit of one") strongly protests against the practice: I have already quoted Mohammed's saying, "Zur ghibban, tazid Hibban" — visits rare keep friendship fair.

*

CONGRESS WITH A CROCODILE

IN KINDNESS

"The king biddeth thee in weal." "To hear is to obey," quoth Al-Abbas and accompanied the officer to the king's palace.

Easterns are always startled by a sudden summons to the presence either of King or Kazi: here the messenger gives the youth to understand that it is in kindness, not in anger.

*

FIGHT AGAINST TIME

THOSE BLOOD-FEUDS ARE most troublesome to the traveller, who may be delayed by them for months: and, until a peace be patched up, he will never be allowed to pass from one tribe to their enemies. A quarrel of the kind prevented my crossing Arabia from Al-Medinah to Maskat (Pilgrimage, ii. 297), and another in Africa from visiting the head of the Tanganyika Lake. In all such journeys the traveller who has to fight against Time is almost sure to lose.

*

FIRST TO MOUNT

THE ARAB OF noble tribe is always the first to mount his own mare: he also greatly fears her being put out to full speed by a stranger, holding that this should be reserved for occasions of life and death; and that it can be done to perfection only once during the animal's life.

*

RED CAMELS

THE RED (AHMAR) dromedary like the white-red (Sabah) were most valued because they are supposed best to bear the heats of noon; and thus "red camels" is proverbially used for wealth. When the head of Abu Jahl was brought in after the Battle of Bedr, Mahommed exclaimed, "'Tis more acceptable to me than a red camel!"

*

SLEEPY LOOKS

EASTERNS ARE RIGHT in regarding a sleepy languorous look as one of the charms of women, and an incitement to love because suggestive only of bed. Some men also find the same pleasure in a lacrymose expression of countenance, seeming always to call for consolation: one of the most successful women I know owes her exceptional good fortune to this charm.

*

FARTHEST LAND

Arab. "Bilád al-Maghrib (al-Aksa," in full) = the Farthest Land of the setting Sun, shortly called Al-Maghrib and the people "Maghribi." The earliest occurrence of our name Morocco or Marocco I find in the "Marákiyah" of Al-Mas'udi (iii. 241), who apparently applies it to a district whither the Berbers migrated.

*

RESPECTABLE

Then they put off that which was upon them of ornaments and laying aside the lutes and other instruments of music, kept to their houses like modest women and veiled, and fared not forth.

In these unregenerate days they would often be summoned to the houses of the royal family; but now they had "got religion" and, becoming freed women, were resolved to be "respectable." In not a few Moslem countries men of wealth and rank marry professional singers who, however loose may have been their artistic lives, mostly distinguish themselves by decency of behaviour often pushed to the extreme of rigour. Also jeune coquette, vieille dévote is a rule of the world, Eastern and Western.

*

RICHARD BURTON

DECENCY FORBIDS

*Then there befel that which befel of his union with the elder
sister, and when he went up to his couch, that he might sleep,
the younger sister said to her elder, "Allah, upon thee, O my
sister, an thou be not asleep, tell us a tale of thy goodly tales,
wherewith we may beguile the watches of our night, ere day
dawn and parting."*

Here, as in the Introduction (vol. i. 24), the king consummates
his marriage in presence of his virgin sister-in-law, a process
which decency forbids amongst Moslems.

*

GOURD USE

THE EASTERN SUCCEDANEUM for swimming corks and other
"life-preservers." The practice is very ancient; we find these
gourds upon the monuments of Egypt and Babylonia.

*

BAD BREATH

IN THE TAMIL version (Babington's translation of the
"Vedála Kadai") there are but two brothers, one of whom
is fastidious in his food, the other in beds: the latter lies on
a bed stuffed with flowers, deprived of their stalks. In the

502

morning he complains of pains all over his body, and on examining the bed one hair is found amongst the flowers. In the Hindí version, the king asks him in the morning whether he had slept comfortably. "O great King," he replied; "I did not sleep all night." "How so?" quoth he. "O great King, in the seventh fold of the bedding there is a hair, which pricked me in the back, therefore I could not sleep." The youth who was fastidious about the fair sex had a lovely damsel laid beside him, and he was on the point of kissing her, but on smelling her breath he turned away his face, and went to sleep. Early in the morning the king (who had observed through a lattice what passed) asked him, "Did you pass the night pleasantly?" He replied that he did not, because the smell of a goat proceeded from the girl's mouth, which made him very uneasy. The king then sent for the procuress and ascertained that the girl had been brought up on goat's milk.

*

SCIENCE OF STRATAGEM

This version occurs in a tale of three artful wives — or, to employ the storyteller's own graphic terms, "three whales of the sea of fraud and deceit: three dragons of the nature of thunder and the quickness of lightning; three defamers of honour and reputation; namely, three men-deceiving, lascivious women, each of whom had from the chicanery of her cunning issued the diploma of turmoil to a hundred cities and countries, and in the arts of fraud they accounted Satan as an admiring spectator in the theatre of their stratagems… "

So, too, in the "Bahár-i-Dánish" a woman is described as being so able a professor in the school of deceit, that she could have instructed the devil in the science of stratagem: of another it is said that by her wiles she could have drawn the devil's claws; and of a third the author declares, that the devil himself would own there was no escaping from her cunning!

*

PRIMITIVE ATTIRE

Herewith he brought forth pouch four strips of a yellow silken stuff and zoning himself with one threw the other over his shoulders; and he gave the two remaining pieces to the Prince that he might do with them on like wise.

I have noted that this is the primitive attire of Eastern man in all hot climates, and that it still holds its ground in that grand survival of heathenry, the Meccan Pilgrimage. In Galland the four strips are of *taffetas jaune*, the Hind. "Taftí."

*

CONGRESS WITH A CROCODILE

AN OARSMAN'S LABOUR

IN EASTERN COUNTRIES the oarsman stands to his work and lessens his labour by applying his weight which cannot be done so forcibly when sitting even upon the sliding-seat. In rowing as in swimming we have forsaken the old custom and have lost instead of gaining.

*

NO ABSURD SHAME

ARAB. "SHAHWAH" THE rawest and most direct term. The Moslem religious has no absurd shame of this natural passion. I have heard of a Persian Imam, who, suddenly excited as he was sleeping in a friend's house, awoke the master with, "Shahwah dáram" = "I am lustful" and was at once gratified by a "Mut'ah," temporary and extempore marriage to one of the slave-girls. These morganatic marriages are not, I may note, allowed to the Sunnis.

*

SEEING MARVELS

"On reaching the saloon thou shalt there find a Lamp hanging from its ceiling; so mount the ladder and take that Lamp and place it in thy breast-pocket after pouring out its contents; nor

505

fear evil from it for thy clothes because its contents are not common oil..."

The idea is borrowed from the lume eterno of the Rosicrucians. It is still prevalent throughout Syria where the little sepulchral lamps buried by the Hebrews, Greeks and Romans are so called. Many tales are told of their being found burning after the lapse of centuries; but the traveller will never see the marvel.

*

SIGNET RINGS

THE FIRST NOTICE of the signet-ring and its adventures is by Herodotus in the Legend of the Samian Polycrates; and here it may be observed that the accident is probably founded on fact; every fisherman knows that fish will seize and swallow spoon-bait and other objects that glitter. The text is the Talmudic version of Solomon's seal-ring. The king of the demons after becoming a "Bottle-imp," prayed to be set free upon condition of teaching a priceless secret, and after cajoling the Wise One flung his signet into the sea and cast the owner into a land four hundred miles distant. Here David's son begged his bread till he was made head cook to the King of Ammon at Mash Kernín. After a while, he eloped with Na'·zah, the daughter of his master, and presently when broiling a fish found therein his missing property. In the Moslem version, Solomon had taken prisoner Amínah, the daughter of a pagan prince, and had homed her in his Harem, where she taught him idolatry. One day before going to the Hammam he entrusted to her his signet-ring presented to him by the four angelic Guardians of sky, air, water and earth when the mighty Jinni Al-Sakhr (see vol. i. 41; v. 36), who was hovering about unseen, snatching away the ring, assumed the king's shape, whereby Solomon's form became so changed that his courtiers drove him from his own doors. Thereupon Al-Sakhr, taking seat upon the throne, began to work all manner of iniquity, till one of the Wazirs, suspecting the transformation, read aloud from a scroll of the law: this caused the demon to fly shrieking and to drop the signet into the sea. Presently Solomon, who had taken service with a fisherman, and received for wages two fishes a day, found his ring and made Al-Sakhr a "Bottle-imp." The legend of St. Kentigern or Mungo of Glasgow, who recovered the Queen's ring from the stomach of a salmon, is a palpable imitation of the Biblical incident which paid tribute to Cæsar.

*

AFRICA PROPRIA

For this Maghrabi was an African of Afrikíyah proper, born in the Inner Sunset-land, and from his earliest age upwards he had been addicted to witchcraft and had studied and practised every manner of occult science, for which unholy lore the city of Africa is notorious.

RICHARD BURTON

Africa (Arab. Afrikíyah) here is used in its old and classical
sense for the limited tract about Carthage (Tunis) net, Africa
Propria. But the scribe imagines it to be the P. N. of a city:
so in Júdar (vol. vi. 222) we find Fás and Miknàs (Fez and
Mequinez) converted into one settlement. The Maghribi,
Mauritanian or Maroccan is famed for sorcery throughout
the Moslem world: see vol. vi. 220. The Moslem "Kingdom
of Afrikiyah" was composed of four provinces, Tunis,
Tripoli, Constantina, and Bugia: and a considerable part of
it was held by the Berber tribe of Sanhája or Sinhága, also
called the Zenag whence our modern "Senegal." Another
noted tribe which held Bajaiyah (Bugia) in Afrikiyah proper
was the "Zawáwah," the European "Zouaves," (Ibn Khall.
iv. 84).

*

STRIPPED OF ONE'S SKIN

*But thou wottest not, my child, that the Jews ever hold lawful
to them the good of Moslems, the Confessors of Allah Almighty's
unity, and, always defraud them; especially this accursed Jew
with whom thou hast relations and into whose hands thou
hast fallen.*

This may be true, but my experience has taught me to
prefer dealing with a Jew than with a Christian. The former
will "jew" me perhaps, but his commercial cleverness will
induce him to allow me some gain in order that I may not

be quite disheartened: the latter will strip me of my skin and will grumble because he cannot gain more.

*

TREASURE TROVE

Alaeddin, however, seeing his parent take courage when he explained to her the workings of the Lamp, feared less she might tattle to the folk thereof; so he said to her, "O my mother, beware how thou talk to any of the properties of the Lamp and its profit, as this is our one great good..."

In Eastern states the mere suspicion of having such an article would expose the suspected at least to torture. Their practical system of treating "treasure trove," as I saw when serving with my regiment in Gujarát (Guzerat), is at once to imprison and "molest" the finder, in order to make sure that he has not hidden any part of his find.

*

ARRIVAL OF THE JINN

"...Therefore I command thee (an thou be a trusty Servitor to the Lamp when thou shalt see bride and bridegroom bedded together this night, at once take them up and bear them hither abed; and this be what I want of thee."

The H. V. gives a sketch of the wedding. "And when the ceremonies ended at the palace with pomp and parade and pageant, and the night was far spent, the eunuchs led the Wazir's son into the bridal chamber. He was the first to seek his couch; then the Queen his mother-in-law, came into him leading the bride, and followed by her suite. She did with her virgin daughter as parents are wont to do, removed her wedding-raiment, and donning a night-dress, placed her in her bridegroom's arms. Then, wishing her all joy, she with her ladies went away and shut the door. At that instant came the Jinni," etc.

*

NAKED SWORD

Presently the youth arose and stripping off his outer dress placed a scimitar between them and lay upon the bed beside the Princess. And he no villain deed, for it sufficed him to prevent the consummation of her nuptuals with the Wazir's son.

For the old knightly practice of sleeping with a drawn sword separating man and maid see vol. vii. 353 and Mr. Clouston's "Popular Tales and Fictions," vol. i. 316. In Poland the intermediary who married by procuration slept alongside the bride in all his armour. The H. V. explains, "He (Alaeddin) also lay a naked sword between him and the Princess so she might perceive that he was ready to die by that blade should he attempt to do aught of villainy by the bride."

*

PURE AND UNSPOTTED

PROFESSIONAL SINGING AND dancing girls: Properly the word is the fem. Of ' lim = a learned man; but it has been anglicised by Byron's

"The long chibouque's dissolving cloud supply,

Where dance the Almahs to wild minstrelsy." — (The Corsair, ii. 2.)

They go about the streets with unveiled faces and are seldom admitted into respectable Harems, although on festal occasions they perform in the court or in front of the house, but even this is objected to by the Mrs. Grundy of Egypt. Lane (M.E. chap. xviii.) derives with Saint Jerome the word from the Heb. or Phoenician Almah = a virgin, a girl, a singing-girl; and thus explains "Alámoth" in Psalms xlvi. and I Chron. xv. 20. Parkhurst (s.v. 'Alamah = an undeflowered virgin) renders Job xxxix. 30, "the way of a man with a maid" (bi-álmah). The way of a man in his virgin state, shunning youthful lust and keeping himself "pure and unspotted."

*

RICHARD BURTON

WELL OF ENGLISH SPEECH

ARAB. DAHAB RAMLI = gold dust washed out of the sand, placer-gold. I must excuse myself for using this Americanism, properly a diluvium or deposit of sand, and improperly (Bartlett) a find of drift gold. The word, like many mining terms in the Far West, is borrowed from the Spaniards; it is not therefore one of the many American vulgarisms which threaten hopelessly to defile the pure well of English speech.

*

THREE CLASSES OF APHRODISIAC

Then he was served with sherbets and ambergris'd coffee and, after drinking, he arose and a party of black slaves came forwards and clad him in the costliest of clothing, then perfumed and fumigated him.

For this aphrodisiac see vol. vi. 60. The subject of aphrodisiacs in the East would fill a small library: almost every medical treatise ends in a long disquisition upon fortifiers, provocatives' etc. We may briefly divide them into three great classes. The first is the medicinal, which may be either external or internal. The second is the mechanical, such as scarification' flagellation, and the application of insects as practiced by certain savage races. There is a venerable Joe Miller of an old Brahmin whose young wife always insisted, each time before he possessed her, upon his being stung by a bee in certain parts. The third is magical superstitious and so forth.

*

MOUTH-WATERING

Then fetch me a stallion fit for the riding of the Chosroes and let his furniture, all thereof, be of crusted with the gold finest gems fetch me also eight and forty thousand dinars that each white slave may carry a thousand gold pieces.

This may sound exaggerated to English ears, but a petty Indian Prince, such as the Gáikwár, or Rajah of Baroda, would be preceded in state processions by several led horses all whose housings and saddles were gold studded with diamonds. The sight made one's mouth water.

*

FORCE OF FANCY

...wherefore he went up to discover what was to do and found the Devotee standing a middlemost the throng, and all who suffered from pain or sickness flocked to her soliciting a blessing and praying for her prayers and each and every she touched became whole of his illness.

Evidently *la force de l'imagination*, of which a curious illustration was given in Paris during the debauched days of the Second Empire. Before a highly "fashionable" assembly of men appeared a youth in fleshings who sat down upon a stool, bared his pudenda and closed his eyes when, by "force of fancy," erection and emission took place. But presently it was suspected and proved that the stool was hollow and admitted from below a hand whose titillating fingers explained the phenomenon.

*

SLEEPING POSTURES

MOSLEMS ARE CURIOUS about sleeping postures and the popular saying is: — Lying upon the right side is proper to Kings; upon the left to Sages, to sleep supine is the position of Allah's Saints and prone upon the belly is peculiar to the Devils.

*

RANK MESMERISM

Hereupon she straightway bade summon Fatimah that the Devotee might impose her hand upon his head; and Alaeddin asked her, "Who may this Fatimah be?"

Rank mesmerism, which has been practiced in the East from ages immemorial. In Christendom Santa Guglielma worshipped at Brunate, "works many miracles, chiefly healing aches of head." In the H. V. Alaeddin feigns that he is ill and fares to the Princess with his head tied up.

*

TURQUOISE

Pírozah = turquoise, is the Persian, Fir·zah and Firuzakh (De Sacy, Chrest. ii. 84) the Arab. forms. The stone is a favourite in the East where, as amongst the Russians (who affect to despise the Eastern origin of their blood to which they owe so much of its peculiar merit), it is supposed to act talisman against wounds and death in battle; and the Persians, who hold it to be a guard against the Evil Eye, are fond of inscribing "turquoise of the old rock" with one or more of the "Holy Names." Of these talismans a modern Spiritualist asks, "Are rings and charms and amulets magnetic, to use an analogue for what we cannot understand, and has the immemorial belief in the power of relics a natural not to say a scientific basis?"

*

RICHARD BURTON

SAMARIA

The King did according to the counsel of his Wazir and despatched his loathed Queen to Samaria 1 accompanied by a writ with the following purport, to his nephew...

Samaria is a well-known name amongst Moslems, who call the city Shamrín and Shamrún. It was built, according to Ibn Batrik, upon Mount Samir by Amri who gave it the first name; and the Taríkh Samírí, by Aba al-Fath Abuú al-Hasan, is a detailed account of its garbled annals. As Nablús (Neapolis of Herod., also called by him Sebaste) it is now familiar to the Cookite.

*

HABSHÍ

IN THE TEXT Zangi-i-Adam-kh'wár afterwards called Habashi = an Abyssinian. Galland simply says un negre. In India the "Habshí" (chief) of Jinjirah (= Al-Jazirah, the Island) was admiral of the Grand Moghul's fleets. These negroids are still dreaded by Hindús and Hindís and, when we have another "Sepoy Mutiny," a few thousands of them bought upon the Zanzibar coast, dressed, drilled and officered by Englishmen, will do us yeomans' service.

*

NOBLEST GAME

THE ONAGER, CONFOUNDED by our older travellers with the zebra, is the Gúr-i-khár of Persia, where it is the noblest game from which kings did not disdain to take a cognomen, e.g., Bahrám-i-Gúr. It is the "wild ass" of Jeremiah (ii. 24: xiv. 6). The meat is famous in poetry for combining the flavours peculiar to all kinds of flesh (Ibn Khallikan iii. 117; iii. 239, etc.) and is noticed by Herodotus (Clio. cxxxiii.) and by Xenophon (Cyro. lib. 1) in sundry passages: the latter describes the *relays of* horses and hounds which were used in chasing it then as now. The traveller Olearius (A. D. 1637) found it more common than in our present day: Shah Abbas turned thirty-two wild asses into an enclosure where they were shot as an item of entertainment to the ambassadors at his court. The skin of the wild ass's back produces the famous shagreen, a word seemingly derived from the Pers. "Saghrí," e.g. "Kyafash-i-Saghri" = slippers of shagreen, fine wear fit for a "young Duke". See in Ibn Khallikan (iv. 245) an account of a "Júr" (the Arabised "Gúr") eight hundred years old.

*

THE RIGHT MOUNT

Accordingly the leech rode on leisurely for the city and on the road he met a lady mounted a she mule whose housings were of the richest and finest, upon while behind her walked confidential servants, followed by a band of horsemen and foot-soldiers and Habashi slaves...

Here and below the Hindostani version mounts the lady upon a camel ("Ushtur" or "Unth") which is not customary in India except when criminals are led about the bazar. An elephant would have been in better form.

*

BLOOD OF THE TARTAR PLAINS

IN THE HINDI, as in Galland's version, the horse is naturally enough of Turcoman blood. I cannot but think that in India we have unwisely limited ourselves for cavalry remounts to the Western market that exports chiefly the mongrel "Gulf Arab" and have neglected the far hardier animal, especially the Gútdán blood of the Tartar plains, which supply "excellent horses whose speed and bottom are" say travellers in general, "so justly celebrated throughout Asia." Our predecessors were too wise to "put all the eggs in one basket."

*

THE MOTHER'S RANK

When Khudadad heard that the Princess his spouse was his father's guest, he rejoiced with exceeding joy cried, "Suffer me first to see my mother; then will I go to the Princess of Daryabar."

Here, after Moslem fashion, the mother ranks before the wife: "A man can have many wives but only one mother." The idea is old amongst Easterns: see Herodotus and his Christian commentators on the history of Intaphernes' wife (Thalia, cap. cxix). "O King," said that lady of mind logical, "I may get me another mate if God will and other children an I lose these; but as my father and my mother are no longer alive, I may not by any means have another brother," etc., etc.

*

THIRST OVER HUNGER

THIRST VERY JUSTLY takes precedence of hunger: a man may fast for forty days, but with out water in a tropical country he would die within a week. For a description of the horrors of thirst see my "First Footsteps in East Africa," pp. 387-8.

*

THE CONCUBINE OF SOLOMON

I.E. THE SECURE (fem.). It was the name of the famous concubine of Solomon to whom he entrusted his ring (vol. vi. 84), also of the mother of Mohammed who having taken her son to Al-Medinah (Yathrib) died on the return journey. I cannot understand why the Apostle of Al-Islam, according to his biographers and commentators, refused to pray for his parent's soul, she having been born in Al-Fitrah (the interval between the fall of Christianity and the birth of Al-Islam), when he had not begun to preach his "dispensation."

*

HYDROPHOBIA

THIS HATE OF the friend of man is inherited from Jewish ancestors; and, wherever the Hebrew element prevails, the muzzle, which has lately made its appearance in London, is strictly enforced, as at Trieste. Amongst the many boons which civilisation has conferred upon Cairo I may note hydrophobia; formerly unknown in Egypt the dreadful disease has lately caused more than one death. In India sporadic cases have at rare times occurred in my own knowledge since 1845.

*

NAILING THE CORPSE

GALLAND NAILS DOWN the corpse in the bier — a Christian practice — and he certainly knew better. Moreover, prayers for the dead are mostly recited over the bier when placed upon the brink of the grave; nor is it usual for a woman to play so prominent a part in the ceremony.

*

ENFANTS TERRIBLES

IN ARAB FOLK-LORE there are many instances of such precocious boys — enfants terribles they must be in real life. In Ibn Khall. (iii. 104) we find notices of a book "Kitáb Nujabá al-Abná" = Treatise on Distinguished Children, by Ibn Zakar al- Sakalli (the Sicilian), ob. A. D. 1169-70. And the boy-Kazi is a favourite role in the plays of peasant-lads who enjoy the irreverent "chaff" almost as much as when "making a Pasha." This reminds us of the boys electing Cyrus as their King in sport (Herodotus, i. 114). For the cycle of "Precocious Children" and their adventures, see Mr. Clouston (Popular Tales, etc., ii. 1- 14), who enters into the pedigree and affiliation. I must, however, differ with that able writer when he remarks at the end, "And now we may regard the story of Valerius Maximus with suspicion, and that of Lloyd as absolutely untrue, so far as William Noy's alleged share in the 'case.' "The jest or the event happening again and again is no valid proof of its untruth; and it is often harder to believe in derivation than in spontaneous growth.

*

FLYING CARPETS

THE GREAT PROTOTYPE of the Flying Carpet is that of Sulayman bin Dáúd, a fable which the Koran (chap. xxi. 81) borrowed from the Talmud, not from "Indian fictions." It was of green sendal embroidered with gold and silver and studded with precious stones, and its length and breadth were such that all the Wise King's host could stand upon it, the men to the left and the Jinns to the right of the throne; and when all were ordered, the Wind, at royal command, raised it and wafted it whither the Prophet would, while an army of birds flying overhead canopied the host from the sun. In the Middle Ages the legend assumed another form. "Duke Richard, surnamed 'Richard sans peur,' walking with his courtiers one evening in the forest of Moulineaux, near one of his castles on the banks of the Seine, hearing a prodigious noise coming towards him, sent one of his esquires to know what was the matter, who brought him word that it was a company of people under a leader or King. Richard, with five hundred of his bravest Normans, went out to see a sight which the peasants were so accustomed to that they viewed it two or three times a week without fear. The sight of the troop, preceded by two men, who spread a cloth on the ground, made all the Normans run away, and leave the Duke alone. He saw the strangers form themselves into a circle on the cloth, and on asking who they were, was told that they were the spirits of Charles V., King of France, and his servants, condemned to expiate their sins by fighting all night against the wicked and the damned. Richard desired to be of their party, and receiving a strict charge not to quit the cloth, was conveyed with them to Mount Sinai, where, leaving them without quitting the cloth, he said his prayers in the Church of St. Catherine's Abbey there, while they were fighting, and returned with them. In proof of the truth of this story, he brought back half the wedding-ring of a knight in that convent, whose wife, after six years, concluded him dead, and was going to take a second husband." (Note in the Lucknow Edition of The Nights.)

*

THE WILL OF MAN

AMONGST EASTERN PEOPLES, and especially adepts, the will of man is not a mere term for a mental or cerebral operation, it takes the rank of a substance; it becomes a mighty motive power, like table-turning and other such phenomena which, now looked upon as child's play, will perform a prime part in the Kinetics of the century to come. If a few pair of hands imposed upon a heavy dinner-table can raise it in the air, as I have often seen, what must we expect to result when the new motive force shall find its Franklin and be shown to the world as real "Vril"? The experiment of silently willing a subject to act in a manner not suggested by speech or sign has been repeatedly tried and succeeded in London drawing-rooms; and it has lately been suggested that atrocious crimes have resulted from overpowering volition. In cases of paralysis the Faculty is agreed upon the fact that local symptoms disappear when the will-power returns to the brain. And here I will boldly and baldly state my theory that, in sundry cases, spectral appearances (ghosts) and abnormal smells and sounds are simply the effect of a Will which has, so to speak, created them.

RICHARD BURTON

*

TELESCOPES

THE ORIGIN OF the lens and its applied use to the telescope and the microscope are "lost" (as the Castle-guides of Edinburgh say) "in the glooms of antiquity." Well ground glasses have been discovered amongst the finds of Egypt and Assyria: indeed much of the finer work of the primeval artists could not have been done without such aid. In Europe the "spy-glass" appears first in the Opus Majus of the learned Roger Bacon (circa A. D. 1270); and his "optic tube" (whence his saying "all things are known by perspective"), chiefly contributed to make his wide-spread fame as a wizard. The telescope was popularised by Galileo who (as mostly happens) carried off and still keeps, amongst the vulgar, all the honours of invention. Some "Illustrators" of The Nights confound this "Nazzárah," the Pers. "Dúr-bín," or far-seer, with the "Magic Mirror," a speculum which according to Gower was set up in Rome by Virgilius the Magician hence the Mirror of Glass in the Squire's tale; Merlin's glassie Mirror of Spenser (F. Q. ii. 24); the mirror in the head of the monstrous fowl which forecast the Spanish invasion to the Mexicans; the glass which in the hands of Cornelius Agrippa (A. D. 1520) showed to the Earl of Surrey fair Geraldine "sick in her bed;" to the globe of glass in The Lusiads; Dr. Dee's show-stone, a bit of cannel-coal; and lastly the zinc and copper disk of the absurdly called "electro-biologist." I have noticed this matter at some length in various places.

*

SUFFERING SECRET CHARMS

THE WISH MIGHT have been highly indiscreet and have exposed the wisher to the resentment of the two other brothers. In parts of Europe it is still the belief of the vulgar that men who use telescopes can see even with the naked eye objects which are better kept hidden; and I have heard of troubles in the South of France because the villagers would not suffer the secret charms of their women to become as it were the public property of the lighthouse employés.

*

FORTUNE'S FAVOURITE

IN FOLK-LORE AND fairy tales the youngest son of mostly three brothers is generally Fortune's favourite: at times also he is the fool or the unlucky one of the family, Cinderella being his counterpart (Mr. Clouston, i. 321).

*

CAGE OF CLAPHAM

THIS IMPRISONMENT OF the good Queen reminds home readers of the "Cage of Clapham" wherein a woman with child was imprisoned in A.D. 1700, and which was noted by Sir George Grove as still in existence about 1830.

RICHARD BURTON

*

BLOOD SPEAKING TO BLOOD

So the Princes farewelled and prayed for him; then rode back home; but they both forgo to tell their sister how they had fallen in with the King; and of all that passed between them they remembered not one word.

A most improbable and absurd detail: its sole excuse is the popular superstition of "blood speaking to blood." The youths being of the royal race felt that they could take unwarrantable liberties.

*

SWALLOWING INSECTS

Pandit S. M. Natésa Sástrí, in "Indian Notes and Queries," for March, 1887, says that women swallow large numbers of an insect called pillai-puchchi (son-insect: gryllas) in the hope of bearing sons, they will also drink the water squeezed from the loin-cloth of a sanyásí devotee after washing it for him! — Another correspondent in the same periodical. Pandit Putlíbái K. Raghunathjé, writes that Hindu women, for the purpose of having children, especially a son, observe the fourth lunar day of every dark fortnight as a fast and break their fast only after seeing the moon, generally before 9 or 10 p.m. A dish of twenty-one small, marble-like balls of rice is prepared, in one of which is put some salt. The whole dish is then served up to the woman, and while eating it she should first lay her hands on the ball containing salt, as it is believed to be a positive sign that she will be blessed with a son. In that case she should give up eating the rest, but otherwise she should go on eating till she lays her hands on the salted ball. The Pandit adds, that the observance of this ball depends on the wish of the woman. She may observe it on only one, five, seven, eleven, or twenty-one lunar fourth days, or chaturthí. Should she altogether fail in picking out the salted ball first, she may be sure of remaining barren all her life long.

*

LUSTRE OF THE EYES

SURMA IS A collyrium applied to the edges of the eyelids to increase the lustre of the eyes. A Persian poet, addressing the damsel of whom he is enamoured, says, "For eyes so intoxicated with love's nectar what need is there of surma?" — This part of the story seems to be garbled; in another text of the romance of Hatim Ta'í it is only after the surma has been applied to the covetous man's eyes that he beholds the hidden treasures.

*

RICHARD BURTON

THE WATER OF LIFE

THE WATER OF Life, the Water of Immortality, the Fountain of Youth — a favourite and wide-spread myth during the Middle Ages. In the romance of Sir Huon of Bordeaux the hero boldly encounters a griffin, and after a desperate fight, in which he is sorely wounded, slays the monster. Close at hand he discovers a clear fountain, at the bottom of which is a gravel of precious stones. "Then he dyde of his helme and dranke of the water his fyll, and he had no sooner dranke therof but incontynent he was hole of all his woundys." Nothing more frequently occurs in folk tales than for the hero to be required to perform three difficult and dangerous tasks — sometimes impossible, without supernatural assistance.

*

FEE FAW FUM!

DEMONS, OGRES, TROLLS, giants, et hoc genus omne, never fail to discover the presence of human beings by their keen sense of smelling. "Fee, faw, fum! I smell the blood of a British man," cries a giant when the renowned hero Jack is concealed in his castle. "Fum! fum! sento odor christianum," exclaims an ogre in Italian folk tales. "Femme, je sens la viande fraîche, la chair de chrétien!" says a giant to his wife in French stories.

*

MAIDENHEAD

She sat down beside me and bent lovingly over me and I rose up for I could no longer contain my passion and wrought that work which was to be worked.

He speaks of taking her maidenhead as if it were porter's work and so defloration was regarded by many ancient peoples. The old Nilotes incised the hymen before congress; the Phœnicians, according to Saint Athanasius, made a slave of the husband's abate it. The American Chibchas and Caribs looked upon virginity as a reproach, proving that the maiden had never inspired love. For these and other examples see p. 72, chap. iii. "L'Amour dans l'Humanité," by P. Mantegazza, a civilised and unprejudiced traveller.

*

LIMBLESS DIVINER

AN OLD PLINIAN fable long current throughout the East. It is the Pers. Ním-chihreh, and the Arab Shikk and possibly Nasnás = nisf al-Nás (?) See vol. v. 333. Shikk had received from Allah only half the form of a man, and his rival diviner Satíh was a shapeless man of flesh without limbs. They lived in the days of a woman named Tarífah, daughter of Al-Khayr al-Himyarí and wife of Amrú bin 'Ámir who was famous for having intercourse with the Jann. When about to die she sent for the two, on account of their deformity and the influence exercised upon them by the demons; and, having spat into their mouths, bequeathed to them her Jinni, after which she departed life and was buried at Al-Johfah. Presently they became noted soothsayers; Shikk had issue but Satih none; they lived 300 (some say 600) years, and both died shortly before the birth of the Prophet concerning whom they prophesied. When the Tobba of Al-Yaman dreamed that a dove flew from a holy place and settled in the Tihámah (lowland-seaboard) of Meccah, Satih interpreted it to signify that a Prophet would arise to destroy idols and to teach the best of faiths. The two also predicted (according to Tabari) to Al-Rabí'ah, son of Nasr, a Jewish king of Al-Yaman, that the Habash (Abyssinians) should conquer the country, govern it, and be expelled, and after this a Prophet should arise amongst the Arabs and bring a new religion which all should embrace and which should endure until Doomsday. Compare this with the divining damsel in Acts xvi. 16-18.

*

MOSLEM SCHOOLS

PAY-DAY FOR THE boys in Egypt. The Moslem school has often been described but it always attracts the curiosity of strangers. The Moorish or Maroccan variety is a simple affair; "no forms, no desks, few books. A number of boards about the size of foolscap, whitewashed on either side, whereon the lessons? from the alphabet to sentences of the

Koran? are plainly written in large black letters; a pen and ink, a book and a switch or two, complete the paraphernalia. The dominie, squatting on the ground, tailor-fashion, like his pupils, who may number from ten to thirty, repeats the lesson in a sonorous sing-song voice, and is imitated by the urchins, who accompany their voices by a rocking to and fro which sometimes enables them to keep time. A sharp application of the cane is wonderfully effectual in recalling wandering attention; and lazy boys are speedily expelled. On the admission of a pupil, the parents pay some small sum, varying according to their means, and every Wednesday, which is a half-holiday, a payment is made from ¼d. to 2d. New moons and feasts are made occasions for larger payments, and are also holidays, which last ten days during the two greater festivals. Thursdays are whole holidays, and no work is done on Friday mornings, that day being the Mohammedan 'Sabbath,' or at least 'meeting day,' as it is called. When the pupils have mastered the first short chapter of the Koran, it is customary for them to be paraded round the town on horseback, with ear-splitting music, and sometimes charitably disposed persons make small presents to the youngster by way of encouragement. After the first, the last is learned, then the last but one, and so on, backwards, as, with the exception of the first, the longest chapters are at the beginning. Though reading and a little writing are taught, at the same time, all the scholars do not arrive at the pitch of perfection necessary to indite a polite letter, so that consequently there is plenty of employment for the numerous scribes or Tálibs who make a profession of writing. These may frequently be seen in small rooms opening on to the street, usually very respectably dressed in a white flowing haik and large turban, and in most cases of venerable appearance, their noses being adorned with huge goggles. Before them are their appliances,? pens made of reeds, ink, paper, and sand in lieu of blotting paper. They usually possess also a knife and scissors, with a case to hold them all. In writing, they place the paper on the knee, or upon a pad of paper in the left hand." The main merit of the village school in Eastern lands is its noises which teach the boy to concentrate his attention. As Dr. Wilson of Bombay said, the young idea is taught to shout as well as to shoot, and this vivâ voce process is a far better mnemonic than silent reading. Moreover it is fine practice in the art of concentrating attention.

*

CLEVERNESS

But she eyed them with the eye of "the physiognomist and said in herself, "Verily these two men are on no wise what they seem and, unless my caution and intelligence and power of knowledge have passed away from me, this must be the Sultan and that his Wazir, for grandeur and majesty are evident on them."

This form of cleverness is a favourite topic in Arabian folk-lore. The model man was Iyás al-Muzani, al-Kazi (of

Bassorah), in the 2nd century A.H., mentioned by Al-Harírí in his 7th Ass. and noted in Arab. Prov. (i. 593) as "more intelligent than Iyás." Ibn Khallikan (i. 233) tells sundry curious tales of him. Hearing a Jew ridicule the Moslem Paradise where the blessed ate and drank ad libitum but passed nothing away, he asked if all his food were voided: the Jew replied that God converted a part of it into nourishment and he rejoined, "Then why not the whole?" Being once in a courtyard he said that there was an animal under the bricks and a serpent was found: he had noted that only two of the tiles showed signs of dampness and this proved that there was something underneath that breathed. Al-Maydáni relates of him that hearing a dog bark, he declared that the beast was tied to the brink of a well; and he judged so because the bark was followed by an echo. Two men came before him, the complainant claimed money received by the defendant who denied the debt. Iyás asked the plaintiff where he had given it, and was answered, "Under a certain tree." The judge told him to go there by way of refreshing his memory and in his absence asked the defendant if his adversary could have reached it. "Not yet," said the rogue, forgetting himself; "'tis a long way off"? which answer convicted him. Seeing three women act upon a sudden alarm, he said, "One of them is pregnant, another is nursing, and the third is a virgin." He explained his diagnosis as follows: "In time of danger persons lay their hands on what they most prize. Now I saw the pregnant woman in her flight place her hand on her belly, which showed me she was with child; the nurse placed her hand on her bosom, whereby I knew that she was suckling, and the third covered her parts with her hand proving to me that she was a maid." (Chenery's Al Hariri, p. 334.)

*

DODGES OF DETECTION

"...and under him in bed I would strew rose-leaves, for an they be found wilted in the morning found wilted in the morning he is a lad, and if they remain as they were he is a lass."

This is a new "fact" in physics and certainly to be counted amongst "things not generally known." But Easterns have a host of "dodges" to detect physiological differences such as between man and maid, virgin and matron, imperfect castratos and perfect eunuchs and so forth. Very Eastern, mutatis mutandis, is the tale of the thief-catcher, who discovered a fellow in feminine attire by throwing an object for him to catch in his lap and by his closing his legs instead of opening them wide as the petticoated ones would do.

*

LEFT TO THE IMAGINATION

By what physical process the author modestly leaves to the reader's imagination. Easterns do not often notice this feminine venereal paroxysm which takes the place of seminal emission in the male. I have seen it happen to a girl when hanging by the arms a trifle too long from a gymnastic cross-bar; and I need hardly say that at such moments (if men only knew them) every woman, even the most modest, is an easy conquest. She will repent it when too late, but the flesh has been too strong for her.

*

KIDNAPPING

THE DARWAYSHES WERE suspected of kidnapping, a practice common in the East, especially with holy men. I have noticed in my Pilgrimage (vols. ii. 273; iii. 327), that both at Meccah and at Al-Medinah the cheeks of babes are decorated with the locally called "Masháli" = three parallel gashes drawn by the barber with the razor down the fleshy portion of each cheek, from the exterior angles of the eyes almost to the corners of the mouth. According to the citizens this "Tashrít" is a modern practice distinctly opposed to the doctrine of Al-Islam; but, like the tattooing of girls, it is intended to save the children from being carried off, for good luck, by kidnapping pilgrims, especially Persians.

*

VELLICATION

THE HAIR BEING shaven or plucked and showing the darker skin. In the case of the axilla-pile, vellication is the popular process: see vol. ix. 139. Europeans who do not adopt this essential part of cleanliness in hot countries are looked upon as impure by Moslems.

*

MASSAGE

HERE IS AN allusion to the "Massage," which in these days has assumed throughout Europe all the pretensions of scientific medical treatment. The word has been needlessly derived from the Arab. "Mas'h" = rubbing, kneading; but we have the Gr. synonym μ?ss? and the Lat. Massare. The text describes child-bed customs amongst Moslem women, and the delivery of the Kazi has all the realism of M. Zola's accouchement in La Joie de Vivre.

*

INDIAN HEMP

FOR THE MANY preparations of this drug, see Herklots, Appendix, pp. lxviii. ciii. It is impossible to say how "Indian hemp," like opium, datura, ether and chloroform, will affect the nervous system of an untried man. I have read a dozen descriptions of the results, from the highly imaginative Monte Cristo to the prose of prosaic travellers; and do not recognise that they are speaking of the same thing.

CONGRESS WITH A CROCODILE

*

MANNERS OF INTOXIFICATION

Now when the next night fell, the Kazi brought the Hashish which he divided into two halves, eating one himself and giving the other to his companion; and both swallowed their portions after supper and then lit the waxen tapers and sat down to take their pleasure.

This tranquil enjoyment is popularly called "Kayf." See my Pilgrimage i. 13. In a coarser sense it is applied to all manners of intoxication; and the French traveller Sonnini says, "The Arabs (by which he means the Egyptians) give the name of Kayf to the voluptuous relaxation, the delicious stupor, produced by the smoking of hemp." I have smoked it and eaten it for months without other effect than a greatly increased appetite and a little drowsiness.

*

HASHÍSH-EATERS

So saying the Bhang-eater arose and loosed the inkle of his bag-trowsers, then approaching the Sultan he drew forth his prickle and proceeded to bepiss him; but the King took flight as the other faced him, and fled before him, he pursuing.

These childish indecencies are often attributed to Bhang-
eaters. See "Bákún's Tale of the Hashísh-eater," vol. ii.
91. Modest Scott (vi. 129) turns the joke into "tweaking
the nose." Respectable Moslems dislike the subject, but
the vulgar relish it as much as the sober Italian enjoys the
description of a drinking bout? in novels.

*

A DATE FOR COFFEE

*On the next night they met again and the two sat down and
ate a quantity of Hashish after they had supped and they lit
the waxen tapers and each of them drank a cup of coffee.*

In the text "Finjál," a vulgarism for "Finján": so the converse
"Isma'ín" for "Ism'aíl" = Ishmael. Mr. J. W. Redhouse (The
Academy No. 764) proposes a new date for coffee in Al-
Yaman. Colonel Playfair (History of Yemen, Bombay 1859)
had carelessly noted that its "first use at Aden was by a judge
of the place who had seen it drunk at Zayla', on the African
coast opposite Aden," and he made the judge die in A.H.
875 = A.D. 1470. This is about the date of the Shaykh al-
Sházalí's tomb at Mocha, and he was the first who brought
the plant from about African Harar to the Arabian seaboard.
But Mr. Redhouse finds in a Turkish work written only
two centuries ago, and printed at Constantinople, in A.D.
1732, that the "ripe fruit was discovered growing wild in the

mountains of Yemen (?) by a company of dervishes banished thither." Finding the berry relieve their hunger and support their vigils the prior, "Shaykh 'Umar advised their stewing it (?) and the use became established. They dried a store of the fruit; and its use spread to other dervish communities, who perhaps (?) sowed the seed wherever it would thrive throughout Africa (N.B. where it is indigenous) and India (N.B. where both use and growth are quite modern). From Africa, two centuries later, its use was reimported to Arabia at Aden (?) by the judge above mentioned, who in a season of scarcity of the dried fruit (?) tried the seed" (N.B. which is the fruit). This is passing strange and utterly unknown to the learned De Sacy (Chrest. Arab. i. 412-481).

*

MASTER-MASONS

The Minister replied, "Hearkening and obeying; and hied to do his lord's bidding taking with him architects and others, and having found a piece of level ground he ordered them to measure an hundred ells of length for the building by a breadth of seventy cubits.

In text "Mu'ammarjiyah" (master-masons), a vulgar Egyptianism for "Mu'ammarin." See "Jáwashiyah," vols. ii. 49; viii. 330. In the third line below we find "Muhandizín" = geometricians, architects, for "Muhandisín." Perhaps a reminiscence of the Persian origin of the word

"Handasah" = geometry, which is derived from "Andázah"
= measurement, etc..

*

CURIOUS SMELLS

*The Wazir cried, "Verily this fellow is a-fizzling and he boweth
his head toward his breast in order that he may savour his
own farts."*

Alluding to the curious phenomenon pithily expressed in
the Latin proverb, "Suus cuique crepitus benè olet," I know
of no exception to the rule, except amongst travellers in
Tibet, where the wild onion, the only procurable green-stuff,
produces an odour so rank and fetid that men run away from
their own crepitations. The subject is not savoury, yet it has
been copiously illustrated: I once dined at a London house
whose nameless owner, a noted bibliophile, especially of
"facetiæ," had placed upon the drawing-room table a dozen
books treating of the "Crepitus ventris." When the guests
came up and drew near the table, and opened the volumes,
their faces were a study. For the Arab. "Faswah" = a silent
break wind, see vol. ix. 11 and 291. It is opposed to "Zirt" =
a loud fart and the vulgar term, see vol. ii. 88.

*

OKRÁ

THE "BÁMIYAH," WHICH = the Gumbo, Occra (Okrá) or Bhendi of Brit. India which names the celebrated bazar of Bombay, is the esculent hibiscus, the polygonal pod (some three inches long and thick as a man's finger) full of seeds and mucilage making it an excellent material for soups and stews. It is a favourite dish in Egypt and usually eaten with a squeeze of lime-juice. See Lane, Mod. Egypt. chapt. v., and Herklots (App. p. xlii.) who notices the curry of "Bandakí" or Hibiscus esculentus.

*

OBSOLETE CUSTOMS

ARAB. "HANÚT:" THIS custom has become almost obsolete: the corpse is now sprinkled with a mixture of water, camphor diluted and the dried and pounded leaves of various trees, especially the "Nabk" (lote-tree or Zizyphus lotus).? Lane M.E. chapt. xxviii.

*

MISS LUCY

THESE COMICAL MEASURES were taken by "Miss Lucy" in order to charm away the Evil Eye which had fascinated the article in question. Such temporary impotence in a vigorous man, which results from an exceptional action of the brain and the nervous system, was called in old French Nouement des aiguilettes (i.e. point-tying, the points which fastened the haut-de-chausses or hose to the jerkin, and its modern equivalent would be to "button up the flap"). For its cure, the "Déliement des aiguilettes" see Davenport "Aphrodisiacs" p. 36, and the French translation of the Shaykh al-Nafzáwi (Jardin Parfumé, chapt. xvii. pp. 251-53). The Moslem heal such impotence by the usual simples, but the girl in the text adopts a moral course of treatment which buries the dead parts in order to resurrect them. A friend of mine, a young and vigorous officer, was healed by a similar process. He had carried off a sergeant's wife, and the husband lurked about the bungalow to shoot him, a copper cap being found under the window: hence a state of nervousness which induced perfect impotence. He applied to the regimental surgeon, happily a practised hand, and was gravely supplied with pills and a draught; his diet was carefully regulated and he was ordered to sleep by the woman but by no means to touch her for ten days. On the fifth he came to his adviser with a sheepish face and told him that he had not wholly followed the course prescribed, as last night he had suddenly?by the blessing of the draught and the pills?recovered and had given palpable evidence of his pristine vigour. The surgeon deprecated such proceeding until the patient should have had full benefit of his drugs?bread pills and cinnamon-water.

*

CONGRESS WITH A CROCODILE

QUESTIONING ANGELS

The Moslem's tomb is an arched vault of plastered brick, large enough for a man to sit up at ease and answer the Questioning Angels; and the earth must not touch the corpse as it is supposed to cause torture. In the graves of the poorer classes a niche (lahad) offsets from the fosse and is rudely roofed with palm-fronds and thatch. The trick played in the text is therefore easy; see Lane's illustration M.E. chapt. xviii. The reader will not forget that all Moslems make water squatting upon their hunkers in a position hardly possible to an untrained European: see vol. i. 259.

*

ON LOCOMOTION

For "'Aun," a high degree amongst the "Genies," see vol. iv. p. 83. Readers will be pleased with this description of a Jinni; and not a few will regret that they have not one at command. Yet the history of man's locomotion compels us to believe that we are progressing towards the time when humanity will become volatile. Pre-historic Adam was condemned to "Shanks his mare," or to "go on footback," as the Boers have it, and his earliest step was the chariot; for, curious to say, driving amongst most peoples preceded riding, as the row-boat forewent the sailer. But as men increased and the world became smaller and time shorter the eighteenth and the nineteenth centuries, after many abortive attempts, converted the chariot into a railway-car and the sailer into a steamer. Aerostatics are still in their infancy and will grow but little until human society shall find some form of flying an absolute necessity when, as is the history of all inventions, the winged woman (and her man) of Peter Wilkins will pass from fiction into fact. But long generations must come and go before "homo sapiens" can expect to perfect a practice which in the present state of mundane society would be fatal to all welfare.

*

CLEVERER THAN EVERYBODY

MODERN SCIENCE WHICH, out of the depths of its self-consciousness, has settled so many disputed questions, speaking by the organs of Messieurs Woodman and Tidy ("Medical Jurisprudence") has decided that none of the lower animals can bear issue to man. But the voice of the world is against them and as Voltaire says one cannot be cleverer than everybody. To begin with there is the will: the she-quadruman shows a distinct lust for man by fondling him and displaying her parts as if to entice him. That carnal connection has actually taken place cannot be doubted: my late friend Mirza Ali Akbar, of Bombay, the famous Munshi to Sir Charles Napier during the conquest of Sind, a man perfectly veracious and trustworthy, assured me that in the Gujarát province he had witnessed a case with his own eyes. He had gone out "to the jungle," as the phrase is, with another Moslem who, after keeping him waiting for an unconscionable time, was found carnally united to a she-monkey. My friend, indignant as a good Moslem should be, reproved him for his bestiality and then asked him how it had come to pass: the man answered that the she-monkey came regularly to look at him on certain occasions, that he was in the habit of throwing her something to eat and that her gratitude displayed such sexuality that he was tempted and "fell." That the male monkey shows an equal desire for the woman is known to every frequenter of the "Zoo." I once led a party of English girls to see a collection of mandrils and other anthropoid apes in the Ménagerie of a well-known Russian millionaire, near Florence, when the Priapism displayed, was such that the girls turned back and fled in fright. In the mother-lands of these anthropoids (the Gaboon, Malacca etc.,) the belief is universal and women have the liveliest fear of them. In 1853 when the Crimean war was brewing a dog-faced baboon in Cairo broke away from his "Kuraydati" (ape-leader), threw a girl in the street and was about to ravish her when a sentinel drew his bayonet and killer the beast. The event was looked upon as an evil omen by the older men, who shook their heads and declared that these were bad times when apes attempted to ravish the daughters of Moslems. But some will say that the grand test, the existence of the mule between man and monkey, though generally believed in, is characteristically absent, absent as the "missing link" which goes so far as to invalidate Darwinism in one and perhaps the most important part of its contention. Of course the offspring of such union would be destroyed, yet the fact of our never having found a trace of it except in legend and idle story seems to militate against its existence. When, however, man shall become "Homo Sapiens" he will cast off the prejudices of the cradle and the nursery and will ascertain by actual experiment if human being and monkey can breed together. The lowest order of bimana, and the highest order of quadrumana may, under most favourable circumstances, bear issue and the "Mule," who would own half a soul, might prove most serviceable as a hewer of wood and a drawer of water, in fact as an agricultural labourer. All we can say is that such "miscegenation" stands in the category of things not proven and we must object to science declaring them non-existing. A correspondent favours me with the following note upon the subject:? Castanheda (Annals of Portugal) relates that a woman was transporter to an island inhabited by monkeys and took up her abode in a cavern where she was visited by a huge baboon. He brought her apples and fruit and at last had connection with her, the result being two children in two to three years; but when she was being carried off by a ship the parent monkey kissed his progeny. The woman was taken to Lisbon and imprisoned for life by the King. Langius, Virgilius Polydorus and others quote many instances of monstrous births in Rome resulting from the connection of women with dogs and bears, and cows with horses, &c. The following relative conditions are deduced on the authority of MM. Jean Polfya and Mauriceau:? 1. If the sexual organism of man or woman be more powerful than that of the monkey, dog, etc., the result will be a monster in the semblance of man. 2. If vice-versâ the appearance will be that of a beast. 3.

If both are equal the result will be a distinct sub-species as of the horse with the ass.

*

CHARMS

ARAB. "TAMÍM" (PLUR. of Tamímat) = spells, charms, amulets, as those hung to a horse's neck, the African Greegree and the Heb. Thummim. As was the case with most of these earliest superstitions, the Serpent, the Ark, the Cherubim, the Golden Calf (Apis) and the Levitical Institution, the Children of Israel derived the now mysterious term "Urím" (lights) and "Thummim" (amulets) from Egypt and the Semitic word (Tamímah) still remains to explain the Hebrew. "Thummim," I may add, is by "general consensus" derived from "Tôm" = completeness and is englished "Perfection," but we can find a better origin near at hand in spoken Arabic.

*

POKETH AND STROKETH

...for by Allah, O my cousin, I will say thee nothing but sooth when I tell thee that the delight of that dog-faced baboon who deflowered hath remained with me ever since.

This appears to be the popular belief in Egypt. See vol. iv. 297, which assures us that "no thing poketh and stroketh more strenuously than the Gird" (or hideous Ahyssinian cynocephalus). But it must be based upon popular ignorance: the private parts of the monkey although they erect stiffly, like the priapus of Osiris when swearing upon his Phallus, are not of the girth sufficient to produce that friction which is essential to a woman's pleasure. I may here allude to the general disappointment in England and America caused by the exhibition of my friend Paul de Chaillu's Gorillas: he had modestly removed penis and testicles, the latter being somewhat like a bull's, and his squeamishness caused not a little grumbling and sense of grievance? especially amongst the curious sex.

*

IN LOWER ANIMALS

So she was delivered of a girl-child, in whom the father rejoiced with great joy and bade bring for her wet-nurses who suckled her; for two years until the milk time was past.

This is the usual term amongst savages and barbarians, and during that period the father has no connection with the mother. Civilisation has abolished this natural practice which is observed by all the lower animals and has not improved human matters. For an excellent dissertation on the subject see the letter on Polygamy by Mrs. Belinda M. Pratt, in "The City of the Saints," p. 525.

*

GUARDING THE JEWEL

S<small>UBAUDI</small>, "<small>THAT HATH</small> not been pierced." "The first night," which is often so portentous a matter in England and upon the Continent (not of North America), is rarely treated as important by Orientals.

Such lore has been carefully cultivated by the "young person" with the able assistance of the ancient dames of the household, of her juvenile companions and co-evals and especially of the slave-girls. Moreover not a few Moslems, even Egyptians, the most lecherous and salacious of men, in all ranks of life from prince to peasant take a pride in respecting the maiden for a few nights after the wedding-feast extending, perhaps to a whole week and sometimes more. A brutal haste is looked upon as "low"; and, as sensible men, they provoke by fondling and toying Nature to speak ere proceeding to the final and critical act. In England it is very different. I have heard of brides over thirty years old who had not the slightest suspicion concerning what complaisance was expected of them: out of mauvaise honte, the besetting sin of the respectable classes, neither mother nor father *would* venture to enlighten the elderly innocents. For a delicate girl to find a man introducing himself into her bedroom and her bed, the shock must be severe and the contact of hirsute breast and hairy limbs with a satiny skin is a strangeness which must often breed loathing and disgust. Too frequently also, instead of showing the utmost regard for virginal modesty and innocence (alias ignorance), the bridegroom will not put a check upon his passions and precipitates matters with the rage of the bull, ruentis in venerem. Even after he hears "the cry" which, as the Arabs say, "must be cried," he has no mercy: the newly made woman lies quivering with mental agitation and physical pain, which not a few describe as resembling the tearing out of a back-tooth, and yet he insists upon repeating the operation, never supposing in his stupidity, that time must pass before the patient can have any sensation of pleasure and before the glories and delights of the sensual orgasm bathe her soul in bliss. Hence complaints, dissatisfaction, disgust, mainly caused by the man's fault, and hence not unfrequently a permanent distaste for the act of carnal congress. All women are by no means equally capable of such enjoyment, and not a few have become mothers of many children without ever being or becoming thoroughly reconciled to it. Especially in the case of highly nervous temperaments — and these seem to be increasing in the United States and notably in New England — the fear of nine months' pains and penalties makes the sex averse to the "deed of kind." The first child is perhaps welcomed, the second is an unpleasant prospect and there is a firm resolve not to conceive a third. But such conjugal chastity is incompatible, except in the case of "married saints," with a bon ménage. The husband, scandalised and offended by the rejection and refusal of the wife, will seek a substitute more complaisant; and the spouse also may "by the decree of Destiny" happen to meet the right man, the man for whom and for whom only every woman will sweep the floor. And then adieu to prudence and virtue, honour and fair fame. For, I repeat, it is the universal custom of civilised and Christian Europeans to plant their womankind upon a pedestal exposed as butts to every possible temptation: and, if they fall, as must often be expected, to assail them with obloquy and contempt for succumbing to trials imposed upon them by the stronger and less sensitive sex. Far more sensible and practical, by the side of these high idealists, shows the Moslem who guards his jewel with jealous care and who, if his "honour," despite every precaution, insist upon disgracing him, draws the sabre and cuts her down with the general approbation and applause of society.

*

HYGIENIC CONNECTION

But one day of the days, my mind was set upon riding out to the waste lands about the town and the gardens thereof, by way of solacing myself; so I embarked in a little caïque upon the river and when we were amid stream I had a longing for coffee so I said to the boatman, "Abide in this place and throw out the anchor while we drink coffee."

Here coffee is mentioned without tobacco, whereas in more modern days the two are intimately connected. And the reason is purely hygienic. Smoking increases the pulsations without strengthening them, and depresses the heart-action with a calming and soothing effect. Coffee, like alcohol, affects the circulation in the reverse way by exciting it through the nervous system; and not a few authorities advise habitual smokers to end the day and prepare for rest with a glass of spirits and water. It is to be desired that the ignorants who write about "that filthy tobacco" would take the trouble to observe its effects on a large scale, and not base the strongest and extremest opinions, as is the wont of the Anglo-Saxon Halb-bildung, upon the narrowest and shakiest of bases. In Egypt, India and other parts of the Eastern world they will find nicotiana used by men, women and children, of all ranks and ages; and the study of these millions would greatly modify the results of observing a few hundreds at home. But, as in the case of opium-eating, populus vult decipi, the philanthrope does not want to know the truth, indeed he shrinks from it and loathes it. All he cares for is his own especial "fad."

*

DANDY

It is related that in Misr there was a Youth, a Shalabí, sans peer for semblance and excellence, and he had to friend a lovely woman whose husband was a Yúzbáshí or captain.

A dandy, a macaroni, from the Turk. Chelebi, see vol. i. 22. Here the word is thoroughly Arabised. In old Turk. it means, a Prince of the blood; in mod. times a gentleman, Greek or European.

*

BUFFOON'S ARTICLE

When they saw him in this condition they doffed turband and crowned him with a cap, and fringes projecting from the peak, which they had brought with them; then they arose and finding in his room a box full of raiment and ready money, they rifled all that was therein.

This is the article usually worn by the professional buffoon. The cap of the "Sutarí" or jester of the Arnaut (Albanian) regiments — who is one of their professional braves — is usually a felt cone garnished with foxes' brushes.

*

RELIABLE CORRUPTION

"'Tis well," said hee; after which he continued to address himself, "Would heaven I knew what hath be left by the mother of our Harím!"

i.e. My wife. In addition to notes in vols. i. 165, and iv. 9, 126, I would observe that "Harím" (women) is the broken plur. of "Hurmah;" from Haram, the honour of the house, forbidden to all save her spouse. But it is also an infinitive (whose plur. is Harîmát = the women of a family); and in places it is still used for the women's apartment, the gynæceum. The latter by way of distinction I have mostly denoted by the good old English corruption "Harem."

*

NEOLOGISMS

Musa did as he was bidden, and thrusting forth his finger gorged out the right eye, whereby Moshin remained purblind withal was he not filleed by a half-scone.

Supposed to be American, but, despite Bartlett, really old English from Lancashire, the land which has supplied many of the so-called "American" neologisms. A gouge is a hollow chisel, a scoop; and to gouge is to poke out the eye: this is done by thrusting the fingers into the side-hair thus acting as a base and by prising out the ball with the thumbnail which is purposely grown long.

*

SENT FROM FAIRY-LAND

As HAS BEEN said (vol. ii. 112) this is a sign of agitation. The tale has extended to remote Guernsey. A sorcier named Hilier Mouton discovers by his art that the King's daughter who had long and beautiful tresses was dying because she had swallowed a hair which had twined round her praecordia. The cure was to cut a small square of bacon from just over the heart, and tie it to a silken thread which the Princess must swallow, when the hair would stick to it and come away with a jerk. See (p. 29) "Folk-lore of Guernsey and Sark," by Louise Lane-Clarke, printed by E. Le Lievre, Guernsey, 1880; and I have to thank for it a kind correspondent, Mr. A. Buchanan Brown, of La Coûture, p. 53, who informs us why the Guernsey lily is scentless, emblem of the maiden who sent it from fairy-land.

*

WALKING THE PLANK

THE "BUCCANEERS," QUITE as humane, made their useless prisoners "walk a plank." The slave-ships, when chased and hard-driven, simply tossed the poor devils overboard; and the latter must often have died, damning the tender mercies of the philanthrope which had doomed them to untimely deaths instead of a comfortable middle passage from Blackland to Whiteland.

*

ROBE OF HONOUR

IN ABYSSINIA THE "Khil'at" = robe of honour (see vol. i. 195) is an extensive affair composed of a dress of lion's pelt with silver-gilt buttons, a pair of silken breeches, a cap and waist-shawl of the same material, a sword, a shield and two spears;

a horse with furniture of silk and silver and a mule similarly equipped. These gifts accompany the insignia of the "Order of Solomon," which are various medals bearing an imperial crown, said to represent the Hierosolymitan Temple of the Wise King, and the reverses show the Amharic legend "Yohanne Negus zei Etiopia" — John, Emperor of Ethiopia. The orders are distinguished as (1) the Grand Cross, a star of 100 grammes in massive gold, hammer-wrought, and studded with gems, given only to royalties; (2) the Knighthood, similar, but of 50 grammes, and without jewels, intended for distinguished foreigners; (3) the Officer's Star, silver-gilt, of 50 grammes; and (4) the Companion's, of pure silver, and the same weight. All are worn round the neck save the last, which hangs upon the chest. This practice of gilding the medals prevails also in Europe, for instance in Austria, where those made of gun-metal are often gilt by the recipients contrary to all official etiquette.

*

NAVEL-STRINGS

In order that the cord might not be subject to the evil eye or fall into the hand of a foe who would use it magically to injure the babe. The navel-string has few superstitions in England. The lower classes mostly place over the wound a bit of cloth wherein a hole has been burned, supposing that the carbon will heal the cut, and make it fast to the babe by a "binder" or swathe round the body, as a preventative to "pot-belly." But throughout the East there are more observances. In India, on the birth of the babe, the midwife demands something shining, as a rupee or piece of silver, and having touched the navel-string therewith she divides it and appropriates the glittering substance, under the pretence that the absence of the illuminating power of some such sparkling object would prevent her seeing to operate. The knife with which the umbilical cord has been cut is not used for common purposes but is left beside the puerpera until the "Chilla" (fortieth day), when "Kajjal" (lamp-black), used by way of Kohl, is collected on it and applied to the child's eyelids. Whenever the babe is bathed or taken out of the house the knife must be carried along with it; and when they are brought in again the instrument is deposited in its former place near the mother. Lastly, on the "Chilla"-day they must slaughter with the same blade a cock or a sheep (Herklots, chapt. i. sec. 3). Equally quaint is the treatment of the navel-string in Egypt; but Lane (M.E.) is too modest to give details.

*

CONUNDRUMS

...whereas if she vanquish she she shall lawfully cut off thy head, even as she hath decapitated so many before thy time.

This series of puzzling questions and clever replies is still as favourite a mental exercise in the East as it was in middle-aged Europe. The riddle or conundrum began, as far as we know, with the Sphinx, through whose mouth the Greeks spoke: nothing less likely than that the grave and mysterious Scribes of Egypt should ascribe aught so puerile to the awful emblem of royal majesty — Abu Haul, the Father of Affright. Josephus relates how Solomon propounded enigmas to Hiram of Tyre which none but Abdimus, son of the captive Abdæmon, could answer. The Tale of Tawaddud offers fair specimens of such exercises, which were not disdained by the most learned of Arabian writers. See Al-Hariri's Ass. xxiv, which proposes twelve enigmas involving abstruse and technical points of Arabic, such as: "What be the word, which as ye will is a particle beloved, or the name of that which compriseth the slender-waisted milch camel!" Na'am = "Yes" or "cattle," the latter word containing the Harf, or slender camel. Chenery, p. 246.

*

FACETIOUS EXAGGERATIONS

In Sindbad the Seaman I have shown that riding men as asses is a facetious exaggeration of an African practice, the Minister being generally the beast of burden for the King. It was the same in the Maldive Islands. "As soon as the lord desires to land, one of the rhief Catibes (Arab. Khatíb = a preacher, not Kátib = a writer) comes forward to offer his shoulder (a function much esteemed) and the other gets upon his shoulders; and so, with a leg on each side, he rides him horse fashion to land, and is there set down." See p. 71, "The Voyage of François Pyrard," etc. The volume is unusually well edited by Mr. Albert Gray, formerly of the Ceylon Civil Service, for the Hakluyt Society, MDCCCLXXXVII: it is, however, regretable that he and Mr. Bell, his collaborateur, did not trace out the Maldive words to their "Aryan" origin showing their relationship to vulgar Hindostani as Mas to Machhí (fish) from the Sanskrit Matsya.

*

BARBAROUS PUNISHMENT

When these had been recovered he commanded that there be set up for them as many stakes in there garden wherein he sat with his bride, and there in their presence he let impale each upon his own pale.

This impalement ("Salb," which elsewhere means crucifying, vol. iii. 25) may be a barbarous punishment but it is highly effective, which after all is its principal object. Old Mohammed Ali of Egypt never could have subjugated and disciplined the ferocious Badawi of Al-Asir, the Ophir region South of Al-Hijáz, without the free use of the stake. The banditti dared to die but they could not endure the idea of their bodies being torn to pieces and devoured by birds and beasts. The stake commonly called "Kházúk", is a stout pole pointed at one end, and the criminal being thrown upon his belly is held firm whilst the end is passed up his fundament. His legs and body are then lashed to it and it is raised by degrees and planted in a hole already dug, an agonising part of the process. If the operation be performed by an expert who avoids injuring any mortal part, the wretch may live for three days suffering the pangs of thirst; but a drink of water causes hemorrhage and instant death. This was the case with the young Moslem student who murdered the excellent Marshal Kleber in the garden attached to Shepherd's Hotel, Cairo, wherein, by the by, he suffered for his patriotic crime. Death as in crucifixion is brought on by cramps and nervous exhaustion, for which see Canon Farrar (Life of Christ, ii. 392 et seqq.).

*

VESTED INTERESTS

"There is an old and trusty saying that 'evil communications corrupt good manners,' and it is a well-known fact that the discussion (?) and reading of depraved literature leads (sic) infalliblably to the depravation of the reader's mind".

It appears to me that our measures, remedial and punitive, against "pornographic publications" result mainly in creating "vested interests" (that English abomination) and thus in fostering the work. The French printer, who now must give name and address, stamps upon the cover Avis aux Libraires under Edition privee and adds Ce volume ne doit pas etre mis en vente ou expose dans les lieux publics

560

(Loi du 29 Juillet, 1881). He also prints upon the back the number of copies for sale We treat "pornology" as we handle prostitution, unwisely ignore it, well knowing the while that it is a natural and universal demand of civilised humanity; and whereas continental peoples regulate it and limit its abuses we pass it by, Pharisee-like, with nez en-l'air. Our laws upon the subject are made only to be broken, and the authorities are unwilling to persecute, because by so doing they advertise what they condemn. Thus they offer a premium to the greedy and unscrupulous publisher and immensely enhance the value of productions ("Fanny Hill" by Richard Cleland for instance) which, if allowed free publication, would fetch pence instead of pounds. With due diffidence, I suggest that the police be directed to remove from booksellers' windows and to confiscate all indecent pictures, prints and photographs; I would forbid them under penalty of heavy fines to expose immoral books for sale, and I would leave "cheap and nasty" literature to the good taste of the publisher and the public. Thus we should also abate the scandal of providing the secretaries and officers of the various anti-vice societies with libraries of pornological works which, supposed to be escheated or burned, find their way into the virtuous hands of those who are supposed to destroy them.

*

RICHARD BURTON

EGYPTIAN OMISSIONS

"Quand aux manuscrits de la rédaction égyptienne, l'omission de cet épisode parait devoir être attribuée à la tendance qui les caractérise géneralement, d'abréger et de condenser la narrative" (loc. cit. p. 7: see also p. 14).

*

TAKING UP THE MANTLE

I would by no means assert that the subject matter of The Nights is exhausted: much has been left for future labourers. It would be easy indeed to add another five volumes to my sixteen as every complete manuscript contains more or less of novelty. Dr. Pertsch, the learned librarian of Saxe-Gotha, informs me that no less than two volumes are taken up by a variant of Judar the Egyptian (in my vol. vi. 213) and by the History of Zahir and Ali. For the Turkish version in the Bibliothèque Nationale see M. Zotenberg (pp. 21-23). The Rich MS. in the British Museum abounds in novelties, of which a specimen was given in my Prospectus to the Supplemental Volumes.

In the French Scholar's "Alâ al-Dîn" (p. 45) we find the MSS. of The Nights divided into three groups. No. i. or the Asian (a total of ten specified) are mostly incomplete and usually end before the half of the text. The second is the Egyptian of modern date, characterised by an especial style and condensed narration and by the nature and ordinance of the tales, by the number of fables and historiettes, and generally by the long chivalrous Romance of Omar bin al-Nu'umán. The third group, also Egyptian, differs only in the distribution of the stories.

Finis

—————— A REQUEST ——————

If you enjoyed this book, please review it on your favourite online retailer or review website.

Reviews are an author's best friend.

To stay in touch with Tahir Shah, and to hear about his upcoming releases before anyone else, please sign up for his mailing list:

 http://tahirshah.com/newsletter

And to follow him on social media, please go to any of the following links:

 http://www.twitter.com/humanstew

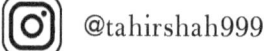 @tahirshah999

http://www.facebook.com/TahirShahAuthor

http://www.youtube.com/user/tahirshah999

http://www.pinterest.com/tahirshah

https://www.goodreads.com/tahirshahauthor

http://www.tahirshah.com